A SCOTTISH
CHRISTIAN
HERITAGE

A SCOTTISH CHRISTIAN HERITAGE

Iain H. Murray

Jean e John
With much love and
thankfulness for you both,

Iain e Jean
September 5, 2006

THE BANNER OF TRUTH TRUST

THE BANNER OF TRUTH TRUST
3 Murrayfield Road, Edinburgh EH12 6EL, UK
P O Box 621, Carlisle, PA 17013, USA

*

© Iain H. Murray 2006

ISBN-10: 0 85151 930 X
ISBN-13: 978 0 85151 930 2

*

Typeset in 11/14 pt Galliard
at the Banner of Truth Trust
Printed in the U.S.A.
by Versa Press, Inc.,
East Peoria, IL

Contents

PART TWO: MISSIONARY

PART THREE: CHURCH ISSUES

Illustrations

Foreword

I have looked on the preparation of this volume as the repayment of a debt. Over fifty years ago, as a young Christian, I first began to read the 'spiritual divinity' of Scotland. Later, in the libraries of Scottish manses and elsewhere, the wealth and extent of that literature became more apparent. Various explanations have been given as to why there were once so many Scottish Christians of 'adoring and heavenly minds'. Foremost among the reasons has to be the recovery of biblical truth, and the persecution that followed, but scarcely less significant was the accompanying literature that moulded successive generations. Books were read, treasured, and then, as their owners approached their closing years, handed on to others. Titles received in this way constituted something of a sacred trust, and that trust came to some of us when we were young.

Today there is a publishing revival that has made a number of older books far more accessible. To have books is not the same, however, as reading them. It is not only books that need to be handed on. Continuing testimony to their worth is no less needed, and I hope this volume will be a help to that end.

These pages are not principally about books. The theme is rather people and movements; yet the books from those times bring the abiding spiritual lessons to us and prevent the history becoming an exercise in nostalgia. The best Christian books never leave us as mere spectators. As one of these authors once advised a friend, 'Study the Spirit's work for the purpose of experiencing it.'

Some disclaimers may be necessary. This is not a book in praise of things Scottish as such. There is no more a natural affinity between Christianity and Scotland than there is in the case of any other nation. By nature we are all equally prone to err. And a Christian who reserves his reading to Scottish literature will necessarily be impoverished. Nor is this in any sense a summary of Scottish church history; it will be enough if I can prompt readers to explore the field further for themselves. Again, while men of Presbyterian persuasion necessarily loom large in these pages, the reader will not find this to be an apologetic for Presbyterianism. What made the Scottish churches so eminent in the Christian world was far more what they held in common with other churches than anything that they held alone.

As I show in the final chapter, before the end of the nineteenth century the foundation which had made the writings of the older evangelical authors of permanent value was largely taken away. A new type of literature arose that did not breathe reverence for the authority of Scripture and, with that omission, books ceased to move hearts and consciences. The reading habits of the nation changed, and in 1887 Robert Louis Stevenson could write in the *British Weekly* (13 May), 'The most influential books, and the truest in their influence, are works of fiction.'[1] With that change a change in the national character itself was unavoidable. Faith in God cannot long survive disbelief in his Word.

One of my guides to the older Scottish Christian literature was Alexander Whyte. In a book on *Bunyan Characters*, published in 1902, Whyte concluded his study of 'Mr Wet-Eyes' with these words:

[1] 'Books Which Influenced Me,' reprinted in *The Works of Robert Louis Stevenson* (London: Chatto and Windus, 1911–25), vol. 16.

There is great intellectual ability in the pulpit of our day, great eloquence, and great earnestness, but spiritual preaching, preaching to the spirit – 'wet-eyed' preaching – is a lost art. At the same time, if that living art is for the present overlaid and lost, the literature of a deeper spiritual day abides to us, and our spiritually minded people are not confined to us, they are not dependent on us.

These words are no less true today. 'The literature of a deeper spiritual day' is still at hand to be rediscovered.

It remains for me to thank colleagues in the work of the Banner of Truth Trust for all their help, including Ian S. Barter and John R. de Witt for reading the material in manuscript form. These pages were completed in the year that my wife and I celebrated our fiftieth wedding anniversary. Jean Ann has ever played a major part in anything I have sought to do. Surely the text is easy to believe, 'Whoso findeth a wife findeth a good thing, and obtaineth favour of the LORD.'

IAIN H. MURRAY
Edinburgh,
April 2006

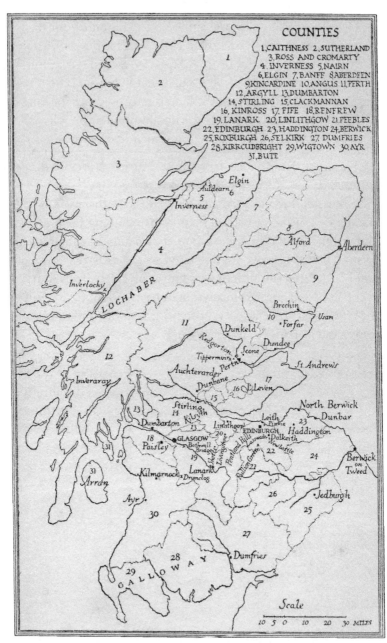

COUNTIES

1. CAITHNESS 2. SUTHERLAND
3. ROSS AND CROMARTY
4. INVERNESS 5. NAIRN
6. ELGIN 7. BANFF 8. ABERDEEN
9. KINCARDINE 10. ANGUS 11. PERTH
12. ARGYLL 13. DUMBARTON
14. STIRLING 15. CLACKMANNAN
16. KINROSS 17. FIFE 18. RENFREW
19. LANARK 20. LINLITHGOW 21. PEEBLES
22. EDINBURGH 23. HADDINGTON 24. BERWICK
25. ROXBURGH 26. SELKIRK 27. DUMFRIES
28. KIRKCUDBRIGHT 29. WIGTOWN 30. AYR
31. BUTE

Elgin
Auldearn
Inverness
Alford
Aberdeen
Inverlochy
LOCHABER
Brechin
Usan
Dunkeld
Forfar
Redgorton
Scone
Dundee
Tippermuir
Perth
Auchterarder
St Andrews
Dunbane
L. Leven
Inveraray
Stirling
North Berwick
Dumbarton
Kilsyth
Dunbar
Linlithgow
Leith
Pinkie
Haddington
GLASGOW
EDINBURGH
Dalkeith
Paisley
Bothwell Bridge
Newbattle
Berwick on Tweed
Kilmarnock
Lanark
Drumclog
Jedburgh
Arran
Ayr
Dumfries
GALLOWAY

Scale
10 5 0   10   20   30 MILES

Outline Map of Scotland

PART ONE

BIOGRAPHY

John Knox and 'the Battle'

Castle Hill, Edinburgh

'Now, O Lord, thou hast revealed thyself and thy beloved Son Jesus Christ, clearly to the world again, by the true preaching of his blessed evangel, which also of thy mercy is offered unto us within this realm of Scotland . . . Give unto us, O Lord, that presently are assembled in thy Name, such abundance of thy holy Spirit, that we may see those things that shall be expedient for the advancement of thy glory, in the midst of this perverse and stubborn generation. Give us grace, O Lord, that universally among our selves, we may agree in the unity of true doctrine. Bless thou so our weak labours, that the fruits of the same may redound to the praise of thy holy Name, to the profit of this present generation, and to the posterity to come, through Jesus Christ; to whom, with Thee and the Holy Ghost, be all honour and praise, now and ever. So be it.'

JOHN KNOX

John Knox remains one of the most controversial figures in history. Even his fellow countrymen are divided over him. Many have asserted that he was 'the greatest of Scotsmen',[1] but the more modern view is that of Dr Charles Warr who wrote, 'Of Christian virtues he had but few.'[2] Connected with this difference is a fundamental disagreement over the state of Scotland in the sixteenth century. History is not only about facts, it is about how they are to be interpreted. Let us begin with some facts. On the last day of February 1528, a young man of twenty-four years was executed by being burned alive at St Andrews. He was Patrick Hamilton, and over the next thirty years some twenty men and a woman were to endure a similar death – sometimes singly, as in Glasgow and Cupar; sometimes in groups, two and then another four in Edinburgh in the 1530s, and finally, in 1558, a man of more than eighty years of age, Walter Milne (sometimes called Mill), endured the last such fire in St Andrews.[3]

The popular interpretation of these facts is that they only illustrate the kind of behaviour that is caused by religious bigotry and superstition. It was part of a dark age that people could be put to death merely for matters of opinion. But there is a very different explanation and it is to be found in the book which was prohibited reading in the Scotland of the 1530s. This was William Tyndale's translation of the New Testament and there, in the book of the Revelation, it speaks of 'witnesses' being put to death, and shows that the sufferings of the Christian church between Christ's first and second advents are not due, in the first instance, to human folly but to demonic evil. Certainly the Devil uses men and the way he does so is set down in that same Scripture. We read in Revelation chapter 13, of Satan's purpose being expressed through two 'beasts', the one nations and their governments, the other false religion – religion that *looks like* a lamb but speaks lies as a dragon (*Rev.* 13:11). By such passages God gave to the martyrs a true understanding of their sufferings.

Patrick Hamilton and those who followed him were put to death by the Church of their day. It was a Church abundant in possessions, revenues and men. In a country where the population was only around 800,000, priests numbered perhaps as many as 3,000. Amid a poor population the Church owned the finest buildings in the land. But it was a Church far gone in moral and intellectual decay. While celibacy was professed by the clergy, living with concubines was common-place among them. Archbishop David Beaton was known to have eight illegitimate children, and the Bishop of Moray had ten. The sons of such liaisons were given lucrative Church positions and for the daughters there was the hope of marriage among the nobility. When in 1549, too late in the day, the Church began to think of reform, the crass ignorance that abounded in the religious orders was openly admitted. Some priests, it appeared, could scarcely say the alphabet. Preaching from the Bible had long since disappeared, and anyone doing so was instantly suspected of being a Protestant. One such suspect, a monk, was examined by the Bishop of Dunkeld who said that he had no objection to preaching provided it stuck to 'any good gospel or any good epistle that setteth forth the liberty of the Holy Church'. The prisoner shrewdly replied that he did not know how to distinguish in the Bible between good gospels and epistles and evil, and asked the Bishop to enlighten him. The Bishop, lost for an answer, could only exclaim, 'Thank God, I never knew what the Old and New Testament was, and I will to know nothing but my breviary and my pontifical.'[4]

Before the middle of the sixteenth century in Scotland the need for reformation was recognized on all hands; what was not recognized was that wrong living was the consequence of wrong believing. The Church could not have grown so fat and bloated had it not been for the money raised from her teaching on the sacraments, purgatory, indulgences and such like. What made the Protestant witnesses so obnoxious to the clergy was the recognition that if their message prevailed then the absolute authority of the Church over the souls of men and women would be at an end. This is clear enough in the charges laid against the martyrs. Patrick Hamilton was condemned for affirming that sacraments cannot save. The first charge against him at his trial was that he said 'the corruption of sin remains in a child after baptism'. Another charge was his statement that 'a man is not justified by works, but by faith alone'.[5] His opponents saw that the evangelicals were moving the whole basis of salvation from the Church to Christ. 'Christ', said Hamilton, 'bare our sins on his back and bought us with his blood.'[6]

The modern idea is that the religious division of the sixteenth century was little more than a difference over terminology, and that both sides have equal entitlement to be regarded as Christian. To say that is to remain ignorant of 'the power of darkness' which prevailed in Scotland before the Reformation. The gospel itself was not known. It was because the Protestant martyrs knew from what they had been delivered that they did not regard the difference with their persecutors as a matter of opinion. The issue was the way of salvation. Speaking of the counsellors of the Queen Regent in 1560, Knox was to say, 'These ignorant Papists that were about her understood nothing of the Mystery of our Redemption.'[7]

To recognize this is to see that the Reformation was no mere disagreement between two groups of men. With the Bible open before them, the Reformers knew that there was an enemy whose great aim was to silence the voice of the gospel. The most frequently used word in John Knox's vocabulary was undoubtedly the word 'battle'; and the battle, as he knew it, was 'not against flesh and blood, but against principalities, against powers, against the rulers of the darkness of this world' (*Eph.* 6:12).

THE EARLY YEARS, 1514–59

John Knox was born about the year 1514,[8] and into a family which knew something of conflicts of a different kind. A native of Haddington in East Lothian, his father and grandfathers had served under the standards of the Hepburns, Earls of Bothwell, and it may be that under those standards one or more of them had died at Flodden in 1513. Few there were in Scotland in those days who had not been in warfare of one kind or another, life was cheap and times were brutal. Sudden death by various means was not uncommon. We read, for instance, of an English soldier who raided a Scots house for provisions and, while he was bent double, peering into a barrel of meal, a female took him by the ankles so that he fell in headfirst and there she put an end to him.

Knox was about fourteen years old when Patrick Hamilton died at St Andrews. It cannot have been long after that event that he became a student in that old university town; yet the burning of Hamilton evidently did not change his religion, for one of the first definite facts we know about Knox is that he was ordained to the priesthood in 1536. He then became a church lawyer, an 'apostolic notary', and there is evidence that in that office he was occupied in East Lothian between 1540 and 1543. At what time it 'pleased God to call me from the puddle of Papistry',[9] he does not tell us. We know that in 1542–43 a change in government allowed a temporary toleration for Protestants and that a friar by the name of Thomas Guylliame preached the gospel in East Lothian and Edinburgh: 'He was the first man,' writes David Calderwood, 'from whom Mr Knox received any taste of the truth.'[10]

If Knox did not become a Christian until about 1543, we can be sure that the next three years were spent in hard study of the Scriptures, for when he first emerges into clear view in 1546–7 it is as a man already able to use the Word of God with telling effect. He was then about thirty-two years of age and no longer earning his living from the Church but from the tuition of pupils. We learn this from his most important book, his *History of the Reformation in Scotland*. This work was not written as an autobiography and his name first enters the pages almost incidentally in connection with the ministry of George Wishart by whose preaching, he says, 'God wrought so wonderfully' at this time.

When Wishart came to East Lothian to preach in the winter of 1545–6 Knox 'waited upon him carefully'. This function included guarding the Reformer with a two-handed sword against would-be assassins. The companionship of Wishart and Knox ended suddenly at the command of the older man who sensed that his work was done and wanted the life of Knox preserved for another day. 'Return to your pupils,' he told Knox, 'and God bless you. One is sufficient for one sacrifice.' That same day a few hours later, at midnight, Wishart was taken, and later burned by Cardinal Beaton, outside Beaton's castle in St Andrews, on 1 March 1546. Among his last words were these:

I beseech thee, Father of heaven! To forgive them that have of any ignorance or else have of any evil mind forged any lies upon me: I forgive them with all my heart. I beseech Christ to forgive them that have condemned me to death this day ignorantly.[11]

Not all professing Protestants were of Wishart's spirit, and two months later David Beaton was also dead, murdered by intruders in his own stronghold. The death of Beaton was one of the first actions by which revolution became confused with Reformation. A connection between the two things would later give the opponents of the gospel excuse to attribute the progress of evangelical Christianity to physical force, but as Merle d'Aubigné has observed of the murder of Beaton: 'Such things are more likely to ruin a cause than to save it. The Christian life and death of Wishart contributed far more powerfully than the death of Beaton to the advancement of the kingdom of God.'[12]

After the death of Beaton the castle of St Andrews became a refuge for a mixed multitude of whom the majority were Protestants. Finding himself increasingly in danger of the same treatment as Wishart suffered, Knox, with three pupils, also went there at Easter, 1547. Here his real life-work began. Others in the castle, hearing the way he taught his pupils, compelled him to take up the public teaching of the Scriptures. This he did from the Gospel of John, but it was not for long. In August of that same year the castle fell before the attack of eighteen French galleons, and the 120 defenders, Knox among them, went as prisoners to France.

What French forces were doing in Scotland in 1547 requires some explanation. It all had to do with royal marriages, which were so often arranged with political aims in view. At the beginning of the sixteenth century, Scotland and England, traditional enemies, were linked by the marriage of Margaret Tudor (sister of Henry VIII of England) to James IV of

Scotland. But good relations with England soon broke down, especially after the son of James IV, James V, married the French noblewoman, Mary of Guise. They had a daughter, Mary, Queen of Scots, who succeeded to the Scottish throne when she was only one week old. King Henry VIII saw the opportunity of uniting the two nations by arranging a marriage between her and his son Edward but, instead, the French connection prevailed and the infant Mary was sent to France by her mother where she remained for thirteen years for education in the dissolute French court.

From 1545, Mary of Guise proceeded to govern Scotland as Regent and to treat it as though it were a part of France. In Knox's words, 'France began to thirst to have the regiment of Scotland in their own hands.'[13] The outcome of these national relationships was to have a close bearing on the recovery of the gospel, for while the Protestant cause was favoured in England, from the throne of France it had only resolute opposition.

A vital part of Knox's preparation for future usefulness lay in his experience of both France and England after his capture in 1547. He can have seen comparatively little of France itself for he tells us that, following his capture, nineteen months were spent as a slave in a French galley. Galleys commonly had about fifty rowers on ten-foot-long benches, four feet apart, and with six men on each bench responsible for an oar fifty feet long (thirteen feet inside the boat and thirty seven outside). To these benches the slaves were chained as the sea washed freely across the low deck.[14] Then, apparently at English intervention, Knox was released and reached England in 1549. These were the days of the young Edward VI, and his Protestant government appointed the Scot to preach in the wild northern borders, first at Berwick, then at Newcastle, and finally he was brought to London where he was a chaplain to the Duke of Northumberland.

These brighter years in England ended in 1553 when Mary Tudor succeeded her half-brother and restored the Roman faith. Leading Protestants were arrested, but for some months Knox went on preaching, only crossing the English Channel to safety at the beginning of March 1554. Before his departure from England, he tried to get back to Berwick. He had a special reason to go there.

One of the people who had come under the power of the gospel during his Berwick ministry was Elizabeth Bowes, who lived in the border fortress of Norham Castle, seven miles from Berwick, where her husband, Richard, was in command. The Bowes family was one of the most influential in the north, and it was their teenage daughter, Marjory, who became the wife of Knox about 1552-3.

He had left her in the north for greater safety and could not get back to her before he was compelled to fly for his life. His flight troubled him:

> Albeit that I have in the beginning of this battle appeared to play the faint-hearted and feeble soldier (the cause I remit to God), yet my prayer is, that I may be restored to the battle again.

For the next few years Knox was in several places, including Dieppe, Frankfurt and Geneva. While a galley slave, God had given him the conviction that he would preach in St Andrews again before he died, but this hope was not fulfilled during a short and hazardous visit to his homeland in 1556. He returned to Europe, and the English congregation at Geneva became his home and congregation.

These twelve hard years of exile from Scotland ended in 1559. Mary Tudor was dead, the Protestant faith was publicly restored in England, and the preparation that Knox needed for 'the battle' in Scotland was now complete.

THE PREPARATION OF THE LEADER

Of the lessons he had learned during that period there are three which stand out:

1. Knox became a man of prayer. Prayer as 'an earnest and familiar talking with God', is not natural to us. It is by sanctified trouble and by the recognition of our own helplessness that we learn to pray. 'Out of weakness made strong' is the biblical principle. 'Call upon me in the day of trouble', became a promise of special significance to Knox. His first writing when the Marian persecution broke in England in 1554, was on *What True Prayer Is, How We Should Pray, and For What We Should Pray*.[15] In another place he says that the Apostle Peter, as he sought to cross the water to Jesus, was allowed to sink because there was in him too much 'presumption and vain trust in his own strength'. 'Unless it had been corrected and partly removed,' he comments, Peter 'had never been apt or meet to feed Christ's flock.'[16] This was surely what Knox himself was being taught. He says that he wrote so much on prayer because,

> I know how hard is the battle between the spirit and the flesh, under the heavy cross of affliction, where no worldly defence but present death does appear. I know the grudging and murmuring complaints of the flesh . . . calling all his promises in doubt, and being ready every hour utterly to fall from God. Against which rests only faith, provoking us to call earnestly and pray for assistance of God's Spirit; wherein, if we continue, our most desperate calamities shall be turned to gladness, and to a prosperous end. To thee alone, O Lord, be praise, for with experience I write this and speak.[17]

Whatever men thought of Knox, none could deny that he was a man of prayer. It is said that even the master of the French galley in which he was a slave, during a severe storm, once called on him to pray for their survival.[18] His future work would not have been possible had he not learned dependence on God.

2. Knox's long exile made him an international Christian. Had he remained always in Scotland he might have remained as parochial as some of his contemporaries. It was in God's design that he spent most of his time away from home among the English. These were the people against whom his forefathers had fought but in Christ the old enmity was gone. He was ahead of his time in foreseeing a common Protestant faith binding the two nations together, and that hope became central to his life. 'Grant, O Lord,' he prayed, 'we never enter into hostility against the realm and nation of England.'[19] He married an English wife, and came to speak English rather than his native Scots. On his brief visit to Scotland in 1556, report spread of a preacher having appeared in Ayrshire. The preacher was an Englishman, some said, going by his accent. 'Nay, no Englishman,' a cleric discerned, 'but it is Knox, that knave.'[20]

3. It was during Knox's exile, and especially in the final years in Geneva, that the master-principles which governed his thought on Reformation came to maturity. In outline, they may be stated as follows:

i. We exist for God's glory; therefore zeal for the honour of God is the essence of true piety; conversely, to despise God, to offend his majesty, is the darkest form of human depravity. The indignation Knox felt against Roman Catholicism sprang from this source. He saw it as a system bound up with giving to men and to idols that which belongs to God alone. The mass is not a mere mistake about the nature of the sacrament; in its insistence that bread becomes Christ, it is idolatry.

ii. Christians are bound to a universal obedience to the Word of God, no matter what the cost, no matter what the consequences. More particularly, nothing is lawful in the church unless it is to be found in Scripture. To quote the Reformer's later words to Queen Elizabeth: 'Whatsoever He approves (by his eternal word) that shall be approved, and what he damneth, shall be condemned, though all men in the earth should hazard the justification of the same.'[21]

iii. The true church is to be distinguished from the false church in this manner: the true has Christ as its living Head, it hears his voice, it follows him, and a stranger it will not follow. This church, further, is to be kept separate from the world by the faithful exercise of discipline in order that reproach is not brought upon God by the character of its members, so that the good is not affected by the evil, and so that those corrected may be recovered.[22]

SUCCESS AND CONFLICT, 1559–72

Knox finally returned to Scotland on May 2, 1559. That very day, at the monastery of the Black Friars in Edinburgh, the Roman bishops and priests were met to discuss reformation in the Church. The decisions they took included the following:

> that none should enjoy benefice ecclesiastical except he be a priest; that if any priest was found in open adultery, for the first fault he should lose a third of his benefice; and none should put his own son in his benefice.

Elsewhere in Scotland a very different kind of Reformation was underway, and in this Reformation there were two differing elements at work. The first was the spiritual movement which had gone on secretly in the years of persecution. Despite the prohibition of Tyndale's New Testament, it was read. 'Their tyranny notwithstanding,' wrote Knox, 'the knowledge of God did wondrously increase within this realm, partly by reading, partly by brotherly conference, which in those dangerous days was used to the comfort of many.'[23] In this way communities of believers came into existence that met in homes or in the fields as hidden congregations or 'privy kirks'. How many such people there were who, at the risk of their lives, abandoned the Roman Catholic faith, it is impossible to know, but judging by the alarm that they caused to the authorities they were not inconsiderable in some parts. Rewards were offered to any who informed on the secret conventicles. In 1554 Archbishop Hamilton informed the Pope how 'a great part of the diocese of Glasgow' was 'infected with heresies'. John Leslie, a Catholic writer of the period, noted how the protestant preaching went on 'in chimney nooks, secret holes and such private places, to trouble the whole country'.[24]

It was the existence of these 'privy kirks' which explains how parish churches could be so readily established once liberty was granted. The other element in the Scottish Reformation that led to liberty was the military and the revolutionary. Whether it is justified to speak in terms of 'revolution' has been debated at length – is it revolution for a people to act against the oppression of an absolute monarchy? In any case, the Scots nobility (often at odds with the throne) had a legitimate title to a share in the government, and there was only a Regent and no monarch in Scotland until 1561 when Mary Queen of Scots returned. Before Knox's return in 1559 a number of the Scottish nobility and landowners, assisted by what he calls 'the Gentlemen of the West' (lairds in the south-west of Scotland), had joined together in self-defence against the persecution of 'professors of the Evangel', and in patriotic opposition to the French domination.

These men, 'the Lords of the Congregation' (i.e., of the evangelicals), now became the leaders of an armed struggle against Mary of Guise. Thus two armies faced each other, one of French and Scots supporting the established power and the Catholic cause, and the other of Scots led by some of their own aristocracy who wanted change. The spiritual leadership of the Lords of the Congregation was now given to Knox, who also employed all his English connections to secure aid from that quarter, including money to maintain the payment of their soldiers in the field. Throughout 1559 the outcome remained highly uncertain. In November it seemed that the cause of the Protestant forces was lost as the French took Edinburgh. The Lords of the Congregation retreated in disarray to Stirling and it was left to Knox to rally their demoralized army by his preaching.

Soon after this, the appeals to England for help bore fruit and in 1560 military support came. Then a sight new for Scotland was that of the old enemies of so many battles standing side by side against the French. It was this combination of the spiritual and the para-military that now changed the course of history. Mary of Guise died, and by the Treaty of Edinburgh the French forces agreed to leave Scotland.

The Protestant cause had triumphed, and at the meeting of the Scots Parliament in 1560 a Confession of Faith, drawn up by Knox and a few colleagues, was ratified. Roman Catholic teaching and practice was henceforth forbidden. The 'privy kirks' now replaced the old parish churches and overnight the congregation of those who professed the evangel became the new national church.

To all appearances this was a sweeping victory, yet the reality was somewhat different. Instead of finding that his 'battle' was over, Knox faced another twelve years of conflict from which only death would deliver him. Mary Queen of Scots returned to Scotland as sovereign in 1561 and took up residence in the palace of Holyrood in Edinburgh. She was well trained in the arts of diplomacy and deception. Almost immediately the coalition which had supported Knox began to falter. Some of the leading nobles who had professed Protestantism now defended the right of the Queen to have the mass and the practice of her religion within her own palaces. Speaking of this new disappointment, Knox wrote to Ann Lock, a friend in London, on October 2, 1561:

> The permission of that odious idol, the Mass, by such as have professed themselves enemies to the same, does hourly threaten a sudden plague. I thirst to change this earthly tabernacle, before that my wretched heart should be assaulted with such new dolours[25] . . . If you, or any other think that I, or any other preacher within this realm, may amend such enormities, you are deceived; for we have discharged our consciences, but remedy there appears none . . . Our nobility (I write with dolour of heart) begin to find ease good service for God . . . I have finished in open preaching the Gospel of Saint John, saving only one chapter. Oft have I craved the miseries of my days to end with the same.[26]

The bright prospects of 1560 were thus already looking dim. For the next six years Knox was to be in continual conflict with Queen Mary and her supporters. Lord Eustace Percy, in his popular biography of Knox, wrote of the years 1562–5:

> Holyrood may well celebrate this prosperous weather with masque and music and dancing. But Knox is in a very different mood. Everywhere Calvin's Reformation hangs on the verge of defeat. All is wrong in Scotland, churches without ministers, ministers without stipends, 'avarice, oppression of the poor, excess, riotous cheer'.[27]

Knox and his helpers had drawn up a Book of Discipline for the Reformed Church in 1560 but it was an ominous portent of the future that Parliament refused to ratify it. A church which ceased to be a sanctuary for the worldly remained a vision for the future and the vision was not forwarded by too many priests who now became nominal Protestants. A historian of the

Scottish Reformation has written: 'The proposals made in 1560 to exclude the existing clergy from the ministry was proved an idle threat . . . it can be said with some confidence that well over 50 per cent of the staff of the Reformed church was recruited from men who had been in orders before the Reformation.'[28] Some of them, indeed, had known a true change of heart, others were rather of the class of those who, to use the words of Knox, made 'flesh and blood their God'.[29]

But for the resolution and courage of Knox the whole Reformation might have failed. In vain the Queen tried to silence him and at length she over-reached herself. Tired of her husband, Lord Darnley, she connived at his murder, and then took the Earl of Bothwell, the man responsible for the murder, for her husband. Once more the Protestant forces took up arms and in 1568 Mary's forces were beaten and she took flight to England where she was eventually executed.

This event introduced another monarch who was only an infant. Mary had left behind her son of two years, James VI (and the future James I of England). Although he had been baptized according to Catholic rites, it was around James that Protestant hopes for the future now settled and his education was in Protestant hands. In the meantime another Regent, the Protestant Earl of Moray, was appointed. Yet opposition was by no means over. Large numbers still adhered to the old religion. A party for the Queen still continued to hold Edinburgh Castle – almost within gunshot of Knox's church of St Giles. Moray was assassinated in 1570 and the next year things were so precarious in Edinburgh that Knox was forced to go to St Andrews with his family. In that place we are told, 'the majority of the university had steadily set themselves against Knox and his preaching'.[30] Knox had good reason to say:

> Above all things, preserve the Kirk from the bondage of the Universities. Persuade them to rule peaceably, and

order their schools in Christ; but subject never the pulpit to their judgment.[31]

In 1572, the year of his death, when he was back in Edinburgh, the majority of the nobility in the land remained against him. Old associates had deserted him, including Kirkcaldy of Grange, the man who held Edinburgh Castle for the Queen. Knox was thankful that the gospel was being preached across Scotland but he had no illusions that a nation had turned to God. In one of his last recorded prayers we hear him saying: 'Be merciful to us, and suffer not Satan utterly to prevail against thy little flock within this realm.'[32] It was one thing to see the Roman Church formally overthrown and quite another to bring such change as would establish a national church that was truly evangelical and Reformed.

KNOX THE MAN

Something must be said on Knox as a person. For his appearance we have the words of a contemporary who tells us he was slightly under medium height, with black hair, broad shoulders, florid complexion and a beard 'a span and a half long'. His forehead stood out over his blue-grey eyes, with their keen gaze. In his face there was a natural dignity and majesty and in anger there was an air of command.

In his temperament Knox was not, as someone has said, a kind of human canon ball, inflexible and insensitive. On the contrary he could recognize situations where the exercise of moderation was a Christian duty. He did not approve, for instance, of those who advocated secession from the Church of England in the 1560s because of differences not essential to salvation.

'God forbid,' he wrote to them, 'that we should damn all for false prophets and heretics that agree not with us in apparel and other opinions, who yet preach the substance of doctrine and salvation in Christ Jesus.'[33]

William Croft Dickinson accused Knox of 'a narrow hate that diminishes the stature of the man'.[34] Certainly he was possessed of an indignation against all that dishonoured God, and while it may be questioned whether this was always rightly directed, he did not exempt himself from the same judgment. In his last publication he confessed:

> In youth, middle age, and now after many battles, I find nothing in me but vanity and corruption.[35]

From such words it should not be deduced that Knox's prevailing spirit was one of gloom. He knew comfort and joy from the reality which Wishart expressed in the words, 'God is friendly minded towards sinners.' Thus Knox could say, 'I am assured my manifold rebellions are defaced, my grievous sins purged, and my soul made the tabernacle of Thy Godly Majesty.' From this assurance came the tenderness with which he sought to comfort others in spiritual distress. In contrast to the representation some give of him as a man who chiefly thundered out judgments, he describes himself rather as an assistant at a banquet of blessing where the Saviour himself is the host:

> I was one of that number whom God appointed to receive that bread (as it was broken by Christ Jesus) to distribute and give the same to such as he had called to this banquet . . . Of this I am assured, that the benediction of Christ so multiplied the portion that I received of his hands, that during that banquet (this I write to the praise of his name, and to the accusation of mine own unthankfulness) the bread never failed when the hungry soul craved or cried for food; and at the end of the banquet, mine own conscience beareth witness, that my hands gathered up the crumbs that were left in such abundance that my basket was full among the rest.[36]

Knox was a man of deep feeling. Listen to these words written to Ann Lock from St Andrews at the end of his first year back in Scotland, 31 December 1559:

> I have read the cares and temptations of Moses, and some times I supposed myself to be well practised in such dangerous battles. But, alas! I now perceive that all my practice before was but mere speculation; for one day of troubles, since my last arrival in Scotland, has more pierced my heart than all the torments of the galleys did the space of nineteen months; for that torment, for the most part, did touch the body, but this pierces the soul and inward affections.[37]

We would know more of the personal side of Knox if his correspondence with his wife, had survived. Marjory Bowes and her mother escaped from England to join Marjory's husband in Geneva during the Marian persecution. Soon after Knox returned to Scotland in 1559 she followed with their two small boys. Besides caring for the family, she acted as his secretary. In the traumatic days when she made a home in Scotland it is not surprising to read that she suffered much from sleeplessness. He wrote from St Andrews on the last day of 1559: 'The rest of my wife has been so unrestful since her arriving here, that scarcely could she tell on the morrow, what she wrote at night.'[38] Still only in her twenties, the health of Marjory Knox failed. Before the end of 1560 she was dead, and Knox had to continue alone. Hearing the news John Calvin wrote to Knox in a letter of condolence, 'You found a wife whose like is not found everywhere.' In a letter to Christopher Goodman, the Genevan Reformer also commented: 'Although I am not a little grieved that our brother Knox has been deprived of the most delightful of wives, yet I rejoice that he has not been so afflicted by her death as to cease his active labours in the cause of Christ and the Church.'[39]

Three years later Knox remarried, and by his second wife, Margaret Stewart (who was seventeen, and he about forty-nine), there were three children, all girls. The youngest of the three, Elizabeth, was to marry John Welsh of Ayr, and as Thomas M'Crie says, she 'seems to have inherited no inconsiderable portion of her father's spirit'.[40]

Many false charges were made against Knox, but no one attempted to accuse him of making money from the gospel. He never owned a house, and moved frequently from one rented building to another, at times harassed by his landlord. The house on the High Street, Edinburgh, where tradition says he died, was owned by a goldsmith named James Mossman – a resolute supporter of Mary and the Catholic cause, who had taken refuge in Edinburgh Castle. In Knox's last Will and Testament, while his books were valued at £130 Scots, his other household effects only amounted to £30. Hume Brown has illustrated the value of these sums by comparing them with the amount that Queen Mary once gave to her secretary, David Rizzio, namely, £200 for the repair of his chamber.[41]

WHAT WE MAY LEARN FROM KNOX

1. In the church situation of today there is an advantage that Knox did not have. Unlike him, we are the inheritors of traditions, and many of them good ones. In the sixteenth century the Reformers had few traditions with which to work. Instead they had to break an existing mould and put another in its place. A similar task faces the church in some countries today, while in Britain we have the aid of nearly five hundred years of Protestant history. Yet while these traditions are an advantage in some respects, they can also be a danger. In an anxiety to conserve them we may lose the freedom and flexibility to make necessary adjustments in the life of the church. We also face the danger that contemporary contempt for tradition may incline us to the opposite extreme, so that

we think it needful to retain every practice that time has honoured.

Knox is not often thought of as an example of fresh and innovative thinking in the life of the church. That is certainly correct if we are thinking of the great issues of truth upon which salvation itself depends. But there are other areas where it may well be legitimate to adapt our plans and organization to the circumstances of the hour, and Knox did this at several points. In other words, he did not believe that what was later to be called the 'regulative principle of Scripture' has so determined everything in the church that we have one permanent blueprint that covers everything. How often the Lord's Supper should be observed is a case in point. Scripture does not lay down precisely how often it is to be received. Once a month, the church at Geneva decided; 'four times in the year we think sufficient', said Knox and his brethren in 1560. Why the difference? The answer was one of expediency rather than of scriptural principle, 'that the superstition of the times may be avoided as far as may'.[42]

Whether expediency was wise in this instance may well be questioned, and there are other questions on which the flexibility of the Scottish Reformers is better illustrated. What part does the church member, who is not an elder or minister, play in the active life of the church? Is any part expected of him other than attending services? The 'privy kirks', through which the spiritual Reformation in Scotland came into being, certainly thought so. In the years of the hidden advance of the gospel, there were no 'church officers', only merchants, bakers, butchers, maltmen and such-like people who could speak from their hearts, exhort, and read the Scriptures to one another even though it might cost their lives. When regular churches were formed, as they were from 1559, this pattern had proved too valuable to be wholly dispensed with. Thus a group of people whom the Book of Discipline of 1560 called 'Readers' was encouraged to continue. 'Their duty', writes David Laing, the editor of Knox's writings, 'was limited to reading the Scriptures and Common Prayers, with liberty, when qualified, to explain the Scriptures read, and exhort the people – hence the name Exhorter.'[43]

This is not all. Once a week, the Book of Discipline laid down, there should be held in towns a meeting similar to what is described in 1 Corinthians, chapter 14, at which 'every man shall have liberty to utter and declare his mind and knowledge to the comfort and edification of the Church . . . These exercises, we say, are things most necessary to the Church of God this day in Scotland; for thereby shall the Church have judgment and knowledge of the graces, gifts, and utterances of every man within their own body.' Rules were recorded for the meeting to be edifying, there was to be 'no invective' and 'exhortations or admonitions' must be short. The principle was that Christians are to be 'willing to communicate the gifts and spiritual graces of God with their brethren . . . For no man may be permitted to live as best pleases him within the Church of God.'[44]

The Scripture does not lay down how men are to be called into the office of the preacher. The Reformers regarded the office of Readers and Exhorters, and the weekly Exercises (or Prophesyings, as they were called), as a valuable means of proving a man's gifts. The idea that a man may be trained for the ministry and licensed before there is any real proof of his gifts was unthinkable to them.

We are not only dependent on the Book of Discipline to know Knox's view on the need for meetings where all men might speak. He urges the very same thing in his 'Letter of Wholesome Counsel' sent to the brethren in Scotland in July 1556, where he says about these meetings, 'If any brother have exhortation, question, or doubt, let him not fear to speak or move the same, so that he do it with moderation, either to edify or to be edified.'[45]

Illustrations of Knox's willingness to be innovative do not stop here. He was ready to lend his authority to the work of the men called superintendents. Was he compromising the regulative principle in so doing? No, the superintendents were simply ministers, they held no higher office. But at a time when preaching was widely needed and able men were few, it was decided that some of the brethren should itinerate, planting new churches and helping existing ones. The innovation claimed no express Scripture warrant but was a good expedient for the situation which confronted them. In some ways the superintendents resembled the travelling preachers who were to be so effective in Methodism two centuries later.

Knox and the Book of Discipline teach us that fresh thinking is sometimes needed for the advancement of the gospel. The contemporary church scene demands it. Not all our traditions are of the same value. In Scotland today the organized church is viewed with almost the same sort of disdain with which the Church of Rome was viewed before the Reformation. We have church buildings but too often the people do not come in. The Scots Reformers would advise us that, along with the truth of the gospel, we need more flexibility; and the aim of flexibility should be that the church as a whole becomes a missionary force.

2. If it were to be asked what is the recurring theme in Knox's words and writings the answer is perhaps a surprising one. Sometimes he could be severe, and sometimes extreme. Given the days and the harshness of the persecution he witnessed it would be understandable if these elements had preponderated in his ministry. But his keynote was of another kind altogether. From the first years that we have anything from his pen, we find him engaged in a ministry of encouragement. It forms the substance of his many letters to his mother-in-law. He handles the doctrines of election and justification as

causes for bright joy in believers. 'Your imperfection shall have no power to damn you,' he writes to Mrs Bowes, 'for Christ's perfection is reputed to be yours by faith, which you have in his blood.'[46] 'God has received already at the hands of his only Son all that is due for our sins, and so cannot his justice require or crave any more of us, other satisfaction or recompence for our sins.'[47] He writes to the believers facing suffering and possible death in the reign of Mary Tudor, likening their situation to that of the disciples in the tempest on the lake of Galilee. He says, 'Be not moved from the sure foundation of your faith. For albeit Christ Jesus be absent from you (as he was from his disciples in that great storm) by his bodily presence, yet he is present by his mighty power and grace . . . and yet he is full of pity and compassion.'[48] Or again he writes:

Stand with Christ Jesus in this day of his battle, which shall be short and the victory everlasting! For the Lord himself shall come in our defence with his mighty power; He shall give us the victory when the battle is most strong; and He shall turn our tears into everlasting joy.[49]

3. One thing stands out above all else in the life of John Knox. At many different points in his life we have the comment of individuals who saw him, and the testimony most frequently repeated has to do with one point, namely, the power of his preaching. One of the first times we hear of Knox's ministry is in a letter of Utenhovius, writing from London to Bullinger in Zurich, on 12 October 1552. He reported how a stranger in London has suddenly caught the public attention:

Some disputes have arisen within these few days among the bishops, in consequence of a sermon of a pious preacher, chaplain to the duke of Northumberland, preached by him before the King and Council, in which

he inveighed with great freedom against kneeling at the
Lord's Supper, which is still retained here by the English.
This good man, however, a Scotsman by nation, has so
wrought upon the minds of many persons, that we may
hope some good to the Church will at length arise from
it.[50]

Another such momentous occasion came seven years later,
at Stirling on Wednesday, 8 November 1559. The Protestant
forces of the Lords of the Congregation had been beaten by
the French outside Edinburgh and had retreated from the city
by night, with insults shouted at them as they departed: 'We
would never have believed,' wrote Knox, 'that our natural
countrymen and women could have wished our destruction
so unmercifully, and have so rejoiced in our adversity.' They
marched to Stirling and regathered, helpless and demoralized,
except for one man. It was at this low point that Knox preached
to them from Psalm 80, 'Turn us again, O God of hosts, and
cause thy face to shine; and we shall be saved.' For years to
come men spoke of the effect of that one sermon. The listeners
acted like men brought back from the dead. The words of the
English ambassador, spoken on a later occasion, describe it
perfectly: 'The voice of one man is able in one hour to put
more life in us than five hundred trumpets continually
blustering in our ears.'[51]

One other account of such preaching is too memorable to
be omitted. As already noted, in July 1571 the Queen's party
had such power in Edinburgh that Knox was forced to stay in
St Andrews for thirteen months. A student there at the time
was fifteen-year-old James Melville, and he would see Knox
walking to church from the old priory, a staff in one hand and
held under his other armpit by a friend, with furs wrapped
round his neck. It was the year before his death and his strength
was gone. Melville wrote in his *Autobiography*:

Of all the benefits I had that year [1571] was the coming of that most notable prophet and apostle of our nation, Mr John Knox, to St Andrews . . . I heard him teach there the prophecy of Daniel that summer and winter following. I had my pen and my little book, and took away such things as I could comprehend. In the opening up of his text he was moderate the space of an half hour; but when he entered to application, he made me so grew [shudder] and tremble, that I could not hold a pen to write.[52]

Melville says further that Knox had to be lifted up into the pulpit 'where it behoved him to lean at his first entry; but before he had done with his sermon he was so active and vigorous, that he was like to ding that pulpit in blads and fly out of it!'[53]

What made Knox this kind of preacher? He had natural gifts, of course, but not more than some others who never made such an impression. 'I am not a good orator in my own cause,' he once wrote to his mother-in-law.[54] When it came to preaching it was *not* his own cause. 'It hath pleased God of his superabundant grace to make me, most wretched of many thousands, a witness, minister and preacher.' His authority came from the conviction that preaching is God's work, the message is His word, and he was sure the Holy Spirit would honour it. This was the certainty which possessed him. I do not say there were not moments of doubt, but at the great crises the Holy Spirit so filled him that nothing could deter him and the result was the transformations that occurred even in the most unpromising and hostile circumstances.

In the summer of 1559, when he first returned to St Andrews, warning was sent to him by the bishop that if he dared to preach the next Sunday there would be a dozen hand guns discharged in his face. His friends advised delay but he went ahead and took for his text Christ driving the buyers and sellers out of the temple. The famous painting of the scene by Sir David Wilkie captured something of that day, 11 June 1559, and the effect of it at the time can be seen in the number of priests of the Roman Church who confessed the faith.

It was due to a similar crisis that we have the only sermon Knox ever prepared for publication. The text was Isaiah 26: 13–21 and the sermon was preached on 19 August 1565 in St Giles. The previous month Lord Darnley had married Queen Mary and was declared King. Darnley has been described as a man who could be either Catholic or Protestant as it suited him, sometimes he went 'to mass with the Queen and sometimes attended the Reformed sermons'.[55] On this particular Sunday he sat listening on a throne in St Giles and, while he was not directly mentioned in the sermon, it so infuriated him that Knox was instantly summoned before the Privy Council and forbidden to preach while the King and Queen were in town. Part of Knox's response was to write down the sermon as fully as he could remember it. It is the only Knox sermon that has survived and in its conclusion he has these memorable sentences:

> Let us now humble ourselves in the presence of our God, and, from the bottom of our hearts, let us desire him to assist us with the power of his Holy Spirit . . . that albeit we see his Church so diminished, that it shall appear to be brought, as it were, to utter extermination, that yet we may be assured that in our God there is power and will to increase the number of his chosen, even while they be enlarged to the uttermost coasts of the earth.

Then, at the end of the sermon Knox added this postscript which was also printed:

> Lord, into thy hands I commend my spirit; for the terrible roaring of guns, and the noise of armour, do so pierce my heart, that my soul thirsts to depart. The last of August

1565, at four at afternoon, written indigestly, but yet truly so far as memory would serve.[56]

The only true explanation of Knox's preaching is in words he applied to others of his fellow countrymen, 'God gave his Holy Spirit to simple men in great abundance.'[57] To read Knox is to be convicted of the smallness of our faith in the power of the Word of God. Unbelief has had too much influence upon us. The modern church needs to relearn the words of 2 Corinthians 4:13: 'We having the same spirit of faith, according as it is written, I believed, and therefore have I spoken; we also believe, and therefore speak.'

4. The history of the church at the time of the Reformation is a singular reminder to us of how God is in history. Christ is in the church and on the throne – directing and governing all person and all events. Standing where we do in time we see Knox's faith in this fact verified, but it was another thing for him to see it in the midst of poverty, when good men were being put to death, and when he endured his twelve years of exile. Yet the truth is that it was the storm of persecution which scattered Christians that was the very means God used to advance his purposes. If Knox had never been a refugee in England he would never have formed the friendships which became so significant in drawing the two long-hostile nations together.

When Knox came back to Scotland in 1559, with his English wife and the English tongue, the world for him was a much bigger place. And it was the exile of Knox and others in Calvin's city which gave Britain the Geneva Bible, the version that was to be the most used through much of the next hundred years. So by persecution the gospel advanced, and it was the means by which God forged an international vision and co-operation among his people. Samuel Rutherford surely stated history accurately when he wrote:

Christ hath a great design of free grace to these lands; but his wheels must move over mountains and rocks. He never yet wooed a bride on earth, but in blood, in fire, and in the wilderness.[58]

* * * * *

In the spring of 1572, while Knox was still in St Andrews, there was a marked decline in his health, yet in August he was able to return to Edinburgh and, after thirteen months absence, preach again in the pulpit of St Giles. But the vast congregation could no longer hear his now feeble voice, and thereafter he chose the pulpit of the much smaller Tolbooth Church where he began to preach on the crucifixion on 21 September. The English ambassador reported on 6 October, 'John Knox is now so feeble as scarce can he stand alone, or speak to be heard of any audience.' Yet he was able, on Sunday, 9 November, to preach at the installation of his successor, James Lawson. It was the last time he was to leave his home. The following Thursday he had to lay aside reading and on the Friday, confused which day it was, he declared he meant to go to church and to preach on the resurrection of Christ. A week later, with increasing difficulty in breathing, he ordered his coffin to be made and waking hours were now spent in hearing Scripture read (especially Isaiah 53, John 17 and Ephesians), saying good-bye to friends, and speaking brief words of testimony and prayer: 'Live in Christ. Live in Christ, and then flesh need not fear death – Lord, grant true pastors to thy Church, that purity of doctrine may be maintained.'

On Monday, 24 November 1572, he insisted on rising and dressing but within half an hour he had to be put back to bed. To the question of a friend, Had he any pain?, he replied: 'It is no painful pain, but such a pain as shall soon, I trust, put an end to the battle.' There was further intermittent conversation that day and a last reading of 1 Corinthians 15 at which he exclaimed, 'Is not that a comfortable chapter?' About eleven o'clock that evening, he said, 'Now it is come', and, lifting up one hand, he passed through his final conflict in peace. In the words of his secretary, Richard Bannatyne,

> In this manner departed this man of God: the light of Scotland, the comfort of the Church within the same, the mirror of godliness, and pattern and example of all true ministers.

[1] James Stalker, *His Ideas and Ideals* (London: Hodder and Stoughton, 1904), p. v. 'For the mass of his countrymen, Knox is the greatest person their country has produced.' P. Hume Brown, *John Knox, A Biography* (London: Black, 1895), vol. 2, p. 298.

[2] Charles L. Warr, *The Presbyterian Tradition* (London: Maclehose, 1933), p. 303.

[3] For summary, see David Hay Fleming, *The Reformation in Scotland* (London: Hodder and Stoughton, 1910), pp. 194–200.

[4] J. H. Merle d'Aubigné, *History of the Reformation in Europe,* vol. 6 (London: Longmans, 1875), p. 123.

[5] A. F. Mitchell, *The Scottish Reformation* (Edinburgh: Blackwood, 1900), p. 31.

[6] d'Aubigné, *History,* vol. 6, p. 50.

[7] John Knox, *History of the Reformation in Scotland,* ed. C. J. Guthrie (repr., Edinburgh: Banner of Truth, 1982) p. 222. Hereafter quoted as Guthrie, *Knox.*

[8] In the seventeenth century a manuscript statement of his age at death was given as '57', but it was misread as '67', thus making the date of his death ten years earlier than it was. This mistake was followed by all writers until Hay Fleming identified it in 1904. That 57 was the correct age of Knox at death is confirmed by a letter from Peter Young to Beza in November 1579. See P. Hume Brown, *John Knox, A Biography,* vol. 2 (London: 1895), pp. 322–3.

[9] *Works of John Knox,* ed. David Laing, vol. 3 (Edinburgh, 1895), p. 439. Hereafter, Laing, *Knox.*

[10] David Calderwood, *History of the Kirk of Scotland,* ed. Thomas Thomson (Edinburgh: Wodrow Soc., 1842), vol. 1, p. 156.

[11] d'Aubigné, *History,* vol. 6, p. 244.

[12] *Ibid.,* p. 257.

[13] Knox, *History of the Reformation in Scotland,* in Laing, Knox, vol. 1, p. 233. There are three versions of Knox's *History.* Guthrie, *Knox,* is a popular abridgement. Laing is complete. William Croft Dickinson produced a fine

edition, *John Knox's History of the Reformation in Scotland* (London: Nelson, 1949), with the spelling of the Laing text modernized throughout.

[14] I am assuming that French galleys changed little between this date and the end of the seventeenth century.

[15] Laing, *Knox*, vol. 3, p. 83.

[16] Ibid., p. 316.

[17] Ibid., p. 102

[18] This was recorded by two contemporary Catholic writers, quoted in Guthrie, *Knox*, p. 96n.

[19] *The Liturgy of John Knox* (Glasgow: Morison, 1886), p. 125.

[20] Laing, *Knox*, vol. 4, p. 439.

[21] Ibid., vol. 6, p. 49.

[22] Ibid., vol. 4, p. 204.

[23] Ibid., vol. 1, p. 61.

[24] This and the preceding quotation I owe to James Kirk's chapter on 'The "Privy Kirks" and Their Antecedents: The Hidden Face of Scottish Protestantism', in his book *Patterns of Reform: Continuity and Change in the Reformation Kirk* (Edinburgh: T. & T. Clark, 1989).

[25] 'Dolour'= pain, grief, sorrow.

[26] Laing, *Knox*, vol. 6, p. 130.

[27] Lord Eustace Percy, *John Knox* (London: Hodder and Stoughton, n.d. [1934]) p. 385. It is true there was a brighter side than this description conveys. It seems that the Reformers were able to fill about a quarter of the parish churches with ministers. See James Kirk, *Patterns of Reform*, p. 130.

[28] Gordon Donaldson, *The Scottish Reformation* (Cambridge: University Press, 1960), p. 85.

[29] Spiritual and other influences were almost chaotically intermingled in the Reformation. There were motives besides the gospel for men to turn Protestant, not least the existence of wealthy Church lands and their revenues that were now defenceless before the nobility. Knox understood this very well.

[30] Hume Brown, *Knox*, vol. 2, p. 277.

[31] Laing, *Knox*, vol. 6, p. 619.

[32] Ibid., p. 569.

[33] Quoted by Peter Lorimer, *John Knox and the Church of England* (London: King, 1875), p. 234. The 'apparell' issue concerned the disagreement over the dress of ministers.

[34] Dickinson, *Knox's History*, vol.1, p. lxxiii.

[35] Laing, *Knox*, vol. 6, p. 483.

[36] Ibid., vol. 3, pp. 268–9.

[37] Ibid., vol. 6, p. 104.

[38] Ibid., vol. 6, p. 104.

[39] Ibid., vol. 6, pp. 124–5.

[40] Thomas M'Crie, *Life of John Knox* (Edinburgh: Blackwood, 1873), p. 294. It was M'Crie's *Life of Knox* that began the recovery of the Reformer's reputation on its first publication in 1811. It remains in print today (Free Presbyterian Publications, Glasgow).

41 Hume Brown, *Knox*, vol. 2, pp. 315–6n. It is not easy to relate the sums quoted with those given by Jasper Ridley who, in the values of 1968, reckoned that Knox left assets worth about £45,000, with some £25,000 of that amount owing to him in debts. Jasper Ridley, *John Knox* (Oxford: Clarendon Press, 1968), p. 518.

42 Laing, *Knox*, vol. 2, p. 239. The General Assembly of 1562 deemed that twice a year was sufficient in rural congregations. Despite protest against the infrequency of the observation of the Lord's Supper, including that of the eighteenth-century evangelical leader, John Erskine ('On frequent Communicating', *Theological Dissertations*, Edinburgh, 1806, pp. 267–339), the tradition still persists in some of the Scottish churches.

43 Laing, *Knox*, vol. 6, p. 386.

44 *Ibid.*, vol. 2, pp. 142–5. Too often a correct insistence on the office of the minister of the Word was to lead to the form of clericalism against which George Gillespie protested in the 1640s: 'The name of clergy appropriate to ministers, is full of pride and vain-glory, and hath made the holy people of God to be despised.' *Assertion of the Government of the Church of Scotland*, p. 9, in *The Presbyterian's Armoury*, vol. 1, *Works of George Gillespie* (Edinburgh: Ogle, Oliver and Boyd, 1846).

45 Laing, *Knox*, vol. 4, p. 138.

46 Ibid., vol. 6, p. 519.

47 Ibid., vol. 3, p. 342.

48 Ibid., p. 287.

49 Ibid., p. 215.

50 Hume Brown, *Knox*, vol. 1, p. 126.

51 A. Taylor Innes, *John Knox* (Edinburgh: Oliphant, 1896), pp. 89–90.

52 *The Autobiography and Diary of James Melvill*, ed. Robert Pitcairn (Edinburgh: Wodrow Soc., 1842), p. 26.

53 Ibid., p. 33.

54 Laing, *Knox*, vol. 3, p. 378.

55 Ibid., vol. 6, p. 223.

56 Ibid., p. 673.

57 Ibid., vol. 1, p. 101.

58 David Hay Fleming, *Critical Reviews Relating Chiefly to Scotland* (London: Hodder and Stoughton, 1912), p. 167.

St Andrews

2

Robert Bruce:
Standing Fast
in Dark Days

Borthwick Castle (akin to Airth)

'Let Tham Say, 1581'

WORDS CUT INTO A WALL IN AIRTH CASTLE, STIRLINGSHIRE, THE YEAR
BRUCE ANSWERED HIS CALL TO THE MINISTRY OF THE WORD.

'Do you remember how James Stuart dragged Robert Bruce about,
seeking a place and a point of view from which that great preacher
and patriot might be got to preach and to pray to the king's dictation?
If our young ministers would have a life-long lesson and illustration
in fearlessness, in fidelity, and in a good conscience to the end of a
life of bribes on one hand, and of persecution and banishment on
the other, let them read themselves deeply into those two narratives
so unsurpassable in effectiveness for a minister, the Life of Balaam in
the history of Israel, and the Life of Robert Bruce in the history of
Scotland and of England.'

ALEXANDER WHYTE, PREACHING ON BALAAM.

B ruce is a noble name which has come down through generations of Scottish history. Most commonly it is first associated with King Robert Bruce who, on the battlefield at Bannockburn in 1314, prevailed over the English with an army less than one third of theirs. Later eminent men of the same name include James Bruce, the eighteenth-century explorer of Ethiopia, and the Rev. John Bruce of Edinburgh whose hearers included the youthful Robert Murray M'Cheyne. But there is another Bruce whom the churches have reason to remember. He is Robert Bruce, 'Minister of Christ's Evangel in the Kirk of Edinburgh', born about the year 1555, and died in 1631. He has been variously described. John Livingstone, a contemporary who often heard him, believed:

No man in his time spake with such evidence and power of the Spirit . . . yea, many of his hearers thought that no man since the apostles spake with such power.[1]

A century later Robert Wodrow, wrote:

There were few, if any Ministers, or Christians, in Mr Bruce's time, or since, that came up his length, far less excelled him.'[2]

William Cunningham, who edited Bruce's writings in 1843, considered he was 'one of the most distinguished men whom Scotland has ever produced'.[3]

Opinions such as these deserve attention. But there is a particular reason why the churches today need to recall Bruce. The period through which he lived was very similar to our own. We tend to think that we live in discouraging and confusing days. We see much false religion and few faithful pulpits. We have a government and a population which shows scant reverence for God and his Word. We face indifference on the one hand and compromise on the other. With features such as these, and worse, Bruce was entirely familiar. After the hopeful beginnings of the Reformed Church of Scotland in the days of Knox, the promise faded and much of Bruce's life was to be spent in a period which his friend James Melville described as one of 'doleful decay'.[4] How did Bruce live and act through such days? What kept him from losing heart? The answer to these questions is a reason why his life and ministry remain of particular relevance. We are not the first generation called upon to stand fast in an evil day.

NOBLEMAN TURNED PREACHER

Bruce was born at Airth Castle in Stirlingshire. Today it is a peaceful hotel and stopping place for tourists. When he was born in the mid-1550s it was a medieval fortress, already three hundred years old. His father, Sir Alexander Bruce, was of royal descent and one of the ancient barons of Scotland. His mother, Janet Livingstone, also came from a royal line, and one of her sisters was a maid-in-waiting to Mary Queen of Scots. Robert Bruce was their second child and it was while he was still a boy that the religious revolution took place which saw Roman Catholicism formally overthrown as the national religion. Acts of Parliament, however, do not change spiritual realities, and as with many others among the nobility, the Bruces of Airth were unsympathetic to the new faith. Their outlook was reflected in the education planned for their second son. When Robert went to the University of St Andrews about 1568, his parents chose that he should enter St Salvator's College, the one College where the old religion still had favour. Then, when he graduated in 1572, 'he was sent by his father to France'.[5] This was for the study of law at Louvain, a university renowned for its religious conservatism and its opposition to Protestantism.

On returning to Scotland, Bruce took up the career arranged for him as a courtier and lawyer. These plans were all over-turned in one night. The date was 31 August 1581 and Bruce has left an account of what happened. After he went to bed in what he calls 'the new loft chamber' of Airth Castle:

> It pleased God to cite me inwardly, judicially, in my conscience, and to present all my sins before me in such a sort, that He omitted not a circumstance, but made my conscience to see time, place, persons, as vivelie [distinctly] as in the hour I did them. He made the devil accuse me so audibly, that I heard his voice as vivelie as ever I heard anything, not being sleeping but awaking. And so far as he spoke true, my conscience bare him record, and testified against me very clearly . . . my conscience condemned me and the condemnator tormented me, and made me feel the wrath of God pressing me down, as it were, to the lower hell; yea, I was so fearfully and extremely tormented, that I would have been content to have been cast into a cauldron of hot melted lead, to have had my soul relieved of that insupportable weight.[6]

These words have been said to give us 'the exact time of his conversion.'[7] The statement has to be a mistake and for two reasons. First, in Bruce's narrative of his experience he was already using the language of a believer. He says, 'I craved

God's mercy, for the merits of Christ; yea, I appealed ever to his mercy, purchased to me by the blood, death and passion of Christ.' Second, he tells us distinctly what this controversy with God was over: it had to do, he says, with his disobedience to God's call to the gospel ministry: 'He made me first a Christian before he made me a minister. I repyned [fretted, murmured] long to my calling to the ministry. Ten years, at the least, I never leaped on horseback, nor lighted, but with a repyning and just accusing conscience.'

The 'ten years' to which he refers must predate the crisis in the 'new loft chamber' at Airth Castle. What happened that last night of August 1581 was that Bruce's long struggle with a call to the ministry of the Word ended and he came to peace as he surrendered himself to the will of God. 'That same night, ere the day dew, or ere the sun rose, he restrained these furies and these outcries of my just accusing conscience, and enabled me to rise in the morning.'

Ten years before 1581 take us to Bruce's student days at St Andrews. The indications are that his parents' desires to preserve him from the new faith had failed at that time. By the beginning of the 1570s the Word of God was let loose in St Andrews. John Knox himself preached there, as already noted in these pages, and spoke personally to the students. In his youth, Bruce says, he was 'drowned in blindness',[8] and we may readily believe that it was at St Andrews that light came which neither the divines of St Salvator's nor those of Louvain could put out. Both James Melville and Calderwood confirm this understanding of events. The latter tells us distinctly that *before* 31 August 1581, Bruce had 'no rest nor comfort but in the Word of God, and company of good men'.[9]

It is not hard to see why God permitted the confirmation of Bruce's call to the gospel ministry to be so unforgettable. A storm of opposition lay ahead and, in part, Bruce must have anticipated it. His change of direction would mean an end to expectations of his being a leader in the King's court or in the legal profession. More painfully, it could end his proud and close relationship with his own family home and lands. In a vault beneath Airth Castle there remains to this day a brief motto cut into the wall. It may have nothing to do with Bruce, but the words, and still more the date, suggest that they do, 'Let Tham Say, 1581.'

Certainly Bruce needed strong resolution to proceed. Once he revealed to his parents the decision taken under their roof there was loud indignation and opposition. Two years were to pass before they would agree to his going to study divinity at St Mary's (the New College) at St Andrews where the Reformed leader, Andrew Melville, was teaching:

> It was long before I could get leave to go, my mother made me such impediment. My father at last con-descended, but my mother would not, until I had denuded my hands of some land and casualties that I was infefted in: and that I did willingly; cast my clothes from me, my vain and glorious apparel, sent my horse to the fair, and emptied my hands of all impediments, and went to the New College.[10]

This was in the winter of the year 1583. It is at this stage of Bruce's life that we have a first-hand report of him. James Melville, nephew of Andrew Melville, was also at the New College at this date. Although about a year younger than Bruce, he was in advance of him and already a teacher in the university. This did not prevent him instantly becoming a friend and admirer. He tells us how a group of students in the College were engaged in the exposition of the Epistles, from Romans onwards, and that before they came to Hebrews, 'Mr Robert took the whole exercise to himself, to our great joy and comfort.' In due course, Melville continues, 'a multitude of the best people of the town' also had opportunity to hear him.

'So it pleased God at that time, to my singular upholding and encouragement in his service, to begin to train up and frame that most notable preacher.'[11]

Four years later, when Bruce was under call to the pastorate in St Andrews, events suddenly brought him into much wider notice. In June 1587 Andrew Melville took him with him to the General Assembly of the Church in Edinburgh and, knowing that Edinburgh needed another leading pastor, he apparently believed that the student from Airth, although not yet ordained, was the man for the place. Along with other candidates, Bruce was required to expound a portion of Scripture; this he did from Ephesians 6 on the Christian armour, and it led almost immediately to a call to the former pulpit of Knox in the Great Kirk of St Giles.[12] A young man in his early thirties, he declined the call, preferring to remain in St Andrews, but finally the insistence was so strong that he says, 'I advised with my God and thought it meet to obey.'

This rapid rise to fame was followed by other honours. The next year, such was the general esteem in which Bruce was held, that he was made Moderator of the General Assembly. Regard for him seemed almost universal. James Melville commented: 'The godly for his puissant [powerful] and most moving doctrine, loved him; the worldlings, for his parentage and place, reverenced him; and his enemies stood in awe of him.'[13]

SHORT FAVOUR, LONG ANGER

The continuance of Bruce's favoured position depended on one individual.

In 1567, the year before the flight of his mother, Mary Queen of Scots, to England, King James VI had been crowned at little more than a year old. Through his minority a confused and divided country had been governed by a succession of regents but, by the time Bruce settled in Edinburgh, James was assuming real power, aided by a Chancellor, John Maitland, who befriended the Reformed leaders. The King, some eleven years Bruce's junior, was prone to adopt favourites and soon the new minister at St Giles was one of his chief. He was often present at St Giles to hear him and when he went to Denmark in 1589 to bring home a bride, he treated the preacher as a leading member of the Council of State to govern in his absence. Letters to Bruce from the King and from the Chancellor make clear how much authority had been invested in him in their absence. In the King's words, 'Good Mr Robert' was his 'trusty and well-beloved Counsellor'. He invested him with a pension for life and affirmed that he was worth a quarter of the kingdom. It was Bruce who presided at the coronation of the new Queen, and in 1590 a first volume of his sermons was dedicated to the King. In his Epistle Dedicatory to James, he wrote, 'God has not only made you an heir to earthly kingdoms, but also has appointed you to be a fellow-heir with Jesus Christ, of that immortal kingdom and glorious Crown that cannot fade or fall away.'[14]

This was the most peaceful period in Bruce's life. The confidence of his family in him appears to have been restored, and on his marriage to Martha Douglas[15] the property of Kinnaird and family lands around Larbert, of which he had been earlier disinherited, were restored to him. Kinnaird, a house close to Larbert, was to be his family home.

But Bruce had anticipated trouble at the time of his call to Edinburgh: 'I liked better to go to St Andrews, for I knew well the court and we could never agree.' Perhaps the trouble now came sooner than he thought. The King, for whom he had expressed high hopes, proved to be a man whose affections and words were as variable as the weather. One day he could praise the Kirk of Scotland as the purest church in the world, and promise to rid the land of all Jesuits, the next he was scheming for the friendship of Catholics both at home and abroad. He knew that perhaps a third of the Scottish nobility were still for the old religion, and they were led by such powerful figures as the Earls of Huntly and Erroll. In 1592, when Huntly was responsible for the murder of the Earl of Moray, the King proposed no action against him and was furious when the Kirk (with Bruce among the leaders) excommunicated him.

The one consistent principle upon which King James came to act was that there should be no authority higher than his own. The rule of the land, exercised largely by the Church in the days when the Papacy reigned, he wanted wholly for himself. No one in the Reformed Church was therefore supposed to speak or act without his leave. To achieve this it became essential to prevent the Church from controlling its own affairs through its representative General Assemblies. Supported by a majority of his nobles, James became committed to the restoration of bishops whom he could appoint and direct.

It was thus inevitable that the King's friendship with Robert Bruce could not last, and soon the transformation in the royal attitude towards the preacher at St Giles was unmistakeable. Praise was replaced by envy and hostility and probably it was Bruce's preaching that he came to dislike most of all. Supposedly a 'Second Solomon', King James possessed no love of the truth. The necessity for obedience to the Word of God, the certainty of God's wrath upon sin, the blood of Christ as man's only remedy – all these were disturbing subjects that had no place in his pedantic knowledge. The preacher's words had evidently got to the royal conscience and he could not shake them off.

At times, seated in the royal gallery of the Great Kirk, the King disguised the unease he felt by indulging in conversation with his courtiers in tones that could be heard even in the pulpit. On one such occasion, it is said, the preacher deliberately paused until the King was quiet. But when Bruce resumed speaking so did the King, at which there was silence again in the pulpit. When this happened for the third time, Bruce addressed these words to the talkers:

> It is said to have been an expression of the wisest of kings, When the lion roars, all the beasts of the field are at ease [quiet]: the Lion of the tribe of Judah is now roaring in the voice of his Gospel, and it becomes all the petty kings of the earth to be silent.[16]

Yet when James missed hearing Bruce he was no more happy for every report of the man's popularity troubled him. He imagined the preacher was exercising more authority than he could from his throne. 'How did he bewitch the people with his harangues?' the King demanded to know on one occasion. 'Sir', replied Mr Robert, 'I use no harangues.'[17] The truth is that James now saw Bruce as a chief obstacle to securing his own way with the Church and before long he even 'vowed he should want his head'. In 1596 when a charge of treason was invented against him, Bruce was compelled to leave Edinburgh for refuge in Yorkshire.

The next year the King permitted Bruce back to his pulpit with the promise, 'Surely, Mr Robert, you shall recover your room which you had in my affection.'[18] The worthlessness of these words was soon seen. By one means or another it was James's intention to have Bruce either subservient or silenced. To that end he forced a reorganization of the congregations meeting in St Giles. He worked successfully to cause other ministers in the Church to side against the preacher. He sought to have the pension he had settled on him removed and, as this required a case in the Court of Session, did his utmost to intimidate the judges. When they expressed judgment against his wishes, he was so enraged that, referring to Bruce, he told them, 'if he had a whinger [a dagger or short sword] he would cast it at his face'.[19]

How far the King was actually willing to use, or to condone, violence became the final issue in a whole series of crises. In August 1600 James made a detour during a day's hunting to visit John, Earl of Gowrie, at his house near Perth. Faithful attendants were with the King. Gowrie was a strong Protestant and widely regarded as a coming leader in the cause of Christ. What happened on their meeting has never been proved but beyond dispute is the fact that before the day was out, both Gowrie and his brother were dead, killed in the presence of the King. The royal explanation was that the two men had met their end in making an attempt on the King's life, and all ministers of the church were commanded to give thanks from their pulpits for the King's escape and his deliverance from treason.

When Bruce and four other Edinburgh ministers declined to condemn the dead men for treason unless they were given evidence, they were ordered to leave the capital and forbidden to preach anywhere in Scotland under pain of death. So the one-time favourite of the King was parted from his pulpit and people. In his autobiographical narrative Bruce wrote: 'I remained not fully twelve years in Edinburgh, when I was chased out, and have now been banished twenty-six years.' Calderwood, also writing in the 1620s, commented: 'Mr Robert Bruce, specially, was hated for his uprightness, and opposition to the episcopal course; for which cause he was never suffered to return to Edinburgh again to this hour.'[20]

The conduct of James VI towards Bruce bore a striking resemblance to the attitude of King Saul towards David.[21] Gone was the early esteem and admiration for his 'well-beloved Counsellor'. Yet, as though recognizing the irrationality of his behaviour, there were times of apparent repentance. Even after Bruce was forced to leave Scotland in 1600, the King allowed him to return the following year although not to enter Edinburgh. When the two met at Brechin, James 'appeared to

Mr Bruce very loving'.[22] But the terms on which he said he would allow Bruce to return to his pulpit were ones which he knew the preacher could not accept. Before he gave him leave to take up his ministry at St Giles, he must preach a sermon to say that he was fully persuaded of the King's innocence in the Gowrie affair.[23] 'The whole Kirk has done it already,' the King insisted, 'you must not be singular.' Calderwood has given us the reply:

> No prince has power to give instructions to another prince's ambassader. I am the Son of God's ambassader. I am discharged [free from obligation] to preach the pleasures of men, place me where God placed me, and I shall teach fruitful doctrine, as God shall give me grace . . . It lieth not in my hand to make a promise: I know not certainly what God will suffer me to speak; I may stand dumb. Therefore, Sir, leave me free, and when I shall find myself moved by God's Spirit, and to have the warrant of his Word, I shall not fail to do it.

Bruce was not quite as isolated in his resistance to the King's wish to rule the church as the monarch had represented, but it is true that those of like conviction were little more than a handful. Calderwood at one point names only three 'as men who would not be boasted [menaced] nor threatened'.[24] Speaking of the royal policy towards the ministers of the Church, another writer says, 'The timid were awed by threats, the ambitious lured by promises of promotion, and the bold silenced by suspension, fine or imprisonment.'[25]

As to restoration to his Edinburgh ministry, Bruce was tantalized by encouragements which were quickly followed by rebuffs. To a relative and confidant of the King he wrote in 1602 of what his exclusion from his pastorate meant to him: 'For these four or five years bygone, I have been continually under a lingering and declining death, which, I am assured, has been more troublesome and tedious to me, both in mind and body, than that hour of death shall be.' Nevertheless he would not, he said, exchange 'divine theology' for 'court theology'.[26] Bruce met King James for the last time in 1603, as the monarch was about to go south to succeed to the English throne. For a year after the King's departure 'he got peace and rest,' but the policy was unchanged and in February 1605, through James' men who were commissioners to the General Assembly, Bruce was formally removed from his position at St Giles: 'They inhibited him to preach thereafter.'

'He obeyed not,' says Calderwood, as Bruce evidently continued to preach around Larbert. There was no other pastor at that location, and at some point he undertook the restoration of the church building where many would gather to hear him. This was too much for the authorities. He was imprisoned, and then ordered on 18 August 1605 to take himself 'to ward' in Inverness or be outlawed.

THE FRUITFUL YEARS OF BANISHMENT

Inverness was in the remote north, only to be reached 'after a journey terrible both for man and beast'.[27] The sentence left Bruce with liberty of movement within the town and its immediate environs. As a situation calculated to leave him ineffective, it was well chosen by his persecutors. He would be far enough away not to exercise any influence in the nation, and as a place it was one of the last where he could be expected to find much local sympathy. The two-street town, with its castle and oak-bridge across the Ness, was in the midst of a wild area, scarcely touched by Protestant and gospel witness. Inter-clan warfare was an age-old tradition. Violence and robbery were commonplace, with respect and fear shown to none save to the powerful chiefs. In the Highlands, Bruce once commented in an Edinburgh sermon, God punishes sin as 'he makes each one of them to be hangmen to other'.[28] Two years before Bruce first arrived in Inverness, the MacDonalds of Glengarry descended on some of their enemies while they were in church and burnt them alive – men, women and children. Yet despite the lawlessness and misery, people clung to the traditional religion and its superstitions. Thus, when a faithful minister named Richard Merchison protested against image worship in Wick at this period, he was seized and drowned in the river.

Bruce remained in Inverness until 1613[29] when the intervention of his son at the Court secured him a licence to return to the south. Unable to enter Edinburgh, he made Larbert his base and appears to have preached in many other places. After three years, Calderwood says, 'The ministers of Edinburgh traduced him, as one that behaved himself as a general bishop, vaging [wandering] from place to place without a warrant.' Another charge from the same men was that when Bruce had preached at Cramond he had 'counted them false apostles'.[30]

One reason why these men-pleasing ministers were disturbed was the knowledge that Bruce's preaching was thinning their own ranks. A notable proof of this was seen at the church's Perth Assembly in 1618 when Alexander Henderson, minister of Leuchars, voted against the prevailing 'court' party. Four or more years earlier Henderson, as a supporter of that party, had been obtruded on the parish of Leuchars against the wishes of the people. On the day of his settlement he found the church doors locked against him and a forced entry had to be made through a window. About a year after that event, Bruce was preaching in the same area at the church of Forgan. Unknown to him, Henderson was there, sitting, it seems, unnoticed in a dark corner of the building. From the moment Bruce gave out his text, he had Henderson's riveted attention. It was John 10:1, which in Bruce's Geneva Version read, 'Verely, verely, I say unto you, He that entreth not in by the doore into the sheepefold, but climeth up another way, he is a thiefe and a robber.' From that day forward Henderson saw Bruce as his father in Christ and the King's party in the Church lost one of its ablest men.

In 1620, after Bruce had been preaching in the Glasgow area, he was threatened with the choice of obedience or a further confinement, this time in Aberdeen. It seems that it was the death of his wife, Martha, that gave him respite from the execution of the threat. During this whole period, Calderwood says, 'the man of God was tossed from place to place'. Before the end of 1621 he was imprisoned without trial in Edinburgh Castle and, early in 1622, ordered to return to Inverness. A personal letter from him to the King had no effect, despite a promise: 'If his Majesty would be graciously pleased to suffer me to spend the few remnant of my aged and wearisome days at my own house, I will be very glad, and willing to be perpetually confined there, and two miles round about; and I shall never transcend these bounds.'[31] When others appealed on his behalf that his removal north be suspended until the end of winter, they received a peremptory response, 'We will have no more popish pilgrimages to Kinnaird; he shall go to Inverness.' Thus Bruce returned north for a second term at about the age of sixty-seven.

The preacher's confinements in the north constitute one of the most significant periods in his life but unhappily little record of what happened in those years has survived. The information that survived consists only of fragments of two different kinds. The first sort concern the difficulties he faced – ill health, hostility from the local minister and magistrates, and even an attempt on his life. A bullet fired at him in the street missed him by inches when, while walking, he suddenly stopped to look at a bird's nest. In a letter written at Inverness in 1613 he speaks of his 'miserable and barbarous' location, which 'almost extinguished both my vital and sensitive spirits . . . I am a man that has tasted many afflictions.'[32] At another time we read, 'he could not get convenient lodging, or at least keep it for long'.[33]

The second set of fragments present a different picture. We read of his preaching Sunday mornings and Wednesdays and of the individuals who came under his influence. They included the Earl and Countess of Sutherland (also confined at Inverness by the King), whose son, the 18th Earl of Sutherland, was to be first to put his name to the National Covenant of 1638. At least one future minister and evangelist in the north was converted through hearing Bruce. He was Alexander Munro, son of the Laird of Kitwell, Kiltearn.[34] But it was not only individuals who were changed, a report has survived which indicates that at some point a considerable turning to Christ attended Bruce's preaching in the town. Robert Fleming, in his work *The Fulfilling of the Scripture*, first published in 1669, wrote: 'While he was confined in Inverness, that poor dark country was marvellously enlightened, many were brought to Christ by his ministry, and a seed sown in these places, which to this day is not worn out.'[35] News of what had happened in Inverness went as far as England for we find Thomas Goodwin referring to one of the individuals brought in there under Bruce's ministry. James Kirkton makes reference to the same individual. He affirmed that Bruce 'rarely preached but to a weeping auditory,' and continued:

> A poor Highlander hearing him, came to him after sermon, and offered him his whole substance (which was only two cows) upon condition Mr Bruce would make God his friend.[36]

Dr Aird, a Highland minister of the mid-nineteenth century, said in an address given in 1888 on 'The Progress of Evangelical Religion in the Highlands':

> It is upwards of half a century since I heard a tradition which astonished me then, that during part of Mr Bruce's

ministry in Inverness, persons from Sutherland and Ross were in the habit of going there to hear him, through bridgeless streams and rivers, and across ferries: but years afterwards I found it verified in *Blair's Autobiography.* 'The memory of that man of God, Mr Bruce, is sweet to this day [1700] in this place, Inverness. He in the days of James was confined in this town and country about, for multitudes of all ranks would have crossed the ferries every Lord's day to hear him, yea they came from Ross and Sutherland.'[37]

Aird's words on 'during part of his ministry' give us a clue to the explanation of the conflicting information which has survived on Bruce's years in Inverness. Hardships were by no means the whole story. Wodrow, without quoting any source, and perhaps mistakenly, refers to 'very great success' with 'many converted and multitudes edified' during his *first* confinement. Other considerations would seem to identify the time of great blessing with his second stay in the town. Wodrow himself gives us a report he heard at Larbert and 'well vouched and believed in that place'. It was that as Bruce was about to leave on horseback for Inverness, he was given a distinct conviction of a commission from Christ, and that he said to a friend he was about to leave, 'I go to sow a seed in Inverness that shall not be rooted out for many ages.' Whether this happened as he went north for his first or second confinement, Wodrow commented, 'I cannot determine, but I incline to think it might be the last.'[38]

'All great awakenings,' it has been said, 'begin in the dawning of the august and terrible aspects of the Deity upon the popular mind.'[39] This is what appears to have happened in Inverness during Bruce's second period there. 'Terrible it is,' wrote Bruce, 'to see the countenance of God in his justice . . . When the Lord wakens thy conscience there is never a sin but it shall start to thy memory, and bring such a horror with it, that of all pains it is the greatest. Yea, the burning of the carcase in a hot lead is nothing to the trouble of conscience.'[40]

This is the explanation of the concern of the 'poor Highlander' who was anxious that God should be 'his friend'. True conviction of sin ever leads to moral transformation and this evidently happened in the area so long a spiritual wilderness. MacNicol writes of Bruce: 'He was ordained to be a pioneer apostle of the north. Nor did the King know, when he sent the great preacher to Inverness, that he was embarking upon a policy which should bring peace to the mountains and the glens, not through extermination, but through the instilling of a new principle of love.'[41]

In 1624 Bruce was given temporary permission to return to his home at Larbert. While he was there King James died in 1625 and, as the reign of Charles I began, he was allowed to remain and preach in Larbert. In 1628 it seems that the injunctions against him were so relaxed that he was once more permitted to preach in Edinburgh, provided he did not reside there. This would have been his first reappearance among his former flock for nearly thirty years. The respite did not last long. His old enemies in the Church informed the King against him and before the end of 1628 he was again restricted to Larbert. In a surviving letter, written in January 1629, he reported to a friend what had happened. His enemies, he wrote, 'have gone about to make me odious to his Majesty, and to all honest men'. But his final parting with the Scottish capital did not overwhelm him with sadness, instead, he could say:

> Howsoever Edinburgh has cast me off, rejected and banished me out of their parts, I leaped no sooner on my horse, but the gates of heaven were cast open to me . . . my God remains my God in a copious manner.[42]

Not content with their actions, at least one of his opponents (whom he calls 'false brethren'), a man named Robert

Monteith, wrote against him. In a letter of 30 March 1629 Bruce commented on how Monteith's words illustrated the difference between a Christian and an unregenerate man. Monteith had accused him of being ignorant, and Bruce responded by referring to Christ's words in John 9:41, 'If ye said that ye were blind, you should have no sin; but now, by reason ye say ye see, therefore your sin remains.' 'Indeed, I say truly, I am blind, and would fain have my eyes opened anew . . . happy am I that I entered to serve him, and sorry am I that I cannot mend my hand; and glad would I be (he knows) to do the thing that might honour him . . . I am of that mind, and look, in his mercy, to keep my credit with His divine Majesty; and that, by renewing my daily repentance, to live and die a penitent sinner.' Yet notwithstanding his persisting ignorance he confessed he could also say: 'I have taken pains to banish it these fifty years; and I may say justly, that I have been a continual student; and I hope I can say it without offence, that he is not within the Isle of Britain, of my age, that takes greater pains upon his Bible.'[43]

We know that Bruce did not keep strictly to the confines of Larbert. He was, for instance, present and preaching during a 'down-pouring of the Spirit' at that memorable weekend of services at Kirk of Shotts in June 1630. That was the occasion when one witness says that 'near five hundred had at that time a discernible change wrought on them, of whom most proved lively Christians afterwards'.[44]

Bruce was now some seventy-five years of age, his wife had been dead for several years and he was also ready for home. 'I wonder why I am kept here so long,' he would say to friends. The following year, while having breakfast, his daughter, Martha, was about to prepare him another egg when he said, 'Hold, daughter, hold; my Master calleth me.' He then asked that the house Bible, the Geneva Version, be brought. Unable himself to read it, he said, 'Cast me up the 8th of Romans,' and he began to recite much of the second half of the chapter until he came to the last two verses: 'For I am persuaded that neither death, nor life, nor angels, nor principalities, nor powers, nor things present, nor things to come, nor height, nor depth, nor any other creature shall be able to separate us from the love of God, which is in Christ Jesus our Lord.' 'Set my finger on these words,' he asked. 'God be with you my children. I have breakfasted with you, and shall sup with my Lord Jesus this night. I die believing these words.'

Thus Robert Bruce departed this life on 27 July 1631, at Gartsherry, a second home at Old Monklands. 'A man as noble by nature as he was by birth,' said Calderwood, 'who won so many thousands to Christ.' The burial took place at Larbert where, it is said, between four and five thousand attended his burial beside the church. There a plain flagstone has his initials and, in Latin, the words of Philippians 1:21:

CHRIST IN LIFE AND DEATH GAIN.

PERSECUTION: 'THE LORD IS A WONDERFUL WORKMAN'

We too often imagine that eminent leaders of the church lived in bright days so unlike our own. The truth is different. The life of Robert Bruce is a reminder that difficulties, affliction and adversity are commonly the characteristic of such men. Suffering marked almost the whole period through which he lived and, as John Laidlaw has written, 'It is partly the gloom and disappointment of the times and his conduct under these which have helped to shed lustre on his name.'[45] The same was true of the small band of faithful men who were his friends; all of them knew banishment, imprisonment and confinement of various kinds. What is striking is the way in which they saw their afflictions, not as a cause for dismay and discouragement, but as a confirmation that they were in the way of Christ, and that the worst the world could do would not prevent his blessing.[46] In the words of Bruce: 'That same fury and rage whereby they think to dishonour God and overwhelm his Kirk, he turneth that same rage to the contrary, and he maketh out of that same fury his own glory and the deliverance of his Kirk to shine. The Lord is a wonderful workman; he bringeth about his purpose in such sort that he can draw out light out of darkness.'[47]

Bruce knew that there is a connection between suffering and the joyful advancement of the gospel. The promise is, 'If ye be reproached for the name of Christ, happy are ye; for the Spirit of glory and of God resteth upon you' (*1 Pet.* 4:14). Writing to one of the flock in Edinburgh from whom he had been finally parted in 1628, he could say:

> My enemies, the worst that they can do the Lord has turned into the best. I never got such access in my time as I have gotten since I went from you. The treasures of his riches have been opened unto me.[48]

His ministry confirms the saying of George Whitefield, 'Persecution and the power of religion will always keep pace.'

It is more surprising, perhaps, to note the chief source of the opposition which had to be endured. While a proud monarchy was at the head, the instigators and instruments were most commonly the 'false brethren' within the Church. Some of them took a lead in the persecution of faithful men; others condoned what was happening by their silence, 'content to be ignorant' of what was going on. There were men enough willing to take the vacant pulpit of St Giles who were not willing to own the cross of Christ. In 1596 we find him writing, 'Fie upon false brethren! These men are the wreck of the kirk, for their graces they have are not sanctified; they will speak the truth a while till they be put at, but incontinent [immediately] they turn and make their graces weapons to fight against Christ and his kingdom.'[49]

In his letter of January 1629, already quoted, to a former member of his church, Bruce says:

> There is a great curse upon Edinburgh, and namely, upon the ministry and magistracy, be learned as they will, and count themselves so. I will assure you, as far as I have learned, they are not taught of God, nor sent in mercy by his Holy Spirit unto you.[50]

In another letter of the same year he wrote: 'There is not now a lawful minister of Edinburgh living except I; for they have all entered in a corrupt way.'[51]

The words of 1629 were written in private, but unfaithfulness in the ministry was not infrequently openly referred to by Bruce in the pulpit. As early as his published sermons of 1591, we find him saying: 'As to the greatest part of our priests, our ministers, their mouths have lost the truth, and their persons have lost their reverence; the Lord has made them contemptible in the eyes of men.'[52]

Such words were undoubtedly the pretext upon which both the King and his servants in the Church repeatedly charged Bruce and his friends with being the authors of 'schism'. James claimed it was his duty to 'prevent discord which was like to arise among pastors, and to knit them up in unity'.[53] One of the charges, justifying Bruce's removal to Inverness in 1605, was 'his censuring the doings of ministers, fostering thereby factions and divisions in the kirk'.[54] Again, in 1622, when the plea was put to the King that Bruce might delay his return to the northern confinement until winter was past, those who wrote the plea were censured with the response, 'It is not for love of Mr Robert that you have written, but to entertain a schism in the kirk.'[55]

For Bruce an unfaithful ministry was of the greatest danger to the cause of Christ. He spoke about it openly because it moved him deeply in private, as John Livingstone mentions:

He told me once in private that he had dreamed, and had seen a great long book with boards flying in the air, and all the black fowls flying about it, and that as it touched any of them they fell down dead; and that he heard a voice which he said was as audible as I heard him speak, 'This is the ire of God upon the ministry of Scotland,' and he presently fell to weeping and crying to God that he might be kept faithful, and not be one of these that were stricken down dead; and he said that when he awaked he found all his pillow wet with his tears.[56]

Behind false brethren in the ministry Bruce saw a deeper problem. It was the extent to which the national Church and the world were confused. Preaching on true Christian experience in his early ministry he said:

This heavenly light and supernatural understanding, whereby we see God, is proper only to the true members of Christ Jesus, who are his kirk; none has this eye of faith but they only. It is so proper to them that it severs them from all other societies in the earth, whether they take to themselves the name of kirk, or are altogether enemies thereunto.[57]

This was the kind of talk that did indeed cause division and, as in England, it brought on Bruce and other faithful men the charge that they were 'Puritans'.[58] The truth is that although Bruce and his colleagues sought to purify the national Church, the necessary remedies were not in their hands.[59] But this did not dismay them for they knew that God had other means to advance his truth. They spoke of the persecution as the way in which real Christians were 'discovered'. True believers would 'rather choose affliction than iniquity', and by permitting their suffering God would distinguish them from the rest. Bearing the cross marks out the true from the false and separates the wheat from the chaff. So when the Countess of Eglinton, a woman faithful in the gospel cause, found herself in the midst of difficulties, Bruce consoled her with these words: 'This is the cross of Christ that is upon your Ladyship . . . Ye would be a formal Christian, Madam, if ye wanted that; a painted sepulchre, an outward professor.'[60]

Bruce would have agreed entirely with words which John Welsh, in exile in France in 1619, wrote to him on the 'desertion so universal' in Scotland:

The persecution there is lamentable; but, without all question, when the chaff is discovered, he will not let the rod of the wicked remain for ever upon the back of the righteous. It is no marvel, if, after so long a peace, so great a liberty, and the enjoyment of the gospel in such abundance, at the last he send the fiery trial.[61]

'THE HAPPIEST MAN THAT EVER WAS BORN'

The secret of Bruce's endurance in such times was the manner in which he was enabled to live in the presence of God. For him such living entailed two things. The first was prayer. In the words of Robert Fleming, he was 'a great wrestler, who had more than ordinary familiarity with his Master'. Bruce exemplified the words of a later Puritan:

Prayer begets and maintains holy courage and magnanimity in evil times. When all things about you tend to discouragement, it is your being with Jesus that makes you bold, *Acts* 4:13. He that uses to be before a great God, will not be afraid to look such little things as men are in the face.[62]

John Livingstone, who could speak from personal knowledge, wrote of Bruce:

He was both in public and private very short in prayer with others, but then every sentence was like a strong bolt shot up to heaven. I have heard him say, he has wearied when others were longsome in prayer, but being alone, he spent much time in prayer and wrestling.

Livingstone illustrates this from an incident known to him at Larbert, where he spent most of the summer of 1627. On a day when Bruce was engaged to preach twice at the church, the interval between the services was extended longer than usual due to the preacher's absence. Some noblemen who were present became anxious about the time on account of the distance they had to ride to their homes later that day. They therefore asked the bellman to find Bruce and request him to begin the service in view of the journey they had before them. The bellman knew where Bruce was – in a room in a house near the church, which he commonly used before the afternoon service. On going to the door the man knocked, but declined to enter when he heard the preacher talking to someone inside. He went back to those who had sent him and explained that he could not tell how long Bruce would be: 'I think he shall not come out the day at all, for I hear him always saying to another that he will not nor cannot go except the other go with him, and I do not hear the other answer him a word at all.' Upon which Livingstone commented, 'The foolish bellman understood not that he was dealing with God.'[63]

The second thing which explains the way Bruce lived in the presence of God was the manner in which he sought 'always to have a clear conscience toward God and toward men' (*Acts* 24:16). He regarded obedience to *conscience* as fundamental to all true Christian living. From that never-forgotten night at Airth in August 1581, acting according to conscience was his watchword. What it meant was the theme of two of his first published sermons:

Our conscience is born with us, is natural to us, and is left in the soul of every man and woman . . . The body shall leave the soul, and the soul shall leave the body; but conscience shall never leave the soul: but wherever the soul goes, to the same place shall the conscience repair; and in whatsoever state thy conscience is when thou diest, in the self-same state shall it meet thee in the great Day.[64]

Although conscience thus belongs to all people, before a man is converted, even when his conscience is 'sleeping', it condemns him and he 'flees from God'. The first need in evangelistic preaching is to awaken conscience so that it 'bites' and 'sendeth thee to seek a remedy'. Once an individual is a Christian, conscience is 'pacified' by faith in the blood of Christ, and 'there comes a calmness and soundness into the heart'. The gospel is 'the oil that should refresh our consciences'. Thereafter, keeping 'a good conscience' is essential to the health and happiness of his soul. It is the ever present witness to our actions and secrets; it gives us the capacity to judge ourselves (*1 Cor.* 11:13), and that judgment leads to joy or pain (*2 Cor.* 1:12). Conscience 'is the best of friends or the worst of enemies in the whole creation'.[65] Bruce has much to say on how a 'sound conscience' is to be preserved. Daily faith in Christ is essential; so is biblical knowledge,[66] and holiness of life. If the mighty God, by his Spirit, dwells in us, he says, 'let us be much more careful that our hearts and consciences may be clean and holy for his remaining'.

What he taught his congregation in this regard in his early ministry he was called to show for another thirty years by his example. Answering critics in 1596 he replies: 'We claim no perfection, but a good conscience in all things.'[67] When he had to refuse obedience to the King it is in the following terms:

I had rather yitt be banished from England and Scotland by his Grace ere they were able to stain the glory of my ministry. For this has been my petition to God, that the Lord Jesus should lead me safely out of this temptation, without impairing my union with him, nor the hurt of the peace of my own conscience . . . I have a body and some goods; let his Majesty use these, as God shall direct him; but as to my inward peace, I would pray his Majesty, in all humility, to suffer me to keep it.[68]

Pressed on another occasion by the Council in Edinburgh to preach so as to satisfy the King, he replied: 'I am resolved by his grace to follow the Word and Spirit of truth; to do there as that Word and Spirit would direct me. If I should promise any other thing, I might well procure the wrath of God, and kindle a fire with my own conscience.'[69]

Prayer and a good conscience were bound up together in Bruce's thinking and in turn they were related to a still more fundamental theme which marks his whole ministry, namely, the Christian's relation to the Holy Spirit. Dependence on the Spirit of God is everywhere in his life and teaching. Prayer is his gift as well as the believer's activity;[70] holiness of life is his enabling as well as our duty. The work of the Spirit and earnest endeavours therefore belong together. 'Walking in the fear of the Lord' and 'the comfort of the Holy Spirit' are conjoined in Scripture (*Acts* 9:31). The Holy Spirit is given 'to them that obey him' (*Acts* 5:32). The resolution of Bruce not to offend Christ, nor to grieve the Holy Spirit, was not the concern of a legalist, unsure of salvation; it was the conviction of one who knew that sin wounds the conscience and mars the enjoyment of God's presence.[71]

Dependence on the Holy Spirit was thus central in Bruce's life. When he was first silenced in Edinburgh, Calderwood reports that his prayer was 'that if it be the Lord's good pleasure to exercise him with a new tentatioun [trial], to pull the people and the ministry both from him, that it would please the Lord instead of the king's, priest's and people's favour, to triple his Spirit upon him, and to let him see in his heart His face brighter and brighter.'[72] Many years later, in the brief period when Bruce was again in Edinburgh in 1628, the petition was still the same. We read of a prayer meeting when Bruce, in the urgency of his plea for God's help, unconsciously knocked upon the table at which they knelt and there was 'so sensible an outpouring of the Spirit, as scarce any present were able to contain themselves.' John Wemyss, a minister present, exclaimed afterwards, 'O! what a strange man is this, for he knocked down the Spirit of God upon us all.'[73]

What Bruce needed as a Christian he needed in a particular way as a preacher. 'We must study to entertain and nourish the Holy Spirit', is his final word addressed to fellow ministers in his early ministry.[74] If the authority and the enabling for preaching – for 'commending ourselves to every man's conscience in the sight of God' (*2 Cor.* 4:2) – comes from God, then his presence and power has to be the first need.[75] So insistent was he on this truth that he regarded powerless preaching as reason enough to question any man's call to the ministry:

> The Spirit in me doth kindle a reverence in the spirit of the hearer; and if it be not in me, the spirit of the hearer will discern me not to be sent, but only to have the word of the commission, and not to have the power; for the power is the evident argument that a man is sent. Therefore, many start to teach this word, who are not sent . . . and therefore the flock of God remains without edification, and the kingdom of God is not built up, because they have only the word of commission and lack the power of the Spirit that should make the Word effectual to the hearer.[76]

An incident in the life of a younger contemporary of Bruce illustrates how seriously he took this principle. Robert Blair was a gifted young man from the Glasgow College, and a candidate for the ministry, when Bruce heard him preach after he had returned to the south from his first exile in Inverness. Afterwards, in conversation with his senior, Blair asked for any advice on his sermon. He received an unforgettable response: 'I found your sermon very polished and digested, but there is one thing I miss in it, to wit, the Spirit of God; I found not *that*.'[77] Far from being alienated, Blair came to admire the man whom he called 'that ancient heroic servant of Christ', and he made the long journey to see him during Bruce's second confinement in Inverness.[78]

The life of Bruce is a testimony to the manner in which joy in Christ can be known whatever the times. Certainly, he knew some dark days and occasional times of 'desertion', but the tenor of his life was the opposite of gloom and sorrow. 'He that has God with him has enough', was the witness of his early ministry and he proved it true. 'Sometimes,' Calderwood says, 'he felt God's presence so sensibly with him, that he could not contain himself in the night from breaking out in these words: "I am the happiest man that ever was born; happy that ever I served God."'[79]

In the last testimony we have from his pen, in a comment which reviews his long life, he wrote in 1629:

> I grant the will was with me, but not so bent as it should have been neither; for I was over timorous, and laden with diversity of infirmities; the spirit in some measure ready, but the flesh weak; yet his Majesty, my gracious God, my God in Christ, accepts of it, as if it had been the most perfect and exact service in the world . . . my sweet Lord has not left me. I never foregathered with a better Master: I never got a sweeter fee and better wages, and I look for a very rich reward. So ye have cause, not only to pray for me, but to praise God greatly for me; that he is so bountiful, and that he meets me above my very expectation.'[80]

The casual observer of the life of Robert Bruce, contrasting the comfort and promise of its beginnings with the hardships that followed, might suppose that by different decisions he could have attained to lasting success. Certainly there is a sense in which he did not become what he might have been. As Laidlaw has written: 'Had he chosen to accommodate himself, even in the least degree, to the contemporary spirit, he might have continued to stand high in royal favour, he might have become in point of influence the first man of his age.'[81]

But Bruce left that kind of success to others, and what a contrast their lives present to his own. John Spottiswoode was one of them. Having started as a minister on the same side as Bruce in the church, he became one of the King's men. He supported the King's plan for bishops in 1600, went south with James for his coronation in England, and rose to become Archbishop of Glasgow and then Primate of Scotland at St Andrews. On his death in England he was buried amid great honour in Westminster Abbey. But Spottiswoode had lived long enough to learn of the downfall of episcopacy in Scotland in 1638, and one of the last things we hear of him was his cry, 'All that we have been doing these thirty years past is thrown down at once.'[82]

For Robert Bruce death brought a simple grave in a country church and, instead of any overthrow of his life's work, there was the assurance of the promise: 'They that be wise shall shine as the brightness of the firmament; and they that turn many to righteousness as the stars for ever and ever' (*Dan.* 12:3).

---

[1] *Select Biographies,* ed. W. K. Tweedie, vol. 1 (Edinburgh: Wodrow Soc., 1845), p. 306. Livingstone, who heard Bruce 'for a greater part of the summer of 1627', elsewhere gives the concluding sentence as his own opinion, Ibid., p. 140.

[2] *Sermons by Robert Bruce, with Collections for His Life by Robert Wodrow,* ed. W. Cunningham (Edinburgh: Wodrow Soc., 1843), p. 3. Hereafter I will refer to this as Wodrow, *Bruce,* and add *Life* when the reference is to the first half of the volume which has separate pagination.   [3] Ibid., p. v.

[4] 'A True Narrative of the Declining Age of the Kirk of Scotland [1610],' in *The Autobiography and Diary of James Melvill*, ed. R. Pitcairn (Edinburgh: Wodrow Soc., 1842), p. 506.

[5] David Calderwood, *History of the Kirk of Scotland*, ed. T. Thomson, 8 vols. (Edinburgh: Wodrow Soc., 1842–9), vol. 4, p.634. Most of the contemporary information we have on Bruce comes from Calderwood (1575–1650), whose *History* covers the years 1527–1625. Much of it is repeated in Wodrow (1679–1734), *Bruce, Life*, with some additions.

[6] Calderwood, *History*, vol. 4, pp. 635–6. This is taken from a few brief pages of autobiography which Bruce wrote in his old age. Other personal words of Bruce, quoted below, are taken from this source unless otherwise stated.

[7] D. C. MacNicol, *Robert Bruce, Minister of the Kirk in Edinburgh* (1907; repr. London: Banner of Truth, 1961), p. 18. MacNicol has provided a helpful biography of Bruce, but not one equal to the stature of his subject.

[8] Wodrow, *Bruce, Life*, p. 123.

[9] Calderwood, vol. 4, p. 635. Calderwood also says that the experience Bruce described was a call to the ministry, 'not after an usual and common manner', vol. 5, p. 724. Melville records how Bruce told him that 'ere he caste himself again in that torment of conscience which was laid on him for resisting the calling of God to the study of theology and ministry, he had rather go through fire and brimstone half a mile long', *Autobiography*, p. 147.

[10] 'Infeft' = put in possession. 'Clothes' = the scarlet clothes worn by courtiers. 'Fair' = a horse market.

[11] Melville, *Autobiography*, p.148.

[12] The building at this period was actually divided into four parts: the Great Kirk, the College Kirk, the Upper Tolbooth and the East or Little Kirk, and so accommodated four distinct congregations. The preacher in the Great Kirk ranked as the senior minister of Edinburgh.

[13] Melville, *Autobiography*, p. 271.

[14] *Sermons upon the Sacrament*, in Wodrow, *Bruce*, p. 4. These five sermons were followed, in 1591, by another eleven, which, together with one more of unknown date, were all that were ever published. The language is a mixture of Scots and English. For an 'Englished' version of the five sermons, see *Robert Bruce's Sermons on the Sacrament, with Biographical Introduction*, John Laidlaw (Edinburgh: Oliphant, 1901).

[15] It is to be wished that we knew more of his wife. She was the daughter of another baron, Douglas of Parkhead, and proved herself able to undertake business for her husband. A letter to her in 1601, when he was in exile, also shows how fully she entered into his thoughts and spirit. He concluded that letter: 'Your loving husband, not weary, I assure you, of the Lord's cross, but weary of the treacherous flattery of men.' Calderwood, vol. 6, p. 135.

[16] Wodrow, *Bruce, Life*, p. 154. Wodrow supposed the preacher was referring to an apocryphal saying attributed to Solomon.

[17] Calderwood, vol. 5, p. 716.

[18] Ibid., vol. 5, p. 653.

[19] Ibid., vol. 5, p. 734. The King's sycophants in the Church, whom he made commissioners of the General Assembly, spoke of Bruce at this time as 'the only pest and troubler of the whole Kirk of Scotland'. Upon which Calderwood comments: 'The truth was they would have been rid of him, because, as long as he stood in that place of ministry, he would be a great impediment to their proceedings', p. 735.

[20] Calderwood, vol. 6, p. 59.

[21] Bruce himself saw the parallel and, on one occasion, speaking to the King on his duty to uphold the law of God, said: 'If you do this, no doubt you will stand, and the Lord will preserve you; if you do it not, I will not say what became of Saul.' Quoted in John Gillies, *Historical Collections of Accounts of Revival* (Kelso: Rutherford, 1845; repr. Edinburgh: Banner of Truth, 1981), p. 178.

[22] Calderwood, vol. 6, p. 146.

[23] At one point, earlier, when this full persuasion was required of Bruce, he replied that more was being asked than he could say of his own creed. 'What,' it was demanded, 'are you not fully persuaded of the articles of your belief?' 'No, my lord,' replied Bruce, 'as I should be: if you and I were both fully persuaded that there were a hell, we should do otherwise than we do.' Ibid., p. 131.

[24] Calderwood, vol. 6, p. 186.

[25] Thomas Thomson in a Life of Calderwood, appended to his *History*, vol. 8, p. v.

[26] Calderwood, vol. 6, pp. 192–3.

[27] This was said of a visit made there by Mary Queen of Scots in 1562.

[28] Wodrow, *Bruce*, p.297.

[29] Except for a quarter of a year in Aberdeen, at one point, where he was invited by the magistrates, but after complaints against his preaching he was charged to return to Inverness. In a letter to the King he explained his absence from Inverness, naming as subsidiary reasons 'my better health, and comfort of my wife and children'. Wodrow, *Bruce, Life*, p. 126.

[30] Calderwood, vol. 7, p. 293.

[31] Wodrow, *Bruce, Life*, p. 132.

[32] Calderwood, vol. 7, pp. 183–4.

[33] Ibid., p. 566. For a time, during his second confinement, this forced him to live at Fortrose, from whence he was entreated to return.

[34] Munro later became minister of Durness in the Reay country, in the far north-west of Scotland, and is spoken of as 'almost the first Protestant minister in that vast territory, now embracing three parishes'. Gustavus Aird, 'The Progess of Evangelical Religion in the Highlands,' in MacRae, *Life of Gustavus Aird* (Stirling: MacKay, n.d.), p. 249.

[35] Quoted in Wodrow, *Bruce, Life*, p. 144.

[36] James Kirkton (1628–99), *The Secret and True History of the Church of Scotland* (Edinburgh, 1817), p. 26. Goodwin probably gives us something closer to the man's actual words, 'I'se give him twenty cows to gree God and me.' *Works of Thomas Goodwin*, vol. 5 (Edinburgh: Nichol, 1863), p. 174. This is an incidental confirmation of the English spoken in the area. In

the Gaelic language there was no New Testament published until 1767, and no Bible until 1801.

[37] MacRae, *Life of Aird*, pp. 248–9. The quotation he gives is not actually from Blair (1593–1666) but from a comment written on 19 June 1700 by John Brand and added as a footnote to *Life of Robert Blair*, ed. Thomas M'Crie (Edinburgh: Wodrow Soc., 1848), pp. 39–40. We have already given above the testimony of Fleming from an earlier date.

[38] Wodrow, *Bruce*, p. 146. Calderwood is silent on the success in Inverness; this may confirm that it came in Bruce's second confinement, which was about the time when Calderwood was writing, but possibly before he heard of it.

[39] W. G. T. Shedd, *Sermons to the Natural Man* (repr. Edinburgh: Banner of Truth, 1977), p. 331.

[40] MacNicol, *Bruce*, pp. 47, 197.   [41] Ibid., p.145.

[42] Wodrow, *Bruce*, pp. 135–6. In the manuscript of this letter possessed by Wodrow an early hand had added against the words, 'Edinburgh has cast me off', 'He means the corrupt ministry of Edinburgh.'

[43] Wodrow, *Bruce, Life*, pp. 137–8. Referring to Monteith's slander, Bruce added, 'I have seen the day, when the best subject in this country durst not have done the like.'

[44] Gillies, *Historical Collections*, p.198. The most used sermon was evidently that of John Livingstone on the Monday night. Another record from the period, written by a Christian in the Glasgow area, noted: 'Two springs of revival of religion in this corner of the country were the famous sermon at Kirk of Shotts; and the labours of Mr Robert Bruce.' Ibid., p. 200.

[45] Laidlaw, *Bruce's Sermons on the Sacrament*, p. lxxv.

[46] Trials themselves are to be seen as blessings for 'bread and drink are no more necessary to sustain this earthly life, than affliction and the cross are necessary to entertain the spiritual life. It is not possible but prosperity shall blind us.' Wodrow, *Bruce*, p. 385.

[47] Wodrow, *Bruce*, p. 316.   [48] Ibid., *Life*, p. 134.

[49] Ibid., *Life*, p. 53.   [50] Ibid., *Life*, p. 136.

[51] MacNicol, *Bruce*, p. 176.   [52] Wodrow, *Bruce*, p. 288.

[53] Calderwood, vol. 5, p. 716.   [54] Ibid., vol. 6, p. 291.

[55] Ibid., vol 7, p. 545.   [56] *Select Biographies*, vol. 1, p. 306.

[57] Wodrow, *Bruce*, p. 282.

[58] On a last visit to Scotland in 1617 King James urged his churchmen to act with severity on the likes of Bruce: 'We took this order with the Puritans of England: they stood out as long as they were deprived only of their benefices, because they preached still on, and lived upon the benevolence of the people affecting their cause. But when we deprived them of their office, many yielded to us, and are now become the best men we have. Let us take the same course with the Puritans here.' Calderwood, vol. 8, appendix, pp. xiii–xiv. As usual, the King's word on what he said succeeded in England is not to be trusted. Calderwood was himself deprived and forced into exile.

[59] The General Assembly of 1596 was the last that was 'free' (i.e., not under royal control) until 1638. It was in 1596 that proposals were drawn

up that ministers 'not given to sanctification and prayer, that study not to be powerful and spiritual . . . be censured according to the degree of their faults, and continuing therein to be deprived.' Calderwood, vol. 5, p. 403. These proposals could never be implemented. See Calderwood on the nature of General Assemblies after 1596, Ibid., pp. 626–8.

[60] MacNicol, *Bruce,* p. 173.

[61] Calderwood, vol. 7, p. 409. Speaking of opponents within the church, Welsh believed, 'They are no more to be counted orthodox, but apostates . . . and therefore not to be heard any more, neither in public, nor in consistories, colleges, nor synods – for what fellowship has light with darkness?'

[62] John Flavel, 'The Best Work in the Worst Times', *Works,* vol. 6, p. 65.

[63] *Select Biographies,* vol., p.307.

[64] Laidlaw, *Bruce's Sermons,* pp. 143, 148.

[65] Flavel, vol.4, p.272. Like Bruce, all the major Puritans dealt much with the heart and conscience of their hearers.

[66] 'If you depend upon the testimony of your conscience, without the examination and rule of his Word, you will be deceived.' 'Knowledge must go before the stroke of conscience . . . solid knowledge, drawn out of the word of God, makes a heavy stroke on the conscience.'

[67] Wodrow, *Bruce,* p. 169.

[68] Calderwood, vol. 6, pp. 134, 141.

[69] Ibid, p. 202.

[70] 'Prayer is God's own gift, it is no gift of ours; for if it were ours, it would be evil: but it is the best gift that ever God gave man; and so it must be the gift of his own Holy Spirit.' Laidlaw, *Bruce's Sermons,* p. 200.

[71] As with all the Puritans, far from setting grace against obedience, Bruce knew that the person who loves grace ever loves obedience also. John Bunyan, near the end of *Pilgrim's Progress,* brings the two so well together in reporting the death of Mr Honest: 'Now the River at that time over-flowed the banks at some places; but Mr Honest in his life-time had spoken to one Good-Conscience to meet him there, the which he also did, and lent him his hand, and so helped him over. The last words of Mr Honest were, *Grace Reigns:* so he left the world.'

[72] Calderwood, vol. 6, p. 192.

[73] Wodrow, *Bruce, Life,* p. 152.

[74] Ibid., p. 378.

[75] 'I longed for a Spirit of *preaching* to descend and rest on ministers, that they might address the consciences of men with closeness and power.' David Brainerd in *Works of Jonathan Edwards* (Edinburgh: Banner of Truth, 1974), vol. 2, p. 383. Kirkton says that Bruce 'made an earthquake upon his hearers'; but it would be a mistake to think that this means he was a dramatic or noisy preacher. On the contrary, we read he was 'not a Boanarges' but 'of a slow and grave delivery' (Wodrow, *Bruce, Life,* p. 154). It was the presence of God which made his preaching what it was. In the words of Robert Fleming: 'The authority of God did so appear in him and in his carriage, with such a majesty in his countenance, as forced fear and respect from the greatest in

the land; even those who were avowed haters of godliness.' Ibid., pp. 143–4.

[76] Ibid., p. 293.

[77] *Life of Robert Blair*, ed. T. M'Crie (Edinburgh: Wodrow Soc.,1848), p. vi. A cause of one of Bruce's collisions with the King and his colleagues in the 1590s was his refusal to receive two young men into the Edinburgh ministry, 'till I have seen some arguments of God's blessing upon your travails'. Calderwood, vol. 5, p. 676. See also Wodrow, *Bruce,* p. 377.

[78] *Life of Blair*, pp. 39–40. Blair says that in Inverness Bruce showed him 'a large book' (i.e., manuscript) relating to his life and correspondence. This has not survived but may have been in the possession of Calderwood and used in his *History*.

[79] Calderwood, vol. 7, p. 393.

[80] Wodrow, *Bruce,* p. 135. 'When I was a young man,' he says in another place, 'I was diligent and lived by faith in the Son of God; but now I am old, and not able to do so much; yet he condescends to feed me with lumps of sense.'

[81] Laidlaw, *Bruce's Sermons*, p. lxxv.

[82] Quoted in 'The King's Bishop', *Patterns of Reform,* James Kirk (Edinburgh: T. & T. Clark: 1989), p. 448.

3

Thomas Chalmers and the Revival of the Church

Anstruther, Fife

'The Moderate and Evangelical parties, differing in their views of Church government, differed also, throughout the whole course of their history, in their cast of sentiment touching the religious life. The one, pushing the supernatural element in Christianity gently into the background, and seeking no more than a general observance of moral precept. The other, throwing the supernatural element into commanding prominence, explicitly declaring the exertion of Divine and creative energy indispensable to the formation of Christian character . . .

Evangelism had to contend against the current of the age: it was alike denounced by the worlds of literature and fashion. The politically powerful exerted themselves to crush it as mischievous; the gay and dissipated denounced it as morose and intolerant; the widely-spread scepticism of the period characterised it as irrational and absurd; historians have written whole volumes to traduce and vilify it; and genius has striven to render it ridiculous in song.'

HUGH MILLER

WHY REMEMBER CHALMERS?

'Thomas Chalmers, as all the world knows, was born in the Fifeshire town of Anstruther in the year 1780.' If William Beveridge was justified in so expressing himself in 1908 then the passing of another century has surely made a vast difference in the knowledge of professing Christians let alone 'the world'. An uncleaned statue of Chalmers still looks down upon the bustle of one of Edinburgh's main thoroughfares, yet the man himself – the man who was 'the greatest spiritual force Scotland saw in the nineteenth century' – is today scarcely remembered even in his own country.

Across the Firth of Forth from Edinburgh, in the little fishing port of Anstruther, a visitor may still find the house where this fourth son of John and Elizabeth Chalmers was born on a Friday, 17 March 1780, but the sight of its dark and broken windows, its overgrown garden, and its general air of neglect, as I saw it on one visit, harmonized with the prevalent forgetfulness. The descendants of those who in 1847 witnessed the burial of Thomas Chalmers, 'amid the tears of a nation, and with more than kingly honours', now have other matters on their minds.

There is not, of course, any difficulty in explaining the indifference of the modern secular mind to Chalmers, neither is it surprising that churchmen of liberal persuasion should lack enthusiasm for his memory. What is more problematical is the question why evangelical Christianity itself should have made so little of him these many years. Certainly Chalmers did not speak only to the narrow interests of one denomination, nor even to one nation. It was the *English* capital which, as William Wilberforce noted in 1817, went 'wild about Dr Chalmers', and while he is rightly associated with the recovery of Presbyterianism in Scotland – a recovery which led to the Disruption of 1843 and the formation of the Free Church of Scotland – his friends and correspondents were always to be found in many denominations. No one, for example, spoke more highly than he of 'the Baptists of England'.[1] Yet though he belonged to the true evangelical succession, and to no sectional interest, this fact has not prevented the neglect to which I have referred.

Undoubtedly many great preachers have been overlooked by posterity because they published little or nothing; after all, the living voice has a short span compared with the life of a book. In Chalmers' case, however, one reason for his eclipse may lie in exactly the opposite direction. His literary work was manifold. *The Works of Thomas Chalmers* (Glasgow: William Collins, 1835–42) run to twenty-five volumes, and they do not contain, by any means, all that he wrote! Certainly, to a reader who has the leisure of an early Victorian, these *Works* will convey the size of his mind and the many-sidedness of his thinking – running as it did into such subjects as economics (including savings banks), pauperism, social reform, education and so on – but for most people what is great and of abiding value is simply buried amidst a mass of paper. An illuminating comment on this point comes from Dr Samuel Miller of Princeton, one of Chalmers' trans-Atlantic correspondents.

Miller read a number of the books that Chalmers put out in his lifetime – books which were frequently hastened to the press by reason of existing 'moods and emergencies'. 'But', Miller later wrote, 'I must say, that those from which I have received the deepest impression of the real glory of his character, have been his *posthumous writings*. Of the vigour and elevation of his mind, I had enjoyed proof enough from the many volumes which had long since fallen under my notice. But from some of his most unstudied writings which have lately met my eye, I have received impressions of his moral and heavenly grandeur, greatly beyond those which I had received from the multiplied and rich productions of his genius.'[2]

The average person can be forgiven for not reading enough of Chalmers to arrive at Miller's discovery. 'Are Dr Chalmers' works now read?' asked David Masson, one of his admirers, in a series of magazine articles in 1864–5. 'They are less read or looked into now', he concludes, 'than it might have once been expected that they would be.'

The extent of Chalmers' writings has also had another effect upon his image at the present time. From his many volumes writers can and have found material enough to write on him as an economist, an educationalist and such like. Dr J. Wilson Harper, in 1910, managed a volume of 368 pages on *The Social Ideal and Dr Chalmers' Contribution to Christian Economics.* Such subjects may not be uninteresting to a select circle but they do next to nothing to present the real heart of his life and vision. If the sum total of Chalmers is the image that plodding writers have furnished who never felt his fire, and if many have assumed *this* image to be the man who once strangely moved a nation, it is no wonder that he lies neglected.

There is an important reason why the life of Thomas Chalmers deserves renewed attention. He was at the centre of a recovery which brought the churches in Scotland from mediocrity, indifference, and unbelief to new conditions of spiritual vitality. To understand Chalmers is not only to understand how that transformation occurred, it is also to learn abiding lessons relating to the subject of revival.

Dr C. H. Waller, one-time Principal of the London School of Divinity and an examining chaplain to Bishop Ryle, is said to have told his students 'that the nearest approach that he knew of in the history of the Church universal to apostolic conditions of faith and living was what was to be seen in the Free Church of Scotland in its early days'.[3] Another independent witness of what happened in mid-nineteenth century Scotland was Dr J. W. Alexander of New York, the son of Archibald Alexander of Princeton. Speaking of the Free Church of Scotland he once wrote: 'That church seems to me all in one great revival . . . I should like to spend three months in the Free Church, to try and find out the secret of their ardour'. In 1851, his wish to visit Scotland was fulfilled and he was not disappointed. He wrote from Glasgow in September of that year:

> These few days in Scotland have shown me a permanent revival of religion, such as proves to me that God has a favour to his covenanting people. The preciousness of it is, that religion is founded on chapter and verse; free from outcry and sanctimony, and even talk about personal feelings, but is so courageous, active, and tender, that I am as certain as that I am writing these lines, that I am among the best people on earth. A thousand times have I said to myself, 'O if my father could just for one hour hear these prayers, and observe these fruits of unadulterated Calvinistic seed!' Here is the fruit of prayers sent up by Rutherfords and Bostons.[4]

Perhaps these words over-state the matter yet it is unquestionable that towards the middle of the nineteenth century many parts of Scotland witnessed a profound awakening and that none stood closer to the spiritual influence which brought this about than Thomas Chalmers. Today the works of not a few of the men who shared in this recovery are being read again across the world. They include those of Robert Murray M'Cheyne, William Cunningham, George Smeaton, Hugh Martin, Andrew and Horatius Bonar, David Brown and James Buchanan. For those who have discovered the value of these writers there cannot but be cause for interest in the man who was, in many respects, their teacher and leader.

THE EARLY YEARS

When Chalmers was born in 1780 it was about the deadest time in the history of the Church of Scotland since the Reformation. The cause of that deadness is not hard to trace. Some ninety-two years earlier, in 1688, the Church of Scotland had emerged from the persecutions of the Covenanting era and been reconstituted. In this re-constitution, clergy who had been submissive to episcopacy when Christians of Presbyterian conviction were being put to death, turned Presbyterian and thus kept their places in the national church. Almost invariably they were men who gave lip confession to a creed – the Westminster Confession – to which they had no heart-attachment. A deadening influence was thus continued in the life of the Church of Scotland and this influence gained increasing sway by an Act of Parliament in 1712 which took away from congregations the right to choose their own ministers. That right was given to patrons, generally the local landowners, who, if they wished, could place a worldly cleric over an evangelical people. Despite some local revivals during the eighteenth century, evangelical pulpits in the national Church were few in number, while 'the Moderates', as the majority of the men-pleasing clergy were called, dominated the life of that Church. When Chalmers was a youth of thirteen, Lachlan Mackenzie of Lochcarron began an ordination sermon with these words:

If people go to perdition in these days it is not for want of ministers. The clergy are likely to become soon as plentiful as the locusts in Egypt, and which of them is the greatest plague of the two, time and the experience of the Church will discover.[5]

The Moderates preached morality, with almost nothing of the supernaturalism of true Christianity. They ignored the Fall of man, sneered at the idea of a new birth and said nothing of the perfection and power of the work of the Son of God. They left their hearers with the impression that man is the author and finisher of his own salvation. Summarizing the results of their influence, Alexander Duff wrote:

> The savour and unction of divine grace was gone; the peculiarities of the gospel were despised as offensive to classic taste and culture, and devotion scorned as fanatical and contemptible . . . Instead of the power and pathos of earnest gospel invitations and appeals, there were substituted cold pretences of academic learning, that froze the generous sympathies of the human heart.

As a consequence of this state of affairs, large areas of the country were left without any gospel preaching. When Robert and James Haldane, members of the Scottish nobility, were converted towards the end of the eighteenth century and began itinerating all over the country, they spoke to multitudes who had never heard of salvation by grace. One old man of ninety-two years told James Haldane that he had prayed eighty years earlier that God would send the gospel to his part of Scotland and, at his death, as he clasped Haldane's hands in his own, he affirmed, 'I believe, I believe!'

It was a striking contrast to many other death-beds of that period. When one enquiring sinner, not far from death, asked his Moderate minister what he must do to be saved, he was met with shocked silence. In his minister's view only the committing of some awful crime could explain why anyone should put such a question.[6]

Not all areas in Scotland were equally dead. In the south there were a number of Secession churches which maintained a faithful witness but, at the time when Chalmers was born, true gospel preaching in Church of Scotland parishes was the exception rather than the rule.

Apart from unusual abilities in the fields of mathematics and chemistry, Chalmers' student days followed the common pattern. Before he was twelve years old he entered the University of St Andrews – ten miles from his birthplace in Fife – and at fifteen he commenced the study of theology with a view to making the ministry his profession. At the age of nineteen he was licensed to preach and in 1802 was settled in the country parish of Kilmany, in his native Fife. In the meantime he had abandoned the beliefs of his godly father and succumbed wholly to the modern school. As he later wrote: 'St Andrews was at this time overrun with Moderatism, under the chilling influences of which we inhaled not a distaste only but a positive contempt for all that is properly and peculiarly gospel.'

One day, while still a student, Chalmers had heard a lecture touching on the subject of Calvinism. Sitting alongside him was another youth by the name of William H. Burns whom he knew to hold the historic faith of the Church of Scotland. In conversation with Burns after the lecture, Chalmers exclaimed, 'You are a sincere Calvinist. There is none in St Andrews that I know. Come down to Anstruther with me on Saturday, and see my father and Mr Hodges [an old elder]. They all agree with you.'

Chalmers' view of the ministry coincided with his Moderatism. The ministry was a helpful profession for a man who wished to make a name in the world. In the case of some of his colleagues, that meant simply being thought a 'good fellow'

and taking a leading part in fox-hunting or other less strenuous
social engagements. But Chalmers was more ambitious and
coveted distinction in the academic world. With this end in
view his main studies remained mathematics, chemistry and
geology, and for as long as six months in a year he might be
absent from his parish in order to teach in St Andrews. When
he was at home he acted on the belief that two days in the
week were quite enough for religious duties and sometimes
his sermon preparation, such as it was, had to be done on the
Sunday morning. In one of his earliest writings, he declared:

> The author of this pamphlet can assert, from what to him
> is the highest of all authority, the authority of experience,
> that after the satisfactory discharge of his parish duties, a
> minister may enjoy five days in the week of uninterrupted
> leisure, for the prosecution of any science in which his
> taste may dispose him to engage.

Not surprisingly, for his first seven years at Kilmany Chalmers
had no personal conversation with people about their souls,
and from the pulpit he would warn his congregation of such
evangelical authors as John Newton, from whom they might
learn 'fanaticism'. Anything like evangelism he openly
nauseated. 'Let us tremble to think that anything but virtue
can recommend us to the Almighty', was the sentiment to
which his hearers were accustomed to listen.

Ineffective as Chalmers' ministry was at this period, that fact
– if he recognized it – did not lead him to question the worth
of his opinions. But in 1808 his plans for his career were
singularly stopped. On July 23rd, we find him writing, 'I
purpose setting off for London about the middle of August.
My great object is to get introduced into some of the literary
circles.' Instead of this, however, August found Chalmers at
the bed-side of a favourite sister in Anstruther and she died
before the month was ended. The London visit was abandoned.

The next summer, death drew even nearer. First an uncle, to whom he was closely attached, passed suddenly into eternity, being found kneeling in the attitude of prayer. Then, returning from a visit to this bereaved home, Chalmers encountered inclement weather that brought to a height an illness to which he had already succumbed. For the next four months he never left his room and his life hung in the balance.

It was now that the great revolution began. After six months' absence from his pulpit, the congregation saw a very different minister and one whose muffled figure walking slowly to the church in the summer of 1810 revealed him to be the invalid that he was. With sunken and sallow countenance, Chalmers now spoke of new themes, and chiefly of the shortness and insignificance of time, and of the nearness and magnitude of eternity. In later years when an opponent in the General Assembly reminded him of his early views on the work of the ministry, from which we quoted above, Chalmers was to confess that he was then blind to the lesson which even those scientific studies should have taught him: 'What, sir, is the object of mathematical science?' he had replied. 'Magnitude and the proportions of magnitude. But then, sir, I had forgotten two magnitudes. I thought not of the littleness of time – I recklessly thought not of the greatness of eternity.'

Yet when these new truths were first heard in the Kilmany pulpit the greatest change was still going on in secret. Smitten with a sense of sin, Chalmers had begun to pray, 'O God, fit a poor, dark, ignorant and wandering creature for being a minister of Thy word.' Gradually the way of salvation by faith in the atonement of Christ was opened up to him and before the close of the year 1811, when he was thirty-one years of age, his journal was recording the joy of assurance and of full commitment: 'O God, make me feel the firmness of the ground I tread upon, and enable me to give all my mind to Thy Word. Above all, may I never recede by a single inch from my Saviour.'

And he notes: 'Had more intimate communion with God in solitary prayer than I had ever felt before; and my sentiment was a total, an unreserved, and a secure dependence on Christ the Saviour.'

The change in the ministry of Kilmany was soon widely known. To Moderates it had the appearance of a bout of insanity and for years the nickname 'mad Chalmers' was to be common. Evangelicals saw it differently. One who visited Chalmers at this time reported:

> He has long been known as a celebrated philosopher and scorner of the peculiar doctrines of Christianity; now, from conviction and with a warm heart, he preaches the faith he once destroyed. I have had serious conversation with him, and am astonished at a man of such superior powers so modest and humble. He is indeed converted, and like a little child.

At no point did Chalmers' life remain the same. Family prayer was established twice a day,[7] anxiety appeared for the souls of others, parish visitation – formerly accomplished in a fortnight each year – became regular and earnest work, and the impenitent dying were warned with tears. His beloved science books now lay closed; instead there was the Westminster Confession of Faith, Jonathan Edwards, John Owen, John Calvin, the once-despised Newton, and supremely, the Bible itself, which he began to read and memorize with an intensity which astonished those who had known his former interests. William Hanna, his biographer writes:

> His regular and earnest study of the Bible was one of the first and most noticeable effects of Mr Chalmers' conversion. His nearest neighbour and most frequent visitor was old John Bonthron, who, having once seen better days, was admitted to an easy and privileged

familiarity, in the exercise of which one day before the memorable illness, he said to Mr Chalmers – 'I find you aye busy, sir, with one thing or another, but come when I may, I never find you at your studies for the Sabbath.' 'Oh, an hour or two on the Saturday evening is quite enough for that,' was the minister's answer. But now the change had come, and John, on entering the manse, often found Mr Chalmers poring eagerly over the pages of the Bible. The difference was too striking to escape notice, and with the freedom given him, which he was ready enough to use, he said, 'I never come in now, sir, but I find you aye at your Bible.' 'All too little, John, all too little', was the significant reply.[8]

Before long a changed spirit also began to appear in Chalmers' parish. In the spring of 1812, as two men were walking away from the church after hearing a sermon on John 3:16, one said to the other, 'Did you feel anything particularly in church today? I never felt myself to be a lost sinner till today, when I was listening to that sermon.' 'It is very strange', replied his companion, 'it was just the same with me.' Both men dated their conversion from that day. The following year, William Carey's friend, Andrew Fuller, visited Kilmany, and after hearing Chalmers preach he declared, 'If that man would but throw away his papers in the pulpit, he might be king of Scotland!'[9]

In 1814, the scene of Chalmers' ministry changed from the quietness of the 150 families of Kilmany to the heart of Scotland's greatest city, Glasgow, and here he was to remain for the next eight years, preaching with passionate eloquence to a crowded church. He opposed unbelief with a boldness that awoke many; church laws which do not come from the Scriptures, he described as 'not worth a straw'; and, above all, he laboured to bring the gospel not only to his hearers but to the multitudes of Glasgow who had no church connection. The fact that the first volume of his sermon sold nearly 20,000 copies in a year gives some idea of the extent of the influence that he was now given.

PREPARING THE NEXT GENERATION

Although William Hanna gives the whole of the second volume of his biography to Chalmers' time in Glasgow, his subject had probably not yet commenced his most important work. In 1823, to the surprise of many and contrary to the judgment of some of his best friends, he left the thousands of Scotland's largest city to undertake the professorship of Moral Philosophy in the University of St Andrews. It was certainly a considerable change. Geographically St Andrews was a backwater and vastly different from Glasgow where, he once complained, 'my bell is ringing every half-minute with inquirers'. Apart from the new-found quiet there were few advantages. His family now grown to six daughters – were to enjoy the 'bathing process', and they were all to value the nearness of Anstruther where his mother was still alive, 'as if at the gate of Heaven, and with such a fund of inward peace and hope as made her nine years' widowhood a perfect feast and foretaste of the blessedness that awaits the righteous'. His parents' religion, however, was still as rare in St Andrews as it had been in his student days, and there was nothing which Thomas and Grace Chalmers felt so much as the change in the spiritual climate when they settled in East Fife. In one of his letters from his new home Chalmers wrote in February 1824: 'Perhaps there is no town in Scotland more cold, and meagre, and moderate in its theology than St Andrews. I do find the Sabbaths to be very heartless in regard to the public services; and Mrs Chalmers half threatens to be a Seceder upon our hands. I will not hinder her . . .' The passing of eight months only deepened this impression as he confides to the same friend in another letter:

I must not disguise it from you that St Andrews has its trials. There is a most inveterate hostility to the evangelical spirit, and a sad public corruption, against which I have hitherto remonstrated ineffectually. Over and above all this, our Sabbaths are truly barren and dreary, from the miserable lack of unction in public services. I have taken up a Sabbath-school which somewhat supplies the want to myself and my family, it being held in my own house, and attended by not more than thirty scholars. I was greatly delighted yesterday by a passage from the excellent Halyburton, who bids us suspect ourselves if our zeal runs all to public, to the neglect of private and personal Christianity. My clear line is to give all my force to the latter when my way is so hedged up against doing much in behalf of the former . . . I forgot to mention that Mrs Chalmers, under the destitution of evangelical truth in our established pulpits, goes very often to the Dissenters, and incurs some obloquy on that account, which we care not for.[10]

Despite these trials Chalmers never seems to have doubted the correctness of his decision to remove from Glasgow. Two principal considerations had swayed his judgment. The first was his conviction that Moral Philosophy is vitally related to sound theology: 'Moral Philosophy stands to Christianity in the relation that Law does to Gospel, that the preaching of John the Baptist did to the preaching of the Saviour.' In this John the Baptist role Chalmers soon had evidence that he had not misjudged the opening which existed. 'I can lift many testimonies on the side of the Gospel,' he wrote to a friend in December 1824, 'my classes give me some precious opportunities.'

A second consideration was more fundamental. For some years he had been convinced that a changed ministry was the primary need if there was to be any general renewal in the Church. While he was still at Kilmany his diary reveals this burden:

> Thy blessing and thy Spirit, O Lord, be on this parish and neighbourhood. O that a day of power and of refreshing were to come amongst them. I implore thy Spirit on behalf of this county. O may its ministers be turned to the Lord. O send them pastors according to thine own heart . . . Stay not thine arm, O God; make it bare. Come forth in the might of thy all-subduing Spirit, and reveal Christ in many hearts, for His sake.

Certainly some ministers could be changed in the midst of their ministries, as he had been, yet the surest hope was for a new generation of preachers – men not trained in the aridity and dead scholarship of Moderatism but in experimental Christianity and in a faith which subordinated everything to the Bible. And as the universities were the only theological schools of the day, it was there, at the 'fountain heads', that a transformation was supremely needed. This was the foremost reason why from 1823 onwards Chalmers was to give the best of his time and thought to helping young men and why, even amidst the difficulties of St Andrews, he did not return to a parish. In June 1825 we find him writing:

> I have of late had several offers to leave the University and return again to the Church . . . But it was not upon light grounds that I relinquished the clerical for the professorial life; and I am more and more confirmed in the belief that a chair in a college is a higher station on the field of Christian usefulness, than a parish anywhere in Scotland. Could one acquit himself rightly of his duties as a professor, it is incalculable the good which might be done to the guides and the clergy of our next generation.[11]

It was not only in Scotland that the 'next generation' were to see the fruit. Of the three hundred students who passed through Chalmers' classes in his five years at St Andrews, six – including the eminent Alexander Duff – were to become pioneer missionaries overseas. The great fulfilment of his vision was, however, to come in Edinburgh. When the professorship of divinity in that university was offered to him towards the close of 1827, he accepted, and on a snow-swept November morning in the following year he gave the first of the many hundreds of lectures which were to be heard by successive classes of students through the next twenty years. William Cunningham, one of the students present on that first occasion was struck most of all by 'the deep, vital consciousness of the glory of the divine presence', and he noted, 'It is impossible not to indulge the hope that the time to favour our Zion, yea, the set time, is come.'

Perhaps the most graphic description of Chalmers' class room at Edinburgh comes from the pen of David Masson:

> When I first knew Edinburgh, one of the great attractions of its University was the classroom of Dr Chalmers, called the Divinity Hall. It was on the right of the quadrangle, immediately after entering through the portico from the street, and the access to it was by a narrow flight of stone stairs leading to a kind of stone-gallery looking upon the quadrangle. In this stone-gallery, or about the portico and quadrangle, would be lounging at an early hour in the forenoon, waiting the doctor's arrival, the members of his audience. They were mostly young Scotsmen of from eighteen to five-and-twenty, destined for the Scottish Kirk; but there was a considerable sprinkling of young Irish Presbyterians, together with a group of oldish military officers, who, after their service in India or elsewhere, had settled for the quiet evenings of their lives in Edinburgh,

and, partly to while away the time, partly from a creditable interest in theological matters awakened at last in their grizzled noddles, had taken to attend Dr Chalmers's lectures. Occasionally there would be a stranger or two of distinction.

Punctually a few minutes before the hour the Doctor would arrive among the gathered groups expecting him. His manner on arriving was generally hurried and absent, and he disappeared at once into his vestry or ante-room, there to put on his gown, and his little white Geneva bands, a pair of which he usually kept in an odd brown-covered old volume of Leibnitz that lay handy for the purpose on a side-table. Sometimes one or two of the strangers would follow the Doctor into the vestry to bid him good morning before lecture, but he did not like the intrusion. Meanwhile, the doors of the Hall having been opened, the audience had entered and filled it. It was more like a dingy ill-contrived little chapel than a classroom, having a gallery raised on iron pillars over the back rows of seats so as to darken them, and a pulpit opposite this gallery rising to a level with it. The students, properly so called, the number of whom was from 100 to 130, occupied the seats below, clear of and under the gallery; and in the comparatively empty gallery, not much noticed by the Doctor, who generally looked downwards to his students, sat the strangers of distinction and the military veterans.

Emerging from the vestry by its private entrance into the Hall, the Doctor, now in his gown and bands, still rather hurried and absent-looking, mounted the pulpit, a sight for any physiognomist to see. Then generally, after a very brief prayer, which he read from a slip of paper, but in such a way that you could hardly detect he was reading, the business of the hour began. Not unfrequently, however, it would turn out that he had forgotten something, and, muttering some hasty intimation to that effect instead of the expected first words of his prayer, he would descend again from the pulpit and go back to his vestry. On such occasions it was a chance if he did not come upon one or two latecomers availing themselves of that quiet means of entrance, engaged while they did so in the interesting process of measuring their heads with his by furtively examining and trying on his vast hat. Suppose all right, however, and the lecture begun. It was a perfectly unique performance – every lecture a revelation, though within so small and dingy a chapel, of all that the world at large had come to wonder at in Chalmers. For the most part he sat and read, either from his manuscript or from some of his printed books, from which he had a most dexterous art of helping himself to relevant passages – sat and read, however, with such a growing excitement of voice and manner that whether he was reading or not reading was never thought of. But every now and then he would interrupt his reading, and, standing up, and catching off his spectacles so that they hung from his little finger, he would interject, with much gesticulation, and sometimes with a flushing of the face, and an audible stamping of the foot, some little passage of extempore exposition or outburst.

To describe the *matter* of his lectures would be more difficult than to give an idea of their form. It was called Theology, and there certainly was a due attempt to go over the topics of a theological course, with frequent references to Butler, Paley, Jonathan Edwards, the *Theologiae Elencticae* of Turretin, and, by way of general text-book, to Dr George Hill's Lectures in Divinity. But really it was a course of Chalmers himself, and of Chalmers in all his characters. Within two or three consecutive sessions, if not in one, every listener was sure to be led so completely and with so much commotion through the whole round of Chalmers's favourite ideas, that, if he remained ignorant of any one of them or unsaturated with some tincture of them all, it could only be because he was a miracle of impassiveness.[12]

Chalmers has been variously assessed as a teacher of theology. He was certainly not without deficiencies. In depth and accuracy of learning he is not in the front rank of Scottish theologians. The course of divinity which he set his students embodied the doubtful procedure of beginning with 'natural theology' before he advanced to the subject matter of Christianity itself. In the lectures themselves he was liable to diverge into matters extraneous to the main theme before him. Yet when this has been said there is a great deal to support the verdict of his biographer when he writes:

> Others have amassed larger stores of learning, and conveyed them to their students in more comprehensive and compendious forms. But who ever lit up the evidences and truths of Christianity with a light so attractive; and who ever filled the youthful breasts of those who were afterwards to occupy the pulpits of the land, with the fire of so generous and so devoted an enthusiasm.[13]

There are many testimonies to support these words of Hanna. John Duncan, who was to serve with Chalmers in New College after the Disruption, spoke thus of his senior: 'Chalmers was not a widely-read divine, but as a practical thinker and teacher of the heart he was unrivalled. We have lost much of him for want of a Boswell. Many of his best sayings are gone for ever. As a man of erudition he might have been better. As a heaven-taught man, he needed little'.[14] W. M. Taylor wrote similarly: 'To the end of his days he had around him a circle of loving and devoted students, all of whom were fired with enthusiasm which they had caught from his lips . . . He was not so much an instructor as a quickener. The other professors laid the materials in the minds of the students, but he brought and struck the match which kindled these materials into a flame that burned with an energy kindred to his own.'[15]

In addition to his more formal class lectures, Chalmers also used what amounted to discussion sessions – class conversations in which he and the students held 'continued parley'. It was probably on these occasions that he did most to direct their minds to the authors that they should master. A few of these authors were contemporaries, his friend the Anglican Charles Bridges, for example, author of *The Christian Ministry*. Among his favourites from the eighteenth century were Edwards, Boston, Newton, Doddridge and Halyburton. But in their sustained biblical thought and fire it was the Puritans who remained his first love and the books of such authors as Joseph Alleine, John Owen,[16] William Guthrie and Richard Baxter, which he had first revelled in at Kilmany, he was to press upon successive generations of students: 'There is a closeness, and a pertinency, and a power in the writings of the good old Puritans, of which we fall greatly short in these days of feebleness and degeneracy . . . From them you are most likely to carry away the impression that a preparation for eternity should be the main business and anxiety of time.'

Along with such 'practical' writers, which he thought should be a main part of the reading of every minister, he also urged the value of the best Christian biographies (amongst which he gave a high place to the *Lives of Philip and Matthew Henry*, and the *Memoir and Correspondence of Henry Venn*). 'I am thankful to say,' he wrote in 1835, 'that no reading so occupies and engages me as the biography of those who have made it most their business to prosecute the sanctification of their souls.'

It is not difficult to discover what were Chalmers' 'favourite ideas' concerning the work of the ministry. They were the great lessons which had been first impressed upon his own heart and they may be stated as follows:

1. The governing principle upon which the strength of all ministerial duties depends is regard for the approval of God. If a minister lacks that principle his public work will be dominated by regard for himself or for the approbation of men. Where that principle is truly present it will operate first in the sphere of the preacher's own inner life; he will not 'strenuously urge sanctification' without attending to that duty himself. His primary concern in all things must be to see that God approves him. 'By far the most effective ingredient of good preaching', he writes, 'is the personal piety of the preacher himself.' 'How little must the presence of God be felt in that place, where the high functions of the pulpit are degraded into a stipulated exchange of entertainment, on the one side, and of admiration, on the other! and surely it were a sight to make angels weep when a weak and vapouring mortal, surrounded by his fellow-sinners, and hastening to the grave and the judgment along with them, finds it a dearer object to his bosom to regale his hearers by the exhibition of himself, than to do, in plain earnest, the work of his Master.'

2. Ministers should never rest satisfied without growth in personal holiness of life. Chalmers' private diary reveals a great deal of this: 'Advance the power and life of religion in my own heart' was his prayer. To friends he writes in similar terms: 'Pray unceasingly for the progress of His work in your heart . . . Strike the high aim of being perfect even as God is perfect . . . Never let go your aspirings . . . Oh! with what unceasing progress towards perfection should we be enabled to advance did we cast all self-seeking and self-confidence away from us – did we consent to be altogether guided by His strength, and be altogether accepted in His pure and unspotted righteousness.'

Andrew Bonar, one of Chalmers' students, used to repeat a saying he heard when he was entering the ministry: 'Remember that very few men, and very few *ministers,* keep up to the end the edge that was on their spirit at the first.' It was a warning which could well have been heard from Chalmers. The prayerfulness and the desires after greater holiness which marked his early Christian life were with him to the end.

3.   Ministers must give themselves wholly to their true work: 'Be assured that a single and undivided attention to the peculiar work of a Christian minister is the way of peace and of pleasantness.' One of the greatest struggles which Chalmers ever had was to break free from the many secular duties and activities which had come to be expected of ministers. For him it was imperative, if the church was to be revived, that preachers should be left to concentrate exclusively upon their proper calling. In Glasgow he had found that ministers were continually required to be at funerals (four at one funeral was considered a 'respectable number'), at committees of all the societies, at public functions of every kind, and so on. At one committee meeting, for example, arranged on behalf of the Town Hospital, he found himself with an honoured place among 'some of the gravest of city ministers, and some of the wisest of the city merchants' to engage in a solemn and, at length, warm discussion on whether pork broth or ox-head broth should be served to the inmates of the Hospital! After such experiences at that time in his life he wrote: 'I am gradually separating myself from all this trash, and long to establish it as a doctrine that the life of a town minister should be what the life of a country minister might be, and his entire time disposable to the purposes to which the Apostles gave themselves wholly, that is, the ministry of the word and prayer.' Speaking again of the secular duties to which so many ministers had given in, and which turned a preacher from being 'a dispenser of the bread of life into a mere dispenser of human benefits', he says,

'This I have set my face against, and though I have a good deal of opposition to encounter, yet I am persuaded that I have the solid countenance and approbation of all who value the pure objects of the Christian ministry.'

4. A minister must deal directly with men concerning their need of salvation. 'Let us pray for that most desirable wisdom, the wisdom of winning souls.' 'A single human being called out of darkness, though he lived in some putrid lane or unheard of obscurity, is a brighter testimony than all the applause of the fashionable.' This meant plain, direct preaching to the heart and conscience. Commending Alleine's *Alarm*, he warned against the 'diseased touchiness' of the age which disliked the urgent preaching of repentance. He told his prospective candidates for the ministry that their work must not be to show their hearers the consistency between geology and the Bible; rather these hearers must be won 'by entering into the chambers of their consciences and telling them of that sin which is their ruin and of that Saviour who can alone hush the alarms of nature'.[17]

But Chalmers' concern for evangelism went beyond giving directions about preaching. He was one of the first nineteenth-century leaders to emphasize that care for the souls of men was not to end in the pulpit. He pressed upon his divinity students what became known as 'the aggressive principle', that is to say, they must take the gospel to the people; the unchurched must not be left alone, rather they must be pursued wherever they are to be found. And this was to be done methodically with accurate records and statistics. During a few years of his Glasgow ministry he sought to visit the 11,000 to 12,000 homes in his parish, an experience which had led him to the conclusion that 'a very deep and universal ignorance on the high matters of faith and eternity obtains over the whole extent of the population'. This kind of practical action he also stimulated in Edinburgh. On Saturday mornings in the 1830s some twelve to twenty of his students would meet for prayer in his vestry at the Divinity Hall and then proceed in twos to visit the poorest districts of the city. Robert M'Cheyne has described his shock on the first occasion that he joined this 'Visiting Society' and discovered 'what imbedded masses of human beings are huddled together, unvisited by friend or minister!' Chalmers was to make important use of the statistics which his students gathered and the General Assembly of 1838 heard that in Glasgow and Edinburgh alone there were 100,000 adults who were totally estranged from the Christian faith.

Few professors of divinity have had such students as crowded Chalmers' classroom in the 1830s. Many of them – as their subsequent biographies reveal – were to become men of outstanding usefulness. In part this usefulness was, of course, due to the considerable natural gifts with which they were endowed, but under other influences such talents might have developed in a different direction. As it was, the 'favourite ideas' they imbibed from Chalmers did much to shape their future lives. Four years' divinity under Chalmers and David Welsh (Professor of Church History) 'afforded no ordinary advantages,' Andrew Bonar could write from experience. 'New fields of thought were daily opened up.' And of M'Cheyne, his fellow student, Bonar says, 'His notes and his diary testify that he endeavoured to retain what he heard, and that he used to read as much of the books recommended by the professors as his time enabled him to overtake.'[18] David Yeaworth writes, 'In Chalmers, more than any other person, M'Cheyne found the mould for his ecclesiastical and religious thought, and a worthy pattern for his own ministerial life'.

Nor did Chalmers' link with his students end when their course was completed. M'Cheyne was a case in point. The new parish of St Peter's, Dundee, to which he went in 1837, had come about through the exertions of John Roxburgh, who, fired by Chalmers, had gone amongst the spiritually destitute in Dundee in 1831. At the time of M'Cheyne's settlement, Chalmers himself was leading the church extension work of the Church of Scotland and St Peter's was one of the 222 new churches which were provided during the seven years when he had this responsibility. By 1843, Chalmers was able to say that he could travel from one end of Scotland to the other and spend each night in the manse of one of his former pupils. And in that same momentous year – the year of the Disruption and of the formation of the Free Church – Hanna believed that 'nine-tenths' of the men whom Chalmers had taught stood with him.

A VISION FULFILLED – THE POWER OF THE SPIRIT OF GOD

We have already noted that in the 1820s Chalmers' hopes and prayers centred upon 'the next generation'. By 1842 he could write,

> I am quite sensible that talent is but secondary to piety – that gifts are but secondary to graces in a minister of the Gospel, and I therefore am all the more thankful that, besides being men of power and high scholarship, very many of our young preachers are men of faith and prayer, who preside at fellowship meetings, and have been the instruments of great and promising revivals in various parts of Scotland.[19]

It remains to speak of some of these revivals and of the lessons which they ought to teach us at this present day. First, however, there is one other recurring theme in Chalmers' thought which needs to be stated. Were any impression to be given that younger men saw revival because they faithfully repeated Chalmers' teaching and copied his example, that would be a travesty of the position. More than anything else, perhaps, Chalmers insisted that nothing truly effective could be done without the personal activity of the Holy Spirit. He had seen enough of a moribund orthodoxy to know that it is not true that if preachers have a correct knowledge of the truth then the Holy Spirit's ministry can be *assumed*. Vast though the importance of sound knowledge is – for the Holy Spirit works by the truth – to view knowledge as the *same* thing as supernatural energy was a profound mistake which had disastrous consequences for preaching. To Charles Bridges he writes in 1834:

> I deeply feel my need of effort and prayer that my whole course may be more and more spiritualized, assured as I am of the possibility of delivering all the lessons of theology in the strictest form of sound words, and with the fullest adherence to the letter of the truth as it is in Jesus, while the real unction and vitality of the Gospel spirit may be altogether wanting.

There is much which could be quoted from Chalmers on this same theme. The following will convey something of his burden:

> I long to realize the joys and the exercises and the habits of experimental religion, to love Christ as fervently as good Samuel Rutherford . . . It comes to me all in word and not in power . . . O that the same God who sent forth His mighty Spirit to convert three thousand at the utterance of one sermon, would so arm me with arguments, and so press them home with efficiency upon the hearts of a people made willing and obedient in the day of His power that the months might witness the accession of many sons and daughters to righteousness.
>
> There is nothing of which I am more thoroughly aware than the utter difference which there is between a speculative and an experimental conviction of the same

truth . . . I long for more of the life and freshness of an actual contact with these things – for the kingdom of God as abundantly in power as it is in word.

These were the feelings which he constantly told his students they needed to possess. Theory and intellect were only the starting point. If men possessed those things alone, instead of 'talking religion' they would merely join the number who 'talk about religion'. There must be much personal dealing with God himself. 'Read Edwards on Prayer,' he would counsel men. 'A season of revival in the Church is generally preceded by a season of prayer.'

Some of Chalmers' strongest statements on this subject occur in his sermon 'The Necessity of the Spirit to Give Effect to the Preaching of the Gospel', in which his text is 1 Corinthians 2:4–5, 'And my speech and my preaching was not with enticing words of man's wisdom, but in demonstration of the Spirit, and of power.' The whole sermon is memorable but an extract here must suffice:

We read of the letter, and we read also of the spirit, of the New Testament. It would require a volume, rather than a single paragraph of a single sermon, to draw the line between the one and the other. But you will readily acknowledge, that there are many things of this book, which a man, though untaught by the Spirit of God, may be made to know. By the natural exercise of his judgment he may compare scripture with scripture, he may learn what its doctrines are, he may demonstrate the orthodoxy of every one article in our national confession, he may store himself with the learning of many generations, he may be familiar with all the systems, and have mingled with all the controversies, and yet, with a mind supporting as it does the burden of the erudition of whole libraries, he may have gotten to himself no other wisdom than the wisdom of the letter of the New Testament. The man's creed, with all its arranged and its well-weighed articles, may be no better than the dry bones in the vision of Ezekiel, put together into a skeleton, and fastened with sinews, and covered with flesh and skin, and exhibiting to the eye of the spectators, the aspect and the lineaments of a man, but without breath, and remaining so, till the Spirit of God breathed into it, and it lived. And it is, in truth, a sight of wonder, to behold a man who has carried his knowledge of Scripture as far as the wisdom of man can carry it – to see him blessed with all the light which nature can give, but labouring under all the darkness which no power of nature can dispel – to see this man of many accomplishments, carrying in his bosom a heart uncheered by any one of its consolations, unmoved by the influence of any one of its truths unshaken out of any one attachment to the world, and an utter stranger to those high resolves, and the power of those great and animating prospects, which shed a glory over the daily walk of a believer, and give to every one of his doings the high character of a candidate for eternity.

The Holy Spirit's office, as defined by the Bible itself, is not to make known to us any truths which are not contained in the Bible; but to make clear to our understandings the truths which are contained in it. He opens our understandings to understand the Scriptures. The Word of God is called the sword of the Spirit. It is the instrument by which the Spirit worketh. He does not tell us any thing that is out of the record; but all that is within it he sends home, with clearness and effect, upon the mind . . .

There is the malignity of the Fall which adheres to us. There is a power of corruption and of blindness along with it, which it is beyond the compass of human means to overthrow. There is a dark and settled depravity in the human character, which maintains its gloomy and obstinate resistance to all our warnings, and all our arguments. There is a spirit working in the children of disobedience, which no power of human eloquence can lay. There is a covering of thick darkness upon the face of all people, a mighty influence abroad upon the world, with which the Prince of the power of the air keeps his thousands and his tens of thousands under him. The minister who enters into this field of conflict, may have zeal, and talents, and eloquence. His heart may be smitten with the love of the truth, and his mind be fully fraught with its arguments. Thus armed, he may come forth among his people, flushed with the mighty enterprise of turning souls from the dominion of Satan unto God. In all the hopes of victory, he may discharge the weapons of his warfare among them. Week after week, he may reason with them out of the Scriptures. Sabbath after Sabbath he may declaim, he may demonstrate, he may put forth every expedient; he may, at one time, set in array before them the terrors of the law, at another, he may try to win them by the free offer of the gospel; and, in the proud confidence of success, he may think that nothing can withstand him, and that the heart of every hearer must give way before the ardour of his zeal, and the power of his invincible arguments. Yes; they may admire him, and they may follow him, but the question we have to ask is, Will they be converted by him? They may even go so far as to allow that all that he says is very true. He may be their favourite preacher; and when he opens his exhortations upon them, there may be a deep and a solemn attention in every countenance. But how is the heart coming on all the while? How do these people live; and what evidence are they giving of being born again

under the power of his ministry? It is not enough to be
told of those momentary convictions which flash from the
pulpit, and carry a thrilling influence along with them
through the hearts of listening admirers. Have these
hearers of the word become the doers of the word? Have
they sunk down into the character of humble, and
sanctified, and penitent, and painstaking Christians?
Where, where is the fruit? And while the preaching of
Christ is all their joy, has the will of Christ become all
their direction? Alas! he may look around him, and, at
the end of the year, after all the tumults of a sounding
popularity, he may find the great bulk of them just where
they were – as listless and unconcerned about the things
of eternity – as obstinately alienated from God – as firmly
devoted to selfish and transitory interests – as exclusively
set upon the farm, and the money, and the merchandise –
and, with the covering of many external decencies to make
them as fair and plausible as their neighbours around
them, proving, by a heart given, with the whole tide of
its affections, to the vanities of the world, that they have
their full share of the wickedness which abounds in it.
After all his sermons, and all his loud and passionate
addresses, he finds that the power of darkness still keeps
its ground among them. He is grieved to learn, that all
he has said has had no more effect than the foolish and
the feeble lispings of infancy. He is overwhelmed by a
sense of his own helplessness, and the lesson is a
wholesome one. It makes him feel that the sufficiency is
not in him, but in God; it makes him understand that
another power must be brought to bear upon the mass of
resistance which is before him.[20]

There was much intellectual ferment in the decade before
the Disruption. A healthy controversy was stirring. Church
government and the spiritual independence of the church were

to claim popular attention, but by the blessing of God the results of Chalmers' teaching work were men who, in the first instance, were gospel preachers, and men of, in his phrase, 'deep and decided piety'. They were no mere imitators or supporters of a movement. They were, rather, themselves taught of God, and, if their thought was akin to that of Chalmers, it was through the media of personal experience and the New Testament itself.

There was certainly a striking unity of thought and of spirit among the large band of men who left Edinburgh's Divinity Hall for parish work in the 1830s. Robert M'Cheyne and Andrew Bonar were only two of a long line of fellow students who shared a common purpose – Horatius Bonar, Alexander Somerville, Thomas Brown, George Smeaton, James Hamilton and a number of others. The subject of revival was in the forefront of their thinking.[21] They had seen something of the magnitude of the need, they believed a theology very different from the old Moderatism, they had studied the spiritual awakenings of earlier periods, and now they looked to Christ to prosper the seed He was sending them out to sow. The letters which passed between them in the early years of their ministries reveal their longings on this subject, nor did they discontinue the petitions to God which had united them in their student days.

'Remember to observe our concerted times of prayer', Andrew Bonar wrote to Somerville in 1837, 'and count it absolutely necessary to be often alone, like Jacob at Jabbok, until you can call your study "Peniel"; for I have seen God face to face.' To another ministerial friend we find him writing, 'I often think of your prayer meetings. Is there any sign of the Spirit poured out?' At the suggestion of M'Cheyne those who shared in this fellowship of prayer united in observing a particular day in each month (frequently the first Monday) for special intercession.

At this same period there were also not a few older Christians and ministers upon whom there rested the same spirit of prayer. One such man was William H. Burns, a fellow student with Chalmers in St Andrews who, as we noted earlier, was invited home to Anstruther. Since that date, unlike Chalmers, Burns had passed a quiet and uneventful life in Kilsyth, a parish some twelve miles from Glasgow. It was an eminently faithful ministry, though one which had to wait long for a rich harvest. When at last it came, a time of reaping commenced which was to renew not Kilsyth only but other areas of the country.

The day which marked the start of this new period of revivals was Tuesday, 23 July 1839. The occasion was the closing day of the communion season at Kilsyth and the preacher was the twenty-four-year-old son of W. H. Burns, William Chalmers Burns. W. C. Burns had been supplying M'Cheyne's pulpit in Dundee since the previous April while the pastor of St Peter's was absent on a deputation to Palestine. An unusual unction seems to have rested upon M'Cheyne's ministry from the first. In his case, the prospect of eminent usefulness appeared early in his Christian life. But with W. C. Burns it was not until the summer of 1839 that he suddenly appeared to be clothed with authority from heaven. Those who knew him spoke of his preaching being lifted to another level during that year. What happened at Kilsyth has been reported by several witnesses. The service, appointed for 10 a.m. was to have been held in the market place, but rain necessitated removal to the church. Here the text of W. C. Burns was Psalm 110:3, 'Thy people shall be willing in the day of thy power.' The sermon was heard in solemn stillness until towards the close when, during a description of the power of the Holy Spirit as displayed in the revivals of former years, it became evident from the faces of many who listened that the God of history was present in their midst to work repentance. W. H. Burns writes:

The eyes of most of the audience were in tears; and those who could observe the countenances of the hearers expected, half an hour before, the scene which followed . . . When he was at the height of his appeal, with the words 'No cross, no crown,' then it was that the emotions of the audience were most overpoweringly expressed. A scene which scarcely can be described took place. I have no doubt, from the effects which have followed, and from the very numerous references to this day's service as the immediate cause of their remarkable change of heart and life, that the convincing and converting influence of the Holy Spirit was at that time most unusually and remarkably conveyed.[22]

Not until three o'clock in the afternoon of that July day could the congregation be dismissed and the old pastor, who had long meditated on the 1742 awakening in Kilsyth, went home believing that his parish had been 'awakened from a dream of a hundred years'. As for W. C. Burns himself, after the scene of that day he could not be the same man: 'The appearance of a great part of the people from the pulpit gave me an awfully vivid picture of the state of the ungodly in the day of Christ's coming to judgment,' and yet accompanying that picture there was also such a view of the glory of God advancing the work of salvation that his soul was filled with 'tranquil joy and praise'.

From July to October, 1839, the work of revival continued in Kilsyth: 'The whole tone and spirit of the place seemed for the moment changed, and an air almost Sabbatic brooded over it, which strangers recognized as with instinctive reverence they approached the spot.'

Before there was opportunity for the churches to regard Kilsyth as an isolated phenomenon, news spread that another general movement of the Spirit had begun in Dundee, where

Burns returned in August. Speaking of the events of August 1839 in his parish, M'Cheyne later wrote: 'The word of God came with such power to the hearts and consciences of the people here, and their thirst for hearing it became so intense, that the evening classes in the schoolroom were changed into densely crowded congregations in the church, and for nearly four months it was found desirable to have public worship almost every night.'[23]

W. C. Burns carried the main burden of the preaching at Dundee, and besides this, he and fellow workers who came to assist him spoke in private with some six to seven hundred individuals who were seeking spiritual help. Some of these enquirers were nominal Christians; far more were men and women who, like so many of Dundee's inhabitants, had lived in open sin.

Of these people, M'Cheyne, who returned from Palestine in November 1839, declared: 'I often think that the change they have undergone might be enough to convince an atheist that there is a God, or an infidel that there is a Saviour . . . The effects that have been produced upon the community are very marked. It seems now to be allowed, even by the ungodly, that there is such a thing as conversion. Men cannot any longer deny it.'

On the last Sunday of 1839 a similar revival began in the church of M'Cheyne's friend, John Milne, at Perth, where services were to continue daily for three months and more than two hundred young people were added to the church. Writes Milne:

During this season there were all the marks of a work of God which we see in the account given of the preaching of the gospel by the apostles. The multitude were divided; families were divided; the people of God were knit together; they were filled with zeal and joy and heavenly-mindedness; they continued steadfast, and increased in doctrine and fellowship, being daily in church and prayer meetings; and numbers were constantly turning to the Lord.[24]

Through the years 1840 and 1841 a quickening influence from above, sometimes as a gentle dew and in other places as a pouring rain, spread across large areas of Scotland. Records exist of powerful movements of the Spirit in Tain and Rosskeen in Ross-shire, on the Small Isles (in the Inner Hebrides), on the Island of Skye (where the foremost preacher, Roderick M'Leod, had earlier come to faith in the gospel through a sermon of Dr Chalmers), and in several parts of Perthshire.

Preaching at Moulin, Perthshire, W. C. Burns reported: 'I spoke for a long time with such assistance that I felt as if I could have shaken the globe to pieces, through the view I got of the glory of the divine person of Christ and of His atoning sacrifice to rescue sinners from eternal death; the people were bent down beneath the Word like corn under the breeze, and many a stout sinner wept bitterly'. After a week at Breadalbane, in August, 1840, he wrote:

> In the evening I walked up the side of Ben Lawers, until I could command a view from the head of Glen Dochart to Dunkeld, having Loch Tay in the centre from Kenmore to Killin. It was a beautiful evening, and the scene was magnificent. However, all my thoughts of external scenery were well-nigh absorbed in the thought of the wonderful works of Jehovah which I had witnessed during the week that was closing among the poor inhabitants of this splendid theatre of the Lord's creation. I could have supposed that I had been in Breadalbane for a month instead of a week; the events that had passed before me were so remarkable and so rapid in succession. It has been indeed a resurrection of the dead, sudden and momentous as the resurrection of the last day – nay, far more momentous than it to the individuals concerned.[25]

Some of these works of grace were set down at the time but there is good reason to believe that the ingathering of these years was greater than has ever been recorded.

THREE MAIN LESSONS

It has been possible here to do little more than allude to the many scenes of spiritual quickening which occurred in the last decade of Chalmers' life. The subject, however, cannot be left without drawing some observations of abiding relevance.

(1) *It was the revival in the Church of Scotland which led to the Disruption of that Church.*

On 18 May 1843, at the General Assembly of the Church of Scotland, the Moderator, Dr Welsh, followed by Dr Chalmers and about 190 other members of Assembly, together with other ministers and elders, formed the Free Church of Scotland. Approximately one-third of the parish ministers of Scotland went into the Free Church.[26]

Behind the events of that day lay ten years of debate and legal procedure, in the course of which the evangelicals had worked to end the abuse of patronage, only to be finally stopped by the civil powers. This long controversy revealed how deep was the traditional division in the national Church. The Moderates, in the final issue, sided with the patrons and counselled submission to the civil law which had long authorized patronage, while the evangelicals, believing in the scriptural right of Christians to elect their own pastors, came to repudiate the interference of the State in a sphere where Christ's authority is supreme.

But this controversy alone does not explain the Disruption. For many years something akin to two different religions had existed side by side in the Church – Moderatism and evangelical Christianity – and it was the renewal of spiritual life which finally made this state of affairs intolerable. The zeal for the salvation of men's souls which the revival brought ended the respect for the parish boundaries of the Moderates which evangelicals had previously shown. For years, men and women had been starved in these lifeless parishes and ecclesiastical etiquette had usually prevented evangelicals from going into them uninvited. Under the impulse of a stronger spiritual life, men such as M'Cheyne and his brethren could no more wait to be invited, and this fact alone was enough to lead to a crisis.

There is also another and even more important, respect in which the revival prepared the way for the Disruption. Formidable and disagreeable practical consequences could be anticipated by any ministers who withdrew from the national Church. Government endowment to the extent of a hundred thousand pounds a year would be forfeited. Churches, manses, and schools would all be lost. Not one divinity hall would remain the property of the evangelicals, nor any of the overseas properties of the Foreign Missions which had been built solely by their effort. And not least, ministers would surrender all the advantages and prestige that the parish system had previously given them. The only influences strong enough to counterbalance these losses were the graces of devotion to Christ and faith in the Holy Spirit. In ages where these graces were only feebly present no event such as the Disruption could have occurred. The ultimate reason why so many ministers in 1843 signed away their earthly possessions, and why the common people followed in such numbers into the Free Church, is that this church was, in the words of one of her ministers, 'nursed in the bosom of religious revival'. Difficulties which would have alarmed another generation were swept away by the new ardour of love to Christ and the joy which men had in the Holy Spirit. Accordingly, the very Disruption day, when all these hazards had now to be faced, was a time of thanksgiving and praise. The Spirit of glory and of God rested upon those who on that 18 May 1843 formed the first Free

Church Assembly. That night they returned home from their meeting, says one who was present, as though from a scene at Pentecost. Dr Landsborough summed up the common feeling when he wrote in his diary, 'Hallelujah! I shall never see the like till heaven.'

Beyond question, the assertion of Samuel Miller of Glasgow is correct, 'If there had been no spiritual and increasing reviving in the Church, the event of 1843 had never taken place.'

(2) *Revivals and their consequences are used by God to restore credibility to the Christian Faith.*

Every period of spiritual declension witnesses a decay in faith in the gospel amongst communities at large. Such decay also operates within the church herself and, consequently, revivals generally give a dramatic turn to the thinking of Christians themselves. In the biography of W. C. Burns, which his son Islay Burns wrote in 1860, it is recorded that from the hour when the remarkable scenes took place in Kilsyth and Dundee in 1839, 'the idea of revival as the great necessity of the Church and of the age – till then but a dim tradition of bygone days – took strong possession of the minds of Christian men, and has never since lost its hold. From that hour it ceased to seem a thing incredible that God should raise the dead.' But revivals not only bring Christians to a surer faith; there is a sense in which they also restore credibility to the church in the eyes of the world.

We have seen how Moderatism reduced Christianity in Scotland to little more than a philosophy of moralism; and its exponents themselves, without belief in the unique and the supernatural facts of the gospel, lived the lives of ordinary worldly men. They differed little from their fellows, unless it was in dry and occasional religious language. Their principal ambitions and interests were just the same as might be seen in any professional class. Accordingly, the common view of a

Christian minister was a long way from the view which the New Testament warrants. Being so much like the world, the calling of such ministers did not expose them to scorn, hardship or sacrifice. Religious beliefs were only matters of opinion, not convictions that they would suffer to uphold.

Before the gospel could gain a general hearing throughout Scotland this debased image of the ministry had to be changed and the means God used to effect the change were the severe trials incurred by those who laid down their privileges by leaving the Church of Scotland in 1843. Before that event took place it was a common opinion that self-interest would prevent a secession on the part of evangelicals – at most, it was said, a hundred might withdraw, and more likely a mere forty. The extent to which these predictions proved erroneous electrified Scotland. When, on the morning of the Disruption, a messenger carried the news of the size of the secession to Lord Jeffrey, a man not accustomed to think highly of evangelicals, he sprang to his feet with the exclamation, 'I am proud of my country.' The event was the beginning of a new respect for Christian ministers and, more important, for the message which they preached.

As already noted, the loss incurred by Free Church ministers was not a small one. Men whose salaries had previously been £200 to £300 p.a. had now no assurance of anything like those figures. Homes had to be left, in many cases, without any suitable alternative accommodation to hand. One minister had to transport his family by boat away from their manse in the Inner Hebrides to the cries of 'Home, home, home' from his sea-sick five-year old son. Such feelings were far from being unique that summer of the Disruption. But the trials did not end there. In many country districts the landowners – the old supporters of patronage – did their utmost to prevent the Free Church ministers gathering congregations. Their reasoning was that if the people could be kept in the parish churches, the secession would soon collapse, so ground for the building of churches was steadfastly refused. One congregation had to endure meeting for five winters in the open air before a building could be erected. Other congregations were compelled, by the refusal of all ground, to meet on sea-shores and in one instance even to buy a ship to employ as 'a floating church'.

Yet these severities only served to deepen the impression that men who were prepared to endure all this for the sake of their message deserved to be heard. There was consequently such a general flocking to the hearing of the gospel in 1843 as had not been seen in Scotland for many years. In two years, 163 new congregations were added to the original number which came out at the Disruption. By 1848, when the position over the refusal of sites had eased, some 700 churches had been built. These conditions of growth amazed onlookers outside Scotland in the 1840s. Instead of everything being lost for evangelicals in 1843, a witness had been established, free from the deadening influence of association with a worldly ministry, and able by the strength of its devotion to purer standards to command the consciences of men in the name of Christ.

(3) *This revival led to a restoration of a true sense of priorities in the Church.*

When the Disruption took place, we might have supposed that with all the problems confronting the new and disorganized denomination – problems in connection with finance, problems in respect to lack of buildings, and problems in many other areas of legitimate business – priority of importance might necessarily be given to these affairs. But such was not the case. The anxiety which was manifested throughout the Free Church was not about how salaries could be paid, nor how churches could be built, it was rather about how vital godliness could be strengthened in the Church and how, in Chalmers' phrase, the gospel might 'be carried to every cottage door'. 'The desire which above all else the Free Church cherished', writes Thomas Brown, 'was to receive some token of His favour in the revival of her spiritual life'.[27]

In other periods, the Church may *profess* that God's blessing is her greatest need but the revived Free Church organized herself so as to make that belief paramount in all her deliberations. The fact was illustrated by a meeting which took place in one of the Edinburgh churches (St Luke's) on the eve of the Disruption in May 1843. The purpose of the gathering was to plead 'for a great outpouring of the Spirit of the Lord upon all the church and especially upon the body of ministers and elders now assembling'. Addressing the gathering on the reason why *this* was the foremost need, W. C. Burns said:

> It is easy to perceive that, if these trials, which are at the door, do come, without a great measure of the Spirit along with them, the most fearful consequences will ensue. Where will ministers be who do not receive *that*, when they lose the influence belonging to their present position? They will either get influence by *carnal* means (and they are to be pitied who get it in that way), or they must get it by being men evidently full of the Spirit of their Master, and publicly *owned* by Him, as those who are winning many souls to Christ.[28]

The same lesson was driven home in the 1844 Free Church General Assembly. Prior to that Assembly, it was agreed that special time should be given during its deliberations to the state of personal religion in the Church and accordingly, the best part of two days were set aside for this purpose. The conference for this purpose on Tuesday, 21 May, commenced with a sermon by Charles Brown. After the measure of success which was attending the work of their new denomination we might suppose that some degree of satisfaction would be revealed in Brown's sermon. Far from it! Taking as his text Habakkuk 2:1,

'I will stand upon my watch, and set me upon the tower, and will watch to see what he will say unto me, and what I shall answer when I am reproved', the preacher proceeded to show what reasons they all had to humble themselves in deep repentance before God. 'Seldom', writes one observer of that day, 'has a more solemn scene been beheld. The vast hall in which the Assembly met was crowded with ministers, elders, and a large number of earnest and devoted worshippers. And as the preacher prosecuted his great work, his faithful and searching confessions and admonitions, urged with all the impressive power of a heart thoroughly in earnest in his Master's cause, and directed, as we fully believe, to the hearts of the assembled audience by the Spirit of God, the whole vast multitude were bowed and shaken like a forest of trees beneath a mighty wind.'

Another who was present from Ireland reported: 'They bowed down before God, and when, instead of railing against their enemies, they confessed, in deep prostration, the plagues of their own hearts and the sins of their own lives, in one universal cry that prayer arose – "God be merciful to us sinners". We never witnessed a scene more solemnly sublime.'[29]

When the sermon concluded, conference did not begin as planned. After a few searching words from Chalmers on the need for unceasing prayer for 'that unction from the Holy One, without which we cannot save our own souls, neither can we save the souls of others', there was silence when the Moderator invited others to speak. Hearts were too full for words, and the meeting was suspended until the evening. Unanimously, the Assembly of 1844 placed on record a statement which concluded:

> With profound humiliation, and in reliance on the great strength of Almighty God, solemnly to devote, dedicate, and consecrate anew themselves and their fellow labourers to the service of God, and His holy purpose of glorifying

His great name, in saving souls through the preaching of the truth, and the operation of the Holy Ghost.[30]

Revival had brought the Church back to her *chief* work. All other discussions and church arrangements had to take a lower place, and men gave themselves first to the real business of the Church of Christ.[31]

CHALMERS AT THE CLOSE OF LIFE

Chalmers' primary interest as his life now drew to its end was the same as it had been in those early years of evangelical fervour at Kilmany. When the Disruption came, he opened his own private house for a church in Morningside and used his hall staircase as a pulpit. He lived to see the Free Church College – of which he was the first Principal – open its splendid building, New College, Edinburgh, in 1846, and declared that the essential equality of human souls would there be strenuously taught: 'In the high court and reckoning of eternity, the soul of the poorest of natural children, the raggedest boy that runs along the pavement, is of like estimation in the eyes of heaven with that of the greatest and the noblest of our land.' This truth he lived out to the end. Though increasingly disengaged from all the public business of the Church, he lent his last energies to seeking to advance the gospel in one of the poorest districts of Edinburgh, where about a dozen adults, most of them elderly women, had commenced a witness after the Disruption, meeting in a loft. Whatever other duties necessity required him to lay down, this one he would not abandon, and when in February, 1847, a church with 132 communicants was opened in the West Port, he spoke of it as 'the most joyful event of my life'.

To the last Chalmers also maintained his primary interest in the young men who would be the future ministers of the Church. In March 1844, by which time the Free Church had her own divinity school in Edinburgh, he says, 'I am obliged to teach two classes, and the whole number of my enrolment is 209'. Declining an invitation to attend the next General Assembly, he wrote in 1845, 'Truly it is a higher department to have to do with the understandings and consciences of my students than to wear out any more of my life in the outward business of the house of God.' When, latterly, his memory was less dependable he still kept up his efforts to have personal contact with the many men who attended his classes. The biographer of Alexander Somerville observed: 'The personal kindness of Dr Chalmers, especially to his students, did more for Somerville and his fellows than the whole training of some professors who, however competent intellectually, fail in this.'[32] In this connection Hanna gives the following amusing anecdote from the concluding years of Chalmers' life:

> He had one morning in the week reserved especially for his students. On meeting with them in his own house, he was often at a loss to recognize them by name, and the mode he took to extricate himself from the difficulty was rather singular. He had a card with the names on it of all the students whom he had that morning invited to breakfast. When all had assembled and were seated, holding the card below the level of the table, as he thought out of sight, he glanced furtively down at it to catch the first name on the list. Then, lifting his eyes and looking eagerly and rapidly around, he would say, – 'Tea or coffee, Mr Johnson?' hoping by this innocent artifice to identify the person so addressed, and to save him the pain of being apparently unknown or forgotten. The device was too transparent to be unnoticed; but which of his students did not love him all the more for the kindliness which dictated it! The recognition once got over, no after difficulty remained.

Chalmers' was never able to fulfil his long-held belief that a man in his sixties should give himself chiefly to preparation for heaven, for he liked to think of a parallel between the seventh decade of life and the purpose of the Sabbath rest. The retirement which his parents enjoyed in their last years was not to be his. Yet the world to come was indeed uppermost in his thoughts. Amidst all the excitement of the Spring of 1843 we find him writing to a friend:

> It should be very solemnizing when one reflects on the nearing of death and eternity. I am as old now as my father was when I was ordained the minister of Kilmany. Let us be awake to the realities before us and above us. I feel more and more the fundamental and all-pervading importance of faith. Let us take God at his word, and we shall believe that Christ's blood washeth from all sin; and that He hath made Him sin for us, that we might be made the righteousness of God in Him. With confidence in these sayings we shall not only have peace and joy, but all the principles within us of new obedience. The benefit of the sacrifice and the gift of the Spirit are inseparable.

To another he writes in 1845,

> I hope we shall meet in heaven; but let us never forget that without holiness no man can see God.

In May of 1847, when he was sixty-seven, Chalmers made his last visit to England and against 9 May his Diary contains the entry, 'Preached with greater comfort than I had ever done before in London.' On his return to Edinburgh at the end of the month he did not seem unduly tired. Sunday, 30 May found him at his home in Church Hill, Morningside. He did not rise as usual in the morning but when a friend observed he was unwell he denied it with the words, 'I only require a little rest.' To the same friend he proceeded to speak, with the kind of liberty more usual in the pulpit, on the election of God, the sacrifice of Christ, and the freeness of the offer of the gospel. During the morning William Cunningham called and the two men went together to the afternoon service at the local Free Church. After tea, and a brief note to an old friend, he walked in the garden, where he was overheard by one of the family saying, 'O Father, my heavenly Father!' The same evening he addressed a friend with a question he must have often asked, 'Are you much acquainted with the Puritan divines?' and went on to speak of Howe's *Delighting in God* which he was currently reading. 'Immediately after prayers he withdrew, and bidding his family remember that they must be early tomorrow, he waved his hand, saying, "A general goodnight".'

The next morning he was found still in his bed, asleep in Christ. When, many years later, Thomas Brown, his former student, wrote his *Annals of the Disruption,* he concluded that account with words which are also our best conclusion here:

> If the Church is to gain over the world, men must recognize her faith and zeal and self-sacrificing love, and in these trace the evidences of Christ's abiding presence with her as her living Head. In Disruption times this was what men lived and prayed for, and they did not pray in vain.

[1] See *A Selection from the Correspondence of Thomas Chalmers,* ed. W. Hanna (Edinburgh: Constable, 1853), p. 32.

[2] Chalmers, *Correspondence,* p. 338. The reference is to Chalmers' *Posthumous Works,* edited by W. Hanna, 9 vols. (Edinburgh: Sutherland and Knox, 1847–9). David Couper held the same opinion as Miller; see 'Thomas Chalmers' in *Disruption Worthies, A Memorial of 1843* (repr. Edinburgh: Jack, 1881), p. 160. The catalogue of New College Library, Edinburgh, contains over 300 entries under Chalmers.

[3] Quoted by John Macleod in *Scottish Theology* (Edinburgh: Banner of Truth, 1974), p. 263.

[4] *Forty Years' Familiar Letters of James W. Alexander,* ed. John Hall (New York: Scribner, 1860, vol. 1), p. 157. Alexander does go on to give some qualifications but his general impression – confirmed by another visit in 1857 (see pp. 267–8) – was high.

[5] *The Happy Man: The Abiding Witness of Lachlan Mackenzie* (Edinburgh: Banner of Truth, 1979), p. 45.

[6] An illustration of the same attitude appears in the life of John MacDonald, 'the Apostle of the North'. In his early life, after preaching as a visitor in the parish of Glenelg, he was told by the minister, 'That was a very good sermon, I suppose, but it was unsuitable here; for you spoke all day to sinners, and I know only one in all my parish.'

[7] In the summer of 1812 he married Grace Pratt whose father, an army officer, was then resident in the parish. The ceremony was conducted in a private house by a clergyman in his 90th year who, says Chalmers, in putting the wedding vows to Grace, 'required of her that she should be a loving and affectionate husband, to which she curtsied!'

[8] William Hanna, *Memoirs of the Life and Writings of Thomas Chalmers*, vol. 1 (Edinburgh: Sutherland and Knox, 1850), p. 262. Most of my biographical material on Chalmers is drawn from this great biography but unhappily its extent – 4 volumes published 1850–2 – has been against its general usefulness.

[9] About this same time, such was the interest in what was happening in Kilmany, that Edward Irving, then a young school-master in Haddington, walked with several of his pupils to hear Chalmers, who was preaching on a week-day in St George's, Edinburgh. They returned home the same night, thus 'accomplishing a distance of about thirty-five miles without any other rest than what was obtained in church'. Mrs Oliphant's *Life of Edward Irving*.

[10] Chalmers, *Correspondence*, p. 196.   [11] Ibid., p. 198.

[12] *Memories of Two Cities*, Edinburgh and Aberdeen, David Masson, 1911, pp. 77–81.

[13] *Memoirs of Chalmers*, vol. 4, p. 420.

[14] *Colloquia Peripatetica, Conversations with John Duncan* (Edinburgh: Oliphant, Anderson & Ferrier, 1907), pp 27–8. 'How did you and Dr Chalmers get on?' a friend once asked Duncan in later years. 'Oh, nobly. Though very inferior, I took the liberty of differing with him sometimes about doctrine. One day, when he came down to my house for a little refreshment, I found fault with his definition of faith. Ah! my doctrine about faith was better than his – but he went to prayer, and his faith was better than mine', *Life of John Duncan*, David Brown (Edinburgh: Edmonston and Douglas, 1872), p. 484.

[15] *The Scottish Pulpit*, 1887, pp. 206–7.

[16] Chalmers seems to have continued reading Owen all his days and with mounting appreciation. 'Have you read Owen on the 130th Psalm?' he said to a friend in 1843. 'This is my last great work, and I would strongly recommend it.'

[17] These words come from M'Cheyne's MS. notes on Chalmers' lectures which are now in New College Library, Edinburgh. They are quoted in the unpublished doctoral thesis of David Victor Yeaworth, *Robert Murray McCheyne (1813–1843): A Study of An Early Nineteenth Century Scottish Evangelical* (Edinburgh, 1957), to whom I am indebted.

[18] *Memoir and Remains of R. M. M'Cheyne*, Andrew A. Bonar (repr. London: Banner of Truth, 1968) p. 31.

19 Chalmers, *Correspondence*, p. 237.

20 *Works of Thomas Chalmers*, vol. 8 (Glasgow: Collins, n.d.), pp. 27–37.

21 An emphasis on the work of the Spirit can be seen in the texts with which several of these men commenced their pastorates. M'Cheyne, for instance, began his historic ministry at St Peter's, Dundee, in November, 1836, with a sermon on Isaiah 61:1–3, 'The Spirit of the Lord GOD is upon me; because the LORD hath anointed me to preach good tidings unto the meek.' His friend Alexander Somerville took as his first text in Glasgow, 'For Zion's sake I will not hold my peace, and for Jerusalem's sake I will not rest, until the righteousness thereof go forth as brightness, and the salvation thereof as a lamp that burneth' (*Isa.* 62:1).

22 *The Pastor of Kilsyth: Memorials of W. H. Burns*, Islay Burns (London: Nelson, 1860), pp. 145–6. This little-known work is one of the best of Scottish ministerial biographies.

23 'Evidence on Revivals' in M'Cheyne's *Memoir and Remains*, p. 543 ff. Testimony from critics as well as supporters of revival can also be seen in *Evidences on the Subject of Revivals Taken Before a Committee of the Presbytery of Aberdeen* (Aberdeen: Gray and Davidson, 1841).

24 *Life of John Milne*, Horatius Bonar (London: Nisbet, n.d. [1868?]), p. 57.

25 *Memoir of William C. Burns*, Islay Burns (London: Nisbet, 1870), pp. 200–1.

26 Hanna says that 470 ministers signed the deed of demission which effected the separation, but not all these men were parish ministers. The figures and the chief areas of Free Church support are discussed by A. L. Drummond and J. Bulloch in *The Scottish Church, 1688–1843* (Edinburgh: St Andrew Press, 1973, pp. 249 ff.

27 *Annals of the Disruption*, Thomas Brown (Edinburgh: McNiven & Wallace, 1893), p. 786.

28 William C. Burns, *Revival Sermons*, ed. M. F. Barbour (repr. Edinburgh: Banner of Truth, 1980), p. 85.

29 *Annals of the Disruption*, pp. 634–5. Recording these events, Thomas Brown cautioned, 'These scenes, it must not be forgotten, were in perfect keeping with what had been going on for years before' (p. 632).

30 H. Bonar, *Life of Milne*, p. 108.

31 In 1868 Horatius Bonar expressed his regret that the priority given to personal religion was no longer so evident in the Free Church: 'For several years the General Assembly set itself in good earnest to do spiritual work for Scotland. Once and again a whole day was set apart for humiliation and prayer. These seasons will never be forgotten, though the number of those who took part in them is diminishing fast . . . "Ecclesiastical" work was not neglected; but it took its lower and more becoming place. WE DID run well; who did hinder us?'

32 *A Modern Apostle, A. N. Somerville*, George Smith (London: John Murray, 1891), p. 18. Chalmers' interest in his former students is also illustrated by the eager support which he gave to the Kelso tracts written by Horatius Bonar.

A View of the Scottish Highlands

4

John MacDonald
and the Awakening
in the North

John MacDonald Preaching at Ferintosh

Culloden was the last battle fought on the British mainland. The date was 16 April 1746 and the scene Drumossie Moor. The combatants are commonly represented as Highland Jacobites, under the command of Charles Edward Stuart ('Bonnie Prince Charlie'), and English troops led by the Duke of Cumberland. It was the final attempt by a descendant of James II (*Jacobus* in Latin) to restore the exiled Stuart dynasty and Roman Catholicism to the British throne. That it failed is common knowledge, less well understood is the composition of the forces that clashed that day a few miles east of Inverness. Certainly most of the men supporting the twenty-four-year-old prince were Highland Scots, clansmen from the wild, Gaelic-speaking west and the central Grampians, but on the other side also were Highlanders, volunteers of Lord Loudoun's regiment, together with Campbells from Argyll. Of the fifteen regular battalions that fought under Cumberland, three were made up of Scots.

These two sides at Culloden thus represented a division within Scotland and within the Highlands themselves. So race alone cannot explain Culloden; religion came into it. The Jacobite cause favoured the religion of pre-Reformation

Scotland, while the opposing army supported Protestant Christianity as well as the continuance of the reign of George II. In religious as well as social terms, for two hundred years before Culloden, time had largely stood still in many parts of northern Scotland. It was from these parts that the clansmen came who charged for the last time on Drumossie Moor. But if spiritual change had not touched their lochs and glens, it was different in the region where they faced the forces of Cumberland. To the east of Inverness, and to the immediate north, lies a rich land, divided by great inlets from the North Sea – the Firths of Moray, Cromarty, and Dornoch – and here there were those who appreciated what the Reformation meant. Patrick Hamilton, the first martyr of the Reformation, was a native of this part of Scotland and from here came some of the landowners who stood by Knox in the Reformation Parliament of 1560.

A CORNER OF THE NORTH-EAST, AN OASIS IN THE DESERT

One reason why the gospel entered the north-east, while it remained shut out of many parts of Scotland's north and west, may well have been connected with language. Ever since Norman times English had been spoken as well as Gaelic by some in the north-east. Thus it is probable that when copies of Tyndale's New Testament began to be smuggled into Britain, in 1526, some came in through the ports of Inverness and Cromarty and found readers. For the exclusively Gaelic-speaking Highlanders elsewhere there was no such opportunity. Not until 1767 was there to be a Gaelic New Testament, followed by the whole Bible in that language in 1801.[1]

As already shown above, the ministry of Robert Bruce brought new life to the Inverness region in the early 1600s, and before that century had ended, aided by Christian patrons such as the earls of Sutherland and the barons of Fowlis, a scattered number of gospel ministries were to be found in the north-east, in Easter Ross, Inverness-shire, Nairn and Sutherland. When episcopacy was restored by Charles II in 1660, five ministers from Ross-shire had been ejected from their charges for their resistance, the best known being Thomas Hog of Kiltearn. While information on these men is meagre, enough is on record to show that their preaching was attended by the authority and power of heaven. Referring to a service led by one of them in a private house, during days of persecution in the 1670s, the historian Robert Wodrow records, 'There were so sensible [i.e. felt] and glorious discoveries made by the Son of Man, and such evident presence of the Master of Assemblies, this day and the preceding, the people seemed to be in a transport, and their souls filled with heaven, and breathing thither while they were upon the earth; and some were almost at that, "Whether in the body or out of the body, I cannot tell."'[2]

Close to the battlefield at Culloden was Kilravock Castle, centre of the Rose clan. Thomas Hog had been welcomed and sheltered there in the previous century and in 1745 it gave Prince Charles no support. The fact was that parishes adjacent to Kilravock were already becoming gospel-centred. Five years before Culloden, James Calder had been called to the nearby congregation of Ardersier, and within thirty miles to the north, across the Moray Firth, a whole brotherhood of like-minded preachers were either settled or soon to be. Referring to this area, Gustavus Aird, who knew the period as well as anyone, wrote: 'Upwards of a generation after the Revolution, in 1740 and thereafter, a real and extensive revival of true religion occurred throughout a very extensive part of the country, and continued until near the close of the century.'[3] One of the first locations where revival was documented was among the population on the north side of the Cromarty Firth. From Nigg, in 1744, a correspondent reported:

There is a like appearance of success to the Gospel in other parishes in this country. . . . The people here were much refreshed with the several accounts they have had of the glorious work of God elsewhere, and particularly in these parts of our native country, where the same appears with such blessed and shining evidences of the divine power and presence.[4]

Twenty years after this, the surviving diaries of James Calder show that he experienced similar blessing after he moved from Ardersier to the parish of Croy (presented to that charge by Hugh Rose of Kilravock in 1746). One entry in Calder's diary, towards the close of 1763, noted: 'Glory to His blessed name! This by-past year has been happier than usual with respect to my flock, there having been some more remarkable instances of conversion-work than usual among them, and more confirmation and consolation, and spiritual prosperity and vivacity, among the Lord's people in this place and this neighbourhood, so that this has been a jubilee year to some – a year that will be remembered and celebrated to the praise of free grace through all the years and ages, if I may so phrase it, of a never-ending eternity.'[5] The following year saw yet larger success.

Calder's diaries show the close fellowship that existed between preachers of like spirit. Several of these men, including Hector Macphail, ministered on 'the Black Isle', the land bounded by the firths of Beauly, Moray and Cromarty. Attending a service in Macphail's congregation at Resolis in 1764, Calder noted: 'A delightful fellowship meeting; more souls awakened . . . Mr Macphail preached one of the best sermons my ears ever heard from Titus 2: "Looking for that blessed hope and the glorious appearing", etc.'[6] When the minister of Resolis died, ten years later, Calder wrote that his friend was, 'the most eminently pious, zealous, active, laborious, minister of Christ I ever saw, and the most lovely, living image of his adorable Lord and Master that ever I was acquainted with.'[7]

The very year of Macphail's death saw another eminent ministry begun on the Black Isle. Charles Calder became minister at Ferintosh in May 1774. Along with his two brothers (John and Hugh also ministers), Charles Calder had come to faith and known the call to serve Christ under his father's preaching at Croy. He had also married the young lady who was frequently noted in his father's diary as 'heavenly Miss Brodie'. She was Margaret Brodie who belonged to one of the leading families of Nairnshire and her conversion may also have occurred at Croy. We do not doubt that she played a major part in her husband's future ministry, of which the 'great theme', it is said, 'was the love of Jesus'.[8]

LOCHCARRON: THE GOSPEL ENTERS THE WEST

It was not love but retribution, in the form of death, transportation and devastation that followed the supporters of the rebellion that had ended at Culloden. The western Highlands would never be the same again. The power of the clan chiefs was broken, new roads gave better access, the carrying of arms was made illegal and even the wearing of clan tartans forbidden. But the abiding spiritual destitution was unmistakeable and it was underlined by a special mission to the area that reported to the General Assembly of the Church of Scotland. While it is true that in all parts of the north a structure of supposedly Protestant parishes existed, often numbers of people had no place of worship, and parishes were so extensive that multitudes lived many miles from any church. Nor were those who lived nearer likely to hear the gospel in a church they could attend. In 1745 probably the only evangelical ministry in the north-west Highlands was at Lochcarron, where an arm of the Atlantic runs inland between mountain ranges, and a village of that name stands on its north-western shore. Eneas Sage became minister there in 1726, in his own words, 'merely to pave the way, if it were practicable, for settling the bounds with a gospel ministry, though it should be at the peril of my life, in which indeed I was. Four nights before my ordination some of the country people set fire to the house where I lodged . . . upon several occasions afterwards there were plots laid either to shoot me on the highway or to drown me.' Addressing an appeal to leave to his presbytery in 1731, Sage concluded, 'It appears to me, to my great grief and sorrow, that my work is at an end in this corner.' This was not countenanced, although he had only one family attending his ministry. Sage struggled on. It was eight years after his arrival before he saw any impression on the few who gathered in his low, thatched church. Most eyed him with suspicion and in 1745 he had still to escape the intent of an assassin. Brighter days were to follow and when he died at the age of eighty-seven in 1774 many of those who mourned 'had become true and vital Christians through his ministry, and were themselves the primitive fathers of the spiritual generations that followed them'.[9]

Lochcarron in the 1770s was only a foothold in the west, for even of the days of his successor, Lachlan MacKenzie, we read, 'Mr MacKenzie was the only minister who preached the gospel with purity and effect.'[10] Like Sage, MacKenzie came from the Black Isle (illustrating how places of powerful preaching are generally the nursery of preachers), and he served at Lochcarron for 38 years until his death in 1819. By that date, as we shall see, the whole prospect in the Western Highlands and Islands was changing and no one was more closely connected with that change than the figure to whom we now turn.

THE NEW MINISTER AT FERINTOSH

The ministry of Charles Calder at Ferintosh (also known by the parish name of Urquhart) ended with his death in 1812. 'For upwards of thirty years,' wrote one of his hearers, 'the church of Urquhart became a central point where many devout worshippers met, exchanged Christian salutations, were animated and refreshed, even by the countenances of each other, and heard the speaker with a riveted and breathless attention.'[11] The fact that Calder's congregation included people from eight to ten parishes shows that even in this area the gospel was by no means in every pulpit. A contemporary who knew the situation described 'Parson Rory', the minister of Knockbain, as orthodox in doctrine, with 'his mind wholly secularised. He was a first-rate shot and deer-stalker.' Of the minister of Avoch, we are told, 'Money-making was the ruling passion of his soul.' The cleric of Rosemarkie, 'not apprehending any evils, temporal, spiritual, or eternal, which might come upon him,' plodded through life, and 'in stoutness of body and inertness of mind' was the same at the age of seventy as the writer had first known him at thirty-seven.[12] Even at Resolis, the man who had followed Hector Macphail had gone to sleep at his post, opposed evangelical ministers, and alienated the best of his people long before his death in 1821. It is no wonder, then, that on Calder's death the Ferintosh congregation feared that gospel light was soon to fade in their midst.

Not long before this date, however, a visitor to the town of Tain, also in Easter Ross, had a surprise that was soon to come to others. The man had walked the sixteen miles to Tain one Sunday to hear its evangelical minister, Dr Angus Mackintosh. But instead of finding Mackintosh in the pulpit he was sadly disappointed to see a stranger, 'a smart looking young man'. Only as the sermon began did the visitor's regret vanish: 'I forgot all but the doctrine I was hearing. As he warmed to his subject, the preacher became most vehement in his action; and suppressed sounds testified to the effect which his sermon was producing. His second discourse was so awe-inspiring that the audience became powerfully affected. Such was the awful solemnity of the doctrine and the vehemence of the preacher's manner, that I expected, ere he was done, every heart would be pierced, and that the very roof of the church would be rent. The sermon over, all were asking who the preacher was. "A young man from Edinburgh of the name of MacDonald", was the only answer given.'

This same 'young man' became Charles Calder's successor at Ferintosh on 1 September 1813. John MacDonald was then thirty-three years of age. Born on the north coast of Caithness in 1779, his retentive memory and ability in mathematics had marked him out for further education at the University of Aberdeen. It was after his first year there, and during the long vacation at home, that he became a Christian, in the autumn of 1798. 'There is reason to believe,' writes his biographer, 'that the reading of President Edwards' works was the means of beginning the work of conviction which issued in his conversion to God.'[13] Licensed to preach in 1805, he first served in Caithness and then, at the Gaelic church in Edinburgh, beneath the walls of the castle.

It was not for the Scottish capital but for the north that MacDonald had been prepared, and almost immediately an unusual degree of usefulness attended his ministry at Ferintosh. In 1814, the week before his first communion season in the new charge, he lost Georgina, the wife of his youth and the mother of his three children, the eldest of whom was only seven. In view of this sorrow the elders proposed a postponement of the communion. 'No, no,' replied MacDonald, 'let not my wife's death interfere with commemorating the death of my Saviour.' According to the usual tradition, several brethren shared in the preaching of this communion season but MacDonald himself took the sermon immediately before the dispensing of the sacrament. Preaching to perhaps as many as ten thousand in the open air, his text was taken from Hosea 2:19, 'I will betroth thee unto me for ever.' 'Unthinking of his own distress,' writes his biographer, John Kennedy, 'he gave himself up to the praise of Christ.' His brethren pressed him to preach again in the evening which he did from Psalm 45:10, 'Hearken, O daughter, and consider, and incline thine ear.' As MacDonald called his hearers to faith in Christ, and urged the question 'Wilt thou go with this man?'(*Gen.* 34:58), 'with extraordinary fervour', an eye-witness reported that 'the great congregation broke down. It was a scene never to be forgotten. The burn of Ferintosh was a Bochim indeed that day. Such was the weeping, the crying, the commotion among the people, that the preacher's voice was drowned.'[14]

ITINERANCY AND THE WIDER AWAKENING

The awakening at Ferintosh appears to have gone on for some time and in January 1816 MacDonald wrote in his diary of some fifty-eight persons 'awakened under my ministry, known to myself, besides others unknown to me'. Inevitably he was now called upon to preach far and wide. Soon we hear of him on the far north coast of Scotland, and then at Dornoch in Sutherland, where, forbidden to preach in the parish, he addressed a multitude from just a few yards from its border, and with such vigour that before he closed his feet had worn the ground on which he stood into a pit. The aged Lachlan Mackenzie, in his own style, urged him to come to Lochcarron with the words, 'I hear that you keep a large store of powder which you use in blasting. I wish you to come and try your skill in breaking the hard rocks of Lochcarron.' One of the most memorable days of his life was in the Breadalbane district of the central mountains of Perthshire, 16 September 1816. His host was Robert Findlater who had been appointed as a missioner to the area six years earlier. Based at Ardeonaig on Loch Tay, Findlater served an area from five to six miles on either side of the loch and with a population of about 1500. The scene was very different from the one he had known at

Ferintosh, where he attended with his parents in the days of his youth, and he wrote to his brother in 1812: 'We have great need of earnest and persevering prayer . . . I am here in a very cold climate, and stand much in need of getting into the reach of some "spiritual atmosphere" that would quicken and enliven me . . . There are a few, but alas! Very few, with whom I can speak with freedom.'[15]

Encouragement came to Findlater from afar, from reports of William Carey's work in India, then from Ferintosh, and before MacDonald came in 1816 there was already a stirring among the 'dry bones' beside Loch Tay. Reporting MacDonald's visit to his brother, Findlater wrote on 21 September 1816:

> There was a vast congregation collected, reckoned between 4000 and 5000; for I spread the information far and wide. He preached two hours and twenty minutes from *Isa.* 54:5 – 'For thy Maker is thine husband'. I may say, during the whole sermon there was hardly a dry eye. Eagerness to attend the word preached was depicted on every countenance, while tears were flowing very copiously, and literally watering the ground. The most hardened in the congregation seemed to bend as one man; and I believe if ever the Holy Ghost was present in a solemn assembly it was there . . . The people of God were themselves as deeply affected as others . . . I could compare it to nothing but the days of the apostles, after the day of Pentecost.[16]

Years later Kennedy could report the testimony of a Gaelic teacher who 'knew fifty persons who were awakened through that sermon at Ardeonaig; that he was one of these; and that he was the only one of them all whose conversion he was tempted to suspect'.[17]

This was not the first or the last time that MacDonald preached in Breadalbane. He was there at least twice in 1817. But the work of grace begun in 1816 did not depend on his presence. Findlater records: 'During the whole of that summer [1817], the same concern was manifested, and every opportunity embraced to hear the preaching of the Gospel.' Few homes appeared to be unaffected. Another eye-witness noted: 'Though chiefly confined to Glenlyon, the revival extended to four or five neighbouring districts.' Proof of the reality of the work did not depend on the appearance of strong emotion. It was rather the moral transformation that made it, in Findlater's words, 'a miracle of grace'. An entire re-orientation of priorities was to be seen, with habits of life and speech all changed according to Scripture.

For MacDonald himself it was a confirmation of the power of the gospel and it increased his conviction that he was called to itinerate as well as be a parish minister. Occasionally he was to be heard in such cities as Aberdeen and Edinburgh, and a much larger salary was promised him if he would return to the latter. In Aberdeen, 'Ferintosh' had probably been best known as the famous brand of whisky formerly distilled there. Robert Burns lamented the end of Ferintosh whisky in his poem on *Scotch Drink* with the words

> Thee, Ferintosh! Oh, sadly lost!
> Scotland lament frae coast to coast!

MacDonald therefore understood the message when, as he was preaching for Dr Kidd in Gilcomston Chapel, Aberdeen, the excited doctor seized the back of his jacket and said, 'Go at them, kilt and bonnet; go at them, kilt and bonnet! Give them the real Ferintosh!'

ST KILDA

Instead of being drawn back to the cities MacDonald gave himself chiefly to areas more spiritually destitute, even going as far as southern Ireland where a Roman Catholic population, commonly hostile to English, readily heard him preach in

Gaelic. 'Why,' he asked, 'should we not love the souls of Catholics as well as Protestants, and do them all the good we can?' This was the spirit in which he entered many of the darkest areas of Scotland. Complaints to the General Assembly of 1818 intended to prevent him entering other parishes without the leave of local ministers had no effect. 'Fired by love to Christ and by pity for perishing souls', is how Kennedy describes him, and it was in this spirit that he accepted an invitation in 1822 to which no one else had responded. The Society for Propagating Christian Knowledge called on him to visit the island of St Kilda, beyond the outer Hebrides, where a population of 108 souls had no Christian teaching. Not without considerable difficulty, and even danger, MacDonald went, preaching en route in Harris where a local minister claimed that St Kilda was in his parish although he had never been there. On the sea journey between Harris and his destination the preacher wrote some verses in Gaelic, including these words, translated by Kennedy:

> Thinking of the island, so remote and lonely, care and sorrow awoke within me, as I remembered the danger of the people. They are as sheep without a shepherd to lead and pasture them . . . Are we guiltless if these people perish before us, and we preach not to them the gospel of peace which shows the only way of life? Hard as flint is the heart that melts not in pity over their sad case. Oh, for the wings of a dove to carry me to them at once! Hunger and hardship I would bear, and the dangers of the sea and storm would I brave, that I might see the people, and preach to them the gospel of peace.

During the month of September 1822 this desire was fulfilled as he preached on St Kilda thirteen times, beginning with the angel's message to the shepherds, 'Fear not: for, behold, I bring you good tidings of great joy' (*Luke* 2:10).

MacDonald understood too much to be discouraged when there was no such response as he had seen elsewhere: 'These poor people cannot read, and how to pray they know not,' he noted in his diary. 'The want of knowledge is a sad bar to conversion . . . The doctrine seemed new to the people.' But he had faith in the seed sown and he had so endeared himself to the people that when he returned two years later, he could write, 'The people flew down to the shore to meet us.' 'Nothing but kindness will melt the heart of man,' was one of his observations while at St Kilda, and before the end of his second visit the truth of those words was confirmed. Before he left, MacDonald told his hearers of the Society's intention to send them a minister. They were overjoyed and said, 'We hope that they will send us a good minister.' 'What kind of minister would you have to be sent?' he asked, and got the response, 'One that will tell us of our danger and preach Christ to us.' MacDonald was back to these much-loved people again in 1827 and for the last time in 1830.

It is no longer possible to trace even a fraction of MacDonald's journeys across the Highland and Islands. Probably the next great revival in which he shared after Breadalbane was the one that began in the Island of Lewis after 1824, but the surviving records of that and other events are very incomplete. What is beyond doubt is the truth of Robert Buchanan's words when he wrote of MacDonald as 'the Whitefield of the Highlands and islands of Scotland', and, referring to the great change witnessed in the north, he went on:

> The proudest and most powerful chieftains of the Celtic race never possessed such a mastery over the clans, which the fiery cross or the wild pibroch summoned into the field in the fierce days of feudal strife, as belonged, in these more peaceful modern times, to this humble minister of

Christ. From Tarbat Ness to the outer Hebrides, – from the Spey to the Pentland Firth, – the fact needed but to be known that John MacDonald had come and was about to preach the Word, in order that the country twenty miles around should gather at his call.[18]

CHANGED LIVES

The change that had taken place since Eneas Sage found Lochcarron and Wester Ross a spiritual wilderness in the 1720s is illustrated by an incident that occurred in the ministry of his successor, Lachlan MacKenzie, who died in 1819. Some time before his death crowds were gathering for a communion season in Lochcarron and among them a blind man from Skye by the name of Donald Munro. Munro was a catechist employed by the Edinburgh branch of the Society for Propagating Christian Knowledge and, as an itinerant preacher, he played a leading part in 'a considerable revival' that affected many parts of his native island in the years 1812–14. In later years he was to be remembered as 'the father of evangelical religion on the Isle of Skye'. When he arrived at Lochcarron, on the occasion to which I am referring, such were the numbers already gathering that the only place he could find to sleep was space in a barn along with many other men. Another visitor who shared the same rough accommodation has left on record the startling awakening he had the next morning. While it was still dark, a voice called, 'Awake! Awake!', and judging from the movement of bodies all round him the summons appeared to have been expected. The same voice then said, 'Let us sing to the praise of God . . . ', and all broke into song with verses of the Psalter long known by heart. Prayer followed, and realizing that all his companions were now on their knees, the newcomer followed their example. But his surprise was only beginning. With no light anywhere, the leader of the worship now repeated a long portion of Scripture: 'He was amazed;

but much more was this the case when he listened to a striking and powerful exposition, with reference to the Scriptures, in proof or in illustration of the doctrine, concluding with an irresistible appeal to the consciences of all who were present.' The speaker, of course, was blind Donald Munro. 'After darkness, light,' had been a watchword of the Reformation and it had become true for many in the Highlands and Islands.

One of the most important parts of MacDonald's ministry was the way he was used to lead others both into the kingdom of God and into ministry to others. Donald Munro's associate in the Skye revival was one of these men, Norman Macleod, who, having fought with the 42nd Highlanders in the Napoleonic Wars, was 'struck with the bullet of love' under MacDonald's ministry. Like Munro, he became an itinerant supported by the Edinburgh branch of the Society for the Propagation of Christian Knowledge.[19] No less eminent in usefulness was John Morrison, the poet/blacksmith of Harris, who came to the knowledge of Christ in 1822 when MacDonald was delayed on that island on his first visit to St Kilda. 'The Harris Blacksmith' was often to assist Alexander Macleod, minister of Uig on the Island of Lewis, where an awakening began and spread in 1824. It was probably a few years later that he wrote to Donald Sage, minister at Resolis, 'Appearances throughout the island furnish very cheering evidences that there is plainly a revival, exhibiting itself under the preaching of the gospel in religious impressions, in a general thirst after instruction, and in a marked and almost incredible change in the morals of the people.'[20] What the ministry of MacDonald meant to Morrison is well illustrated by an event in 1830 which the latter told to a friend:

> Some one came one evening to the smithy, where I was hard at work on the anvil, and mentioned that Dr MacDonald had come. I tried to subdue my emotion, and I longed for the absence of the messenger; and whenever

the messenger had gone, I ran to the smithy door and bolted it. I could then, when alone, give scope to my emotions. I danced for joy – danced round and round the smithy floor, for I felt a load taken off my spirit suddenly. I danced till I felt fatigued, and I knelt down and prayed and gave thanks.[21]

Donald Sage, the recipient of this letter, had a relationship to MacDonald worthy of being mentioned. Resolis was an adjoining parish to Ferintosh on the Black Isle. Robert Arthur served that charge from 1774, on the death of Macphail. In his last days, we read, Mr MacDonald sometimes preached in the open air close to the manse, Mr Arthur sitting at the window and listening. He was a sound theologian, and admired Mr MacDonald as a preacher, but he gave no sign of any change of heart. On Arthur's death, Donald Sage (grandson of Eneas Sage) succeeded him in 1822. But Sage was scarcely settled in the parish when his wife, Harriet, died giving birth to a stillborn child. Her husband, who reports the event, was so overwhelmed that he could not even attend the funeral. MacDonald's involvement at that point shows how he cared for individuals: 'Mr MacDonald of Ferintosh often visited me, and preached to my people. Shortly after the death of my beloved wife, he passed on his way to Cromarty, and I accompanied him on horseback.' Perhaps MacDonald thought that the exercise would aid his friend's low spirits, in the event it proved the opposite, although the outcome was still more important. The ride to Cromarty and back in one day so exhausted Sage that he took to his bed completely exhausted and 'wishing that I might die'. He regarded his prostration, he says, with delight, hoping it might be the precursor of death and re-union with his wife. But these feelings were to be shaken:

> Conscience began to ask, 'Why did I wish to die?' My sorrows at once responded to the inquiry – 'just to be

with Harriet'. 'But was I sure of that? If Harriet was in heaven, as I could not but hope that she was, was nothing else to be the consequence of death to me but to go to heaven merely to be with her?' I was struck dumb; I was confounded with my own folly. So then, the only enjoyment I looked for after death was, not to be with Christ, but to be with Harriet!

Now Sage faced a more serious problem, not the sorrow of despondency but a conviction of sin that brought all the failures of a lifetime before him. 'Oh, what a God had I, then, to deal with – how like Himself – how unlike me!' Whether this was a first or a second conversion is not clear from his account but it ended as every true experience must, resting on Christ alone. In the midst of a struggle that he graphically describes, a text came into his mind and 'like a light, dim at first, it gradually and rapidly brightened. "*I am the door* . . . " God was gracious. I laid hold of the hope set before me. I thought, believed and felt that I had entered the "Door". I found it was wide enough for the sinner, and high enough as a door set open by *God* and not *man*, by which to enter.'[22]

A bright evangelical ministry followed at Resolis.

JOHN MACDONALD, JR. OF INDIA

One of the greatest blessings of MacDonald's ministry was to see his own life and convictions so largely reproduced in his eldest son John whose mother had died when he was a child. His father had married again, and more children were born, but his closeness to John was abiding. The latter went to King's College, Aberdeen, to study, and, no doubt on his father's advice, was a serious reader of Jonathan Edwards. But rather than meeting evangelical Christianity in the university he was to find his home district regarded as 'the focus of fanaticism' and his father 'the central point of the whole'. His biographer says that 'idolatry of the intellect' reigned. 'It was supposed to be capable of achieving everything', and the training he received 'favoured that delusion'.[23] Young John MacDonald did not give up his religious profession and his moral life but it now went together with a love of the world, and his subsequent diary shows the place that dances and parties came to have in his life. That he did not possess what his father knew also figures in his diaries. After the latter came to visit him when he was a tutor to a family in Nairn in 1825, he noted:

> August 23 [1825]. Walked over to the top of a hill above the Priory, to enjoy the view. He prayed on top of the hill, and I thought I never felt so much impressed as I did there. Oh! what an enviable state of mind, always to find pleasure in addressing our Maker! This is true filial affection. O Lord! Do thou give me that spirit of adoption whereby I may say unto thee, Abba, Father.[24]

Three years later John MacDonald, Jr., was still to be found at balls but a great change was at hand. He wrote on 8 January 1828, after 'the Academic Ball at Elgin', 'I feel my mind becoming more and more dissatisfied with such things. I have no enjoyment in them. A flash of another world will sometimes strike upon me in the midst of the gay dissipation.' Before that year had ended he had passed through the new birth and had taken up the prayer to which his father had drawn his attention, 'Lord, here I am, send me.' The answer to that prayer was unexpected. After an interim period of serving the Scots Kirk in London, he left for the mission field of India in 1837.

Before this happened there was a series of exchanges by correspondence with his hesitant father whose heart was set on the need of the mission field in the Highlands. To the reservations expressed by his father, John replied: 'It has hitherto been as a *rule* in the Church that no ordained, tried, or accepted minister, should think of carrying the gospel out of his own land; but *who* had made this rule? Should it any longer exist?'[25] Eventually his father came to see his son's decision as the will of God.[26] As John sailed on the *Marion* from Portsmouth, his father accompanied him on the first part of the journey. John wrote:

> After the interval of an hour we were obliged to part, and thanks be to God that it was to some degree as conquerors: the last time I saw my beloved father, as the pilot-boat moved off, was smiling with one of his own sweet smiles, and I could not but smile too with joy that the love of Christ was still triumphant.[27]

Calcutta was to be John MacDonald, Jr.'s 'St Kilda', where, in the words of his father, 'The tide of Christian prayer in this country has followed you.' All his work was to be done there, and at Serampore. After the Disruption of 1843, the witness of his denomination had so grown in India that in September of that year a 32-page twice-monthly magazine, *The Free Churchman*, began to be published in Calcutta, price 'four annas'.[28] In 1847, when his father was about to enter a pulpit in Glenlyon, a letter was put in his hand that he left unopened. Only the next day, travelling to Edinburgh, did he remember it, and read the news of John's death. Commenting on this, his biographer says:

> A few tears from a fond father's eyes, and the Christian triumphed over the man, and with his heart he said, 'It is well.' That was his first text when he got back to Ferintosh. In the course of that sermon, referring to the son his hearers knew so well, he said: 'It is well that he was born; "it is well" that he was educated; it is better that he was born again; "it is well" that he was licensed to preach the gospel; "it is well" that he was ordained as a pastor; "it is well" that he went to India; and above all, "it is well" for him that he died; for thus, though away from us, and "absent from the body", he has secured the gain of being for ever with the Lord.'[29]

A CALLING COMPLETED

The closing years of the life of MacDonald of Ferintosh were marked by several trials, including illness, opposition, and false accusations. Back in 1815 Robert Findlater had said of him, 'He has been the means of raising up a host of friends and enemies.'[30] But the last decade of his life also saw him, as we have noted, engaged in the revivals seen in Kilsyth and other places in the south from 1839. His biographer writes: 'The power of the Breadalbane days came back to his preaching again. Texts from which he had not preached since then were now resumed. Hundreds were asking for the first time, "What must we do to be saved?" Never were more alarming sermons preached than those which he then delivered.'[31] Much nearer to Ferintosh, he also shared in revivals at Tain and Rosskeen in 1840–1.

The autumn of 1848 found him still itinerating, prior to resuming his work at Ferintosh and in neighbouring congregations through the winter. By this date he had preached over ten thousand sermons. He often preached three or four times a week, and never, Kennedy says, without careful preparation. His main themes now were 'the shortness of time, the glory of heaven, and the Father's love'. The following spring a blistered foot led to infection which quickly spread beyond the aid of medical treatment. A friend, visiting him near the last, said: 'He looked to me, as he lay there, with his massive heaving chest, like the hull of some mighty war-ship, that fought triumphantly in many a battle and outrode victoriously many a storm, and that now lay stranded on some beach, with all her masts and rigging gone.' 'Was there any cloud between him and the Saviour?' another friend asked, noticing a restlessness in the sufferer. 'No,' he replied, 'I feel as much assured of being for ever with the Saviour as I am lying on this bed; but I know not how I can look Him in the face, when I think how little I have done for Him.' These were among his last recorded words before delirium and unconsciousness. He died on 18 April 1849, just two years after his son John.

SOME LESSONS FROM MACDONALD'S MINISTRY: 1. THE CENTRALITY OF THE LOVE OF GOD IN THE GOSPEL

Outstanding among the lessons to be noted from MacDonald's life and this period of history is the manner in which gospel preaching dominated the ministry. MacDonald excelled, as Kennedy says, 'in fervent appeals to the Christless'. Calvinists he and his colleagues certainly were. They were opponents of an easy religion that has no place for divine grace and sovereignty, but preeminent in their preaching was the fact that all were addressed as those whom God was willing to save. The free offer of a loving Saviour was at the heart of their ministries, and the provision of the atonement was pressed upon all for their acceptance. The warrant of Christ's invitation was all that the unconverted needed. 'The Lord grant,' writes MacDonald, 'that we who preach the gospel may not be the means of subverting it by clogging its free calls with conditions.'[32] 'The cross, I see, is that chiefly which moves the sinner,' he noted at St Kilda in 1817.[33] Years later, after a visit to his son John's church in London, the latter wrote in his diary, 'March 7 [1832], I bless the Lord for my father's visit; it has refreshed and edified me much . . . I have learned that I have been very *unfaithful* as to the grand doctrines of the *cross*, and the grand object of saving sinners.'[34]

No volume of MacDonald's sermons was ever published but we can see something of what this free gospel preaching meant in practice from the surviving sermons of some of his friends. One of these was Charles Calder Mackintosh of Tain. On one of the early occasions when this younger man was to preach at Ferintosh, MacDonald told his people, 'Be sure to come all of you to hear him; for his words are with the unction of the Holy Ghost.' In his sermons, Mackintosh urged all to believe that 'the infinite worth' of Christ's atonement, 'has made it possible for you and me to be saved'. God spared not his own Son, so that mercy might stoop 'to save those who were like the very devils, offering them pardon, receiving them with open arms; pardoning them freely, fully, heartily, and unalterably'. Pointing his hearers to Christ's words, He 'would have gathered them' (*Luke* 13:34), he affirmed, 'Christ's tears over Jerusalem now assure the most guilt-laden sinner of His readiness to receive him, and that he cannot perish because of want of willingness in Christ to save him.' Let it not be thought that the holiness and wrath of God were missing from such sermons. They were not. 'But,' in the words of the same preacher, 'I would rather make use of the *love of Jesus*, as exhibited here, to move, to awaken, to melt, and to draw you. This is the loving Saviour who now invites you . . . Think what a heaven it must be to be with Him! Think what a hell, were there nothing else in hell, to be separated from Him for ever!'[35]

Gustavus Aird, a leading authority on the Christianity of the Highlands, said in an address to the General Assembly of the Free Church in 1888: 'Those in the north Highlands whose ministrations were most acknowledged were distinguished for their soundness in the faith, and specially for proclaiming the free, unfettered call of the Gospel to lost sinners . . . One of the most eminent of them could say, when on his deathbed, giving his successor a dying charge, "I have at times felt, when proclaiming the free call of the Gospel to every sinner in my hearing, as if breathing the very air of heaven."'[36]

Under such preaching multitudes felt as a hearer tells us he did on first hearing James Calder at Croy. This visitor, doubtful about committing himself to Christ, was surprised at his first sight of 'the great Mr Calder', for there was nothing significant about his appearance. The greatness, he soon learned, lay rather in the preacher's message. Standing in the open air, above the water of the Moray Firth, Calder spoke of the vastness of the merit to be found in the sacrifice of Christ, and told the people by way of his own testimony: 'When I got an entrance into this truth, though I had as many souls as there are drops of water in the Firth down there, and every one of them a thousand times worse than the poor soul I have, I would willingly entrust them all to Christ.' 'It was then,' said his hearer, 'that I saw that I had the great Mr Calder before me. I could not entrust my own miserable soul to Christ, while Mr Calder, if he had so many, would entrust them all to Him.'

These preachers offered no explanation as to how the blessings of the gospel could be both sovereign and universally free to all, but they knew it was true, and saw God himself bearing witness to it in the salvation of thousands. John Kennedy, in describing the mind of such an evangelistic preacher as MacDonald, wrote:

> He cannot reconcile the good will [of God] declared to all, with the saving love confined to the elect; but he takes the revealed will of God as it is given to him. He would have others, he would have all, to come in. For the salvation he himself has found is more sure and free – sure as the covenant secures it, free as the gospel offers it.[37]

2: THE INNER LIFE

MacDonald reminds us that when God is pleased to use the preaching of Christ to the salvation of many, his messengers are men whose spirit and experience is in harmony with the truth they preach. This period of history in the Scottish Highlands was marked by a recovery of the real nature of the Christian ministry. A new race of men appeared, for whom the reality of God's great love in the sending of his Son was the motivating experience of their lives. What was said of Charles

Calder Mackintosh might have been said of them all: 'The motives and the strength of his ministry grew out of his inner life.' His own father had first impressed that truth on him, telling him before his settlement at Tain: 'Charles, let your face shine; be much on the mount with God; the praying minister is the preaching minister; let your face shine, Charles.'[38]

Personal experience of the truth preached was a first imperative. In the words of John Bunyan:

> Let him speak of love that is taken with love, that is captivated with love, that is *carried away* with love. If this man speaks of it, his speaking signifies something; the powers and bands of love are upon him, and he shews to all that he know what he is speaking of.[39]

In this connection, dependence upon the Holy Spirit, and the place of prayer, were characteristics of their daily living.[40] Although they were averse to saying much about their personal experience, there is enough evidence to show that this was true. In MacDonald's case, for instance, it is known that before he ever came to Ferintosh, a private experience lay behind a striking change in his preaching in Edinburgh. Kennedy identifies it with other instances 'of renewed men becoming other men under a fresh baptism of the Spirit'. He writes of MacDonald at that time: 'Always clear and sound in his statements of objective truth, his preaching now became instinct with life . . . His statements of gospel truth were now the warm utterances of one who deeply felt its power. The Lord's people could now testify that he spoke from his own heart to theirs.'[41]

This is not to imply that these preachers attained to the stature that they desired as Christians, nor that they taught that any *one* second experience of the Spirit established them on a higher level of life. A true work of the Spirit, they taught, far from imparting greater independence, causes the Christian more earnestly to 'make use of [God] as having the Spirit to give'. The Christian life is progressive, and they considered themselves to fall far short of what they ought to be. 'I have been shamefully *cold* and powerless in my ministry', was a common complaint in their diaries. But they knew what the standard ought to be – Christ himself; they aspired towards him, and believed in more grace to be received. The influence resulting from such examples was great. The biographer of John MacDonald, Jr. tells us that after his conversion he had a period at home in the manse at Ferintosh when 'the giants of Ross-shire made him appear a mere dwarf in the divine life. But the discovery was salutary – it humbled him more and more, and he glorified God on that account. His prayer still was – "Bring down self, and exalt Christ in me, and by me." '[42]

3: NOT MINISTERS ALONE

In every period of awakening since apostolic times, the spread of the gospel is by no means confined to the instrumentality of ordained preachers. The importance of preaching cannot be estimated too highly, yet a danger is connected with that truth. Because records most commonly concern ministers, the way in which the activity of all Christians is involved in such periods can too easily be overlooked. It would be a great mistake to suppose that such men as MacDonald pioneered in virgin ground singlehanded. In many cases there were Gaelic schoolmasters who prepared the way before preachers ever came. Similarly there were home missionaries, often known as catechists, supported by the Society for the Propagation of Christian Knowledge, and also, from 1800, by Robert and James Haldane.[43] Besides such full-time workers there grew up a whole category of faithful witnesses who, holding no office, were simply know as 'the men': 'They were the most gifted and godly among the Lord's people, who had enlarged views of divine truth, and deep experience of its power.'[44] Commonly they were known

by their ability to speak and pray with unction, and this they did
in fellowship and society meetings, as well as by personal
conversation. The kind of counsel they gave is well illustrated
by the words of one of them, 'See that you bring not down to
the world a bad report of the good land, but seek to press so
near the "Tree of Life" as to taste of its fruit, so that others,
perceiving about you the flavour of Zion's provision may be
induced to go thither also.'[45] Given such Christians, it is not
surprising that in several instances revivals were known to begin
before there was any ministerial involvement. As William Taylor
has written, the gospel was

> commended to the sympathies of the people by lay
> influence as cordially recognised as in Wesleyan Methodism
> . . . As it has been found among the Wesleyan Methodists
> that the class meetings for conference on matters of
> Christian experience are essential to the vitality of their
> system, and form one of the most important means of its
> continuance and extension, so in the Highlands was it with
> these fellowship meetings. Awakened souls were there
> introduced to experienced believers, to find their cases
> understood and described, their doubts resolved, their
> desires stimulated, and their faith confirmed.[46]

The strength of the gospel in any given district was often
judged by how many men could speak to others to edification.
One visitor who had attended a fellowship meeting in
Strathnaver was asked how many men had spoken. 'Seventy'
was the reply, on which his questioner, who knew the
neighbourhood, commented, 'You could get seventy men to
engage in a conference, and double that number of eminent
women.' This statement highlights the fact that throughout
this whole period, behind all events were the support and
prayer of godly women. Quietly exercised although their
ministry commonly was, they were true 'helpers in the gospel'

as much as women in apostolic times and, while deferring to faithful ministers, they were quite able to speak up when they judged it necessary. At a meal in a manse, after an uplifting service on a Monday evening, Peggy McDermid thought the amount of conversation of a worldly kind was inappropriate for the occasion and said so. When a minister present reminded her of Paul's words, 'Women are not to speak in public', she ignored the misquotation and replied, 'Indeed, Sir, if the Apostle Paul were here, no woman had need to speak.' Another woman had for her minister the eminent Alexander MacColl, but that did not prevent her from giving him advice. When MacColl in her hearing once rebuked a young woman for the kind of hat she was wearing, Kate Gordon told him, 'You should allure them to the Lord first before you begin to attack their hats!'

Lay agency had a vital place in the evangelization of the Highlands. In later years it was evident that a decline had set in when almost all devolved upon ministers, and the idea became current (though unspoken) that listening to sermons fulfilled the main part of a church member's duty. Great affection for ministers was the understandable feeling of many who benefited so largely from them in bright days but this feeling, if unguarded, could become an idolizing of men and consequently lead to a wrong estimate of the ministry itself. The common attachment by Gaelic-speaking people of the word *Mor*, meaning 'great' or 'big', to the names of some of their most eminent ministers, including MacDonald (*Ministear Mor na Toisidheachd* – The Great Minister of Ferintosh) was unwise.

4: THE SOVEREIGNTY OF GOD

There is a great deal in the history of the evangelization of the Northern Highlands to impress us with the truth of divine sovereignty. The collapse of the feudal power of the chiefs of the Jacobite clans after 1746 certainly helped to open the way for the gospel in those regions, but it does not explain why God chose that time and not another. Some are prone to explain revivals in terms of the influence of prominent personalities and to see MacDonald of Ferintosh in that light. But had MacDonald been an originator rather than only an instrument, uniform effects would have resulted from his ministry. This was not the case. There were many years when nothing occurred under his preaching to equal Breadalbane in 1817 or Kilsyth in 1839. And there were powerful awakenings in the west, as in Arran in 1812, in which MacDonald appears to have played no part at all. As one writer on this period rightly says: 'The movement was not organised by man. Indeed, there was no organisation of any kind for the production of such a movement.'[47]

It is said that Charler Calder saw more blessing in other parts than he did in his own parish at Ferintosh. And when the awakening began in that place, only one year after MacDonald's settlement, Calder's widow, while rejoicing in what was happening, was concerned by 'what seemed the comparative unfruitfulness of her husband's labours'. When she expressed this feeling to MacDonald, the new minister, who was often in her home, gave this response: 'What you now see, my dear Mrs Calder, is the upspringing of the seed which your husband was sowing. The farmer sends his best man to sow the seed; but the field once sown, he sends any boy who may happen to be at hand to harrow it. The field must be harrowed as well as sown, but the sowing is the more important work. It was thus "the Lord of the harvest" dealt in appointing work for your husband and for me.'[48]

The truth is that, in appointing a work, God also appoints gifts. MacDonald's gifts were supremely those of an evangelist; this was so much the case that there were even to be times when it might raise mild complaints among his people. An instance has been recorded of the elders at Ferintosh asking one of the female members during MacDonald's ministry why she was too often absent from the church and attending other evangelical ministers in the neighbourhood. In her reply she contrasted the benefits of those congregations with her own. At Killearnan, she told the session, the sheep are fed, and at Resolis the lambs are provided with the sincere milk of the Word. 'And what happens here?' was the inevitable question. To which she replied, 'Here the dead are raised.'[49]

'The Lord,' wrote Robert Findlater, shows 'the freeness and sovereignty of divine grace, not only as to the *objects* of his mercy, but as to the *time* and the *instruments* to be employed.'[50] Within this sovereignty, yet in a manner hidden from us, is the place of prayer. MacDonald had no hesitation in seeing a connection between outpourings of the Spirit and a praying people. Prayer to the 'Lord of the harvest' had gone before the appearance of men anointed by the Spirit of God.

Great lessons on the subject of revival were learned from this period and were recorded in the Scottish literature that remains with us. One of the foremost of these lessons was the one underlined at an earlier date by Jonathan Edwards: a work of God is not to be judged by the amount of excitement or by the height of the emotion, but by the long-term moral and spiritual results. The people who heard the ministry of MacDonald and his colleagues 'became', it could be said, 'externally at least, the most religious, and, at the same time, the most moral population in Scotland'. Nor did it end there. From this evangelized region came many of Britain's most dependable regiments of the nineteenth century, composed in many cases of men who were witnesses as well as soldiers in far corners of the earth – men who often surprised locals by their preference for Bible studies over public houses.[51] In one sense soldiers were volunteer emigrants, but many others who left the Highlands at this same period did so under the compulsion of absolute poverty. In the infamous Highland 'clearances', rapacious landowners, with the law on their side, forced families from their traditional homes in order to make way for more profitable sheep. Donald Sage, who was a distressed witness of one of the worst of the 'clearances' in Sutherland, wrote of the sufferers, 'The truly pious noted the mighty hand of God in the matter. In their prayers and religious conferences not a solitary expression could be heard of anger or vindictiveness.'[52] In the same way the island of Skye was deprived of 'some of the best of its inhabitants'. On the mainland, Dr Aird reported in 1884 that in the previous thirty years, from his parish alone, upwards of 266 people had gone to Australia, and one hundred to America. Scottish Christians, thus painfully scattered across the earth, from Canada to New Zealand, were to play a leading part in the furtherance of the kingdom of God. Their Catechism had long taught them that God's sovereignty and eternal counsel guides every detail of life, and they knew his promise, 'Instead of thy fathers shall be thy children, whom thou mayest make princes in all the earth' (*Psa.* 45:16).

[1] Even if the Scriptures had been available in Gaelic at an earlier date, large sections of the population were illiterate. In 1811 Lachlan Mackenzie stated that of 877 parishioners in Lochcarron, excluding children, only two could read Gaelic. A Government census in 1821 found 78,609 families in the Highland area, of which only one third understood English.

[2] Quoted in John Kennedy, *The Days of the Fathers in Ross-shire* (Inverness: Northern Chronicle, 1927), p. 32.

[3] Alexander MacRae, *Life of Gustavus Aird* (Stirling: MacKay, n.d.), p. 258.

[4] John Gillies, *Historical Collections of Accounts of Revival* (1754; repr. Edinburgh: Banner of Truth, 1981).

[5] 'Diary of James Calder', in *Banner of Truth* magazine, Issue 139, July–August 1974, p. 20.   [6] Ibid., p. 24.

[7] Ibid., p. 55. It was not always so with Macphail for he was in the ministry before he became a real Christian.

[8] Kennedy, *Days of the Fathers*, p. 55.

[9] Donald Sage, *Memorabilia Domestica; or Parish Life in the North of Scotland* (Wick: Rae, 1899), p. 22.   [10] Ibid., p. 188.

[11] William Findlater, *Memoir of the Rev. Robert Findlater* (Glasgow: Collins. 1840), p. 35.

[12] Sage, *Memorabilia*, pp. 285–8. Sage died in 1869 in his eightieth year. His work was published posthumously.

[13] John Kennedy, *The 'Apostle of the North': The Life and Labours of the Rev. Dr John MacDonald* (London: Nelson, 1866), p. 18. Reviewing this biography, after reading it on a train journey home to London from Glasgow,

Spurgeon said it had 'a marvellous power of shortening the journey', and he blessed the giver of the book to him 'many times on the road home from Scotland for furnishing us with spiritual refreshment so enjoyable and strengthening'. *The Sword and the Trowel* (London: Passmore and Alabaster, 1866), p. 149.

[14] *Disruption Worthies of the Highlands, Another Memorial of 1843* (Edinburgh: Greig, 1877), p. 23. A sheltered glen by the burn (stream) at Ferintosh continued to be used for occasional open-air services for many years.

[15] *Memoir of Findlater*, p. 160.

[16] Ibid., p. 182. Apart from a few biographies, the main source of information on revivals in the Highlands was a series of tracts published in Glasgow early in the nineteenth century, subsequently reprinted in the *Scottish Christian Herald*, and used by Mary Duncan in *History of Revivals of Religion in the British Isles* (Edinburgh: Oliphant, 1836). The most recent comprehensive source is Richard Owen Roberts, *Scotland Saw His Glory* (Wheaton: International Awakening Press, 1995).

[17] Kennedy, *'Apostle of the North'*, pp. 92–3.

[18] Robert Buchanan, *The Ten Years' Conflict: Being the History of the Disruption of the Church of Scotland*, vol. 2 (Glasgow: Blackie, 1852), p. 389.

[19] See Roderick MacGowan, *Men of Skye* (Glasgow: MacNeilage, 1902), pp. 65-85. On the morning of his death in 1858 he said, 'Before this day ends I will be with Donald Munro.' Munro had died in 1830.

[20] Sage, *Memorabilia*, p. 297.

[21] Alexander MacRae, *The Fire Among the Heather, or, The Spiritual Awakening of the Highland People* (Inverness: Carruthers, n.d.), p. 77.

[22] Sage, *Memorabilia*, p. 268.

[23] W. K. Tweedie, *The Life of the Rev. John MacDonald, Late Missionary of the Free Church of Scotland at Calcutta* (Edinburgh: Johnston and Hunter, 1849), pp. 54, 116. About ten years earlier Donald Sage had studied divinity at Aberdeen and he was to write of the theological lectures he heard from Principal William Brown, 'I never heard from his lips three consecutive sentences illustrative of any of the doctrines of the Bible; and I can conscientiously say that I never heard him pronounce, even once, the name of Jesus Christ in his lectures.' *Memorabilia*, p. 168. Sage's first-hand description of the Moderate clergy is graphic and he confirms the statement made above: 'The Moderate party in the church were wont to point the finger of scorn at that county [Ross-shire], and say, "Behold the hot-bed of fanaticism."' p. 262.

[24] Tweedie, *Life of John MacDonald*, p. 62.

[25] Kennedy, *Days of the Fathers*, pp. 258–9.

[26] When MacDonald, Jr., published a speech he made to the Scotch Presbytery in London in January 1837 called 'A Statement of Reasons for Accepting a Call to Go to India as a Missionary', his father responded, 'Your Pamphlet has silenced us all.' The Statement was reprinted in John MacDonald [Jr.], *A Pastor's Memorial to his Former Flock: Consisting of Sermons and Addresses , the Relics of a Bygone Ministry* (London: Cotes, 1842).

[27] Tweedie, *Life of John MacDonald*, p. 338.

[28] Volume 1 (Calcutta: W. Rushton, 1843) was made up of issues to the end of the year, the 30 December issue containing a long supplement.

[29] Kennedy, 'Apostle of the North', p. 269.

[30] Memoir of Findlater, p. 171.   [31] Ibid., p. 231.

[32] Kennedy, 'Apostle of the North', p. 150.   [33] Ibid., p. 122.

[34] Tweedie, Life of John MacDonald, p. 234.

[35] William Taylor, Memorials of the Life and Ministry of Charles Calder Mackintosh (Edinburgh: Edmonston and Douglas, 1870), pp. 46, 79, 91–2, 127, 131, 134.   [36] MacRae, Life of Aird, p. 269.

[37] Kennedy, 'Apostle of the North', p. 332. Despite his long conviction, MacDonald was to say in one of the last sermons he preached that, 'looking back on his preaching, there was nothing he regretted more than how little he had said regarding the love of God the Father' (ibid., p. 317).

[38] Taylor, Memorials of Mackintosh , p. 43.

[39] 'The Saints' Knowledge of Christ's Love,' Works of John Bunyan, vol. 2 (repr. Edinburgh: Banner of Truth, 1991), p. 39. 'Such men are, at this day, wanting in the churches. These are the men that sweeten churches, and that bring glory to God and to religion' (Ibid., p. 35).

[40] 'Remember,' Robert Findlater's father wrote to his son, 'a minister that preaches much should pray much.' Memoir of Findlater, p. 69.

[41] Kennedy, 'Apostle of the North', p. 53.

[42] Tweedie, Life of MacDonald, p. 193.

[43] See Alexander Haldane, The Lives of Robert and James Haldane (repr. Edinburgh: Banner of Truth, 1990). One of the Haldane missionaries was a Mr Farquharson who was used in a work of grace in the Loch Tay region fourteen years before the revival of 1816, and again in Skye, where he was the means of the conversion of blind Donald Munro. Because Haldane's men were generally Independents or Baptists their work tended to be recognized too little by Presbyterian writers.

[44] Alexander Auld, Ministers and Men in the Far North (repr. Glasgow: Free Presbyterian, 1956), p. 96. Commenting on this passage of Auld's book when first published in 1869, Spurgeon wrote, 'These men were the ministers' best assistants; or, if he failed to preach the Gospel, they were his most terrible critics.'   [45] Ibid., pp. 109–10.

[46] Taylor, Memorials of Mackintosh, pp. 14–5. I have written further on this subject in Wesley and Men Who Followed (Edinburgh: Banner of Truth, 2003).

[47] MacRae, Fire Among the Heather, p. 82.

[48] Kennedy, 'Apostle of the North', p. 86. The remark illustrates the truth that the work of Christ is not confined to periods which we call revivals. The remark of Alexander Macleod, who saw the wonderful change in the Isle of Lewis, is important: 'There is a danger of underrating revivals on the one hand, and of exaggerating them on the other.' Memorabilia Domestica, p. 297.

[49] Murdoch Campbell, Gleanings of Highland Harvest (Ross-shire Printing, 1961), p. 79.

[50] Memoir of Findlater, p. 197.

[51] Of the 93rd Highlanders, or Sutherland Regiment, made up in 1800, it is said that over a period of twenty years not a single man warranted punishment. Sage, Memorabilia, p. 100.

[52] Sage, Memorabilia, p. 215.

5

Horatius Bonar and the Love of God in Evangelism

Remains of Old Broughton Village, 1852

'He helped me to understand how St John could be at once the apostle of love and a son of thunder; and how in our Lord there could be both the love and the wrath of the Lamb.'

DR GEORGE WILSON ON HORATIUS BONAR

O Love that casts out fear
O love that casts out sin.
Tarry no more without,
But come and dwell within.

True sunlight of the soul,
Surround me as I go;
So shall my way be safe,
My feet no sliding know.

Great love of God, come in,
Well-spring of heavenly peace,
Thou Living Water, come,
Spring up, and never cease.

HORATIUS BONAR

On a November evening in 1852 Andrew Bonar, Free Church minister in Collace, Perthshire, was driving in a gig along a country road to Blairgowrie with his older brother Horatius, when the horse veered off the road, and the gig overturned on top of them. Although unable to walk for a week, Andrew commented in his diary on 'a marvellous deliverance', and was especially thankful for his brother's entire escape: 'I could depart without being missed beyond my narrow circle, but his would be a general loss.'[1]

Andrew's assessment of his brother does not coincide with the extent to which the two men have been remembered in more recent times. If hymns are excluded from the reckoning, Andrew Bonar's writings have often been better known, not least because he was the author of the book which Spurgeon described as the best ministerial biography ever written, the life of Robert Murray M'Cheyne. Yet it would certainly be a mistake to take this as a true guide to the respective importance of the two men. Horatius Bonar, while first an evangelist, has to be ranked as one of the finest writers that Scotland ever produced, in addition to being her greatest hymn writer.

It was Horatius Bonar's own instruction that no biography of him should be written and, in the words of a relative, he 'effectually secured the fulfilment of his wish'. Probably his personal papers were destroyed. Certainly no biography was to appear, and today it is only the main facts of his life that can be told. Born 19 December 1808, he was one of five sons to survive infancy, James, John, Horatius (Horace to the family), Andrew and William. Of the two others who became preachers, John was born in 1803 and Andrew in 1810. Their home was in Paterson's Court, Broughton, a village now swallowed up by the north side of Edinburgh's New Town.

James Bonar (1757–1821), the father of the family, was a solicitor in the Excise Office. A relative says of him: 'Cheerful, sagacious, devout, he spent a blameless life in the pursuits of business, philanthropy, study, and authorship.'[2] We are also told that he was a gifted linguist and 'a member of almost all the literary societies in Edinburgh'. At one time it was his habit to walk every morning to Trinity, on the Firth of Forth, to swim. Time was not lost on the walk for he read all the way, and became known by people on his route as the 'reading gentleman'.

At the centre of the family's life was Lady Glenorchy's Chapel where James Bonar served as an elder. In the late eighteenth century there were few evangelical churches in Edinburgh, and in 1774 this had led Lady Glenorchy to build a church below the east end of Princes Street; it was to be connected to the Church of Scotland yet independent of it. Her rank entitled her to such a privilege and allowed her to settle an evangelical Welshman, Dr Thomas Snell Jones, in the pulpit. Lady Glenorchy's (as the church became known) was the spiritual home of the Bonar family; they filled Pew 88 – for there were four daughters as well as the five sons – amid a congregation of more than a thousand. Dr Jones served Lady Glenorchy's Chapel for upwards of fifty years, and Horatius

Bonar was later to describe him as 'a vigorous, earnest preacher, to whom multitudes from many parts resorted in those days'.

In the childhood years of the Bonar brothers, Edinburgh was awakening from the long night of Moderatism. In that process the publication of Thomas M'Crie's *Life of John Knox* in 1811 played a significant part. With that book in their hands, others could say as James Fraser of Brea had once done, 'When I read Knox, I thought I saw another scheme of divinity, much more agreeable to the Scriptures and to my experience than the modern.' Still more important, the year 1810 had seen the beginning of Andrew Thomson's influential ministry in the capital and his commencement of a monthly magazine, the *Christian Instructor.*

No record exists of the time when Horatius Bonar's new life as a Christian began. He wrote in after years of how much he owed to both parents,

> I thank Thee for a holy ancestry;
> I bless Thee for a godly parentage;
> For seeds of truth and light and purity,
> Sown in this heart from childhood's earliest age.

But it would be reading too much into these words to suppose that he passed from death to life before he reached teenage years. There is much in other verses that he wrote to suggest that he had 'wasted years' to regret. He was twelve when his father died in 1821, and this was followed three years later by the death of the eldest sister, Marjory (named after her mother). It may well be that these events contributed to conversion and a definite crisis in his later school days at Edinburgh High School. One who knew him said that, while he reverenced his parents, 'he did not and could not merely glide into their understanding. He read his way, he thought his way, he fought his way, he reasoned his way, he prayed his way to his anchorage in Christ.'[3]

After the bereavement of 1821, the eldest brother, James, became a second father to the family, which now removed to 3 London Street.[4] Mrs Marjory Bonar, is spoken of as 'a woman of child-like faith, gentle spirit, and over-flowing kindness.' Her hands were surely full with a family of nine young people and children, and most of them still at school. At school Horace shone in English literature and classics, and these gifts developed further at Edinburgh University where he was an undergraduate by the mid-1820s. In 1826 he gained a prize in Moral Philosophy in the class of Professor Wilson.[5] The next year he appears to have been one of the editors of a student magazine, *The College Observer*, and it was in its pages that some of his first poems were published. A friend from university days remembered him as being already a committed Christian when he entered the university and, that being so, we can be sure that the year 1828 was particularly significant for him.

That year marked the arrival of Thomas Chalmers in the university. It was also the year when, at the time of the Church of Scotland's General Assembly in May, Edward Irving startled the country by preaching at 6 a.m. on successive mornings in St Cuthbert's, the largest church in Edinburgh, on the subject of unfulfilled prophecy. This procedure Irving repeated in the two subsequent years and among his hearers were the Bonar brothers, Robert M'Cheyne, and many other young people.

University degrees meant less at this date, and the M.A. degree was commonly not thought to be worth the money it cost. Accordingly, after passing through the Arts course, Bonar proceeded without a degree to the Divinity Hall in 1829, and to Dr Chalmers, 'the greatest man he had ever met'. Academically his younger brother, Andrew, seems to have been ahead of him, but spiritually Horace was the leader. As we have seen, he was a definite Christian by the time he entered the university, and we know that he became a communicant member at Lady Glenorchy's in January 1830. At that point,

Andrew envied his brother's commitment, judging himself to be still unregenerate. But with Horace's guidance and encouragement, Andrew took the same step at the end of 1830, and the next year followed his brother into the Divinity Hall. Horatius also appears to have been a leader among a group of the divinity students who introduced a significant extra-curricular activity in 1831, 'a society, the sole object of which was to stir up each other to set apart an hour or two every week for visiting the careless and needy in the most neglected portions of the town'.[6] The outreach of this 'Visiting Society', as it became known, followed a missionary prayer meeting on Saturday mornings in Dr Chalmers' vestry.

No doubt in connection with Chalmers' influence, Andrew Bonar's thoughts and ambitions, at this date, were much taken up with the foreign mission field and on this also the counsel of Horatius carried weight: 'A remark of my brother Horace went far to satisfy me about missionary labour. He spoke about the need for labourers and ministers at home.' The impression the comment made must have been deepened by Andrew's joining in the weekly visitation among the poor. 'All of us', he writes, 'felt the work to be trying to the flesh at the outset; but none ever repented of persevering in it.'[7] Although Robert M'Cheyne had also entered the Divinity Hall in 1831, it was not until 1834 that he accompanied Andrew 'through some of the most miserable habitations I ever beheld' and saw scenes he had 'never before dreamed of'.

MINISTRY AT LEITH AND SETTLEMENT AT KELSO

Referring to M'Cheyne, Andrew Bonar commented that 'the Visiting Society was much blessed to the cultivation of his soul'. The same was true for all who shared in it. Certainly it prepared Horatius for his first charge. Even more important in that preparation was what one writer calls the 'life-long impulse to the proclamation of God's love in its gracious simplicity', received in Chalmers' classes. In that connection it is significant that the earliest manuscript of Bonar's that has survived is a 'Popular Sermon' on the pre-eminent need for love from 1 Corinthians 13:3. Dated 29 November 1831, it was evidently required as part of his training in the Divinity Hall.

This training concluded, he was licensed by the Edinburgh Presbytery on 27 April 1833, and became assistant to the Rev. James Lewis at St John's, the parish church of South Leith. This was a congregation described as 'one of the most energetic and useful in the Church', and Bonar was given special responsibility for mission work. Leith, the grimy port of Edinburgh, quite equalled the heathenism he had already witnessed in the city.

Speaking of the direction he received from Lewis on his arrival, Bonar recalled the experience at the end of his life in these words:

> The district which he allotted to me had a population of more than 3000; its streets and lanes were among the very worst in the town. But the work soon became pleasant, and we were welcomed even by the worst and the wickedest. My commencement was of a peculiar kind. Mr Lewis had secured a hall, which held about 200, in one of these lanes; and I was to occupy it every Sabbath, forenoon and afternoon, with the Sabbath school in the evening. It had hitherto been used by a small body of Roman Catholics. I had scarcely begun the forenoon service, when the door was thrown open, and a furious woman walked in, shouting, 'My curse and the curse of God be upon you.' But there was no disturbance and the curse did not come; but in many ways, both among old and young, the blessing followed. That was the starting point of my work in Leith.[8]

While sharing in the work of church services and house-to-house visitation, the opportunities for Sunday schools among the young seems to have taken much of his attention. Numbers multiplied and he relied on 'fellow workmen' from the Divinity Hall, including his brother Andrew.

For four years Horatius remained an assistant at Leith, and the length of time may reflect the difficulty that some of Dr Chalmers' students had in receiving calls. Word circulated among the churches of a new school of young preachers whose message could disturb congregations long unfamiliar with anything disturbing; in addition, some of these young men (not least the two Bonar brothers) had been convinced by Irving's preaching that there would be no long millennium before Christians need expect Christ's coming. This earned them the label, unusual for Scottish evangelicals, of being 'pre-millenarians', or, more slightingly, of being 'the Evangelical Light Infantry'. Undisturbed by the reproach they incurred, Horatius urged on his brother Andrew the likelihood that 'witness for Christ's Second Coming, borne by few in this land . . . may be part of our work.' When Andrew finished at the Divinity Hall he was to find himself 'kept out of several appointments' on account of this belief, and when the newly-formed North Parish Church of Kelso showed interest in Horace in 1837, he feared the same belief would prevent his brother's settlement there. In the event the fear was unfulfilled. At a farewell children's meeting in Leith in November 1837, 283 boys and girls (their names all carefully listed in his notebook) witnessed the conclusion of Bonar's work among them. On Sunday, 3 December 1837, Andrew wrote in his diary:

> Last Thursday God permitted me to see Horace ordained at Kelso. At the moment of laying on of hands I felt a strange thrill of solemnity and love towards him. The prayer was most excellent; I think the Lord was there.[9]

The parish of Kelso, a Border town 52 miles south-east of Edinburgh, where the river Teviot joins the river Tweed, had at this time a population of around five thousand. Sir Walter Scott had spoken of it as, 'the most beautiful, if not the most romantic, village in Scotland', and Bonar concurred. It was situated, in his opinion, 'amid scenes of beauty such as few spots can rival'. Floors Castle and a ruined Benedictine abbey stood close to rich and wooded farmland, and a five-arched bridge crosses the river today as it has done since 1803. Bonar revelled in these surroundings and in the view from his first home on a terrace above the confluence of the Teviot with the Tweed. A friend who visited him in those early days, recalled his 'rapture' as they went out of doors on a moonlight night to survey the scene.

Bonar's first sermon at Kelso was on the words, 'And he said unto them, This kind can come forth by nothing, but by prayer and fasting.' The message included a note which seems to have been characteristic of his life. He did not believe in working alone. 'In coming amongst you here,' he told the congregation, 'the first thing I ask of you is *your prayers*. Not your customary, your general, your formal prayers. Keep these idle compliments, – these regular, it may be, but too often unmeaning pieces of courtesy, to yourselves. These I ask not. If these are all you have to give, I shall be poor indeed. What I ask is your unwearied, your believing, wrestling prayers. Nothing else will do, for "this kind cometh out by nothing but by prayer and fasting".'[10] The hope expressed in these plain words was to be fulfilled. 'I found there plenty of work, plenty of workmen, and plenty of sympathy, – zealous elders, zealous teachers, and zealous friends. The key-note which I struck was, "Ye must be born again:" and that message found its way into many hearts. It repelled some, but it drew many together, in what I may call the bond of regeneration.' Without such helpers Bonar could never have accomplished the work that lay ahead.

Other help came from further afield, as Bonar kept in close
touch with the band of like-minded men – Robert M'Cheyne,
John Milne, Alexander Somerville and others – who were first
united in their days together in Edinburgh. Speaking of this
group, James Stalker was later to say that they 'were all, or
nearly all, highly cultivated men, though they sank their culture
in something better, and therefore sometimes received less
credit than they deserved'.[11] Alexander Whyte referred to them
as a school of preachers that 'had an immense influence on the
religious life of Scotland'; and another summarized their work
in the words, 'Their ministry produced seekers after God,
produced saints of God, and produced servants of God to staff
the Churches and missions of Christ at home and abroad.'[12]
This brotherhood of men continued to look to Bonar; they
shared in a union of prayer and visited each other whenever
possible.

M'Cheyne was one of his visiting preachers at Kelso and
was a regular correspondent. In a letter of 18 August 1842,
the pastor of St Peter's, Dundee, wrote: 'I have great desire
for personal growth in faith and holiness. I love the word of
God, and find it sweet nourishment to my soul. Can you help
me to study it more successfully?' In another letter, later that
year, M'Cheyne expressed his disappointment at not being able
to be in Kelso in November, and continued: 'Oh that my soul
were new moulded, and I were effectually called a second time,
and made a vessel full of the Spirit, to tell only of Jesus and
His love! I fear I shall never be in this world what I desire.'[13]
The following March every desire was met when he fell asleep
in Christ at the age of twenty-nine.

Still closer to Horatius than these friends were his two
brothers, John and Andrew, both now in the ministry. At least
once a year they shared in the communion seasons of one
another's churches – times when, according to the older
Scottish tradition, there were successive days of preaching.

These years were ones of general reviving in several parts of Scotland. Andrew Bonar speaks of a service at his church in Collace in 1840 when Horace preached on the Samaritan woman who was never to thirst again as Jesus gave her 'living water' beside the well of Sychar: 'There was a dead silence in the congregation, then there was weeping, and no less than sixty grown-up persons waited behind. It was the beginning of our first awakening in the parish – quite a new era in the place.'[14] The following year there were similar events at Kelso and the blessing was not temporary. One visitor described what he found there in these words:

> It was not so much the stir and excitement of one or more revivals, as the spiritual power, the still solemnity, the continuous life and action of a revived church, that made it the centre of life and refreshing to all the district round, through many a successive year. The Spirit came less as 'the rushing of a mighty wind,' or 'as floods on dry ground,' than as 'rain upon mown grass, as showers that water the earth'. Prayer meetings abounded, and 'they that feared the Lord spake often one to another', so that to some of us who had only begun our ministry, a visit to Kelso was felt to be a season of refreshing, whence we returned to our own work with new encouragement and hope.[15]

Bonar, referring to the general scene at this same period, spoke of 'widespread interest, full churches, a fervent ministry, the preaching of the gospel everywhere, in barns, field, moors, highways; large and manifest blessing on the word spoken'.[16] And more particularly of Kelso:

> The tide of blessing which, from 1837, had been flowing without intermission, had not yet begun to ebb. Many were daily added to our living membership. The Church's true work went on happily in parts where it had already

commenced; and it began in many places to which it had not yet reached. We look back on these months with thankful joy. Gladly should we live them over again, with all their tear and wear of body and mind, had we but our former strength, and the hope of like success. No one who passed through them would wish either to forget or under-estimate the privilege of having been one of the "labourers" in the reaping of that blessed harvest.

During this season there were all the marks of a work of God which we see in the account given of the preaching of the gospel by the apostles. The multitude was divided, families were divided; the people of God were knit together, they were filled with zeal and joy and heavenly-mindedness; they continued steadfast, and increased in doctrine and fellowship, being daily in church and in prayer-meetings; and numbers were constantly turning to the Lord.[17]

It is no wonder that people said of the Kelso manse that the lamp in his study burned far into the night and that early in the morning Bonar was again at his work. 'I should have taken more rest', he was heard to say in his latter years. It would not have been in his make up to have done so.

FROM THE BORDERS TO THE WORLD

As noted already in these pages, in the midst of the reviving of the late 1830s and early 1840s, the Disruption of the Church of Scotland took place in 1843. Bonar and his brothers were among the 450 or so ministers who left the Established Church, and he seems to have had no difficulty in taking his congregation into the newly-formed Free Church of Scotland. That event had unforeseen effects upon his ministry. Prior to 1843, deference to colleagues had kept him out of most other parishes in the Borders. After the division, in which only three other ministers of the presbytery joined him, he had no more scruples over parish boundaries, and he discovered, in his own words, 'open doors and open ears in that populous district among all ranks of people'. In this way an itinerant ministry, far and wide, was added to his Kelso work. William Robertson Nicoll, one of his successors at Kelso, remembered it in these words:

> He set himself to evangelize the Borderland. His name was fragrant in every little village, and at most of the farms. He conducted many meetings in farm kitchens and village schoolrooms, and often preached in the open air. The memory of some sermons lingered, one in particular on the Plant of Renown. The chief characteristic of his preaching was its strange solemnity. It was full of entreaty and of warning. Dr Bonar exhibited with faithful simplicity and decision the great things of the Gospel.[18]

As this itinerating developed, and Bonar 'found the work too great', he resorted to his old habit of gaining helpers, two of whom he names as Mr Stoddart and Alexander Murray. 'These two', he wrote in later years, 'were truly the evangelists of the Borders, and traversed the three counties of Roxburgh, Berwick, and Northumberland, with blessed success; and the fruit of their labours remains to this day all over these Borders . . . The missionary work which thus went on for ten or twelve years was of the most striking kind; and the journals of these two men of God, in that wide Border district, would furnish narratives which the Church would rejoice to read.'[19]

Bonar's other helpers were more occasional and whoever was suitable to exercise any service was encouraged to give their time. One of these fellow-workers was the future Lord Polwarth, who, with reference to the evangelizing of the Borders, said that the minister of Kelso 'was revered, respected, and beloved by all, no matter to what denomination they belonged'. The statement is not altogether correct, for Bonar himself remembered, 'Many rebuffs we got, many angry letters, many threats of ecclesiastical censure.'

Women also played their part. One of these warrants particular mention. From time to time a Madeleine Ballantyne stayed in Kelso, and in writing to a friend in 1844 she reported, 'Mr Bonar has given me a district, and I go nearly every day to speak to the people, and to read to them, and give them tracts.' This young woman had spent her infancy in Kelso and, after living in France, had returned to visit a friend in June 1841. Well educated, widely travelled and thoroughly worldly, she may have known her friend had been converted under Bonar's ministry before she made this visit and seems to have been determined to remain untouched by her 'religion'. Nonetheless she consented to attend the evening service on the first Sunday after her arrival.

Bonar was preaching on the misery of man in sin and the visitor's verdict on the sermon was 'too awful for her – she would not go back'. But when individuals become angry under preaching it can be a good sign, and it was so in this case. There was something hollow about her protest, 'Don't suppose that I care anything for that man's words – I am determined not to mind him.' Soon she met the man she intended to ignore and a few weeks later, 'She went back to the world no more – but after a little delay, straight forward to the Cross, there to deposit all her sins and fears.'

The subsequent bright witness of Madeleine Ballantyne was a blessing, not only to people in Kelso, but to a much larger number after her death in 1849 when Bonar wrote an account of her life.[20] What gives the book added interest is that it contains many letters to another friend in Kelso by the name of Jane Lundie, daughter of a former minister of the town.[21] It was Jane Lundie that Bonar married in 1843, and it may have been through his wife that valuable letters for the biography of Madeleine Ballantyne came into his possession.

It is extraordinary that, in a period when Bonar was at full stretch in his public ministry, another side of his work should have developed as it did. Thus far his writing was largely confined to articles in the *Presbyterian Review,* a magazine published from 1831 to 1848, and which for a time he edited. But the felt need in Kelso was for clear evangelistic material and this led him to write a first lengthy tract in 1838; it was based on Isaiah 55:1 and entitled, 'The Well of Living Water'. As openings for the gospel increased in the Borders, so did the need for such material, and in 1846 a large number of the tracts were published in book form as the *Kelso Tracts.* The note they strike is well introduced in his Preface:

> The idea which many have of religion is, that it is a most necessary and becoming thing, by means of which they hope, in course of time, to work themselves into God's favour, and so to obtain forgiveness before they die. But this is man's religion, not God's. It has no resemblance to that in which God delights, and which he alone will accept. The chief feature is a direct contradiction to that which the Bible presents to us. It is an entire inversion of God's order. It *ends* with securing forgiveness, whereas God's religion *begins* with securing it.[22]

The distance which Bonar's tracts were to travel can be judged by the fact that a million copies of one of them, 'Believe and Live', were circulated. The freeness with which Bonar pressed an acceptance of the gospel upon sinners was startling to some, and offensive to others, but the message was the power of God unto salvation. 'I am truly delighted with your tract, "Believe and Live"', Chalmers wrote to him. 'I hold by that theology.'

Bonar's first book, published in 1844, was on the ministry needed by the churches: *The School of the Prophets; or, Training for the Ministry.* The main part of this had first appeared as an article in the *Presbyterian Review*. With revision, it was later reprinted by him as *Words to Winners of Souls.*[23] Two years later, the same year as the collection of *Kelso Tracts,* two more titles appeared. They were, *The Night of Weeping,* and *Truth and Error.* The former was written out of the conviction that Christians 'are all cross-bearers'. His experience had already taught him that all members of the 'household of faith' will know sorrow and suffering, either personally or in sharing the burdens of others. *Truth and Error* was a very different kind of book. A subtitle explained its purpose: *Letters to a Friend on Some of the Controversies of the Day.* It is a forceful work, intended to explain biblical teaching over against the superficial evangelism already becoming popular which claimed that the sinner must co-operate with God in order to be saved – 'He begins the work by becoming willing, and God does the rest.' 'We think if we can but get men converted, it does not much matter how.' Our whole anxiety is, 'not how shall we secure the glory of Jehovah, but how shall we multiply conversions?'[24] Yet, at the same time as emphasizing human inability, and holding to a definite atonement, Bonar insisted on the gospel as a message of universal compassion. He quoted with approval words of Jonathan Edwards on how that spirit becomes stronger in Christians in times of revival: 'There was found an universal benevolence to mankind, with a longing to embrace the whole world in the arms of pity and love.'

From this date onwards, items of one kind or another were published by Bonar almost every year. Evangelistic literature remained prominent, one of the best known books being *God's Way of Peace: A Book for the Anxious* (1861). In the Preface to this book, which sold 285,000 copies by 1889, he wrote:

> Some have tried to give directions to sinners on 'how to get converted', multiplying words without wisdom, leading the sinner away from the cross, by setting him

upon *doing,* not upon *believing.* Our business is not to give any such directions, but, as the apostles did, to preach Christ crucified, a *present* Saviour, and a *present* salvation.

It is an indication of Bonar's range of gifts that, as well as writing on the popular level, he was able to produce material requiring research and scholarship. In this category was his publication of an enlarged edition of John Gillies' *Historical Collections of Accounts of Revival* (1855), and his *Catechisms of the Scottish Reformation* (1866). The latter work he edited with notes and a lengthy preface, written, in Alexander Whyte's words, 'with such scholarly sympathy that I cannot but call that book a classic in the religious literature of Scotland'. I think the same writer is correct in saying, 'I do not know that anywhere in Dr Bonar's writings you will find his masculine power as a writer of English, his great ability as a theologian, and his grasp of evangelical truth better exemplified than in the powerful preface he has written to his edition of those Catechisms.'[25] The University of Aberdeen had the wisdom to be the first university to recognize Bonar's all-round stature when they conferred the degree of D.D. on him in April 1853.

Nothing seemed to deter Bonar's commitment to writing, and few books can have been written in the circumstances that produced his titles, *The Desert of Sinai* (1857), and *The Land of Promise* (1858). Both were written in the form of journals while on the backs of camels! This was in the Middle East where he travelled for five months in 1856 for the sake of his health.[26]

Perhaps it reflects the condition of the churches of the last century that Bonar's hymns were allowed to overshadow the importance of his many other writings. Certainly it was through his hymns that his name became renowned throughout the English-speaking world, and in translation they were to be sung from Spain to Russia. Most who sang them knew nothing of their author. One admirer of his hymns, an Anglican lady in Torquay, was astonished to meet a member of his congregation.

'What!' she exclaimed, 'is Bonar the hymn writer still alive? I always thought he was a mediaeval saint.'

It was not until 1857 that Bonar put his name to hymns he had written, but their origin, and his interest in hymnology, belongs to a much earlier date. Although, with the exception of paraphrases, hymns were not sung in church of his childhood, there was a long Scottish tradition for their use in families. To the Bonar children's early training they owed 'the stores of paraphrases and hymns which they held in their memory'.[27] When his twenty-four-year-old sister died in 1824 it was ever remembered how Isaac Watts' hymn, 'There is a land of pure delight,' brought comfort to them all at her bedside. Bonar's own first hymns were written for children in his mission district in Leith. They were prompted by the need to combat the listlessness of their singing during services, compared with the exuberance they showed in singing other songs, with bright tunes, at other times. Taking some of the lively tunes with which they were familiar, he put new words to them. The interest and improvement were immediate, so he gathered a number of further hymns for them, including some of his own. Among his first were, 'I was a wandering sheep', and. 'I lay my sins on Jesus'.

Convinced of the teaching value of hymns, he early introduced at Kelso 'a little unbound hymn book for the young'. This was followed in 1845 by the publication of *The Bible Hymn Book*, containing three hundred hymns, with sixteen or seventeen of his own, yet none bearing the author's name.[28] A few of the items were by his wife, for Jane Bonar also had a poetic gift. It was her sister, Mary Lundie Duncan, who wrote the widely-used evening hymn for children, 'Jesus, tender Shepherd, hear me'. In 1857 Bonar put out the first collection of hymns bearing his name. Although it had the title *Hymns of Faith and Hope* it did not have a hymn-book format. Many of the items were poems for spiritual reflection and meditation, and we may judge that much of the book was primarily intended for reading rather than singing. Bonar did nothing to introduce hymns into the regular services of his church and several of what were to be his most popular hymns were first read in Free Church congregations rather than sung. Thus he read the words of his hymn, 'Here, O my Lord, I see Thee face to face,' first at a communion service at his brother John's church in Greenock in October 1855.[29]

Bonar's poems are in some ways the closest thing we have to autobiography from his pen. They were not written as part of his ordinary work but were rather personal thoughts jotted down in a notebook he always carried in his pocket, perhaps on a country walk or by a sea-shore. Elements of confession, prayer, thankfulness and testimony are intermingled. The love of God, the Person of Christ and the thought of his speedy Coming are dominant themes. It was more as an afterthought that these poems were brought together for others, so that Christians everywhere have been able to repeat so many of his sentiments. The gospel was surely never put more simply in uninspired words than in his verse:

> Upon a life I did not live,
> Upon a death I did not die;
> Another's life, another's death,
> I stake my whole eternity.

There is a pervasive seriousness about his poems, born of a sense of the brevity of time and what has been called 'nostalgia for heaven'. He surely cannot be a Christian who reads his verse as pessimistic. The following lines represent a hope that is characteristic:

> Well pleased I find years rolling o'er me,
> And hear, each day, time's measured tread;
> Far fewer clouds now stretch before me,
> *Behind* me is the darkness spread.

Even so, the modern reader of Bonar's verse might think he shows an abnormal interest in death. But in that connection it needs to be remembered that death was a much closer event to his generation. They regularly saw its reality in a way that cannot be conveyed by a television screen, for life expectancy was of a very different order in the mid-nineteenth century. His wife's sister, Mary, died at the age of twenty-six. One of his own surviving sisters died in the Kelso manse, with her five brothers at her bedside. Andrew Bonar's wife died so suddenly that, he told Jane, the wife of Horatius, 'Dear Isabella could not bid me farewell.' Of the nine children of his marriage, only four reached adulthood. Two died in infancy, one at three years of age, one at four and one at seventeen. Some of these deaths were probably due to tuberculosis (then known as 'consumption'), there being no recognition of infected cows as the source. They did not all die of that lingering illness. Only after arriving to preach for Andrew at Collace, on one occasion, did Bonar hear of the sudden illness of his son James and the next news was of his death. Slow to express his feelings to others, the father on these occasions found therapeutic value in setting down his sorrow in verse. One such bereavement poem is headed 'Taken Away from the Evil to Come', another, 'The Blank'. On 'Lucy' he wrote eleven verses after her death at the age of four in August 1858, and I will quote the opening and concluding verses:

> All night we watched the ebbing life,
> As if its flight to stay;
> Till, as the dawn was coming up,
> Our last hope passed away.
>
> She was the music of our home,
> A day that knew no night,
> The fragrance of our garden bower,
> A thing all smiles and light . . .

> Farewell, with weeping hearts we said,
> Child of our love and care!
> And then we ceased to kiss those lips,
> For Lucy was not there.
>
> But years are moving quickly past,
> And time will soon be o'er;
> Death shall be swallowed up of life
> On the immortal shore.
>
> Then shall we clasp that hand once more,
> And smooth that golden hair;
> Then shall we kiss those lips again,
> When Lucy will be there.

When Bonar went to Kelso in 1837 no one supposed a world-wide ministry in writing also lay before him; but, looking back, we can see evidence of divine planning and that in more than one respect. The settlement in that quiet place was the means of putting him in touch with the publisher who would play an indispensable part in Bonar's work as an author. James Nisbet was a Kelso man who had removed to London where he established a prosperous evangelical publishing firm. Troubled at the lack of spiritual provision for many in his native town, which he revisited in 1834, Nisbet, anonymously, provided half the funds for the building of Bonar's church. Thereafter the two men became close friends, and it meant that Bonar was never to lose any time in finding a publisher for his writings. The vast majority were to carry the name of 'James Nisbet, London'. Nisbet was also to take the major share in the republication of the sets of leading Puritans that went on from the 1850s to the 1870s. Without Nisbet the Christian world would have been immensely poorer.

Given Bonar's seriousness, and the element of reserve in his character, it might be thought that his ministry would have little appeal to children and young people. The opposite was the case and the affection shown for children in his early ministry at Leith only deepened with the years. At Kelso it is said that 'his sermons to the young were peculiarly attractive'. On Wednesday afternoons it was his custom at Kelso to hold a Bible class and many years later one of the young people who attended recalled the 'bright, happy band of schoolgirls, sitting around listening to his earnest, loving, faithful teaching'. She went on: 'I see Dr Bonar seated at the end of a long table with the large Bible spread out before him, the Bible-hymnbook in his hand, his dear handsome face beaming, and the pleasant smile which lighted it up, as some of us gave a fuller, clearer answer than he expected to the question asked.'

REMOVAL TO EDINBURGH

Much seemed to indicate that Bonar would spend all his ministry in Kelso. He showed no interest in calls elsewhere. When a Presbyterian church in Newcastle invited him he replied, 'Here I am, and here I must remain till my Lord come to me or for me.' However in the 1860s he experienced what one who knew him called 'a great trial' in Kelso. Although Bonar's North Parish Church had been built so largely by money from those who adhered to the Free Church, it was claimed by the Church of Scotland and had to be relinquished. A last service was held in the building on 25 September 1864. By this time there was a congregation of 432 members, and perhaps an equal number of non-communicants, including children. The loan of a school building and another church helped out in the emergency, and 'Bonar and his friends subscribed largely' to the erection of a new building. Before it was completed, however, he was asked to face the challenge of taking on another church extension charge, the newly formed Free Church at Grange, a growing district on the south side of Edinburgh, to be named the Chalmers' Memorial Church after his much-loved mentor.[30] This call he could not refuse. Edinburgh was, for him, 'the flower of cities'. Much as he loved the beauty of the Borders, there were attractions higher than nature, as he had written in a poem of 1855 entitled 'The City':

> There seems, in yon city's motion,
> Yet a mightier truth for me:
> 'Tis the sound of life's great ocean,
> 'Tis the tides of the human sea.
>
> My heart, in its inmost beatings,
> Ever lingers around its homes:
> My soul wakes up in its greetings,
> To the gleam of its spires and domes.

There is no record of whether or not the building trouble in Kelso unsettled Bonar. What is clear is that after twenty-eight years there was no lessening of affection between the pastor and his people. The testimony of one of his elders before the Presbytery of Kelso was published in the *Kelso Chronicle* (2 March 1866) and included the words:

> Our attachment to his ministry exists to this day in its unbroken strength. Our sense of the value of his teaching continues to increase. His ministrations have lost to us nothing of their freshness and power. As a man of God – pre-eminently a man of prayer – we give him all honour. His pure, unselfish, holy walk and conversation among us have gained our entire respect.

Bonar was inducted to the new charge on 7 June 1866. The call had come to him from sixty communicants who first met in a hired hall. By December their new building, able to hold a thousand, was opened. The following year there were seventy-four additional communicants; ten years later the figure was 700.[31] A church manse was acquired close by at 10 Palmerston Road. The witness of the congregation was also extended through a mission hall established in a poorer part of the parish, and for this Bonar brought Alexander Murray, the Borders evangelist, to join him. Bonar himself was not content only with evangelism through Sunday services. We read that, 'He often went on Sunday evenings or in the week-time to the Meadows or some other open space, and preached in the open air.'

Even in this city charge, Bonar's literary output remained immense. It was at its height in the 1860s. Since 1848 he had been editor and main contributor to the *Quarterly Journal of Prophecy*. Unfulfilled prophecy was much more to him than a matter of study; as Marcus Loane has written, 'He looked for the second coming of Christ as the event towards which all history gravitates.'[32] To his editorship of this journal was added, in 1859, the editorship of the *Christian Treasury*. This was one of the most widely read Christian magazines of the period, published simultaneously every month in Edinburgh and London, and then issued in an annual volume. Anonymity was far more common in literature at that date, and the 1859 volume gives no indication of the new editor apart from the initials 'H.B.' at the conclusion of the Preface. For those who knew Bonar, however, the identification of the editor was not needed, for there was much that showed his hand in the contents, not least the attention to the revival that took place that year in Ulster and part of Britain.[33] While he terminated his editorship of the *Quarterly Journal of Prophecy* in 1873, the *Christian Treasury* remained a monthly duty right down to 1879.

By no means all, but a good part of Bonar's own contributions to these periodicals were of material first preached to his people. Two of his major publications of the later years originated in the same way, *Fifty-two Short Sermons for Family Reading* (1863),[34] and *Light and Truth: Bible Thoughts and Themes*, in five volumes (1868–72).[35] In his *Commenting and*

Commentaries, Spurgeon classified the latter work in his first category for value, while adding, 'The volumes will be more prized by the ordinary reader than by the minister.' Even although not intended for them, there are many preachers who would not be without these volumes. The only Bonar work to approach the style of a commentary was his book on the first six chapters of Genesis entitled, *Earth's Morning: Or, Thoughts on Genesis* (1875). Two additions to this volume, on 'The Sabbath' and on 'Satan', are too valuable to be appendices.

For the Edinburgh period of Bonar's life there are insights from his son, Horace Ninian, who was only six at the time of the family removal from Kelso. The son would later write:

> When I look back on the way his day was filled with the affairs of his own ministerial work, I wonder how he could possibly make room in his life for anything else. Yet he edited a magazine (for a considerable time, two of them), and was, in addition, perpetually publishing prose works. In fact, one special table in his study was entirely devoted to proof-sheets, and he used to say that for a period of thirty years he had been continually in the hands of three separate printers, of his editorial, his prose and his poetical work.[36]

Although Bonar was fifty-two years old when Horatius Ninian was born the son did not lack fellowship and recreation with his father. They swam together, for his father (like his grandfather) still loved the sea, and the family would head for the beaches of Arran, East Lothian, or Fife for summer holidays. When the exercise was over, his son continues, 'I used to watch my father pacing up and down some level beach or stretch of turf, sometimes repeating a line or two aloud to try how it sounded to the ear, ere he committed it to paper.' Another feature of the father is reported that we would not otherwise have known: 'He had a strong sense of humour, which he very rarely allowed to show itself in public.' One proof of this was the merry lines he would contribute to 'a little family manuscript magazine which was maintained among a circle of relatives for many years'.[37]

Horatius Ninian also wrote of his father's happy disposition and of the skill with which he guided his children:

> He very rarely said 'Don't' to me – not that he did not indicate very strongly what he would like me to do. . . . All my holidays were passed with him. We boated together, we walked together, we swam together, we climbed hills together. Stern! No, he was never stern in my boyish eyes. I can remember another little personal incident – you will pardon me for mentioning it in this connection. Once an officious neighbour came to him to complain of one of my misdeeds. I fancy I had been climbing to the rooks' nests in Warrender Park, then unbuilt on. He reported this to my father, and wound up by saying, 'I hope you will give the boy a good thrashing.' My father replied, 'If I thrashed the boy for that, what would I do if he told me a lie?'[38]

Bonar's ready identification with children showed itself in the work of his congregation. Besides the Sunday Schools, once a month he would hold an evening service for children, who filled the body of the church, while adults were permitted in the galleries. 'In the children's meetings he especially delighted. Together with his gown he threw off something of the awe-inspiring solemnity which usually characterized him, and going amongst the little ones he would talk to them individually and settle them in their seats, and then ascending the pulpit he would give his fancy freer play than at other times, and deliver an address which always secured interested attention.'[39]

The same eye-witness has described Bonar's usual pulpit manner in his later years:

The minister with thought-lined face, keen eye and white hair, was a striking figure. Holding in his hand a small Bible, from which he read, he would often lean his elbow on the pulpit desk, while with gestures of the other hand he would enforce his simple but weighty utterances. He spoke in terse language, in deep measured tones, and his manner was profoundly reverential. Deep silence reigned; often the clock could be heard to tick in the long pauses between the sentences.

CONTROVERSIES

Controversy was a business that Bonar shunned, and commonly he took no part in the debates of church courts. When differences of opinion among Christians were public it was 'conference' that he advised, and the spirit in which he edited the *Quarterly Journal of Prophecy* was exemplary in that regard. Nevertheless, after his arrival in Edinburgh in 1866 he could not in good conscience avoid an involvement in more than one controversy. The first was the so-called 'Union movement'. In the 1860s a Free Church proposal for uniting with the United Presbyterian Church (descendants of the Secession of the previous century) became a matter of constant discussion. One issue that seemed to prevent union was the relationship of the church to the state. Both denominations held that it was the obligation of the civil powers to obey and profess the Christian religion but there was disagreement over how this obligation should express itself in practice. Many in the Free Church, favouring the proposed union, argued that the disagreement was not of a nature to justify a continued separation. Although Bonar had long been an advocate of closer unity between believers, he believed that the proposed union would involve doctrinal compromise, and in a motion to the Presbytery of Edinburgh (February 1868) he spoke against it. He had a powerful seconder in James Buchanan,

Professor of Systematic Theology at New College, whose argument urged the principle that had been missed in the church-government debates of the seventeenth century.[40] But, despite men of known godliness on both sides, the discussion in the Free Church descended into prolonged controversy. In 1870, the veteran missionary Alexander Duff pleaded that the interest of Satan in the dispute be recognized, and asked, If the energy being expended were 'directed to the evangelization of the multitudes . . . who have never yet heard the Saviour's name, – how soon might any minor differences that may exist between us and other churches that "hold the head" as much as we do, vanish out of sight?'[41] This and other pleas for peace were without avail and it became clear that union with the United Presbyterians could only be achieved at the cost of a division within the Free Church itself. For this reason the proposal was abandoned in 1873.

But other controversies were also current and these began to converge. A hymn book had been authorized in the United Presbyterian Church in the 1850s and was in general use in that denomination. The Free Church, however, while allowing paraphrases in addition to the Metrical Psalms, had no practice of hymn singing in public worship. When an overture to the General Assembly of the Free Church in 1866 asked leave for the use of hymns, it was noticeable that a number of the leading ministers in opposition belonged to the same minority that opposed the Union movement. In the ensuing debate Bonar spoke for the allowance of hymns but it was indicative of his retiring nature, and of his unwillingness to see division, that he made no attempt to introduce his own hymns, or those of others, in his congregation. This was a matter of surprise to observers in other denominations, in England and America, where his hymns were already widely sung.

Before the end of 1873 yet another controversy arose in which Bonar was to play a decided part, and to this we must give fuller attention. On 22 November 1873, D. L. Moody and Ira D. Sankey, accompanied by their wives, arrived in Edinburgh. It was Moody's first preaching visit to Britain and through much of the following winter his home was to be with Professor W. G. Blaikie of New College, while the Sankeys stayed at the Bonars' home. Evangelistic services, and afternoon Bible Readings, began under the oversight of a local committee of which Bonar was a member. For more than a month a succession of churches were used, and numbers and spiritual interest increased week by week, in a work that was to go on for many months after Moody had moved on to Dundee and Glasgow early in 1874. All the main denominations were involved. Prayer meetings for the work were held in the Free Church of Scotland's Assembly Hall in Edinburgh, a building able to hold more than a thousand. After Andrew Bonar attended one of these prayer meetings he wrote in his diary: Wednesday, 17th [December 1873] 'Have been since morning in Edinburgh attending the remarkable meetings of Moody and Sankey. What a sight! Our great Assembly Hall crowded with eager, praying, listening souls from ten o'clock till four.' It was, he believed, the revival for which they had been praying since the end of 'the Union strife'. Moody stayed in Scotland into the summer of 1874, preaching often to immense numbers – allegedly to as many as 20,000 to 30,000 in the Botanic Gardens in Glasgow on one occasion. 'But,' Blaikie observed, 'the numbers that attend are not the most remarkable feature. It is the presence and power of the Holy Ghost, the solemn awe, the prayerful, believing, expectant spirit, the anxious inquiry of unsaved souls, and the longing of believers to grow more like Christ . . . All this is of the grace of God.'[42]

Andrew Bonar, like Blaikie, was not taken up with numbers. In another diary entry he wrote: 'The most memorable part of the day was our Bible Reading with Mr Moody in the forenoon; about thirty Christian friends present. We were like

Acts 20:7, talking for two hours, and then dispensing the Lord's Supper. Mr Moody closed with prayer. Most solemn scene, never to be forgotten.'[43]

Robertson Nicoll, speaking of Horatius Bonar's Edinburgh ministry, was of the opinion that 'perhaps his happiest time was in the revival of 1874'.[44] But this assessment of 1874 as a year of revival was not the universal belief. During that year, a thirty-one page pamphlet appeared from the pen of Dr John Kennedy of Dingwall, entitled, *Hyper-Evangelism: 'Another Gospel,' Though a Mighty Power. A Review of the Recent Religious Movement in Scotland* (Edinburgh: Grant, 1874). Moody had not been without lesser critics, but here was a leading – probably *the* leading – evangelical of the Scottish Highlands, taking issue with his brethren of the Free Church and other denominations in the south.

Kennedy's name was, in Bonar's words, an 'honoured' one. We have met him earlier in these pages as the biographer of John MacDonald of Ferintosh, and since 1844 he had exercised a ministry of wide influence in Dingwall, the county town of Ross-shire. When a larger church building had to be opened there in 1870 it was C. H. Spurgeon who had preached. If criticism from such a quarter was to be answered, it needed no lightweight person to do it. When Bonar replied in a pamphlet of seventy-eight pages, *The Old Gospel: Not 'Another Gospel,' but the Power of God unto Salvation* (Edinburgh: Elliot/London: Nisbet, 1874) it was akin to a collision of giants. Kennedy was not satisfied and responded with *A Reply to Dr Bonar's Defence of Hyper-Evangelism* (Edinburgh: Lyon and Gemmell, 1875).[45]

Without naming Moody, or anyone else, Kennedy argued that the message at the centre of the 'religious movement' was *another gospel*: it was produced, he believed, mainly by 'an extreme application of some truths, to the neglect of others', and by the adoption of unscriptural methods. He thought the character of God as Lawgiver, Judge and Sovereign was being by-passed in the preaching, with a consequent absence of any insistence upon repentance. He did not deny that the answer to 'the legal difficulty' in the way of a sinner's forgiveness was presented in terms of Christ crucified as the Substitute, but claimed that 'the moral difficulty' (man's fallen nature), which necessitates a new birth, was left out of view in order to make conversion instantly possible for all. 'Sudden conversion', he complained, was being treated as the biblical norm, and he thought that the adoption of inquiry rooms led to individuals being 'pressed and hurried into public profession' (p. 28). With 'grief' he concluded, 'I look on my Church, in a spasmodic state, subject to convulsions, which only indicate that her life is departing, the result of revivals got up by men' (p. 31).

In replying to this assessment Bonar insisted that the 'evidence' given by Kennedy rested upon misquotations, upon words taken out of context, or simply on sweeping generalizations. 'A call to repentance never issues from their trumpet,' Kennedy wrote. 'This is quite at variance with fact,' Bonar replied. 'That word "repent" – how I have heard it ring through the Assembly Hall in the ears of thousands!'(p. 58). While Kennedy affirmed that in Moody one 'never hears any confession of sin', Bonar heard 'full and fervent confessions of sin at Mr Moody's meetings (p. 42).' The correctness of other claims made by Kennedy was similarly challenged. Bonar repeatedly urged that, while Kennedy brought forward no witnesses to substantiate words attributed to Moody, there were hundreds of ministers able to verify what was actually said. 'I am not aware that Dr Kennedy was present at one of these central meetings, in which the work was mainly carried on. It was certainly, then, somewhat incautious in him to affirm that certain doctrines were never taught at these meetings. He who was not present at any declares that they were *not* taught; we who were present at hundreds of them declare *that they were taught*. Who is to be believed?'(p. 59).

It is apparent in Bonar's reply that his concern was larger than providing a defence of Moody. Nor was it his intention to justify every word casually spoken by the visitor who spoke of himself as an evangelist, not a teacher.[46] Bonar's main concern had to do with Kennedy's charge that the work was the result of 'another gospel', and with the belief that it was this that the ministers in the south had tolerated and supported: 'The pamphlet is not directed against Mr Moody merely, but *against the brethren of all Churches who gathered round him*.' To support this allegation Bonar quotes Kennedy's words, 'Hundreds of ministers have I seen, sitting as disciples at the feet of one whose teaching only showed his ignorance even of "the first principles of the doctrines of Christ"'(p. 26) These men were thus all to be presumed guilty of conniving at 'another gospel'.

In Kennedy's *Reply to Dr Bonar's Defence of Hyper-Evangelism,* there is some ambiguity in his response to the claim of Bonar that hundreds of orthodox ministers were being condemned. Kennedy denied that it was his purpose to accuse any of the ministers who supported Moody, and yet he went on to confirm what Bonar had pointed out. He claimed that Bonar's very response supplied 'proof of the dangerous influence of the teaching to which I referred' (p. 13). Bonar's pamphlet, he said, gave him reason to doubt his adherence to the teaching of the Shorter Catechism, and it confirmed his 'opinion regarding the recent religious movement in Scotland' (p. 21). 'What I condemned, as the teaching of another, is held by Dr Bonar himself' (p. 23).

Kennedy was correct in asserting that there was some doctrinal disagreement involved in their differing assessments. Dr Bonar, he wrote in his *Reply,* 'charges me with hyper-Calvinism' (p. 23). In Bonar's *The Old Gospel* there are, in fact, only passing references to hyper-Calvinism, the longest being the words: 'We may dread "hyper-evangelism"; but is hyper-

Calvinism innocuous? If the former is to be charged with drawing many who are not drawn by the Father, the latter may with more truth be charged with repelling many to whom the Saviour says, "Come unto me"' (pp. 7, 27, 57).

Kennedy was not named in connection with these references but there can be no doubt that there was an important doctrinal issue upon which the two men disagreed. Kennedy objected to Moody's preaching of 'immediate salvation' as though there was no prior need for conviction of sin. In this connection he instanced a newspaper report that at a meeting in Glasgow, Moody asked the question, 'Was there any hindrance to the conversion of all present that night?' Bonar, present on the platform, had audibly replied, 'None.' But surely, Kennedy urged, a work of conviction – 'law-work' – must precede conversion. He accused Bonar of denying this (*Reply*, p. 25) and with teaching that 'faith is mere belief, and no more' (p. 28).

This was surely a misunderstanding. Certainly Bonar believed in the necessity of conviction, and had long preached the gospel from that standpoint; but he did not believe that conviction was a *qualification* required of sinners before the duty of believing the gospel is pressed upon them. The *way* in which God bring men to Christ, is not to be confused with the *warrant* men have to believe on him for salvation. Nothing is required *of the sinner* before that warrant is addressed to him. Certainly, those who call men to receive Christ need to know that grace alone makes the invitation effective, but as far as the hearer is concerned, Moody saw correctly that 'there is no need of long intervals or intervals of any kind between the sense of need and the experience of redeeming grace'.[47]

Understanding the process of conversion is important for the Christian, for it makes clear the truth that it is all of God, but understanding the theology is not necessary for the sinner in order to a true conversion. The disciple has to begin in the primary school, not at the university. Bonar was not compromising his Calvinism in supporting Moody's insistence that the gospel preaching should look for an immediacy of response. In the words of one of his tracts, 'The news which God sends you, is, like every other piece of news, to put you in the attitude of a *listener*, and not a *doer*; in the attitude of a *receiver*, not of a worker at all.'[48] In his *Old Gospel*, Bonar had replied to Kennedy:

> We believe in Christ's redemption of His chosen Church . . . in the enmity of the human heart to God . . . in the absolute necessity of the Holy Spirit's work, alike before and after conversion. At the same time we preach a free and world-wide gospel; we proclaim a free and world-wide invitation to sinners; we present to every sinner a gracious welcome to Christ, without any preliminary qualification whatsoever. We bid no man wait till he has ascertained his election, or can produce evidence of his regeneration, or sufficient repentance, or deep conviction. We tell every man, *as he is,* to go to the Saviour this moment, assured that he will not be cast out or sent away (p. 23).

But there was more to Kennedy's criticism of 'immediate salvation', and this is where the question of hyper-Calvinism comes in. In his encouragement of the 'immediate', Moody spoke of the gospel invitation as an expression of the love of God to all who heard it. This brings us to the nub of the disagreement with Dr Kennedy. The Highland preacher denied the belief of those who regard '*the call of the gospel as expressive of the love of God to each individual to whom it is addressed*'.[49] The love of God in the invitation is *not* to be presented to sinners as a reason why they are to receive Christ for salvation, because, he believed, the *only* love of God taught in Scripture is the saving love that must be traced back to the election of particular people. Those who remain unsaved have never, therefore, been loved. 'It is one love, and only one, which is revealed in Scripture – the love that gave the Son, and that giveth all things with him.'[50] 'The Calvinist does not profess to base the gospel call on aught else than the revealed command of God . . . He believes that there is a peculiar love to a chosen people, and he believes in no love besides.'[51]

Had Bonar wished to score points he might have replied that Calvinism, so defined, would exclude John Calvin, who believed in a love extending to all men, as well as a special love to the elect.[52] More important, the invitations of Jesus spoken indiscriminately to multitudes did not express compassion for the elect alone. He loved those who turned away (*Mark* 10:21); he mourned the unwillingness of sinners to come, 'I would . . . you would not!' (*Matt.* 23:37). 'You will not come unto me that you might have life' (*John* 5:40). Bonar had ever believed this, as had Chalmers and so many others before him. He had no wish to fix the perjorative label of hyper-Calvinistm on Kennedy and did not engage him further on this point. What was of major concern to him was the impediment that his opponent's belief presented to the reception of 'the word of salvation' on the part of all who hear it. For if the invitation contains no expression of divine love for the individual hearer, then some *other* evidence that the invitation to believe is *really* for him becomes necessary, which evidence can only be found in his own life. Introspection – looking for 'signs of grace' within before there can be trust in Christ without – is the consequence. The inevitable tendency is for the question, 'Am I one of the elect?' to come before, 'Can I trust in Christ?'

This question was not uncommon in Scotland in the 1870s, and not least where a form of Calvinistic teaching was strongest.[53] Moody's emphasis was a necessary corrective and the reason Bonar supported that emphasis was not that there was any weakening in his Calvinism. On the contrary, he continued to warn against an evangelicalism that 'oscillates between Calvinism and Arminianism.'[54] Now Kennedy would have denied that faith needs subjective corroboration before it can be exercised, and he held there was a warrant for all to believe. But why, he would ask, need love be introduced into gospel invitations? Is not the command of God to repent and believe enough? It was upon that question that a division of opinion centred. The *Shorter Catechism* (Q. 87), defines 'repentance unto life' as 'a saving grace, whereby a sinner, out of a true sense of sin, and *apprehension of the mercy of God in Christ*' turns to God (my italics). Will a sinner who has only reason to believe that God is hostile towards him turn to him? If 'apprehension' of something besides God's justice and authority is necessary, must it not be his character as love? and how is that character to be known unless it is presented to all that hear? Our Lord's parable shows that the return of the prodigal begins with a re-assessment of the Father's character. 'How excellent is thy loving-kindness, O God! therefore the children of men put their trust under the shadow of thy wings' (*Psa.* 36:7).

Now it would be a monstrous injustice to imply that Dr Kennedy did not preach the love of God. He did, and yet with care not to individualize it. He held that while 'the love of God was displayed before men' in the gospel, 'it can be expressed to them only when they are in Christ'.[55] This can only mean that the preacher must not give the impression that divine love and compassion extends to all who hear him. Rather, in applying the gospel, Kennedy seemed to believe, the preacher should only go as far as asserting that God will receive all who come to him through Christ.[56] He should not go beyond that, to seek to persuade all of the love of God towards them in the gospel. The element of God pleading with men, which warrants the preacher to say, 'We pray you in Christ's stead, be ye reconciled to God' (*1 Cor.* 5:20), was necessarily overshadowed, to the extent that Kennedy was consistent with his principles. According to John Duncan's message: 'The Gospel does not say, "There is a Saviour, if you wish to be saved"; but, "Sir, you have no right to go to hell – you can't go there without trampling on the Son of God."'[57] This note was muted in Kennedy.

Calvinistic ministers who, like Bonar, supported Moody, did so because they believed that the evangelist's emphasis was much needed. Blaikie summarized what they thought when he spoke of the current need to counter a 'lurking distrust of the generosity of God in the free offer of salvation. The heart is naturally so suspicious of God, so unwilling to believe in his infinite love and goodness, that it is apt to lag behind the understanding, and prevent the soul from closing with the offer. The remedy for this must be found in urging passages of Scripture in which the love of God to sinners is expressed very clearly, and his desire that they should at once accept his salvation in all its fullness of blessing.'[58] It was to this point that Moody gave prominence. Canon Hobson of Liverpool put his finger on it when he recorded in his autobiography: 'I once said to an intelligent Scotchman, "Tell me how you hard-headed Scotchmen could listen to a Moody." His answer was "Who could resist love?" That is it.'[59] Bonar approved the words of his friend, W. H. Hewitson, who said, 'It is as sinful to doubt God's willingness to save me as to doubt his existence.'[60]

On the central doctrinal point, it is my belief that Bonar was right in this controversy but it is noticeable that he did not justify Moody in every respect, and there is a point where he meets Kennedy's concern with comparative silence. Kennedy in *Hyper-Evangelism* condemned 'the novelty of the "inquiry room"', and the way it sought to separate people publicly as 'seeking salvation' or as 'converts'. Bonar replied that the use of an inquiry room was no new thing, and he instanced the practice of Robert M'Cheyne and others. But there was surely an important difference between advising people, concerned and awakened, to meet for further counsel (as was often done in earlier history), and making inquirers publicly identify themselves, with a later announcement of how many had done so, or had subsequently confessed faith in the inquiry room.

How far this was the norm in Moody's practice at this date is not clear. But occasionally, at least, he would say, 'Anyone who wants to take Christ as their Saviour, you all come forward now, so we can pray for you. Let us bow our heads as they come.'[61] Another time he asked those who wished to acknowledge Christ as the Son of God and trust him as Saviour to rise in their places 'that we may pray for you'.[62] While something like this was a well-established practice in revivalism in the United States, it was new in Scotland. Moody, unlike C. G. Finney, did not teach that regeneration was by human decision, and he told counsellors, 'Urge immediate decision, but never tell a man he is converted. Never tell him he is saved. Let the Holy Spirit reveal that to him. You cannot see when a man receives eternal life. You can't afford to deceive anyone about this great question.'[63] Yet even without Finney's theology, the call for a public 'decision' of some kind, to be followed by attending the inquiry room, was bound to give the impression that the procedure was all part of becoming a Christian. Knowing, as he did, the history of revivalism, Kennedy was right to be dismayed that his brethren in the south appeared to make little of this danger. Bonar, as I have said, did not address the point. Another leading supporter of Moody, Dr John Cairns, expressed this private opinion on Moody's work to a friend: 'The only feature that all might not approve of has been the coming forward of persons to be prayed for. Yet I have become used to this, and everything else is so decorous that I am satisfied and even thankful.'[64]

How far the appeal for some kind of public response was a uniform part of Moody's evangelism is not clear but, given that Finney's theology and practice, with its inevitable tendency to confuse a physical act with regeneration and saving faith, had already gained some popularity, Kennedy was right to fear that the inquiry room was being used as a method to make conversion easier. Bonar said nothing to approve the practice of singling out individuals publicly though he did express disapproval of 'hasty or premature announcement of conversions' (*Old Gospel*, p. 66). Able as we are to take a longer-term view, it cannot be doubted that the endorsement that Moody gave to the public appeal was to contribute to a significant long-term deterioration in evangelism.[65] Conversion was to become identified with an instant decision made at an evangelistic meeting.

Yet when this is said, I believe the Highland leader was seriously wrong in characterizing the evangelistic movement of 1873–4 as the product of 'another gospel'. Bonar did not need to exonerate Moody on every point to repudiate that characterization: 'That extreme statements may have been made, and one-sided views of truth occasionally exhibited, I might admit' (p. 66), but 'the imperfections of infirm instruments' has ever been true. 'Can the Holy Spirit not work by poor and defective instruments?' (p. 10).[66] The number of well-attested conversions was simply too great to support Kennedy's main allegation. Whatever did, or did not happen, in the inquiry room, Bonar was convinced that the testimony of ministers, Sunday School teachers, and parents, on the changed lives of individuals personally known to them, made the idea of a mass deception impossible. There was, he observed of converts, new love for the Bible and prayer; new eagerness for the means of grace; a tender conscience and a turning from the world; family worship begun; communicants greatly increased, and so on. After Moody's work in Glasgow, Andrew Bonar believed that there were 'more than seventy under my care converted.'[67] Among the many other ministers who believed they saw new converts added to their congregations was W. S. McDougall, a personal friend of Kennedy's, and minister of the parishes of Fodderty and Contin, adjacent to Dingwall. McDougall welcomed Moody to his area in July 1874 and the evangelist preached in the open-air at Strathpeffer, at Jameston, and later twice in the Strathpeffer Pavilion. McDougall's biographer records: 'There was much impression in connection with these services, and Mr McDougall had reason to believe that it was made a time in which some members of his own family, and several others of his congregation, were led to decide for the Lord.' As these words were not written until 1897, it is hardly likely the biographer would have referred in this way to three members of McDougall's family had they not lived up to their profession. He quotes McDougall's notes, written in 1874, 'Oh, if these should prove true converts, what cause I have to praise the Lord for any little trial endured in connection with these devoted men' – 'the American evangelists'. The 'trial', his biographer adds, 'arose from some of his brethren and office-bearers who rather opposed the evangelists, because they feared that their teaching was unsound and their methods unscriptural.'[68] Happily the relationship with Kennedy was not broken for, on his death, in April 1884, McDougall preached at the funeral of his 'beloved friend and nearest brother-minister'.

There were other good friends of Kennedy's who disagreed with him over Moody. They included C. H. Spurgeon who wrote: 'We are very sorry that our esteemed friend, Dr Kennedy, issued a pamphlet severely criticizing the labours of Messrs Moody and Sankey, whom we judge to be sent of God to bless our land in an unusual degree.'[69] The biographer of the veteran preacher Dr Moody Stuart of Edinburgh, another friend of Kennedy's, said of his relationship with the two Americans: 'While his ripe Christian experience and his exact theological knowledge were eminently useful in guiding these honoured evangelists, they in turn exercised a very beneficial influence upon him. I can clearly recall that his preaching at this period became distinctly less introspective, and that while he had always preached a free salvation, the Gospel invitations and appeals which fell from his lips now became more full and free and touchingly persuasive.'[70]

From the above it should be seen that the controversy between Bonar and Kennedy has complex aspects to it. It arose in part out of a differing emphasis in the ministries of the two men. Of Bonar it was rightly said: 'As a teacher he was a follower of the Reformers rather than of the Puritans.[71] His strength lay in his insistence on the objective facts and truths of the Gospel, rather than in an analysis of human experience, or in the skill with which he laid bare the deceitfulness of the human heart. His main teaching ever was, "Look away from self to Christ".'[72] Kennedy, on the other hand, as well as being Highland in temperament, was conscious of the need for stronger emphasis on subjective experience in the region where he ministered. His fears over the entrance of an 'easy believism' in the south were not without some justification, yet in his aversion to 'revivalism' I think there was ground for Bonar's claim that he gave too little place to the phenomenon of real revival.

Kennedy had written, as noted above, of how an enduement of the Spirit had transformed the ministry of John Mac-Donald,[73] yet a theology of revival as a larger giving of the Holy Spirit does not seem to have been prominent in his thinking. Bonar believed that such a giving of the Spirit had repeatedly been seen in Scottish history, transforming preachers, and that he had seen this personally in 1839 when both William C. Burns and John Milne suddenly 'received power', and 'rose up to another level both in life and service'.[74] Bonar probably understood Moody in a similar way, though he did not believe that such experiences and times of revival rendered any man free from error or mistake. In the biography of Milne, which gives Bonar's best account of the revival years before the Disruption of 1843, he commented: 'We prayed for a revival of truth and faith. It has come. But with it there has come a revival of error and unbelief; of superstition and rationalism. We were not prepared for this. It has taken many by surprise. Ought it to have done so? Did we expect the enemy to sleep?'[75] In his perception of the negative, Dr Kennedy, it seems to me, sometimes missed the good that others saw and experienced.

Another difference in viewpoint between the two men was the encouragement Bonar had ever given to young converts to become active witnesses for Christ. Moody followed the same practice, urging that, 'In Scotland there are piety and education and money enough to evangelize the whole world.'[76] Kennedy, on the other hand, was concerned that inexperienced novices were being thrust into gospel work. This difference was a matter of judgment rather than of belief. A new generation of workers and missionaries arises out of every revival, and there is reason to think this was not absent from the work of 1873–4.

Had Dr Kennedy moderated his criticism, had he not characterized the work as 'another gospel', had he given more place to the love of God, his insight into dangers might have been more widely received and done more permanent good. This opinion is akin to Bonar's own conclusion: 'He might have hit some blots, and, with less indiscriminate condem-nation, might have at least prevented the recoil which his sharp words must produce' (*Old Gospel*, p. 72).

The greatest controversy that Bonar faced in his latter years was not over evangelism, but with a movement that threatened the whole future of the churches in Scotland. It was not about the different views of brethren who held equally to Scripture as the Word of God, such as Dr Kennedy, rather it concerned the trustworthiness of Scripture itself.

Bonar had long regarded unbelief as the greatest danger to true Christianity; that it should arise and spread as it came to do in the Free Church, very few had anticipated. How this happened will be taken up in later pages and I only mention it here to note that Bonar saw the fundamental nature of the controversy over Scripture and where, if unchecked, it would lead. Scottish critics of Moody have supposed that his work in Scotland served to bring on this greater controversy. The contrary opinion appears to me to be true. As W. Robertson Nicoll observed, a crisis was sure to come and that it did not come earlier 'was due largely to the influence of one man – the American evangelist, Mr Moody'.[77] For whatever weaknesses Moody had, there was no hesitation in his message on the authority of Scripture. It may well be, as Nicoll thought, that Moody delayed what was developing. Far from being blind to the threat on the horizon, from the 1860s Bonar's warnings on unbelief within the Church were definite, and as Moderator of the General Assembly in 1883 he repeated them again. In a Preface to his two addresses given at that Assembly, when they were published, he wrote:

> Man is now thinking out a Bible for himself; framing a religion in harmony with the development of liberal thought; constructing a worship on the principles of taste and culture; shaping a god to suit the expanding aspirations of the age. The process of evolution on all these points is so satisfactory and so well advanced that disguise is no longer needful.[78]

On the great issue of the authority of Scripture, Bonar and Kennedy were one. But it seems to us that previous controversies had done their damage. There was now an element of distrust between Bible-believing men in the

Lowlands and the Highlands that hindered a united front. The growing toleration of what became known as 'Higher Criticism' in southern Scotland drove the best men in the Highlands further away, and, as we shall see in later pages, it was not without reason that the North lost all confidence in the denomination's theological colleges. On this account, a section of the Highland Free Church seceded to become the Free Presbyterian Church in 1892, and when the Free Church majority united with the United Presbyterian Church in 1900, few evangelicals in the south supported the Highland Christians who continued in a greatly-reduced Free Church. But this is to go well beyond Bonar's lifetime.

THE CLOSING YEARS

When Bonar turned seventy years of age in 1878 he was far from looking for retirement. Forty years earlier he had quoted the question once put to Rowland Hill, 'When do you intend to stop?' To which the answer was, 'Not before we have carried all before us.' As a young man Bonar had added, 'Such is our answer too.' While he would have used different words now, the spirit was the same. The concern to be 'useful' was abiding. As late as 1883 his church news pages for November, attached to the *Free Church Monthly Record*, show he was preaching at least once every Sunday and continuing his evening service for children on the first Sunday of the month.

Bonar was less seen in the wider Christian scene in the 1880s and, while his writing diminished, it was by no means ended. Of the items published in the last decade of his life the largest was a fine biography of his son-in-law, George Theophilus Dodds, who after training at St Andrews and New College, Edinburgh, married the eldest Bonar daughter, Margaret, in 1870 and led the mission work of Bonar's congregation for 'a year and more', before joining the McAll Mission in Paris.[79] At the time of the census of 1881, the Dodds happened to be back in Edinburgh at the Bonar home, and the census figures give us a glimpse of the full house at 10 Palmerston Road. Bonar was then 72 and his wife, Jane, 59; there were the two unmarried daughters, Eliza, aged 23, Emily, 19, and the one surviving son, Horatius Ninian.[80] The Dodds family was made up of the father, aged 30, his wife, Margaret, 36, and their three sons, aged 1 to 3. In addition four female servants whose ages ranged from 15 to 19 lived in the house.

The whole family were not to be united in this way again. When the Dodds family returned to Paris that same year, the conclusion of his fruitful ministry was near, for he died there in September of the next year, 1882. His widow, now with five fatherless children, returned to her family home in Edinburgh. Bonar wrote to a friend: 'God took five children from me some years ago, and He has given me other five to bring up for Him in my old age.' His love for children was undiminished but two years later, in December 1884, Jane, the chief helper of his lifetime, was taken from him. It is to be wished we knew more of Jane Bonar. A few letters to her from her brother-in-law, Andrew Bonar, indicate that they were kindred spirits.[81] All the Bonar brothers were close-knit, and Horace did not fail that month to send the usual parcel as a New Year gift to Andrew, who replied on December 31:

Last night your parcel came. All felt that it was very kind of you to remember us amidst your trials, and when we began our family worship, the passage in course was (2 Corinthians 1:4): 'Who comforteth us in all our tribulation, that we may be able to comfort them which are in any trouble.' I thought of you as the latest instance of the kind; and then I looked a little back and saw each of us four brothers, drinking each in turn the same cup of sorrow, and made to drink at the same time of the same cup of blessing, so as to be able to say, 'our consolation aboundeth by Christ'.

A trial for Bonar in this closing period of his ministry was a division of opinion in his congregation over the use of a hymn book. We have noticed how, in the 1840s, Bonar produced a hymn book, but had not used hymns in his own congregations apart from reading them aloud, and had not agitated for their adoption. By the 1880s, however, hymns were accepted in the Free Church and a denominational hymn book had been produced. The extent to which it would be used was left to congregations. For Bonar's church at Grange, the liberty thus given became the source of division when a memorial, signed by 17 out of 28 or 29 elders, asked for a meeting of session to consider introducing the Free Church Hymnal. Before that session meeting took place on 22 November 1883, Bonar, in the congregation's monthly news pages, addressed one common argument for the exclusive use of the Metrical Psalter, namely, that the faith recovered at the Reformation had ended the use of hymns in Scotland and elsewhere. He set out evidence, as he saw it, against that idea. A few weeks later, at the session meeting, a motion that Dr Bonar use the Free Church Hymnal was carried by 14 to 7 and thereafter hymns were occasionally sung as well as psalms.

Those who believed in the exclusive use of metrical psalms objected and controversy was quickly carried outside the local congregation by a monthly magazine, *The Signal: Devoted to the Maintenance of Sound Doctrine and Pure Worship*. This periodical, prepared by Free Church people, was now in the second year of its existence and wholly opposed to any use of hymns in church worship. In the December 1883 number of *The Signal*, Bonar's article on the historical issue was condemned as a 'flood of dim medieval light', and his statement that he had held this view of Scottish history all his life brought down upon him the unjust charge that he had hitherto practised an unworthy concealment of his true position. The possibility that Bonar had not previously raised the issue at congregational level out of due regard to the peace and unity of the church was not so much as considered.

In successive months in 1884 *The Signal* sought to shred the evidence Bonar had alleged from history, and in the May issue it headed an article, 'The Story of the Grange Free Church: A Tragedy'. This reported things that had happened in the congregation since the previous November, blaming Bonar for a division in the congregation, and publishing a letter from William Martin, an elder who had resigned as Superintendent of the Sabbath School. Bonar made no reply, either to *The Signal* or in the congregation's news pages. Perhaps he wished that some of his elders of earlier years had still been with him, for even John Duncan, who died in 1870, was on record as saying, 'Hymnologies are of great use; but we should have a better selection of hymns.'[82] Certainly the tension in the congregation would have been painful to Bonar. When a sharp reflection was made on a member of his flock on one occasion he responded: 'Hush, do not speak so. You do not know how a minister feels to the members of his congregation over whom he has watched and prayed. It is like speaking against my own children.'

By 1886, with Bonar approaching seventy-eight years, it was becoming apparent that he could not long continue caring for a congregation whose communion roll had now risen to eight hundred. No one knew better than he did the labour involved. When a candidate was under discussion as an assistant and colleague, he questioned whether the man had the physical strength necessary. He doubted, he wrote to the Convener of the Congregational Committee, the candidate 'being able to undertake at once the greater part of the work, not only in preaching, but in visiting, holding classes, and caring for our large Sabbath Schools, and ultimately the whole ministerial and pastoral burden' (21 June 1886).

In 1887, a suitable colleague and successor, John M. Sloan, was appointed, and it was none too soon. Andrew Bonar had noted in his Diary the previous March, 'My brother Horace seems much stricken down in health', and in April 1887 he recorded that for the first time Horace had not been able to come and preach at his communion. Bonar's last sermon in his own pulpit, on 11 September 1887, was on the words, 'But as the days of Noah were, so shall also the coming of the Son of man be' (*Matt.* 24:37–39). The final sentence, characteristically, was 'In such an hour as ye think not the Son of Man cometh.'

At the end of the year he started a last tract for the New Year headed, 'My Funeral: Shall It Be This Year?', but it was never finished. In April 1888 a meeting to celebrate his Jubilee in the Christian ministry was held in his church, for which he prepared the 'Fragment of Speech' already mentioned, but this, too, was unfinished, and although he was present at the meeting, he was unable to deliver it. 'Here,' he wrote, 'I have spent twenty-two chequered years of my ministerial life. To recall its events, joyful and sorrowful, would be impossible. God has not disowned the work and the message. Righteousness without works to the sinner, simply on his acceptance of the divine message concerning Jesus and His sufficiency, – this has been the burden of our good news.'

Referring to this Jubilee meeting, Andrew Bonar noted on 6 April 1888: 'It was a singular gathering. Every one testified to the hymns which the Master had given him for the Church. The Lord helped me to say a few words about the very uncommon fact that *three* brothers of us had each for about fifty years preached the same Gospel.'

Another of the congregation who was there described Horatius as they saw him now for the last time, a 'bony framework, the wreck of the grand physique we all remembered, dominated by the noble head, now skull-like in its outline, with pinched and pallid face. He looked like a dying man.'

For fifteen months longer he lingered in much pain confined to his bed where, prone, he would still conduct family worship, forgetting at times his earthly hearers. If he did not repeat the words, the truths he had once expressed to a dying friend were with him:

> The darkness seemeth long, and even the light
> No respite brings with it, no soothing rest
> For this worn frame: yet in the midst of all
> Thy love revives. Father, Thy will is best.
> 'In Me ye shall have peace!'[83]

In his sufferings he was not as useless as he sometimes felt, for he would say, 'Oh, how many people are in pain! I never knew how to pray for them enough before.' After getting rest from sleep, on another occasion, he exclaimed, 'Oh, what a mercy to be free from pain! Let us say the 103rd Psalm.' Once, we are told, 'in great weakness, he asked half-despondingly, "How long is this to last?" and then, before anyone had time to reply, he answered himself in the words of Scripture, "Until the day break and the shadows flee away."' He 'fell asleep' in Jesus on 31 July 1889. On the Sunday after his funeral, his aged brother Andrew sat in the vestry of the Chalmers Memorial Church during the morning service 'listening to the prayers and singing of the congregation assembled for devotion. Once or twice,' he wrote in his *Diary,* 'I almost realized what it may be to hear the great congregation singing together as they welcome a brother arrived in glory!' And his memory went back to the 'beloved companions' who had gone before – 'M'Cheyne, John Milne, William Burns, Dr Chalmers, James Hamilton and hundreds of such.'

Considering how much Horatius Bonar valued biographies, one may wonder at his prohibition to contemporaries with regard to his own life. In part his wish was a reflection of his natural privacy. In temperament, as in other respects, he was akin to his brother Andrew who, when he gained the Dux Gold Medal in his High School days, said nothing of the fact at home until his mother elicited the information. In part, also, his embargo came from what has been called his dread of unreal words, and his shrinking from 'biographical flattery'. In unison with Andrew he would say, 'Imperfection stamped upon everything I ever undertook; omission running through my life. My place is under the shadow of the Righteous One.' But although what might have been gained from a fuller record has been lost, we know enough both to humble and uplift us. For Bonar the most important thing was the work he had been given and he wanted no other memorial:

My name, and my place, and my tomb, all forgotten,
The brief race of time well and patiently run;
So let me pass away, peacefully, silently,
Only remembered by what I have done.

Needs there the praise of the love-written record,
The name and the epitaph graved on the stone?
The things we have lived for, let them be our story,
We ourselves but remembered by what we have done.

Not myself, but the truth that in life I have spoken,
Not myself, but the seed that in life I have sown,
Shall pass on to ages, – all about me forgotten,
Save the truth I have spoken, the things I have done.[84]

[1] *Andrew A. Bonar, Diary and Life*, ed. Marjory Bonar (1893; repr. London: Banner of Truth, 1960), p. 151 (see note 27 below).

[2] 'Horatius Bonar' by the Rev. James Bonar in the *Presbyterian Record*, 1899, quoted from the CD-Rom 'Life and Works of Horatius Bonar,' Lux Publications (http://bonar.luxpub.com). I am indebted to this extensive and invaluable source of Bonar material. Almost all the Bonar titles cited below can be found on this CD. Perhaps the two best, though brief, accounts of Bonar are those of his brother-in-law, R. H. Lundie, in *Horatius Bonar: A Memorial* (London: Nisbet, 1889), and W. R. Bowman, *Horatius Bonar* (London: Religious Tract Soc., 1894). These sources are also on the CD.

[3] The Rev. George Wilson in *Memories of Dr Horatius Bonar by Relatives and Public Men* (Edinburgh: Oliphant, 1909), p. 121. It is not difficult to suppose there is a note of autobiography in Bonar's best-known hymn, 'I heard the voice of Jesus say.'

[4] Subsequently to 24 Gayfield Square and, finally, 15 York Place.

[5] *Hymns by Horatius Bonar*, H. N. Bonar (London: Froude, 1904), pp. viii, xxviii.

[6] Andrew A. Bonar, *Memoir and Remains of Robert Murray M'Cheyne* (1892; repr. London: Banner of Truth, 1966), p. 24.   [7] Ibid.

[8] Almost at the end of his life Bonar partially prepared a speech of an autobiographical nature. It was never finished but has survived in five pages as 'Fragment of a Speech' in *Bonar: A Memorial* (London: Nisbet, 1889) p. 90.

[9] *Andrew Bonar: Diary and Life*, p. 57.

[10] *Memorial*, p. 76.

[11] Quoted in F. Ferguson, *Life of Andrew Bonar* (Glasgow: Rae, n.d.), p. 202. Stalker says of Andrew Bonar that he heard him 'state that in the entire course of his ministry he had never once preached without reading his text beforehand in the Hebrew and Greek original'.

[12] *Memories of Horatius Bonar*, pp. 78, 115. W. R. Bowman said, 'Dr Bonar was the spiritual father of many ministers.'

[13] See M'Cheyne, *Memoir and Remains*, pp. 137, 145.

[14] *Report of Celebration of Ministerial Jubilee of Dr H. Bonar.*

[15] *Disruption Worthies; A Memorial of 1843* (Edinburgh: Jack, 1881), p. 44.

[16] H. Bonar, *The Life of John Milne* (London: Nisbet, 1869), pp. 82–3.

[17] Ibid., pp. 86–7.

[18] *Memories of Bonar*, p. 99.

[19] 'Fragment of a Speech,' *Memorial*, pp. 91–2.

[20] H. Bonar, *A Stranger Here: The Memorial of One to Whom to Live Was Christ and to Die Is Gain* (London: Nisbet, 1853). This volume of 411 pages is largely taken up with letters, in the editing of which Bonar removed names of correspondents, and even Madeleine Ballantyne's own name is not given. I owe the identifications I have given above to the first owner of my copy of the book who has pencilled in the blanks. In January 1846 Bonar conducted her marriage to Adam Gregor, a Free Church minister, and her death only twelve months later was in childbirth. A son survived her only for a day.

[21] Robert Lundie, who died in 1832.

[22] *Kelso Tracts* (repr. London: Nisbet, 1868), p. x.

[23] This title seems to have had constant reprints. It went, for instance, through nine printings by the American Tract Society between 1950 and 1971 and was reissued by Presbyterian and Reformed (Phillipsburg, NJ) in 1995.

[24] H. Bonar, *Truth and Error* (repr. Edinburgh: Kennedy, 1861), pp. 15–16. Bonar names C. G. Finney as largely involved in the changed views of evangelism (pp. 136, 153). I have written more fully on this subject in *Revival and Revivalism: The Making and Marring of American Evangelicalism, 1750-1858* (Edinburgh: Banner of Truth, 1994).

[25] *Memories of Bonar*, pp. 80–1.

[26] From this date comes a brief 'snapshot' of Bonar written by Dr W. C. Prime of New York: 'One dark night, in the year 1856, in the earthly city of Jerusalem, I wandered into a lighted mission-room on Mount Zion, where a small number of men and women of different countries and complexions were gathered. In the desk was a man of impressive countenance, whose voice seemed to me remarkably forcible, though low and musical. The preacher, as I later learned, was Dr Horatius Bonar. Learned and eloquent, there was a wonderful charm in what he said that night . . . My memories of him are memories of great respect and admiration.' Quoted in Bowman, *Horatius Bonar.*

[27] *Reminiscences of Andrew A. Bonar*, ed. Marjory Bonar (London: Hodder and Stoughton, 1895), p. 101. Andrew Bonar's *Diary* and the most of the *Reminiscences* were reprinted by the Banner of Truth in 1984 under the title *Andrew Bonar: Diary and Life*. There was no encouragement to sing paraphrases, let alone hymns, at Lady Glenorchy's Chapel. On one occasion a visiting minister gave out a paraphrase only to be interrupted by the words of Dr Jones, 'We sing no paraphrases here!'

[28] The best account of Bonar as a hymn writer is by his son, H. N. Bonar in *Hymns of Horatius Bonar.*

[29] Andrew Bonar recalled how John Milne of Perth brought from Perth a leaf of paper that he held up to his people and read the verses of 'I lay my sins on Jesus', adding, 'That was the way in which these hymns came to the public.' *Report of Celebration of Jubilee of Dr H. Bonar*, p. 31.

[30] The building remains today as St Catherine's Argyle Church, and holds some Bonar manuscripts which have enriched the Bonar CD published by Lux.

[31] This was the figure of the communicant members which, it should be remembered, was considerably less in that period than the actual numbers attending. None but members (or visiting members from other churches) came to the Lord's table.

[32] Marcus L. Loane, *They Were Pilgrims* (repr. Edinburgh: Banner of Truth, 2006), p. 165.

[33] An unsigned item, 'Reminiscences of Robert M'Cheyne', was surely from his hand. *Christian Treasury* (Edinburgh: Johnstone, 1859), pp. 63–4.

[34] Republished Grand Rapids: Baker Book House, 1954, as *Fifty-Two Sermons.*

[35] Beautifully republished recently (Muskegon:Dust and Ashes Publications, 2002).

[36] *Hymns by Horatius Bonar*, p. xxiii.

[37] H. N. Bonar, *Hymns of Horatius Bonar*, p. xxxv.

[38] *Memories of Horatius Bonar*, p. 55.

[39] W. R. Bowman, *Horatius Bonar.* Lux CD. The regular services of worship in Scotland at this date were still morning and afternoon. The monthly evening service for children had commenced at Kelso. There were also occasional evening services in Edinburgh for young men.

[40] 'It is manifest, I think, that it was not the design of the Head of the Church, in so far as His design is either revealed in His Word, or made known by His Providence, that all his Churches should be united under one external

organization; and consequently, that the Unity and Catholicity which are ascribed to His spiritual body, have no dependence whatever on that external unity, but rest on a far deeper ground – their vital union to Him as their living and life-giving Head, and their indissoluble relation to one another , as members of His body.' J. Buchanan, *Substance of a Speech on the Union Question* (Edinburgh: Johnstone, 1868), p. 29.

[41] Alexander Duff, *Union Not Incompatible with Free Church Principles, and Suggestions with a View to Peace and Harmony*, a Speech in the F. C. Edinburgh Presbytery (Edinburgh: MacLaren, 1870), p. 21.

[42] W. R. Moody, *The Life of Dwight L. Moody* (London: Morgan and Scott, n.d.), p. 170.

[43] Andrew Bonar, *Diary and Life*, p. 300.

[44] *Memories of Bonar*, p. 103. See also W. Robertson Nicoll, *Princes of the Church* (London: Hodder and Stoughton, 1921).

[45] These three pamphlets were republished in 1997 by the James Begg Society (Port Dinorwic, N. Wales) under the title *Reformed Evangelism*.

[46] On this point Blaikie wrote of Moody: 'He is an evangelist, not a pastor, and no one would more readily acknowledge than himself that, however fitted to rouse, his evangelistic addresses have not the fullness, breadth, and depth needful for building up all classes over a series of years in the Christian life.' *The Preachers of Scotland* (repr. Edinburgh: Banner of Truth, 2001), p. 326. Elsewhere the same writer speaks more fully of Moody who spent 'most of the winter of 1873-74' in their home. 'We came very soon to see what a genuine man Moody was – unworldly, unaffected, unambitious; and how thoroughly his whole heart was set on the evangelistic work to which he had devoted his life.' *William Garden Blaikie: An Autobiography* (London: Hodder and Stoughton, 1901), p. 331.

[47] The words are Blaikie's on Moody's beliefs, *Blaikie*, p. 334. Speaking of this point a few years earlier (1869), Dr John Duncan said to a friend: 'If Dr Bonar says a good deal about immediate believing, he gets up afterwards and prays very earnestly for the Holy Ghost. Dr B. and I could very easily work ourselves up into a controversy, but neither of us is disposed to do it.' David Brown, *Life of John Duncan* (Edinburgh: Edmonston, 1872), p. 218.

[48] Bonar, *Kelso Tracts* (repr. London: Nisbet, 1868), Tract 3, p. 5.

[49] Kennedy, *Unionism and the Union* (repr. Dingwall: Ross, 1900), p. 32. Italics belong to the original.

[50] John Kennedy, *Man's Relations to God: Traced in the Light of 'The Present Truth'* (Edinburgh: Maclaren, 1869), p. 82.

[51] Kennedy, *The Present Cast and Tendency of Religious Thought and Feeling in Scotland*, Eight Articles to the *Perthshire Courier*, 1879 (repr. Inverness: MacQuarrie, 1955), p. 27.

[52] See, for instance, Calvin on John 3:15 and his *Sermons on Deuteronomy*, p. 167. I have written more fully on this point in *The Old Evangelicalism* (Edinburgh: Banner of Truth, 2005), chapter 4.

[53] Alexander Somerville, speaking of what he observed in the Highlands in 1887, wrote: 'What seemed to me to be needful was a bright and winning gospel, and that they should be encouraged to go at once to Jesus. The tendency of a great many in the region visited may be summed up in the

word "Wait"; whereas, is it not true the distinctive voice of the gospel is "Come"?' George Smith, *A Modern Apostle: Alexander N. Somerville, 1813–1889* (London: John Murray, 1891), p. 339. Deputies of the Free Church General Assembly, sent to visit Sutherland in the 1860s, reported 'a tendency to understate the love and freeness of the Gospel call, in the rigid assertion and exposition of systematic doctrine,' and thereby imparting 'a deadening and gloomy tone to the Christian life.' Quoted in Kennedy, *Unionism and the Union* (repr., Dingwall, Ross-shire: Ross, 1900), p. 37.

[54] 'Our Last', in the final issue of the *Quarterly Journal of Prophecy*, 1873.

[55] *Man's Relations to God*, pp. 83–4.

[56] I say 'seemed' because in Kennedy's book, *The Apostle of the North*, published in 1866, he commended 'fervent declarations of God's good will to all'. Controversy can make men stricter than their pulpit ministry.

[57] Duncan, *In the Pulpit and at the Communion Table*, ed. David Brown (Edinburgh: Edmonston, 1874), p. 63.

[58] Blaikie, *Work of the Ministry* , p. 274. In a diary note, Andrew Bonar observed: 'I felt a sort of fear to dedicate myself to the Lord, to give up myself wholly to Him, till in a moment I saw that the Lord is love itself, and cannot but require me to do what is best.' *Diary and Life*, pp. 148–9.

[59] *Richard Hobson of Liverpool: The Autobiography of a Faithful Pastor* (Edinburgh: Banner of Truth, 2003), p. 190.

[60] H. Bonar, *Words Old and New* (repr., Edinburgh:Banner of Truth, 1994), p. 348.

[61] J. C. Pollock, *Moody Without Sankey* (Hodder and Stoughton, 1963), p. 115.   [62] Ibid., p. 158.

[63] *Life of Dwight L. Moody*, p. 421.

[64] Alexander R. MacEwen, *Life and Letters of John Cairns* (London: Hodder and Stoughton, 1895), p. 721.

[65] Long term effects of 'Moodyism' are well discussed by David R. Breed in 'The New Era in Evangelism,' *Princeton Theological Review*, vol. 1, pp. 227–38. 'I believe in Moody, but not in Moodyism,' Breed wrote. The problem was that so many took Moody as the leader he was not designed to be. Introduced in London as 'Reverend Mr Moody,' he replied, 'I am not Reverend Mr Moody at all. I am plain Dwight L. Moody, a Sunday-school worker.'

[66] Bonar added: 'He wrought not only by the Calvinistic Whitefield, but by the Arminian Wesley. We are not, surely, reckoned to be further gone in "error", or more peculiar in practice, or more unguarded in statement, than the preachers of Methodism.' Years earlier he had heard M'Cheyne say, 'The Lord can show us how to catch fish with a broken net.'

[67] *Diary and Life*, p. 296.

[68] John S. McPhail, *Memorial Sermons of W. S. McDougall*, with a Sketch of His Life (Edinburgh: Macleod, 1897), p. 23.

[69] C. H. Spurgeon, *The Sword and the Trowel*, 1875, p. 142. See also p. 190, and in the volume for 1876, pp. 1, 84–7. For his later reflection on Moody's mission in London, see his letter of 1 April 1882, in *Letters of Charles Haddon Spurgeon* (Edinburgh: Banner of Truth, 1992), p. 155. Spurgeon did not agree with everything to do with the Moody missions,

and saw the danger of turning inquiry rooms into a method to gain conversions. 'I would warn Churches against *trusting* in spasmodic effort,' he wrote in 1882, 'but at the same time against refusing such special help as the Lord puts in their way. There is a medium.' I have written of this in *The Forgotten Spurgeon* (London: Banner of Truth, 1966), pp. 176–82. On 26 February 1886, Spurgeon wrote to Mrs Kennedy of her late husband, 'His death was a loss to the Highlands greater than could have befallen by the death of any other hundred men.' Alexander Auld, *Life of John Kennedy* (London: Nelson, 1887).

[70] K. Moody Stuart, *Alexander Moody Stuart: A Memoir* (London: Hodder and Stoughton, 1899), p. 140. That Moody Stuart also had some words of warning is clear from his address on 'Counsels on Conducting Revivals', given in 1875 when he was Moderator of the Free Church of Scotland.

[71] This should not be misunderstood. He was well read in the Puritans and often quoted them. When new teaching on sanctification was launched by Pearsall Smith and others, in the 1870s, Bonar was among the first to oppose it from the Puritan standpoint. See his long letter letter to G. T. Fox published in *Plain Words* (Dublin: Bible and Colportage Soc., 1875), pp. 219–22.

[72] W. R. Bowman, *Horatius Bonar.*

[73] See above, chapter 4.

[74] Bonar, *Life of Milne*, pp. 105–6.

[75] Ibid., pp. 65-6.

[76] W. R. Moody, *Life of Moody*, p. 176.

[77] In Henry Drummond, *The Ideal Life and Other Unpublished Addresses* (London: Hodder and Stoughton, 1897), p. 8.

[78] Bonar, *Our Ministry: How It Touches the Questions of the Age* (Edinburgh: MacNiven & Wallace, 1883), p. vi.

[79] *The Life and Work of the Rev. G. Theophilus Dodds, Missionary* (London: Nisbet, 1884). It was more than admiration for his son-in-law which led Bonar to take on this extended biography: it gave him the opportunity to show the effect of devotion to Scripture as contrasted with the effect of unbelief. For Dodds, he wrote, 'Unsettlement as to that Book which professed to reveal the mind of God, and on which the security of his eternal future was involved, could not be contemplated without dismay' (Ibid., p. 114).

[80] Eliza never married and died at the age of 82 in 1941. Emily was to marry the Rev. D. C. MacNicol, author of *Robert Bruce, Minister of the Kirk of Edinburgh,* republished by Banner of Truth in 1961. Horatius Ninian became minister at Saltoun, 1890–1914, and then a Home Mission Worker in Edinburgh until his death in 1930.

[81] See *Reminiscences of Andrew Bonar*, pp. 211, 217.

[82] Duncan, *Colloquia Peripatetica*, ed. W. Knight (Edinburgh: Oliphant, 1907), p. 60. I have argued the case against an exclusive use of Metrical Psalms in a booklet, *Should the Psalter Be the Only Hymnal of the Church?* (Edinburgh: Banner of Truth, 2001).

[83] Part of a poem written in 1880 for his friend James Watson, an executive of James Nisbet the publishers.

[84] From 'The Everlasting Memorial' in Bonar, *Hymns of Faith and Hope* (London: Nisbet, 1872), pp. 46–7.

PART TWO

MISSIONARY

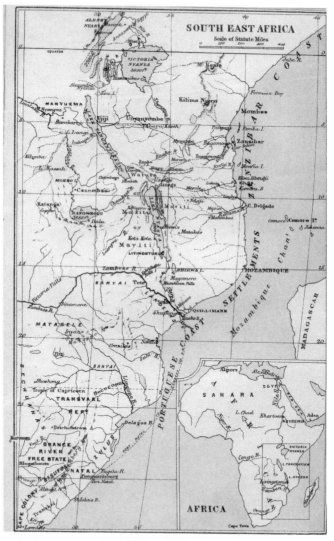

South-East Africa, 1880

6

The Missionary Spirit
and the New Hebrides

Dundee, from Broughty Ferry

'Oh, the dear homeland, shall I really be there and worship in its churches again! How I long for a wee look at a winter landscape, to feel the cold wind, and see the frost in the cart-ruts, to hear the ring of shoes on the hard frozen ground, to see the glare of the shops, and the hurrying scurrying crowd, to take a back seat in a church, and hear without a care of my own the congregations singing, and hear how they preach and pray and rest their souls in the hush and solemnity.'

MARY SLESSOR, WRITING FROM CALABAR, WEST AFRICA, 1907.

'The missionary of Jesus will have cause to reproach himself that he served not his Lord more fully, but not that he was a missionary. O Calvary, Calvary, when I view the blood of Jesus streaming down thy sides, I am amazed at my coldness of affection towards the Lord, and of my slothful performance of the duties which the authority of God, but shall I say, which the love of Jesus more strongly imposes upon me. Yes, O Father, Thy love in sending Jesus, and O my Saviour, Thy love in giving Thyself for me, and Thine, O Holy Spirit, in applying the salvation of Jesus to my guilty conscience, unitedly overcome me, and constrain me to live not to myself but to Thee.'

ROBERT MORRISON, PIONEER TRANSLATOR OF THE BIBLE INTO CHINESE.

Jessie Inglis

For his Moderator's Address at the Free Church of Scotland General Assembly at Edinburgh in 1886, Alexander Somerville, spoke on 'Evangelization for the World'. When he had been born in the year 1813 the missionary age was only dawning; seventy years later numbers of the best of Scotland's sons and daughters were taking the gospel to the far corners of the earth. Somerville, himself a missionary, reminded the Assembly that Lake Nyasa, although 350 miles long, was so small 'as almost required to be searched for, as we scan the map of Africa'. The land surface of diminutive Scotland, he continued, could all be packed within the limits of that one African lake: 'Yet see what God has already done by Scotland. Scotland, small as she is, has already told on the destinies of the world.'[1]

If it is true that 'the missionary movement is arguably the single most important event in the history of Western Christianity',[2] then Scotland certainly played no small part in that movement. Referring to the rise of the missionary spirit in that land, a journalist could write in the 1840s, 'The great movement in Scotland is a new thing under the sun. It is little less than the breaking up and recasting of a nation. It is developing events which mere politicians cannot understand.'[3]

Six years before Somerville's address, George Smith, the Secretary of the Foreign Missions of the Free Church, had written on the mission fields of his denomination in a book of seventy-eight pages, published in 1880.[4] It showed a division of the work into four main fields: India, Africa, Syria and Melanesia (in the southern Pacific). Within these fields there were sub-divisions, as in India where there were thirty-one mission stations and twenty-four missionaries. But the Free Church was far from being the only source of Scottish missionaries at this date. The Church of Scotland had its own operations (reorganized after the Disruption of 1843), and the Secession Churches (which mostly became the United Presbyterian Church), provided a number of the first men to enter the foreign fields.

Yet if the Presbyterians were prominent, they were not alone in sharing the missionary awakening.[5] Leaders of Congregationalist persuasion played a vital part. They included: David Bogue, who, at his academy at Gosport, trained 115 for missionary service (including fifty for India); John Campbell, John Philip, Robert Moffat and David Livingstone, all linked with Africa.[6] Among those of Baptist convictions, the brothers Robert and James Haldane, already mentioned in these pages, were among the first to raise missionary concern. Robert Haldane inspired many, including William Wilberforce. It is said that when Haldane visited Wilberforce to lay before him his vision for a mission in Bengal, the latter was suffering so badly from gout, with his feet wrapped in flannel, that he could not rise to greet him. But Haldane had not spoken long before Wilberforce forgot all else and began to walk about the room! The Haldanes' witness ensured that Scottish Baptists would not be missing in the world-wide enterprise. In 1926 there were 180 Scottish Baptists in various missionary agencies.

The Scottish Brethren also gave some of their best to the mission fields of the world, men such as F. S. Arnot and Dan Crawford who were pioneers in Africa. Then there were Scots whose work overseas was connected with the Church of England, such men as Claudius Buchanan in India, Temple Gairdner of Cairo, and Alexander Mackay of Uganda.

Once men went overseas the distance from home commonly lessened denominational differences. In the words of George Smith, 'A Christ-like charity has been the unbroken law of the army of the Evangel, in front of the common enemy.'[7] While this was not invariably the case, Smith himself gave the right example. His full-length biographies of such Presbyterians as John Wilson (1875), Alexander Duff (1889) and Alexander Somerville (1890), were matched by his works on the Baptist, William Carey (1885), and the Anglican, Henry Martyn (1892). In admiration of Carey, Smith's home at Merchiston in Edinburgh was named 'Serampore'.[8]

If George Smith was the most prolific of missionary writers, he was preceded and followed by a multitude of other authors, and it would be a very large library that could house all the literature that has been produced on Scottish missions and missionaries. Sometimes the names of individual pioneers stand out because they were among the earliest to enter certain regions: John Paterson and Ebenezer Henderson went to Denmark and Russia; David Cargill to Fiji; Robert Kalley to Brazil; James Gilmour to Mongolia; James Chalmers to parts of New Guinea. On occasion the honour of being unmistakeably the first belonged to Scots: Robert Morrison was the first translator of Scripture into Chinese; John Ross the first translator into Korean; William C. Burns was the first to reach Nieu-chwang on the border of Manchuria, and David Livingstone the first to the Victoria Falls in the heart of Africa. Many of these men, along with hundreds more, are forgotten today but, as was once said, there will be a resurrection of reputations as well as of bodies.

THE ORIGIN OF THE MISSIONARY SPIRIT

The question deserves comment why, within a hundred years, such a small country, with a small population, produced so many missionaries. The explanation cannot simply be that the world had opened for travel in a new way. That was true, yet history shows that openness of itself does not produce evangelization. A pointer to the true explanation lies in the fact that the missionary era began in Scotland before any denomination took official action. Not until 1824 was there any commitment by the General Assembly of the Church of Scotland; yet more than a quarter of a century before that date individuals had formed the Glasgow and the Edinburgh (later Scottish) Missionary Societies in 1796, and such was the rise of concern at the 'grass-roots' level that between that date and 1825, no fewer than sixty-one local mission societies sprang up in Scotland, including one in each of the four universities. Movements of the Spirit of God are generally to be recognized by their spontaneity and this was to be seen in Scotland in the early nineteenth century. In the words of one observer: 'In the end of the last [i.e. 18th] century and the beginning of this, when the missionary spirit awoke, missions were undertaken and carried on by societies, not Churches; but, as the missionary spirit increased and spread, the Churches were aroused to a sense of their duties and responsibilities, and missions began to be undertaken by Churches.'[9]

The first of these non-denominational societies, in time and importance, was actually established in London in 1795, subsequently to be known as the London Missionary Society (LMS), but one of the prime movers was a Scot (David Bogue) and from the outset there was a large Scots presence both among the missionaries who went out and among the Directors. 'Almost half the original committee were Scots.'[10]

This widespread new concern can only be explained in terms of the increased hold of the gospel on the Scottish population.

In the Lowlands, the Secession churches, originating from evangelical recovery in the mid-eighteenth century, had spread their influence and, as already said, provided a number of the first Scots missionaries. Before the end of the eighteenth century it is notable how many ministers of the Secession, who had excluded Whitefield in 1742, were breathing his same spirit. Without such a change the age of interdenominational co-operation would never have come. The Evangelical Revival had brought a new standpoint. Rowland Hill said of Whitefield:

> It pleased God to give him a most enlarged mind, and liberated him from all the wretched shackles of education. He knew no party; his glory was to preach the gospel to every creature. Bigotry his soul abhorred; and, like a second Samson, he had so made her main pillars to totter, that we may rejoice that she trembles to the very foundation.[11]

This new catholicity was related to the recovery of the truth of God's love to all men. The special interest in the missionary movement early shown by Secession churches came in no small degree from the tradition that Thomas Boston and others had revived early in the eighteenth century. The gospel is not a message simply intended for the elect: it is an offer of salvation, flowing from divine love, for all men. Those at the forefront of the new missionary endeavour commonly had no doubt about this truth. As Henry Martyn could preach beside the Ganges, 'God loved the Hindoos',[12] so could the Scottish evangelicals take the same good news to other corners of the earth.

The recovery of the gospel in parts of the Church of Scotland, after 1800, inspired the same missionary spirit, and this was no less evident in the North where the revival lay behind the formation of the Highland Missionary Society. Nominal Christians, who think little of their own souls, are not going to be concerned for others, least of all for people whom they never saw. The indifference to foreign needs which affected many in the eighteenth century was the direct result of unbelief; and the new zeal to take the gospel to the world was born out of a new experience of its power. The pattern of the book of Acts was thus repeated: the indwelling of the Holy Spirit leads to compassion and to outreach. Before this time, as John Campbell noted, professing Christians had been 'busy repairing and adding to their walls of separation, and now and then throwing *squibs* at each other from their battlements.'[13] Now the true spirit of Christianity appeared at the popular level:

> Friends, parents, neighbours first it will embrace
> Our country next, and next the human race.

The gospel does affect homes first. In Scotland it led to a type of home life and family religion fitted to produce young men and women whose great interest was the service of Christ. There can be little more moving in missionary literature than the picture which John G. Paton gives us of the piety of his cottage home near Dumfries. His autobiography provides an unforgettable account of the prayerfulness of his father, who, as John finally left home for Glasgow, so lovingly watched him till he was out of sight up the road. Paton's biographers write:

> The Lowland cotter's lad cherished and guarded in his heart the spell of his father's habit of communion with God, and the vision of his mother's absorbed passion to win her children to fear and love the Most High. These were his main equipment in life. No science can produce them; no money can purchase them.[14]

One of the most remembered sounds of Paton's childhood was of his father's voice, at family worship, as 'he poured out his whole soul with tears for the conversion of the Heathen world to the service of Jesus'. The thatched cottage of the Patons was only one of many such nurseries. Most of the

Scottish missionaries came from homes and backgrounds where simple living, hard work, ready sacrifice and earnest devotion were the everyday experiences of youth. A few, it should be added, came from less humble backgrounds; they belong with the exceptions noted by Paul in 1 Corinthians 1:26. Robert Moffat, in the heart of Africa in 1854, wrote in his Journal: 'Was much interested in reading a review of the lives of the Haldanes. What nobles they were in the kingdom of Christ! How few have been so highly favoured, and all brought about by, or through the instrumentality of a praying mother!'[15] The Hon. Ion Keith-Falconer, the son of the Earl of Kintore, was reared by parents of the same spirit. He became an Arabic scholar/missionary, before he died in South Arabia in 1887 at the age of twenty-nine. What is certain is that a home like that of Eli, the high priest, will rarely produce a missionary.

FAITH IN DIVINE REVELATION

The origins of the new spirit involved something more than a recovery of compassion and the nurture of godly homes. The driving impulse was *faith* in Scripture as the Word of God, and in the teaching it contains. 'I *believed*, and therefore have I spoken', has to be where the missionary spirit begins. It is bound up with being 'not ashamed of the gospel of Christ', and the confidence that it has power that depends on no man for its accomplishment.

When metal gates, to the memory of John G. Paton, were erected at the peaceful cemetery at Torthorwald, Dumfriesshire, they bore the text: 'Other sheep I have which are not of this fold; them also I must bring' (*John* 10:16). These words of Christ are at the heart of the missionary movement. Peter Cameron Scott, and his brother John, went as missionaries to the Congo from Glasgow in 1890. Very soon John died and Peter, alone in the jungle, with his own health broken, gave up in discouragement. He returned to Britain where, in London, he visited the grave of David Livingstone in Westminster Abbey. There he read the same words as are on the gates at Torthorwald: 'Other sheep I have which are not of this fold: them also I must bring.' The promise was enough for him to spend the remainder of his life in Africa.

Christ is *the* 'missionary'. Without him there would be no others. It is his sheep who are to be gathered, and for whose salvation he is responsible. That his voice should be heard is the reason he sends messengers (*Rom.* 10:14–15); he is both the agent and the pattern for all who carry the message. In the words of John MacDonald, Jr., explaining to his London congregation the reason for his departure to India, 'The standard of that interest which we ought to take in the matter of *publishing* the Gospel of salvation, is surely to be found in the interest the Son of God took in *working* out that salvation.'[16] 'What is the object of the missionary enterprise on which the Church of Scotland has embarked?', asked Alexander Duff, and he answered:

> It is, to announce to those millions, who are still enslaved in sin and exposed to eternal misery, that, to restore and save them, the Son of God himself came down from heaven, to proclaim liberty to captives, and shed his precious blood for their ransom. It is, to beseech them to renounce their numberless penances, and soul-deceiving works of merit, and flee for refuge to the atoning sacrifice and justifying righteousness of the divine Redeemer.[17]

The proof that faith in Scripture and its message is supreme in the motivation of mission can be seen in what happens when that faith is absent. When faith was undermined in so many of the Scottish churches towards the end of the nineteenth century a great era of Scottish missionary endeavour slowly came to a close. The World's Missionary Conference in Edinburgh in 1910 was supposed to be a high point in the evangelization of the world, but it was not so. The veteran missionary, Mary Slessor, watching events at home from afar in Calabar in West Africa, was disappointed that so little practical result followed that much-publicized occasion. Yet she was not altogether surprised:

> After all, it is not committees and organizations from without that are to bring the revival, and to send the Gospel to the heathen at home and abroad, but the living Spirit of God working from within the heart . . . Surely there is something very far wrong with our Church, the largest in Scotland. Where are the men? Are there no heroes in the making among us? No hearts beating high with the enthusiasm of the Gospel? Men smile nowadays at the old-fashioned idea of sin and hell and broken law and a perishing world, but these made men, men of purpose, of power and achievement, and self-denying devotion to the highest ideals earth has known.[18]

What had happened in Scotland was parallel with what had happened in Germany a century earlier. Germany had led the world in the zeal shown in the eighteenth century by the Danish-Halle Mission. That Mission had sent out some sixty missionaries, supported by about 15,000 people at home, and the work continued in strength, as Dr Warneck wrote, 'until in the last quarter of the century and afterwards rationalism at home dug up its roots. Only when the universities, having fallen completely under the sway of this withering movement, ceased to furnish theologians, was the first trial made in 1803 of a missionary who had not been a university student.'[19] The same thing happened in the Scottish universities. In the 1820s and 30s it was enthusiasm for foreign mission that excited student minds; sixty years later, as already noted in these pages, German 'scholarship' replaced the enthusiasm of the earlier generation.

In 1870 the veteran Free Church missionary in Bombay, John Wilson, pointed the young W. Robertson Smith to India as a field needing his great linguistic gifts.[20] Instead Robertson Smith, as described in a later chapter, became a leader in the Higher-Critical approach to the Bible.[21] George Adam Smith, born in India in 1856, might have followed his missionary-minded father, George Smith, but, as Professor of Old Testament in the Free and then the United Free Church College in Glasgow, he also undermined faith in the Word of God. The 'faith', as he claimed, is now left 'clear, practical and without mystery'. A different description would be a truer description of what his students learned. On the basis of such teaching there would be no need for missionaries.

In the Free Church of Scotland, as in others, unbelief went far to kill missionary enterprise. 'Send us men "full of faith and of the Holy Spirit"', the mission fields asked, but in the course of time there was little of the missionary spirit left to respond.[22]

THE NEW HEBRIDES, AN ILLUSTRATION OF THE MISSIONARY SPIRIT

It was the voyages of Captain James Cook (son of a Scottish father) that brought the Pacific to the attention of Britain. Three times Cook reached Tahiti, near the southern centre of that vast ocean, and it was to Tahiti that the LMS sent her first eighteen missionaries in 1796. One of the first two secretaries of the LMS was the Rev. John Love of Glasgow, at that date serving a London church. It was Love's work, *Addresses to the People of Otaheiti* [Tahiti], *Designed to Assist the Labour of Missionaries,* that the first missionaries took with them. In its printed form, a book of more than a hundred pages, it was written as a guide to how the Christian message should be stated. After seventeen pages on the character of God and on fallen man, to whom God at the dawn of history promised a Saviour, Love said:

Men and women of Tahiti, you are our brethren and sisters, our flesh and blood; and we bring you the joyful news of that man whom Jehovah promised to send into the world. That wonderful Man has come into those parts of the world which are far off from Tahiti. He was the image of God. He was bright and glorious like the sun. When he walked up and down in the world, it was as if the sun had come down from the skies to earth, not to scorch it and burn it but, shrouded in clouds, to cherish and delight in it. But you were very far off, and many seas were between him and you, and you could not see him. When he spake and smiled, it was the voice of God, and the sweet face of Jehovah; when he rebuked wicked men and frowned upon them, they were struck with terror, they felt the anger of God.[23]

Love went on to deal with the law of God, the history of Israel, leading to the cross of Christ and the revelation of all this given in Scripture:

You ask us, how we know that this book is Jehovah's book? We ask you, how do you know that the sun now shines in the heavens? How do you know that the fruit of these trees is pleasant, and wholesome and suited to strengthen and to nourish you? You wonder that we should ask such questions, because the matter is plain. It is equally plain to us that this writing is Divine.[24]

This first attempt to establish a foothold in the Pacific was a failure yet a salutary one. The people of Tahiti – two hundred and eight days sailing from England – were not irreligious and simply awaiting further instruction. They already had beliefs, demonically strong, all well-suited to the kind of life they followed. The words of one missionary were true of conditions throughout the south Pacific:

Their deities, like themselves, were all selfish and malignant; they breathed no spirit of benevolence, and the rewards and punishments of the future state were connected more with ritual observance than with moral character. Their religion contained no principle that could lead to a holy life; they certainly thought that their gods were like themselves, and that they approved their sins. It would have been morally impossible on Aneityum for any man to have conceived of such a character, morally and religiously, as that of Jesus Christ.[25]

Faced with conditions indescribably dark, all remaining missionaries were withdrawn from Tahiti in 1809, and an end to mission in the South Seas was proposed. Individuals of unusual ability and spiritual strength would be needed if it were to continue, and just such a man now came forward in the person of John Williams.

Converted at Whitefield's Tabernacle in 1814, he was ready to sail under the LMS three years later. Beginning near Tahiti, he worked steadily westwards, through Raratonga and Samoa, where he saw churches formed. After nearly eighteen years Williams returned to Britain, but he could not remain. His mind was set on reaching the New Hebrides, a group of some thirty inhabited islands scattered over four hundred miles of ocean in the area known as Melanesia.[26] This hope was fulfilled simultaneously with his death, for when he first landed at Dillon's Bay, Eromanga, he was killed by the natives of that island. A monument erected by the Christians in Samoa read:

> Sacred to the memory of the Rev. John Williams, father of the Samoan and other missions, aged 43 years and 5 months, who was killed by the cruel natives of Eromanga, on the 20th November 1839, while endeavouring to plant the Gospel of Peace on its shores.

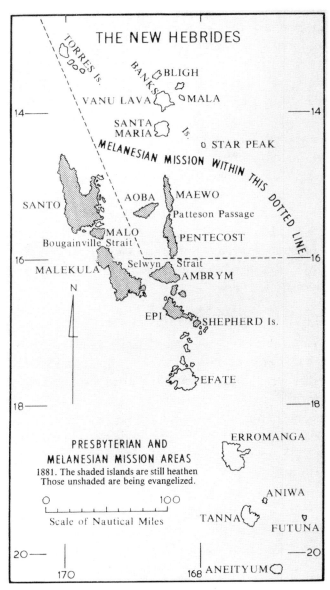

THE NEW HEBRIDES

TORRES IS.

BANKS IS.

BLIGH

VANU LAVA   MALA

14

SANTA
MARIA   o STAR PEAK

MELANESIAN MISSION WITHIN THIS DOTTED LINE

SANTO   AOBA   MAEWO

Patteson Passage

MALO
Bougainville Strait   PENTECOST

16

MALEKULA   Selwyn Strait
                          AMBRYM

N

EPI   SHEPHERD Is.

EFATE

18

PRESBYTERIAN AND
MELANESIAN MISSION AREAS
1881. The shaded islands are still heathen
Those unshaded are being evangelized.

ERROMANGA

0   100

Scale of Nautical Miles

ANIWA

TANNA
                          FUTUNA

20

170   168 ANEITYUM

THE NEW HEBRIDES IN 1881

The conclusion which the native Samoan Christians drew from this sorrow was that the people of the New Hebrides were in great need of help, and in the years that followed about one hundred volunteered to go as 'teachers'. Despite the murder of some of them, and the early death of others from diseases to which they had no resistance, these Polynesian Christians were steadfast as the first missionaries to the New Hebrides. At the same time, in far-off Scotland, Williams' mission was taken up by others. Speaking of Williams' time in Britain, his biographer says: 'Of all the missionary journeys which Mr Williams undertook, none awakened greater anxiety, or produced a better influence than that to Scotland.'[27] By 1842, the first Scots, George Turner and Henry Nisbet, arrived in the New Hebrides and spent seven months on the cannibal island of Tanna. Forced to retreat to Samoa, Turner's leadership went into a Teachers' Training Institution for the preparation of missionary teachers.

ANEITYUM – 'THE ANTIOCH OF THE PACIFIC'

Four Samoan missionary-teachers, Tavita, Fotauyasi, and their wives, had been left on the island of Aneityum in 1841, and in 1848 they were joined by the first white missionaries to settle permanently in the New Hebrides. Their leader was John Geddie, born in Banff, Scotland, where his father was a watch and clock maker. 'Both his father and mother were God-fearing people, and strongly imbued with a missionary spirit.'[28] The family subsequently emigrated to Canada where they were members of the Presbyterian Church of Nova Scotia. With Geddie on his arrival at Aneityum were his wife and two other missionary couples. After a year, only the Geddies were left of this party when the others departed, and he wrote in his journal, 'It was a sad prospect to us to be left alone on a heathen island, 1500 miles from our nearest missionary brethren, and at the very time when clouds thicken around us which will sooner or later burst, and the result will be the destruction of the mission or the triumph of the gospel.'[29]

The danger on Aneityum was not exaggerated. In every sense the people were naked before the powers of darkness. Evil spirits known as *natmasses*, which they imagined dwelt in the stones they worshipped, ruled their lives. Human life was valued no more highly than the life of a pig; abortion was commonplace; men, in fear of others, all carried weapons; women were degraded and often strangled on the death of their husbands. At death, the body, unless that of a chief, was simply thrown into the sea, while that of an enemy would be eaten. Geddie noted: 'Satan will not give up his dominion over this people without a struggle; he never did that either in the case of individuals or nations . . . Every crime seems to be perpetrated among the people without scruple or remorse. The Apostle's dark description of heathen character in Rom. 1:23–32, will apply to these islanders in all its fullness.'[30]

During 1850 a British ship visited Aneityum with a minister on board looking for a field of labour that might be supported by the Reformed Presbyterian Church of Scotland. This was John Inglis. 'I had previously written to him,' wrote Geddie, 'and strongly urged him to unite with us in the New Hebrides Mission.' No decision was reached but two years later when Inglis unexpectedly returned to stay, Geddie was overjoyed: 'We feel thankful to God that he has sent this excellent missionary and his wife.'

The wife of John Inglis warrants more than a passing reference. Jessie M'Clymont, of Kirkcudbrightshire, was typical of many of the Scots wives of the first missionary generation. Her husband's account of her after her death brings her photograph to life. 'Nothing was so distasteful to her,' he wrote, 'as a Christless sermon, or one in which the atonement was ignored. Her religion was of the strong Puritanical type; there was nothing feeble or sentimental about it . . . Her religion made her earnest, truthful, devout, practical. She was hopeful, cheerful, joyful.' Mrs Inglis was 'always a Bible student' and an eager reader of Christian books. On one occasion she asked a lady friend what books she was reading and received the answer: 'Books! I read no books; the housework and the baby occupy all my time.' To this Jessie Inglis replied in astonishment, 'Read no books! and what do you think you will become? Your husband is a great reader; he is reading daily; and if you read none, will you be any companion to him ten years hence? No, do what you like, but you must read.' John Inglis lists some of the authors with which his wife was familiar; they included Thomas Chalmers, William Cunningham and Robert Moffat. When, in later years, they were on a visit to their homeland, at the time when Robertson Smith's Higher Criticism 'was moving ecclesiastical society in Scotland to its lowest depths', she assessed the whole controversy for herself, reading both sides, and remained 'with increased satisfaction' in her conviction of the plenary inspiration of the Bible.[31]

The Inglises were only the first of a number of men and women from their denomination to reach the New Hebrides. In the words of J. Graham Miller, the modern Christian historian of Vanuatu (formerly New Hebrides): 'The Reformed Presbyterian church of about forty small Scottish congregations poured its life into the New Hebrides Mission.'[32] The first of the reinforcements from this source after Inglis, were John and Mary Paton, and Joseph Copeland in 1858. Altogether this denomination sent eleven missionaries to New Zealand and the New Hebrides before it merged with the Free Church of Scotland in 1876. The first man to be sent by the Free Church was Peter Milne who was to serve for fifty-five years before his death in 1924 at the age of ninety. These men, together with colleagues, first from Canada, then from New Zealand and Australia, often at great personal cost, lived to see the

transformation of the islands they came to serve. Five
Presbyterian denominations were co-operating harmoniously
in the Mission by 1880.

What kind of struggle this was became known to the world
by the deputation work, and then the autobiography, of John
G. Paton. Forced to retreat after four years on Tanna, Paton
saw much success on Aniwa (1866–81). The testimony of
Namuri, which Paton records, was by no means untypical:

> Misi, I am not afraid to die. I love the things of God, and
> so I do not fear. Long ago I did much bad conduct; I was
> very wicked. But since Misi Gete [Geddie] taught me what
> was right and wrong, I have hated evil and loved good. I
> lean on Jesus.[33]

The words were spoken as Namuri was dying from club
wounds received on the island of Tanna. The reason why he
was on that island rather than on his native Aneityum, and
with Paton rather than with Geddie, is the key to understanding
how the gospel spread. During the 1850s, Aneityum had
become like a second Antioch where 'a great number believed
and turned to the Lord' (*Acts* 11:21). A first church had been
formed there in May 1852, with the baptism of thirteen natives.
A few months later Geddie wrote: 'This island will, I trust in
due time furnish many teachers for the dark islands around. It
is delightful to see even now a missionary spirit in embryo.'[34]
By 1860 there were 500 attending public worship, and Geddie
had 179 church members in his district. Inglis, responsible for
another district, had completed a translation of the New
Testament. Before this date Geddie's hope that the island –
like Antioch – would become a missionary base was being
fulfilled. As natives from Samoa and Raratonga had first reached
the New Hebrides, so the converts of Aneityum became the
evangelists to other islands. Thus when Paton landed on Tanna
in 1858 he had the help of twelve native Christians from

Aneityum, including Namuri. Of these helpers Paton wrote: 'These teachers had all been Cannibals once; yet, with one exception, they proved themselves to the best of my judgment to be a band of faithful and devoted followers of Christ. Nothing known to men under heaven could have produced their new character and disposition, except only the grace of God in Christ Jesus.'[35] Namuri was not alone among them in giving his life.

Not at the time, but in after years, Paton was to be revered on Tanna. He was to become the best-known of the New Hebridean missionaries, and Patons were to serve that field through four generations; yet their work was, in a sense, all due to the success first given to Geddie and Inglis on Aneityum. From the converts of that one island came the witnesses who went and stood where Europeans might never have stood alone. It is estimated that there were no less than 200 missionaries from Aneityum, including wives, by the year 1879.[36] Yet this did not strip the home base of natives prepared to lead in Christian work. Inglis speaks of having forty such men in his district on Aneityum.

OBSERVATIONS

1. A missionary spirit appears first in the lives of individual men and women, and its strength will ever be found to correspond with their spiritual stature. This has been true in every part of the world and it stands out in the men and women who went from the northern hemisphere to the south Pacific. The common features were single-mindedness, determination, and the conviction that 'every Christian is a soldier'. They were of the same spirit as W. C. Burns in China who told disciples, 'We must not study comfort: they that go to the front of the battle get the blessing.'[37] For the Scots, this mindset no doubt had some connection with nationality, belonging, as it is said they did, to a race 'free from everything like sentimentalism,

and distinguished rather by zealous decision and thorough activity'. Yet flesh and blood alone of any race would have been useless before what was faced in the South Seas. Nor were these men free from faults, as John Inglis points out in his tribute to his friend John Geddie. It was the grace of God that made them what they were, and pre-eminently that large measure of the selfless love that comes from Christ. For Geddie and Inglis love is the chief motivation for Christian life and service: they sought to live in the spirit of 1 John 3:16: 'Hereby perceive we the love of God, because he laid down his life for us; and we ought to lay down our lives for the brethren.'[38]

This same spirit was engendered in those who became Christians; hence it was that Inglis could write, 'On Aneityum every convert, as far as it was practicable, was made a missionary.'[39] And it was the effect of the lives of these former heathens that was so telling on others. When a large canoe of heathen natives stopped at Aneityum on one occasion, the visitors were astonished at what they heard and what they saw: a religion that made people happy was entirely new to them. Speaking of the character of the Aneityumese missionaries, Graham Miller writes:

> These were men and women of influence, the best the church on Aneityum could provide. They left all. The love of Christ constrained them . . . love knew no bounds, kept no accounts, suffered and was kind, did not behave itself unseemly, bore all things. And when love's last sacrifice was asked, it was gladly given.

Archibald Alexander was not thinking of the New Hebrides, but he exactly summarized the point we are seeking to make when he wrote: 'In vain do we seek to awaken in our churches zeal for missions as a separate thing. To be genuine, it must flow from love to Christ. It is when a sense of personal communion with the Son of God is highest, that we shall be most fit for missionary work, either to go ourselves or to stir up others.'[41]

2. A missionary spirit is inspired by biblical truth. While the first missionaries to the New Hebrides were practical men, they believed intensely in the necessity of the theology of the Bible that had been recovered in Scotland at the Reformation and subsequently revived. They read Christian doctrine, taught it, and published it as soon as they could.[42] They believed in the Fall of man, and knew that the new birth was the work of God and not of man. Conversion is the *result* of regeneration. As John Paton wrote, 'Regeneration is the sole work of the Holy Spirit in the human heart and soul.'[43] 'They felt,' says Graham Miller, 'that they were helpless unless the Spirit of God breathed upon the dry bones and caused them to live. Those pioneers toiled as few servants of God have done. But they rested all their hope of spiritual success upon the sovereign power and grace of God.'

The balance of the teaching of the first missionaries is noteworthy. They kept back nothing of the seriousness of sin, which they defined in the light of the character of God; they insisted on the Ten Commandments as a standard required of all men;[44] at the same time, the love of God, and the happiness of the Christian life, were their prominent themes. Instruction in gospel-believing was the dynamic for Christian living. When John Geddie died in 1872, his colleague, John Inglis described the tenor of his teaching on Aneityum in these words:

He gave great prominence in all his ministrations to the primary, vital truths of the gospel – sin and grace; the fall of man; the love of God; the atonement of Christ; the work of the Spirit; the necessity of a new heart and a holy life. He exhibited Christianity, not as a code of restrictions, but as a religion of privileges, breathing nothing but blessings. He gave prominence to the fact that Christ came not to destroy men's lives but to save them.[45]

Speaking of his black helpers, Inglis wrote:

If salvation were of works, none of these would be eligible for heaven; but as it is of grace, the irresistible efficacy of this Divine power can accomplish anything; it can transmute the chief of sinners into the most eminent of saints, change the most ferocious of murderers to be the mildest and meekest of martyrs, and render the wildest of savages to be the gentlest of human kind.[46]

John Paton summarized all we have been seeking to say in the words,

Did the church of God but fully realise her wondrous heritage in the gospel, she would send ten thousand fresh messengers to the farthest bounds of earth to proclaim, by word and example, this glorious gospel to the millions still in the thraldom of heathen darkness and superstition.[47]

There lies the explanation for the presence or absence of the missionary spirit.

---

[1] George Smith, *A Modern Apostle, Alexander N. Somerville* (London: John Murray, 1891), p. 311. I quote from the second edition, published only a year after the first.

[2] 'Missions', *Dictionary of Scottish Church History & Theology* (Edinburgh: T. &T. Clark, 1993), p. 573.

[3] George Smith, *Life of John Wilson of Bombay* (London: John Murray, 1879), p. 226. The quotation is from a review of a published sermon preached by Wilson at Oxford University.

[4] George Smith, *Fifty Years of Foreign Missions: or the Foreign Missions of the Free Church of Scotland in Their Year of Jubilee, 1879–80* (Edinburgh: MacLaren, 1880). At least twelve printings were issued in the first year of publication.

[5] For a comprehensive survey of Presbyterians, see Elizabeth G. K. Hewat, *Vision and Achievement 1796–1956: A History of the Foreign Missions of the Churches United in the Church of Scotland* (London: Nelson, 1960).

[6] For South Africa, and the part played by Scottish missions, see J. du Plessis, *A History of Christian Missions in South Africa* (repr. Cape Town: Struik, 1965).

[7] Smith, *Fifty Years*, p. 9.

[8] After an early career in India, where he was editor of the *Calcutta Review*, Smith returned to Scotland in 1858. He was also author of a *Short History of Christian Missions* (Edinburgh: T. & T. Clark, 1884). The omission of his life from the *Dictionary of Church History and Theology* is one of the few oversights in that fine volume; the section on 'Missions' is particularly full and valuable.

[9] John Inglis, *In the New Hebrides, Reminiscences of Missionary Life and Work* (London: Nelson, 1887), p. 43.

[10] 'Missions', *Dictionary of Scottish Church History & Theology*, p. 568.

[11] John Morrison, *The Fathers and Founders of the London Missionary Society* (London: Fisher, n.d.), vol. 2, p. 150. Morrison says that the Scottish Missionary Society 'was chiefly supported by members of the Secession Church', but, 'It embraced, in its direction and membership, persons belonging to all the orthodox denominations' (pp. 593, 595).

[12] John Sargent, *Life and Letters of Henry Martyn* (repr. Edinburgh: Banner of Truth, 1985). I have commented on Boston's teaching on the universality of divine love in the gospel in *The Old Evangelicalism* (Edinburgh: Banner of Truth, 2005), pp. 159–60.

[13] James Gardner, *Memoirs of Christian Missionaries* (Edinburgh: Johnstone, 1848), p. 141. Campbell (1766–1840), initially an ironmonger in Edinburgh, became a director of the LMS, was twice in Africa, and was a key figure in the missionary enterprise.

[14] A. K. Langridge and F. L. Paton, *Later Years and Farewell* (London: Hodder and Stoughton, 1912), pp. 269–70. How similar this is to what we read of C. H. Spurgeon. When asked how he accounted for the position God had given him in the world, he replied, 'My Mother, and the truth of my message.'

[15] *The Matabele Journals of Robert Moffat*, ed. J. P. R. Wallis, vol. 1 (London: Chatto & Windus, 1945), p. 221.

[16] MacDonald, *A Pastor's Memorial*, p. 248. These men all believed what J. H. Thornwell wrote on 'The Type and Model of Missionary Effort', 'To suppose that the benefits of redemption can be imparted where the knowledge of redemption is not found, is to violate all the analogies of providence and to contradict the express teachings of Revelation.' *Collected Writings of J. H. Thornwell*, vol. 2 (repr. Edinburgh: Banner of Truth, 1974), p. 435.

[17] Duff, *Missions the Chief End of the Christian Church* (Edinburgh: Johnstone, 1840), p. 50. Forty thousand copies of this work were quickly in circulation.

[18] W. P. Livingstone, *Mary Slessor of Calabar* (London: Hodder and Stoughton, 34th ed., 1931), pp. 319–20.

[19] C. H. Robinson, *History of Christian Missions* (Edinburgh: T. & T. Clark, 1915), p. 49.

[20] George Smith, *Life of John Wilson of Bombay*, pp. 341-2.

[21] See below, chapter 11.

[22] For a view of how 'enlightened' scholarship regards the spirit of the missionary movement see Gavin White, 'Scottish Overseas Missions: A Select Bibliography,' *Scottish Church History Society Records*, vol. xx, Part 3, 1980. Eminent missionaries are described in such terms as 'scatty and inaccurate', 'naïve and bumptious', 'intolerant and intolerable'. Of George Smith (father of G. A. Smith) it is said that he 'gives the facts but fails to interpret the meaning'. But at least this armchair critic is right in saying that unless the reader of the Scottish missionary literature keeps the 'changing theologies' in mind he will never 'grasp the issues'. One of the few leaders who spoke clearly on the effect of unbelief on world mission was J. Gresham Machen. See his *Modernism and the Board of Foreign Missions of the Presbyterian Church in the U.S.A.* (Philadelphia, 1933).

[23] John Love, *Sermons Preached on Various Occasions; with Fifteen Addresses to the People of Otaheite* (Edinburgh: Ogle,1846), p. 18.

[24] Ibid., p. 86.

[25] Inglis, *In the New Hebrides*, p. 32.

[26] Melanesia = 'black islands', due to the dark skin of the natives. Williams' field had been in Polynesia (= 'many islands'). It was subsequently seen by the missionaries as divine guidance that the work had begun among the lighter-coloured people of Polynesia, where one language was commonly spoken, whereas in the New Hebrides there were twenty, besides other difficulties.

[27] Ebenezer Prout, *Memoirs of the Life of John Williams* (London: Snow, 1843), p. 438.

[28] Inglis, *In the New Hebrides*, p. 247.

[29] R. S. Miller, *Misi Gete, John Geddie: Pioneer Missionary to the New Hebrides* (Launceston, Tasmania: Presbyterian Church of Tasmania, 1975), p. 37.

[30] Ibid., pp. 33, 43.

[31] 'Mrs Inglis', *In the New Hebrides*, pp. 261–94. The book was dedicated to her memory.

[32] J. Graham Miller, *Live: A History of Church Planting in the New Hebrides, Now the Republic of Vanuatu*, Book 2 (Sydney: General Assembly of Presbyterian Church of Australia), p. 15.

[33] *Misi Gete*, p. 255. A fuller account of Namuri is given in *John G. Paton, Missionary to the New Hebrides, An Autobiography* (repr. London: Banner of Truth, 1965), pp. 118–20.

[34] *Misi Gete*, p.145.

[35] *John G. Paton, Missionary to the New Hebrides*, pp. 136–7.

[36] *Live*, Book 1, p. 186. Paton gives the figure as one hundred and thirty-three; the number cannot be exact. It is not always clear whether a wife was included. It was found indispensable for missionaries of all nationalities to be married.

[37] Islay Burns, *Memoir of Wm. C. Burns* (London: Nisbet,1870), p. 523.

[38] The same truth was exemplified in the missionary advance in China:

'Love first, then suffering, then a deeper love – thus only can God's work be done.' Dr and Mrs Howard Taylor, *Hudson Taylor in Early Years* (London: China Inland Mission, 1911), p. 291.

[39] John Inglis, *Bible Illustrations from the New Hebrides* (London: Nelson, 1890), p. 219.

[40] *Live*, Book 1, pp. 186–7.

[41] Archibald Alexander, *Practical Truths* (repr. Keyser, West Virginia: Odom, n.d.), pp. 21–2.

[42] The Shorter Catechism was one of the earliest publications in the New Hebrides. Writing of his wife, John Inglis could say of their leisure hours, 'We read together the Life and most of the practical writings of Chalmers, the Life and the whole of the theological works of Principal Cunningham.' *In the New Hebrides*, p. 267.

[43] *Paton, Missionary to the New Hebrides*, p. 372.

[44] Among the blessings indicated by the law of God, the fourth commandment was especially emphasized. 'I have no doubt', wrote John Inglis, 'that the steady and rapid progress of the gospel on Aneityum was due, in no small degree, to the manner in which we emphasised the Scripture doctrine of the Sabbath, and established its observance. We thus secured time for religious instruction, quietness for devotional exercises . . . and, above all, brought down upon us the influences of the Holy Spirit, in accordance with the divine promise.' *In the New Hebrides*, p. 73.

[45] Inglis, *In the New Hebrides*, pp. 253–4.

[46] Inglis, *Bible Illustrations*, p. 253.

[47] Quoted in *John G. Paton, Later Years and Farewell* (London: Hodder and Stoughton, 1912), p. 178.

7

Robert Moffat
'Africanus'

Robert Moffat Preaching in Mosheu's Village

'Oh! Christians of England, can you as subjects of divine love, as possessing the blessed Gospel of the Son of God, and as holding his last commission from the Mount of Olives to publish it to the ends of the earth, – can you gaze on these fields of human blood, these regions of unutterable woe, without emotion? Ah! brethren, could you behold the scenes your missionaries witness, you would wake up with a power of pity which would impel you to deeds of compassion, compared with which your past exertions would appear as nothing.'

ROBERT MOFFAT, 1842.

'You must be either writing, reading, working, walking or talking.'

MOSELEKATSE, MATABELE CHIEF, TO ROBERT MOFFAT.

O n a Day of Intercession for Missions, 30 November 1873, Robert Moffat, Congregational minister and veteran missionary, spoke at a service in Westminster Abbey. He was possibly the first Nonconformist minister to have done so since the ejection of the Puritans from the national church in 1662. Unknown to him, at that very time, the body of his son-in-law was being carried by loving African hands to the coast for its return to Britain. Five months later it was Moffat who had to identify those remains before they were buried at the Abbey under a slab which bore the words:

> Brought by Faithful Hands over Land and Sea,
> Here Rests DAVID LIVINGSTONE . . .
> For thirty years his life was spent in an unwearied
> effort to evangelize the native races.

Both Moffat and his son-in-law were missionaries of the London Missionary Society – the Society which was the pioneer to the South Sea Islands and to China, as well as to the tribes beyond the Cape Colony in South Africa. Today it is Livingstone who is the better remembered, and yet J. Du

Plessis could write in his classic *History of Christian Missions in South Africa*, 'Robert Moffat was undeniably the greatest missionary which that Society sent to South Africa – the greatest in natural ability, in patient devotion to duty, and in deep, transparent piety.'[1]

It is one of the mysteries of divine providence that while the gospel entered parts of North Africa within the apostolic age, it was only in recent centuries that it penetrated the darkness of the centre and the South. The unknown nature of the terrain was undoubtedly part of the explanation, a fact which led Livingstone to 'contribute more towards the construction of the map of Africa than perhaps any three other explorers who could be named'.[2]

In the far South it was the Dutch who first colonized at Cape Town. Van Riebeck, who arrived in 1652, was one of the first to be concerned to see the knowledge of Christ spread among the native population. But, apart from the labours of some Moravians, little of a missionary character seems to have been done until early in the nineteenth century. In January 1806 the Cape was violently taken from the Dutch East India Company by the British. An unhappy eyewitness of that event was the twenty-five-year-old Henry Martyn, *en route* to India. At the Cape, he wrote in his journal for 10 January:

> I had a happy season of prayer. I prayed that the capture of the Cape might be ordered to the advancement of Christ's kingdom; and that England whilst she sent the thunder of her arms to the distant regions of the globe, might not remain proud and ungodly at home; but might show herself great indeed, by sending forth the ministers of her church to diffuse the gospel of peace.[3]

When Martyn wrote these words Robert Moffat was a child of ten in Scotland. Born on 21 December 1795, at Ormiston, East Lothian, there is no record that he ever knew of that prayer, but other prayers were part of his early life. Over fifty years later he would write to his mother: 'Wherever I am I never forget how much I owe to your prayers. The first dawn of reflection respecting my soul commenced with hearing you pray.'[4] The son of poor parents, Moffat early left school and by the age of thirteen was apprentice to the trade of a gardener – an occupation for which Scotland at this date was famous. This led him in 1814 to appointments in nursery gardens in Cheshire, England, where Methodist preaching, the reading of the Bible, and contact with the Rev. William Roby (one of the founders of the London Missionary Society), were the means by which he came to ambitions wholly new:

> I had undergone a great change of heart . . . Beyond visitors to see the gardens, and the men in daily employ who returned home after their labours of the day, I saw no one. I occupied my leisure in studying the Scriptures, and when opportunities offered I did not fail to try and convince others of the necessity of repentance towards God and faith in the Lord Jesus Christ. I thought I had only to tell them what Christ had done for them and what was required of them to be saved. I wondered they could not see what I saw, and feel what I felt, after explaining to them the great truths of the everlasting gospel.[5]

Roby, the minister of a Congregational Church in Manchester, befriended Moffat, tutored him, and introduced him to a Scottish Christian, William Smith, who owned a nursery at Dukinfield in Cheshire. While this was a better post it led to a major difficulty when Moffat was accepted as a missionary with LMS. Roby wrote to the General Secretary of the Society on 31 August 1816: 'Poor Moffat's amiable disposition and eminent devotedness have attracted the affectionate regards of his Master's daughter, a young lady of high piety, of polished manners, and the expectant of a considerable fortune. She possesses as truly a missionary spirit as he does and is eager to accompany him; but her parents forbid it.' Moffat had to go forward alone, and 13 September 1816 found him standing beside other future missionaries at a farewell service in Surrey Chapel, London. One of the others was John Williams, the martyr of Eromanga. It had been proposed that Williams and Moffat should go together to the South Pacific, but this was overruled by the counsel of an elder statesman of the LMS, Alexander Waugh (1754–1827) who, in language Moffat could well understand, judged 'thae twa lads ower young tae gang thegither'. Moffat respected the decision and refers to Waugh as 'that worthy Scotsman, like another John Knox'.[6] So it was that Moffat sailed for South Africa and arrived at the Cape on 13 January 1817. He would not see England again until the summer of 1839.

A COUNTRY 'LIKE AN OCEAN IN A STORM'

At the time of Moffat's arrival there was only one missionary beyond the border of the Cape Colony, and the purpose of the LMS was that Moffat, with another man and his family (the Ebners), should enter the area of Namaqualand, north of the Orange river, which was under the control of half-breed Hottentots known as Afrikaners.[7]

First, he had to learn Dutch, the only language understood by many in the Colony, and only in January 1818 did he reach Namaqualand. One mission among the Afrikaners had already failed, leaving 'the baptized', in the opinion of some, as 'wicked and dangerous as the unbaptized'. Moffat's colleague soon decided not to remain, and thus, as he later remembered, 'I was left alone with a people suspicious in the extreme; jealous of their rights, which they had obtained at the point of the sword; and the best of whom Mr Ebner described as a sharp thorn. I had no friend or brother with whom I could participate in the communion of saints, none to whom I could look for counsel or advice . . . I was wont to pour out my soul among the granite rocks surrounding this station, now in sorrow, and then in joy.'[8]

A letter which he wrote home on 15 December 1818, tells us a little of how the isolation affected him: 'I long to hear from you. I have now been nearly two years in Africa, and only received one letter from you . . . Write me fully, and forget me not in your approaches to the throne of grace.' The same letter carried the news that his hopes that his Cheshire sweetheart, Mary Smith, might yet join him had again failed: 'Her last two letters have been completely effectual in blasting my hopes. She has most reluctantly renounced the idea of ever going abroad, her father determining never to allow her.'

But in this desolate situation encouragement came in an unexpected way. God gave Moffat the friendship of the greatly-feared chief of the Afrikaners. Moffat's capacity for friendship was to be a characteristic of his future work. 'The shy and somewhat silent Scotch lad' (as his son would later describe him in his early years) would repeatedly gain the confidence of tribal despots who kept thousands in terror. 'Afrikaner', as Moffat called this Hottentot chief, had given Moffat a cool reception, despite some previous Christian influence. Yet when the missionary commenced services and 'school' to teach reading this was the pupil who was always present. Now the New Testament became Afrikaner's constant companion: 'Often I have seen him under the shadow of a great rock, nearly the livelong day, eagerly perusing the pages of Divine inspiration . . . Many were the nights he sat with me, on a great stone at the door of my habitation, conversing with me till the dawn of another day, on creation, providence, redemption, and the glories of the heavenly world.'

Moffat had practical and mechanical gifts that were to prove essential to his future work. If his years of formal education had been few, the many experiences of his youth had prepared him well for the situation he described in a letter to his parents: 'Daily I do a little in the garden, daily I am doing something for the people in mending guns. I am carpenter, smith, cooper, tailor, shoemaker, miller, baker and housekeeper – the last is the most burdensome of any. An old Namaqua woman milks my cows, makes a fire and washes. All other things I do myself.'

When Moffat visited the Cape in April 1819, Afrikaner went with him. The latter had previously been known and sought by the Cape government as a 'public terror' but now Moffat could write to his father, 'everyone is pleased to see him, and no less astonished to witness the effect of Divine grace manifesting itself in him.' That same letter carried the news that Mary Smith's parents had relented, and that he hoped he might see her soon, 'for a missionary in this country without a wife is like a boat with one oar'. In December 1819 Mary arrived. Moffat's prayers for her were turned to praise, and they were married that month in Cape Town. Next to his conversion it was the most important event in his life. The pair were, as their son John was to write, 'in many ways a great contrast. He was tall and strong, with dark piercing eyes, with more than ordinary endurance. She was under ordinary height, with blue eyes, and a complexion that never lost its delicate girlish bloom. She was never strong, and latterly lived and worked only by dint of great care and method.' Constitutionally, he continued, she was timid, 'I have seen her effectually routed by a turkey-cock . . . but once let her see the path of duty, and nothing could turn her aside.'[9]

Mary's companionship came in time for the many hard years that lay ahead. Afrikaner had proposed to move his nomadic people eastwards, where there was more prospect of water and fertility but he died before this could be done, and the Moffats' lifelong field of labour came to be among the Batlaping people, part of the Bechuanas,[10] to be found some 700 miles north from the Cape and eight weeks' travel by ox wagon. In that region a base was eventually established at Kuruman, close to the Kalahari Desert. Discouragements abounded. Initial threats from the Batlaping subsided into constant thieving, allied with stony indifference to anything spiritual: 'The moment a word was said about divine things their ears seemed to become deaf at once.' Still more disturbing was the poor testimony of the professing Christian Hottentots, employed by the mission from other parts to be with him as interpreters – they proved 'too weak in the faith to meet the demands which were made upon their constancy, surrounded as they were by a heathen and corrupt people'. By the exercise of discipline, the little Christian community was reduced to a 'mere fraction' and so it remained year after year. There were days when Moffat and his mission colleague and fellow Scot, Robert Hamilton, wondered if they were in the right path. But Mary Moffat permitted no such doubts. Pointing to the promises of God, she would say, 'We may not live to see it, but the awakening will come as sure as the sun will rise tomorrow.'

The nature of the barriers to the gospel that Moffat countered are graphically described in his *Missionary Labours*. The tribes beyond the Cape Colony were nomadic in their living, in part the result of the constant search for water supplies, and in part, the effect of the nearly-constant warfare in which tribes and nations were successively threatened and devoured by one another. The Cape's original white settlers, the Boers, felt pressured by the British to move further inland where they, in turn, intimidated and sometimes decimated the native people. Zulus, moving west from Natal, threatened and slew the Bapedi and Basuto. Chaka, the Zulu chief, had the reputation of being responsible for the deaths of two million fellow Africans. Similarly the terrible Matabele fell on both Bapedi and Bechuanas. Some tribes utterly disappeared. Lands were abandoned and emigrations were commonplace as fugitives sought new homes. In Moffat's view: 'The whole country appeared like the ocean in a storm; – its inhabitants like the waves, alternately rolling forward, and receding, carrying with them devastation and misery . . . O Africa! the world's great mart of rapine, bondage, blood, and murder! Thy skies have been obscured with smoke of towns in flames! thy burning deserts bedewed with the agonizing tears of bereaved mothers!'

Without effective interpreters, the most immediate problem was that of language, and as Moffat learned Sechuana there was a sense in which it increased his difficulty, for he discovered that the people had no religion at all, no words at all to correspond with any spiritual truths. But the greatest barrier of all was the nature of fallen, unregenerate man. When Moffat knew enough of the language to preach, the message was met with incomprehension or derision. Or he might be told, 'These fables are very wonderful but not more so than our own.' The natural man anywhere in the world is activated by no principle other than self-love. Repeatedly the missionary found that an initial degree of welcome was based only on the expectation of the temporal benefits that might come from white people. This response led some missionaries to become traders, a practice which Moffat regarded as a disastrous mistake. He knew that when his hearers began to understand the effect that believing the truth would have upon their lives – 'making terrible havoc with his darling pleasures' – they would react with all the opposition of the heart of the natural man.[11] But the reality, and the Satanic power behind it, had to be faced. To soften the message to win a better response was not an option. He observed with feeling: 'This is a period in which the faith and patience of the missionary are put to the test.' The power of God in the gospel message was the only hope.

This hope was certainly severely tested. After some five years among the Bechuanas, Moffat could write: 'A sameness marks the events of each returning day. No conversions, no inquiry after God, no objections raised to exercise our powers in defence . . . We preach, we converse, we catechise, we pray, but without the least apparent success . . . It did indeed produce a melancholy feeling, when we looked around us, on so many immortal beings, not one of whom loved us, none sympathised, none considered the day of their merciful visitation; but with their lives as well as their lips, were saying to the Almighty, "Depart from us, we desire not the knowledge of thy ways." . . . "I will be exalted among the heathen," cheered our often baffled and drooping spirits.'

Mary Moffat, now with a babe in arms, had additional trials. Often the home would be crowded with uninvited guests 'who would seize a stone, and dare interference on her part'. When she asked a woman to leave the kitchen on one occasion as she was about to go to worship, the response was a piece of wood thrown at her head. She was learning the same lesson as her husband, as she wrote to her father: 'Patience and perseverance are two essential qualities in a missionary in this country.'

It was 1826 before Moffat could speak of their hope of a true convert, but with the general prospect unchanged, the LMS considered abandoning the mission at Kuruman. When unofficial news of this reached Moffat and Hamilton, they could say, 'We felt our souls riveted to the country and people.' Their faith in divine intervention was deepening and in 1829 they saw the unmistakeable beginning of a new day. 'We were favoured,' Moffat writes, 'with the manifest outpouring of the Spirit from on high. The moral wilderness was now about to blossom. To see females weep was nothing extraordinary; it was, according to Bechuana notions, their province and theirs alone. Men would not weep . . . The simple Gospel now melted their flinty hearts; and eyes now wept, which never before shed the tear of hallowed sorrow. Notwithstanding our earnest desires and fervent prayers, we were taken by surprise.' Speaking of this same event, many years later, John Moffat wrote:

At length in 1829, a marvellous awakening began. It came, as such things do come, without any human or visible existing cause. There was a wave of tumultuous and simultaneous enthusiasm. The two brethren who witnessed it were sober-minded and hard-headed Scotchmen, by disposition not willing to lend themselves to any movement which might seem to have the taint of mere sensationalism. They had been schooled to adversity, and they could but dread some new device of the devil to obstruct their path; but it was not long before they were forced to admit that there was something that could not be gainsaid. In a few months the whole aspect of the mission had changed. The meeting-house was crowded before the service had begun. Heathen songs and dancing had ceased, and everywhere were to be heard the songs of Zion and the outpouring of impassioned prayers. The missionaries were beset even in their own houses by those who were seeking fuller instruction in things which had become to them all at once of paramount importance. The moral condition of the community rapidly improved, and the dirt and indecency of heathen costume were exchanged for cleanliness and European habits of clothing, as far as the supply could be met by the visit of occasional traders.

At the time, Moffat and Hamilton proceeded with a great deal of caution and watchfulness, aware of how often there had been premature professions of conversion. But in June 1829, after 'much prayer and deliberation', six individuals who gave 'very satisfactory proofs of a change of heart' were baptized (with five of their children). Twelve people in all now sat down at the Lord's table and the first church among the Bechuanas came into being. It was on the Friday previous to that event that a communion cup and plates had arrived from Sheffield, England. Mary Moffat had requested them two years earlier 'in the confidence of faith', her husband noted, 'that they would some time be needed, dark as things then appeared.'

Every faithful church is a missionary agency and Kuruman was now to become a springboard for outreach further inland. Sometimes the new openings came unexpectedly, as on the day in 1829 when two headmen of the Matabele, sent by their master, Moselekatse, arrived at the mission. The reputation of their sender and his 70,000 people was well known. Once a lieutenant of the great Zulu king, Chaka, Moselekatse had moved into the uplands of what is now the Transvaal and, behaving 'like a wolf among a flock of sheep, deluged the Bakwena country with blood'. News of the white men at Kuruman had prompted him to find out what they were doing.

It was providential that these trusted servants came after the awakening at the mission station, otherwise it might have been only such things as the houses, the water-carrying ditches, the smithy's forge, and a mirror in which to see their faces, that would have impressed them. As it was there was nothing more new to them than the sight of public worship in the chapel: 'They saw men like themselves meet together with great decorum; mothers hushing their babies, or hastily retiring if they made a noise, and the elder children sitting perfectly silent.' Instead of war-songs and masculine feats, there were hymns; and, although they understood not the language, they could recognize that a message was being treated with great importance. The days had gone when Moffat's hearers laughed at what they heard.

Before the two Matabele were ready to leave Kuruman, information came that some of the Bechuana were planning to kill them on their homeward route. Such an event would have brought down the overwhelming power of Moselekatse, and so there was nothing for it but for Moffat to accompany and shield them through the most dangerous part of their journey. This done, he was about to turn round for the return to Kuruman, when Moselekatse's servants informed him that their master would be ready to kill them if they allowed Moffat to go back without meeting him.

The journey to the Matabele headquarters through lion-infested country, mountain ranges and ruins of once-populous 'towns' desolated by war, is one of the most colourful parts of Moffat's *Missionary Travels*. At length the destination was reached, a kraal near Pretoria, capable of holding ten thousand cattle. There were a thousand warriors to meet them, not in their normal nudity but standing silent and dressed for war. Moffat stayed for eight days and later reported, 'I had never before come into contact with such savage and degraded minds.'

Yet those days established the most unlikely friendship with the Matabele chief, whose reputation for crime was well deserved. On one occasion when six hundred of his men failed to defeat an enemy, he put the remnant to death on their return. One of his four hundred wives, who told him that he should not have so many women, had her head severed from her body. It seems it was the care Moffat had shown for the king's two headmen that won a way to the tyrant's heart: 'What you did to them you did to me,' he declared, 'I am still wondering at the love of a stranger who never saw me.' This was the man who now came to treat Moffat – 'Moshete' – as a father and, though his heart remained unchanged, a life-long bond was established between the two.

The reputation of Moselekatse's friendship with Moffat gave the missionary more openings in the latitudes north of Kuruman. Other chiefs were not only to be favourable but in some cases truly converted. In the midst of much danger and confusion the Scotsman was one of the very few who could move among warring factions. In addition to his gift in winning friends it needs to be said that he loved and trusted the blacks in a manner they had never known before. This often gave him an entrance where others would have feared to go.

THE MESSAGE PREACHED

Moffat gives a valuable comment on the often-repeated story concerning the preaching of the Moravians in Greenland. It is said that for five years the Moravian missionaries spoke of the existence and attributes of God, the Fall of man, and the demands of God's law, without any effect. It was only when they resolved 'simply to preach Christ crucified' that they saw conversions. Moffat believed the lesson drawn from that experience of preaching to heathen to be 'very erroneous'. He pointed out other missionaries who also emphasized 'God so loved the world', yet saw no quick success. He was sure that preaching the character and commandments of God prepared the way for the preaching of redemption. Speaking of a conversation with Moselekatse, he says, 'I told him of the Sabbath and to whom we kept it, our duty to acknowledge God and keep his commandments.'[12] The most alarming and solemn parts of the whole counsel of God were all necessary, and Moffat spoke of death, judgment and eternity, themes not appreciated by his hearers. He reports: 'One day, while describing the day of judgment, several of my hearers expressed great concern at the idea of all their cattle being destroyed, together with their ornaments. They never for one moment allow their thoughts to dwell on death, which is according to their views nothing less than annihilation.'

But conscience had to be awakened and sometimes it was the truth about last things that did it. Take, for example, his speaking with Makaba, the powerful chief of the Bangwaketsi:

> In the course of my remarks, the ear of the monarch caught the startling sound of a resurrection. 'What!' he exclaimed with astonishment, 'what are these words about? The dead,

the dead, arise!' 'Yes,' was my reply, 'all the dead shall arise.' 'Will my father arise?' 'Yes,' I answered, 'your father will arise.' 'Will all the slain in battle arise?' 'Yes.' 'And will all that have been killed and devoured by lions, tigers, hyenas, and crocodiles, again revive?' 'Yes; and come to judgment.' 'And will those whose bodies have been left to waste and wither on the desert plains, and scattered to the winds, again arise?' he asked, with a kind of triumph, as if he had now fixed me. 'Yes,' I replied, 'not one will be left behind.' This I repeated with increased emphasis. After looking at me for a few moments, he turned to his people, to whom he spake with stentorian voice: 'Hark, ye wise men, whosoever is among you, the wisest of past generations, did ever your ears hear such strange and unheard of news?' And addressing himself to one, whose countenance and attire showed that he had seen many years, and was a person of no common order, 'Have you ever heard such strange news as this?' 'No,' was the sage's answer, 'Surely he must have lived long before the period when we were born.'

Makaba, then turning and addressing himself to me, and laying his hand on my breast, said, 'Father, I love you much. Your visit and your presence have made my heart white like milk. The words of your mouth are sweet as honey, but the words of a resurrection are too great to be heard. I do not wish to hear again about the dead rising! The dead cannot arise! The dead must not arise!' 'Why,' I enquired, 'can so great a man refuse knowledge, and turn away from wisdom? Tell me my friend, why I must not add to words and speak of a resurrection?' Raising and uncovering his arm, which had been strong in battle, and shaking his hand as if quivering a spear, he replied, 'I have slain my thousands, and shall they arise?' Never before had the light of divine revelation dawned upon his mind, and of course his conscience had never accused him, no, not for one of the thousands of deeds of rapine and murder which had marked his course.[13]

Yet although Moffat aimed to make known all fundamental truths, the special prominence of what he called 'the Gospel of love and good-will to all men' was unmistakeable. No idea of God among his hearers was more alien to them than that of love. The one word Moffat could find, used to express the Deity in the language of the Hottentots, was 'Thiko', meaning, literally, 'one that induces pain'. Here were people who were attributing the essential character of the devil to their Creator, the author of all good. Contrary to such a falsehood, as Moffat wrote to his brother in 1834, we 'have received the ministry of reconciliation, assured that God our Saviour willeth the salvation of all'. He had seen men and women raised from the abyss of degradation 'aroused by the voice of love, and drawn by the attractions of the cross'. Mosheu, chief of the Corunna tribe, visited Kuruman to hear Moffat in 1834. He returned a second time, saying, 'When I first visited you I had only one heart, but now I come with two,' and Moffat commented, 'All the powers of his soul seemed overwhelmed with the contemplation of the love of God.'

It was this part of Moffat's message that was so eminently transmuted into his character. His son, John, affirmed, 'He was just full of his Saviour's love and mercy all through his life.' In the crowded pages of his *Missionary Travels,* Moffat himself draws no attention to this but the repeated instances of men being 'subdued by kindness' tell their own story. He witnessed 'the omnipotence of love, even among the most barbarous of the human race'.

INCREASING LABOURS

The measure of awakening at Kuruman in 1829 and the care of young converts that ensued brought Moffat much additional work. At last familiar with the language of the people, the translation of the Bible now became a main focus in his life. Never, he said, had 'such a treasure' been brought to the Bechuana people as the translation of the Gospel of Luke which he was able to give them in 1831. But finding printers had been a major problem and so, that same year, he determined to be a printer himself and hauled a printing press by wagon from Cape Town.

Mary Moffat wrote home in 1834: 'Robert is in a perpetual bustle: the printing is a wonderful addition to the work here, and the extreme anxiety of his mind to give everything as correctly as possible causes him incessant mental labour . . . If my dear Robert had not had an iron constitution he must long ago have sunk under his manifold labours.' Two years later she reported: 'The translating and printing are going on. The Scripture lessons which were in hand are finished, a volume of 443 pages. The Assembly's Catechism [that is, the Shorter Catechism] is also in print and in use; readers are increasing in every direction.'[14]

The translation of the New Testament and Psalms into Sechuana was at last complete in 1840. It was a work of immense difficulty, for he was the first to put the language of the Bechuanas into written form. Moffat felt at times as if the task had 'shattered his brain'. It is remarkable that a man whose initial education had been so slender could become a translator, using both Greek and Hebrew, yet there is no doubt he had been given a natural aptitude for languages. Desk work in Kuruman was far from easy:

> Writing was a work of great difficulty, owing to the flies crowding into the inkhorn or clustering around the point of the pen, and pursuing it on the paper, drinking the ink as fast as it flowed. The night brought little relief, for as soon as the candle was lighted, innumerable insects swarmed around so as to put it out.

At the same time, all his other work continued, and it was as varied as his gifts. At Kuruman he might be found in the pulpit, supervising agriculture and drainage, doing the work of a blacksmith, putting roofs on buildings, corresponding with native teachers, visiting out-stations, giving medical advice, extracting teeth, and welcoming visitors. 'My situation,' he noted tersely, 'was not very well suited to study.' Nor was this all. At heart he remained the pioneer and was not infrequently long distances away from his beloved Mary, befriending those who were to hear the gospel for the first time. Even when he was turned sixty, he 'seemed', says his son, 'to have the strength of three men, and was here, there, and everywhere in turn.' Yet this was the man who was conscious

> that we want in zeal. The work of conversion, or endeav-
> ours to convert sinners, is not so much the primary object
> of our souls as it ought to be. If I speak for myself I must
> say that I do not feel that sympathy for the awful condition
> of my fellow-men which their state ought to excite in every
> Christian bosom. When I look at the Man of Sorrows,
> His toilsome days and midnight prayers, and the burning
> zeal of the first ministers of the gospel, I feel as if I had
> not the same mind or spirit.

THE MATABELE JOURNALS

Moffat's first journey to Moselekatse we have already noted. Four more such lengthy journeys to the chief of the Matabele were to be made, and each one, like the first, Moffat recorded in a journal kept almost daily. John Moffat employed these journals in his biography of his father, but they contain a far greater wealth of material than he could use. In 1941 the originals were rediscovered at a farm in Cape Province and published in 1945 under the auspices of the Government Archives of Southern Rhodesia. Their editor commented,

'They are not easy reading in an age that has largely forgotten their primitive evangelicalism, but they may help to explain the man, his endeavours and his methods.'[15] This they certainly do, and the two volumes are classics in Christian missionary literature. They were not, in fact, journals, written for publication, so much as letters addressed to 'My Dear Mary', and sent to her at Kuruman in regular instalments. His wife was never with him on the five journeys to Moselekatse. The second journey was in 1835 when he acted as a guide to an official acting for an Association for Exploring Central Africa. The third was not made until 1854; its purpose, in Moffat's words, 'my health, visit my old friend Moselekatse, see what Livingstone is doing, and preach to the natives'. This journey (and the two that followed) involved far more difficulty, for Moselekatse, worsted in fighting with Zulus when he lost some five thousand men, had moved far north. His head-quarters were now at Inyati, about 50 miles from the modern Bulawayo in Zimbabwe, and approaching a thousand from Kuruman.[16] His headmen had assured him he would never see Moffat again, and great was the tyrant's joy when 'Moshete' arrived. Twenty years had brought a major change in appearance to both men, as Moffat noted at their meeting:

> There he sat – how changed! the vigorous active and nimble monarch of the Matabele, now aged, sitting on a skin, with feet lame, unable to walk or even to stand. I entered, when he grasped my hand, gave one earnest look, drew his mantle over his face. It would have been an awful sight to see the hero of a hundred battles wipe from his eye the falling tear. None saw the whole of the scene, except one or two of his wives, who sat behind their lord to minister to his wants. He spoke not, except pronouncing my name, Moshete, again and again. Withdrawing his head, he looked at me again, his hand still in mine,

and again covered his face. My heart yearned in compassion for his soul.[17]

Moselekatse was still a powerful monarch, with warriors
numbered by the thousand at his command. With such a man
favourable to Moffat, the LMS proposed in 1857 that a mission
be established in his territory. But Moffat was uncertain.
Moselekatse's affection to him was one thing, but his evasiveness
over permitting others to settle as Christian missionaries
confirmed that he did not want the message he had often heard:
As 'the servants of God, [we] had all one object in view, namely,
to tell him and his people the good news of God's love to a
sinful world, and how he and his people could be saved.'[18] In
accordance with the Society's wish, however, Moffat, at the age
of sixty-two, made a fourth visit in 1857, to seek a response to
the proposal that missionaries should come to Inyati, and this
he secured. By 1859 a missionary party, made up of his son John
with his wife Emily, William Sykes, and Thomas Thomas (with
wife and infant), were ready to leave and settle among the
Matabele. Yet Moffat remained hesitant. While determination
was part of his make-up, and 'Nothing ventured, nothing won,'
one of his favourite sayings, he was not rash. While thankful for
the favour of the Matabele king he had no confidence in his
character; and he had never been given leave to preach to his
people. If the party were to go, then at least he must go with
them and introduce them personally. Moselekatse himself
demanded, 'Moshete must come. These new men, I do not
know them. All men are not alike.'

The fifth visit proved that Moffat's caution was not
unfounded. After the hazardous journey in which oxen (twelve
needed for pulling each wagon) died, and they were plagued
by small rats – not to speak of danger from larger animals –
the party of about thirty in all reached the headquarters of
Moselekatse. But it was only to find the king unready to

confirm his promise. He did not deny it, he simply did nothing to allocate anywhere that the new arrivals could unload and settle. It seemed that the chief's suspicions of missionaries had deepened; in part because some had told him that missionaries were only spies sent in advance of the Boers.[19] The language barrier increased the problem, for Moffat could speak little Setebele (the language of the Matabele), and the interpreter who had helped him before had been murdered.

In the suspense that followed their arrival at Inyati there was nothing for them to do but to wait with their wagons, as days turned into weeks and their food supplies dwindled. Bearing responsibility for the whole party, it is no wonder that Moffat had sleepless nights. His letters to Mary show that it was one of the most critical periods of his life:

> [27 October 1859] The planting of a mission among the Matabele, I need scarcely say, weighs *very heavy* on my mind . . . I could not help sometimes observing shadows of coming events, but the finances of the Society and the distant and isolated position of the Matabele would not permit me to hope. Their dreadfully savage state – this is not exaggeration – seemed sometimes to require a faith I did not possess; and, added to this, the peculiar character of their government, worshipping a king with the idea that he is superhuman . . . *I cannot help having my fears,* and often, like the man, pray, 'Lord, help my unbelief'. Why should we doubt? Is it because we look at the instruments? 'Go ye!' 'Lo, I am with you.' 'I will be exalted among the heathen.'[20]

> [30 October] *Patience, patience, patience! Lord increase our faith.*

But things grew worse. Frustration and disagreement arose among the missionaries and Moffat faced criticism; he refers only briefly to the latter in writing to Mary:

[8 November] I feel not the shadow of inclination to communicate the mental trials I have had to endure, and the deep waters through which I am passing. The trial of faith and patience ought, according to Scripture, to be 'precious' unto us. At some distant day, I may, if spared – at some distant day when the horned spectre of *contention*, which haunts my nights' repose and terrifies me with dreams, has ceased – record the mental exercises of one who has ceased to contend. I leave my cause to the judgment of Him who will not condemn the innocent . . . What a pity that men who have had so much time at colleges, do not find a few leisure hours to read the apostolic acts and sufferings and conquests of earlier missionaries, the advance guard of that army which is to subdue every nation, kindred and tongue, and bring all to the obedience of faith! Would that some knew, even if it were a tithe, of what you have had to suffer for the cause, for Christ's sake among the Bechuana.[21]

Later, it appears that unity among the party was restored and he could write: 'Whatever may be the results of our attempt to introduce the gospel among the Matabele, we are all, I believe, of one mind not to be scared by appearances, but resolved, through divine help, to bear patiently and see what the Lord intends us to do – to remain or return.'

[24 November] Satan is making a desperate attempt to shut the door against the blessed Gospel. We are troubled verily, but we are not distressed; we are perplexed, but we do not despair. Though it was not at my recommendation to commence a mission among the Matabele, yet I believe the Directors of our Society were divinely directed, and therefore I pursue that object with my whole soul; if I perish in the attempt, what am I? – an unworthy servant, a debtor to divine grace.

Part of the trial in these events was that through all the weeks of waiting Moselekatse's conduct was mystifying to Moffat. He wrote to Mary, 'If he has changed his mind, he cannot put on a face to tell me so.' Of the despot's continued affection for Moshete there could be no doubt; the man before whom others crawled and trembled, would still sit contentedly beside the missionary for hours on end at the front of his wagon. The explanation for the king's behaviour seems never to have been clearly understood. For two months his tantalizing inaction continued until, on 23 December, Moffat could report that the party had been given a valley where they could begin to set up a mission station. Moffat waited with them a further six months before leaving on 18 June 1860. To the last, Moselekatse sought to keep him there. 'Why should such good friends part?' he asked the missionary. 'I replied', Moffat reported, 'that I desired to meet him in the other world, the heavenly, where there would be no more parting, and therefore I brought teachers.' John Moffat saw the parting of the two men and later described it:

> The old chief was, as usual, in his courtyard and gave kindly greeting. They were a strange contrast as they sat side by side – the Matabele tyrant and the messenger of peace. The word of command was given; the warriors filed in and ranged themselves in a great semicircle, sitting on the ground; the women crept as near as they could, behind huts and other points of concealment, and all listened in breathless silence to the last words of 'Moshete'. He himself knew that they were his last words, and that his work in Matabele land was now given over to younger hands. It was a solemn service, and closed the long series of such, in which the friend of Moselekatse had striven to pierce the dense darkness of soul which covered him and his people.

The return journey by Moffat to Kuruman took from 18 June to 21 August 1860. He had been away from Mary for a little over a year. It is a strange comment of the twentieth-century editor of the *Journals* to say that Moffat's missionary journeys 'would have been more eminent' if he had 'just so much more of his son-in-law Livingstone's spirit as would have reconciled him to a longer absence from his wife'.[22] The truth is that the couple endured many deprivations in their family life. It cannot have been easy for them to see their son John, and his young bride, settle at Inyati when they had only come from England. 'Persevere till you see the influences of the Holy Spirit descending,' his mother urged John. It would be over six years before she saw him and Emily again, when poor health brought them south.[23]

FAMILY AND LATTER YEARS

Commitment to his wife and family were very much a part of Moffat's Christian life, though the closeness of his attachment to Mary and to their children is partly veiled in Scottish reticence. Two of the children, who died in infancy, are very briefly mentioned. David Livingstone, having met Moffat on the latter's only visit home in 1839, subsequently joined him in Kuruman. There he met young Mary Moffat (the eldest daughter) and they married in 1845. Another Moffat daughter married a French missionary, Jean Fredoux (her father kept up warm relationships with all evangelical missions in South Africa). As the years passed the family circle was subject to many cares and anxieties. In 1862 the eldest son, Robert, who was a valuable help to the mission station as a trader, died suddenly. Only weeks after this the news came that Mary Livingstone had succumbed to malaria on the fever-stricken Zambezi. A further blow was the death of their other missionary son-in-law, Fredoux, who was blown up while trying to settle a dispute, leaving seven orphan children.

After Moffat's fifth visit to Moselekatse, there was still another ten years of work ahead although the Moffats were conscious that the time was short. 'It will soon be said of us,' Mary wrote to her far-off brother, '"They are gone." Well, the grand thing is to be found prepared. If I had not felt it before, I should do so now, that all earthly things are vain and trifling, except we are enabled by Divine grace to use them to His glory. My strength is gone, and I begin to feel myself of so little use in the world that my affections are more and more loosened from it, and I feel that I could very willingly leave it; for I know in whom I have believed.'

By this time Moffat's great work in the translation of the whole Bible into Sechuana had been completed.[24] The first volume of the Old Testament was completed in 1853 and the second in 1857. But revision, in order to improve the translation, continued. Nothing, in Moffat's estimation, began to approach the importance of Scripture, 'the only guide from earth to heaven'. The following words, written to Mary, tell us something of what Scripture meant to him personally:

It was only yesterday, after laying down the Bible, that I wondered what kind of mind I would have had if I had not the Book of God, the Book containing the astounding idea of 'from everlasting to everlasting', the development of all that is worth knowing . . . One would think, that as I have critically, and, I think, devoutly read and examined every verse, every word in the Bible, some a score of times over, I should not require to open the pages of that unspeakable blessed Book. Alas, for the human memory! I read the Bible today with the same feeling I ever did, like the hungry when seeking food, the thirsty when seeking drink, the bewildered when seeking counsel and the mourner when seeking comfort. Don't you believe all this? For alas, I read it sometimes as a formal thing, though my heart condemns me afterwards . . . I am yet astonished at my own ignorance of the Bible![25]

It was in these latter years that Moffat suffered a physical attack. As he returned one night from church in the dark at Kuruman, he was savagely beaten by an assailant with a knobkerrie. Such a thing had never happened before in Kuruman where the Moffats 'maintained an almost absolute rule, though wielding no other sceptre than that of gratitude and affection'. The attacker proved to be a lunatic and while Moffat's 'iron frame' saved him from such consequences as others might have suffered, the sorrow that such a thing could happen lingered with him.

Although Kuruman was now far more home than Britain could ever be, the conclusion was slowly reached that their work there was done. Moffat took his last service on 20 March 1870. John Moffat, who was to continue at his parents' station, spoke of the great congregation gathered that day:

> The older people were for the most part children at the time when they had first seen the missionaries. With a pathetic grace peculiarly his own, he pleaded with those still unbelieving amid the gospel privileges they had now enjoyed so many years. With a fatherly benediction he commended to the grace of God those who had been to him a joy and crown. Many years must pass before that service can be forgotten in Bechwanaland.

Then there was the one last wagon trek to the Cape before they sailed in June 1870, more than fifty-four years after Moffat's first arrival. He had lived to see large parts of southern Africa 'occupied by an army, not merely of missionaries, but of missionary societies; while his own Bechwanaland is through its length and breadth feeling the influences of his work and that of his companions, a work which has extended its operations to the very banks of the Zambezi River'.

Mary Moffat had scarce time to adjust to England, praying to the last, before she was gone to a brighter world in the autumn of 1871. At the end, 'her mind occasionally wandered, but it was always in the right direction: the Redeemer's reign among the heathen, the printing of the Scriptures, Kuruman and the Bechwanas.' Her husband's first words to others on her death were, 'For fifty-three years I have had her to pray for me.' He was to remain busy, serving his 'two masters', the LMS and the British and Foreign Bible Society and travelling to speak for them all over the country. Other Christian agencies and churches received his willing help and he delighted to welcome visitors from overseas. Scotland was, of course, revisited on several occasions,[26] although he chose to make his home at Park Cottage in the grounds of Samuel Morley's home at Leigh in Kent. He reached the age of eighty in 1875. In July 1883 we find him writing, 'Some seem to suppose that I do not get old like other folks, as applications still come in for services at public meetings. My platform and public days are over, and I have had a tolerable share.' One month later he was where

> Our best friends and kindred dwell,
> And Christ our Saviour reigns.

Moffat's character is clear enough from all the above, but there is one feature which must be added. John Moffat speaks of the 'life-long impression' made on him by his father's 'reverence for holy things'. He continued: 'No man relished a joke more than he – there was a good deal of fun hidden away under that long beard; but woe to the man who thought to approach the ark of God in a jesting spirit. The Word of the Lord was too real and too great for triviality. Even when I was alone with him on the journeys spoken of, no meal was commenced without a reverent doffing of the Scotch bonnet, his usual head-dress in those days, and the solemn blessing;

our morning and evening worship were never missed or hurried.'

John Moffat was a worthy biographer of his father and his work contrasted with more superficial writing on missionary work. The son wrote of the father in 1921:

> The glamour that had gathered round missionary enterprise in the early and middle years of the last century appeared to him uncalled for and unhealthy, as tending to appeal to mere emotionalism. He detested everything in the shape of cant and humbug; for this reason he held that the naked truth should be told no matter how unpleasant or depressing, and the brightly pictured, often grossly exaggerated, reports that sometimes appear in missionary books and magazines caused him real distress and shame. A good cause should require no such fictitious aids.[27]

CONCLUSIONS

Two conclusions must be mentioned. The first concerns the argument put forward when foreign missions were first proposed in the General Assembly of the Church of Scotland, that civilization needed to precede the gospel. The expectation of any moral change could therefore only be a very slow process. Moffat, along with other pioneer missionaries, challenged that belief. What no government powers could do in establishing peace, purifying life and uplifting womanhood, their message saw accomplished. The work was not that of the LMS, or of any one denomination, but of all 'the noble band of Church, Wesleyan, and Baptist missionaries'. 'It is now demonstrated,' he could write of all these agencies in 1842, 'that the Gospel can transform these aceldamas [fields of blood], these dens of crime, weeping and woe, into abodes of purity, happiness, and love . . . We are warranted to expect, from what has already occurred, great and glorious results.' A moral improvement in society in general is not needed to prepare the way for spiritual success. On this point Moffat wrote:

> Much has been said about civilizing savages before attempting to evangelize them. This is a theory which has obtained extensive prevalence among the wise men of this world, but we have never yet seen a practical demonstration of its truth. We ourselves are convinced that evangelization must precede civilization. It is very easy in a country of high refinement to speculate on what might be done among rude and savage men, but the Christian missionary, the only experimentalist, has invariably found that to make the fruit good the tree must first be made good. Nothing less than the power of Divine grace can reform the hearts of savages, after which the mind is susceptible of those instructions which teach them to adorn the gospel they profess.

This lesson needs to be remembered wherever the moral decay of society tempts Christians to suppose the plain preaching of the gospel cannot meet the situation. Moffat was certain that only one source is adequate to answer the effects of sin upon society, whether these are among 'barbarians' or 'the civilized nations of Europe': 'Nothing but the Bible can save man from these woes.'

This leads to the second observation. If the ultimate purpose of creation is the praise and worship of God, and if salvation serves the same purpose as God is glorified in lives recovered by grace, then joyful song will ever follow the accomplishment of God's purposes. Moffat's generation began to see the fulfilment of words previously only read in faith: 'From the uttermost part of the earth have we heard songs, even glory to the righteous'; or, in another translation, 'From the ends of the earth we hear songs of praise, of glory to the Righteous One' (*Isa.* 24:16).

With just such promises in view, we find him writing to Mary on one journey: 'After a review of most of the inhabitants, who are verily in gross darkness, I was, when wending my way through these villages amidst bald rocky hills, forcibly reminded of the passage, "The inhabitants of the rock shall sing". My imagination pictured these thousands rejoicing in God's salvation and making the high praises of Jehovah echo from rock to rock.'

One of Moffat's first endeavours in translation was with hymns. The result was the hymn book that came from Cape Town with Luke's Gospel in 1831. But even before that, the thatched roof of the chapel in Kuruman resounded with song, as Moselekatse's men heard with such surprise in 1829. He prepared another Sechuana hymn book at a later date.[28]

The song did not stop while the long wagon treks were made to other places. When they stopped at night, says his son, all would assemble at one fire and a hymn be sung. On one such trek one of the young men from Kuruman took seriously ill with fever. For two days he lay motionless in a comatose state. On the evening of the second day, when Moffat was working about thirty yards away, he says, 'I heard someone singing with a strong, clear voice.' Inquiring who was singing, he found it was the sick man:

> I hastened to the spot, and found it was even so. He was lying as I had left him about an hour before, but with a firm voice he was still singing one of our hymns, which embodied some of the striking parts of the 84th Psalm. When I entered and knelt down beside him he was singing the last verse. I felt his pulse – it was performing its last beats: and while I was looking at his motionless lips, his spirit departed to that heavenly Zion about which he had just been singing.

It was in the same spirit of praise that Moffat himself finally ended his testimony to Christ. Speaking of a Sunday shortly before his death, his biographer wrote:

> In the evening he enjoyed the singing of a few hymns, after our usual stroll round the garden. He could not join in the singing, but chose the hymns – 'The sands of time are sinking', as it is in the Presbyterian Hymnal, and he seemed to enjoy it peculiarly; also, 'Come, Thou Fount of every blessing', 'How sweet the name of Jesus sounds," 'At even when the sun was set', and 'Nearer, my God, to Thee'. He was very fond of hymns, and at home, even when quite well, it was his habit when most of the household had gone to bed, and he smoked his pipe before going himself, to repeat hymn after hymn.

At his death, we read, 'He repeated many hymns . . . one hymn he would have us read to him was, "Hail, sovereign love", his mother's favourite hymn.'

In so many ways Moffat can stand as representative of his generation of Scottish missionaries. They were diffident in speaking of themselves. Their hearts concurred with their theology in adopting the affirmation of the psalmist: 'Not unto us, O Lord, not unto us, but unto thy name give glory.' But his love for the people of Africa was bound up with his love of God. W. G. Blaikie has said that, if we were to re-adopt the old Roman custom of giving heroes the names of countries, then this pioneer, preacher and Bible translator, should be called 'Robert Moffat Africanus'. To that title this faithful Christian would surely not have objected.

---

[1] J. Du Plessis, *A History of Christian Missions in South Africa* (London, 1911; repr., Cape Town, C. Struik, 1965), p. 154.

[2] C. H. Robinson, *History of Christian Missions,* (Edinburgh: T. & T. Clark, 1915), p. 320. Livingstone, introduced to Africa by Moffat, travelled 29,000 miles in that continent. It is a mistake, however, to view him primarily as an explorer. In his own words, 'I will place no value on anything I have or may possess, except in relation to the kingdom of Christ . . . Viewed in relation

to my calling, the end of the geographical feat is only the beginning of the enterprise.' W. G. Blaikie, *The Personal Life of David Livingstone* (London: John Murray, 1880), pp. 139, 193.

[3] John Sargent, *The Life and Letters of Henry Martyn* (1819; repr. Edinburgh: Banner of Truth, 1985), p. 132.

[4] John S. Moffat, *The Lives of Robert and Mary Moffat*, eleventh edition (London: Unwin, n.d.), p. 175.

[5] Ibid., p. 12. All unidentified quotations which follow are taken from this same volume by Moffat's fourth son.

[6] For Waugh see J. Hay and Henry Belfrage, *A Memoir of John Waugh* (London: Hamilton, Adams and Co., 1830).

[7] The people are not, of course, to be confused with white, especially Dutch, natives of South Africa, to whom the same name is more commonly given.

[8] Robert Moffat, *Missionary Labours and Scenes in Southern Africa* (London: Snow, 1842), pp. 107–8.

[9] John Moffat was the fourth son in a family of ten children born to the Moffats. His own biography, which contains autobiography, reveals him as a humble Christian who sought to avoid giving glory to his family. Some thought his classic life of his parents was too 'sober', but, as his own son wrote, 'He felt strongly that the prominence given to his father's name in South Africa had, to some extent, unjustifiably overshadowed those of some others as worthy, perhaps, of honour.' Robert U. Moffat, *John Smith Moffat* (London: Murray, 1921), p. 368.

[10] For this, and a number of other names, I am retaining Robert Moffat's spelling. It was by no means standardized when he wrote and has varied since in a number of instances.

[11] It was this truth that explained to Moffat why chiefs of distant tribes could be willing to receive missionaries while those near at hand remained opposed. The former 'being sensible only of the temporal benefits enjoyed by those who received the Gospel, but comparatively ignorant of the strict requirements of the word of God; while such as live nearer, and have mingled with Christians, often have the enmity of their carnal hearts aroused by witnessing the havoc it makes among their heathenish customs and darling sins, without having tasted the blessedness of being turned from them to serve the living God.' *Missionary Labours,* p. 608.

[12] *Matabele Journals of Robert Moffat,* ed. J. P. R. Wallis, vol. 1 (London: Chatto and Windus, 1945), p. 246.

[13] *Missionary Labours*, pp. 404–5.

[14] We tend to forget the revolution which literacy and printing were to bring. In one tribe an old chief, who was told that spoken words could be made 'visible', denounced the claim as lies! But when one of his statements was written on the sand, and another literate person was called to read it 'he burst forth into a torrent of invective against his subjects and his family for not having informed him of the miracles which were being performed in his country'. Du Plessis, *Missions in South Africa,* p. 197.

[15] *Matabele Journals*, vol. 1, p. x.

[16] Various estimates of the distance are possible, for although it was about 640 miles directly, on the map, no direct routes were physically possible.

[17] Ibid., p. 229.   [18] ibid., vol. 2, p. 230.

[19] As in other parts of the world, the conduct of white colonists was often a major hindrance to missionaries. Black people understandably assumed that all whites were in league with one another, which was not the case as far as Moffat was concerned. He was critical of the Boers who, despite a Christian profession, were often lacking in missionary sympathy. John Moffat wrote in 1913: 'Happily there is a strong missionary party in the Dutch Church now, thanks to the influence of Dr Andrew Murray and his school.' *John Smith Moffat*, p. 368.

[20] *Matabele Journals*, vol. 2, pp. 202–3.

[21] Ibid., p. 213.   [22] Ibid., vol. 1, p. 140.

[23] John and Emily Moffat left Inyati in 1865. Twenty years later John wrote that both Moselekatse (who died in 1866) and his successor remained friends to the missionaries, 'but the mission has as yet been without visible success. Time only will tell what has been the meaning of this strange history. The day will declare it!' *Lives of Robert and Mary Moffat*, p. 233.

[24] In this he was closely aided by William Ashton who served in Bechuanaland for fifty-four years before his death in 1897.

[25] *Matabele Journals*, vol. 2, pp. 234–5.

[26] One of the places revisited was the old family home at Carronshore, on the Firth of Forth, where his parents had moved when he was still an infant. An old tailor in the village declined to believe that he was Moffat, the missionary from Africa, telling the stranger who made the claim, 'Are you aware, Sir! that if you were really the person you represent yourself to be, you would be the father-in-law of Livingstone, the African explorer?' Seeing the Carron river, on this same visit, Moffat exclaimed: 'Is it possible that this really narrow stream is what I have so long thought of as a broad river; and that I could think myself to be a man when I was able sixty-three years ago to swim from the one bank to the other! But, after all, I need not wonder at the difference between my conception of the size of the Carron and the reality, for it seems to me that even the Firth of Forth has shrunk woefully since I first knew it!'

[27] R. U. Moffat, *John Smith Moffat*, p. 45.

[28] How widely these hymns were sung will never be known. In 1883, Fred Arnot was surprised to find, among unevangelized Barotse, an old woman who knew the Sechuana hymn 'Jesus, King of Galilee'. Ernest Baker, *Life and Explorations of Frederick S. Arnot* (London: Seeley, Service & Co, 1921), p. 81.

PART THREE

CHURCH ISSUES

8

The Churches and Christian Unity in Scottish Church History

The Westminster Assembly (an artist's impression)

'It is a sweet meditation to think . . . that though we understand not one another, yet we have one loving and living Father that understands all our meanings; and so the different languages and dialects of the members of this body make no confusion in heaven, but meet together in his heart and affection, and are one perfume, one incense, sent up from the whole Catholic Church which is here scattered on the earth.'

HUGH BINNING

In his book, *Scottish Theology*, Principal John Macleod wrote: 'There is scarcely any segment of the circle of Christian truth that has had more abundant heed paid to it in the Theology of Scotland than that which takes to do with the Church of God.'[1] While accepting in general the truth of this statement, it is my opinion that Scottish Presbyterian discussion on the church has not given the same degree of attention to *all* aspects of the subject. On the headship of Christ in the church there is a rich and abundant literature. Fully stated in that same literature is the collateral truth that Christ's will, as revealed in his Word, is the sole rule for service in his church. On the question of church government, and especially for one order of Christian ministry over against episcopacy, there is also very full treatment. What these convictions meant is further elaborated and illustrated in records of the way men and women have upheld them at such cost at various times in Scottish history.

We turn here, however, to an aspect of the church question which appears to have received less attention, namely, what is the relation between the churches, considered as denominations, and the unity of the church universal? As a historical subject the matter is interesting but it might scarcely warrant time and renewed thought if it was not also relevant to present problems. I hope to show that it is both relevant and important.

For a starting point let us take the church scene in Scotland in the early months of the year 1559. The pre-Reformation church, still the official church of the nation, was divided into some 1,028 parishes. Apart from that church, there were groups of Protestant believers who had been worshipping in private houses or in the fields in different parts of the country. In the words of their Roman Catholic opponent, John Leslie, these people met 'in chimney nooks, secret holes and such private places, to trouble the whole country, quench all quietness, banish peace out of the land.'[2] But during 1559, such was the growing support of local town authorities, and of the so-called Lords of the Congregation, that the 'privy kirks' became publicly established as reformed congregations in at least seven towns. The next year, 1560, saw 'the Confession of Faith, Professed and Believed by the Protestants within the Realm of Scotland'. This crucial document gave the biblical basis for the reformed congregations over against the Roman church. It stated that according to Scripture the church has to be understood in two ways: first, the church universal, containing true believers, 'the elect of all ages, of all realms, nations and tongues,' and, second, particular churches, 'such as was in Corinth, Galatia, Ephesus, and other places . . . and such kirks we, the inhabitants of the realm of Scotland, professors of Christ Jesus, profess ourselves to have in our cities, towns, and places reformed. For the doctrine taught in our kirks is contained in the written word of God.'[3]

If this definition was correct then the Roman church had no biblical standing. It was not the church universal and it was devoid of the scriptural marks that the Confession held to be necessary for the recognition of a particular church – 'true preaching, right administration of the sacraments, and ecclesiastical discipline uprightly ministered as God his Word prescribes'. Behind this difference in definition is a profound and irreconcilable theological difference. Protestants held that it is through faith in the gospel that men are saved and make up the church; Roman Catholicism, on the contrary, insisted that men must first attach themselves to the church in order that through her they may be saved. And because salvation depended upon the Roman church, it was impossible that she could ever become – as the Reformers charged – 'a synagogue of Satan'. Cardinal Bellarmine, the eminent Roman Catholic apologist, wrote that the Protestants, 'to constitute anyone a member of the church, require internal graces', but we [Roman

Catholics] think that what is required is 'only an external profession and the partaking of the sacraments'. For Bellarmine, as John Macpherson has said, 'The Church is an outward institution in which men are made holy, and of which good and bad are alike members.'[4] At the heart of the Reformation was a protest against such teaching. In the words of Luther: 'Were I the only man on earth that held by the Word, *I alone would be the church*, and I would be justified in pronouncing of all the rest of the world that it was not the church.'

'The Confession of Faith', although only the work of six men was endorsed by Parliament in Edinburgh in August 1560, and that same Parliament effectively ended the pre-Reformation church. Any further administration of the sacraments according to that church was forbidden and all priests were required to recant. Those who continued to say mass were threatened with confiscation of property, banishment and, for the third offence, death. Yet for the most part the clergy and parishes as they had been seem to have remained in a kind of limbo: stipends were still paid; the dioceses remained in existence; while the faith so recently persecuted was the only one now declared lawful.

As is well known, Queen Mary defied this legislation and it was only after her flight in 1568 that the position slowly became more regularized. The Act of Parliament of 15 December 1567 declared 'the Reformed Kirks of this realm . . . to be the only true and holy Kirk of Jesus Christ within this realm'. The traditional machinery of over a thousand parishes now passed into the spiritual care of the Reformed. Not wholly into their care, it should be added, for the right to present churches ('benefices') to men still belonged to patrons (nobles, clan chiefs and others) who might hold no position in the church at all. All benefice holders were required to subscribe to the Reformed Confession although, as in previous times, they might draw the stipend of the benefice without ever ministering within its boundaries.

THE NATIONAL PROTESTANT CHURCH – A NEW SITUATION

Here was a vast change from the official church situation of 1559. Previously the 'privy kirks' had prospered despite the persecution of the state. Now the support of Parliament had transformed the situation. Reformed kirks merged into the pre-Reformation church structure and introduced a new national religion and a new national church. From one point of view this was very desirable for the Reformers – a reformed church co-extensive with the nation was a noble vision. But the problems involved were immense. In the first place there was the sheer lack of personnel to serve the whole country. Only Knox and five others drew up the Confession of 1560. One historian has assessed that there was a 'total of 85 Presbyterian workers [including readers and teachers] to whom was entrusted the Christian evangelization of Scotland'.[5] Even if, as James Kirk has more recently written, 'Many more ministers were employed by 1561 than has previously been appreciated',[6] the number by no means approximated to what was needed to serve the pre-Reformation structure with which the Reformed kirks were now merged.

Another problem was more serious. An Act of Parliament cannot change hearts and make Christian pastors, but it can and did produce many former Roman clergy who were willing to confess to being 'Reformed ministers' in order to retain their livings in the re-constituted national church. Hugh Miller, that keen observer of Scottish life, has commented on how easily many clergy made this exchange, 'Every one should know it is quite a possible thing to be a Protestant, sound enough for all the purposes of party, without being a Christian at all.'[7]

The rank and file of the population did not need to change their faith in order to secure employment. In their case a different motive existed for them to change to Protestantism. For centuries they had been taught that the sacraments were essential to salvation and now no one was permitted to receive the sacraments except in the new national church. Indeed in all parishes it was a requirement rather than a question of permission. For a non-use of the sacraments people could be fined. The result was inevitable. As a later observer wrote, 'The fiction of a national faith, requiring no homage of the heart and life, has been the fruitful source of nominal Christianity.'[8]

Out of this came an abuse in the administration of the sacraments which was to persist. Over a century later Thomas Boston faced it after he became minister at Simprin in 1699. The prevailing laxity in administration brought him to write, 'From that time I had little fondness for national churches strictly and properly so called, and wished for an amendment of the constitution of our own church, as to the membership thereof.'[9] A hundred years after Boston, James Alexander Haldane protested concerning how the making of the church virtually co-extensive with the nation hindered a right understanding of Christianity, because, he wrote:

It leads the great bulk of the inhabitants of a country to suppose themselves real Christians. All the ordinances are dispensed to them, if not grossly immoral, and that even by good men. There is not, I suppose, one child born in Scotland, who has not been baptized. This indiscriminate administration of ordinances counteracts, in a great measure, the most faithful preaching. In the latter, the minister separates between the precious and the vile; in the former he confounds them together.[10]

This is not the place to discuss why the leaders of the Reformed Church of Scotland in the sixteenth century came to allow a situation which could not do otherwise than compromise their own convictions. The Confession of 1560 had spoken of the church as a 'communion, not of profane persons, but of saints, who, as citizens of the heavenly Jerusalem, have the fruition of the most inestimable benefits'.[11] Without question the Reformation had seen a powerful revival of true Christianity in various parts of Scotland but it was nothing like co-extensive with the whole population now to be regarded as the national church.[12] Sooner or later to justify the toleration of this situation there had to be some adjustment in teaching on the church.

ONLY ONE VISIBLE CHURCH

Seventeenth-century Scottish Presbyterians came to justify the condition of the mixed national church by means of a distinction between the church visible and the church invisible. Genuine believers, they said, belong to the invisible church, but all who profess Christ without any open scandal in their lives are valid members of the church visible. Supposing, argued Samuel Rutherford, a congregation of forty, served by true preaching, should have within it twenty-four who are 'hypocrites for a time', or should all forty members be unconverted, it is nevertheless 'a true visible church'. Because, 'A visible church does not essentially and necessarily consist of believers; but only of professors of belief.'[13] Accordingly, in the words of John Macpherson:

> A community professing the faith in which the word is preached, the sacraments are administered, and discipline is exercised may not have in it one sincere believer, but only formal and heartless professors, and yet it is a true visible Church . . . It is not the profession of the possession of grace, but only the waiting upon the ordinances of grace that makes one a member of the Church. In short,

the Church of Rutherford and Brown[14] was made up of all baptized adherents, all, that is to say, of Christian descent.[15]

Circumstances often make an argument appealing. It is hard to believe that eminent men of the seventeenth century could have accepted this justification for their national church had it not been for the situation with which they were trying to wrestle. The issue was not whether the unregenerate are to be found within true churches. (They are, for God has not entrusted to men an unerring ability to judge the reality of a profession of Christ.) The issue was whether a distinction between the church visible and invisible can be used to justify the presence of unbelievers in the church in the manner a national church required. The biblical simplicity of the Confession of 1560, which knew only a universal church and particular local churches, required no such breadth. David Calderwood (1575–1650) spoke for the earlier view when he wrote in 1621 that the New Testament nowhere knows 'a visible Church endowed with power of ecclesiastical government taken for a whole shire, or Countie . . . City churches and town churches the Scripture knoweth, but not countrie churches. For when the Scripture speaketh of a province or country, it speaketh in the plural number.'[16]

The distinction made between the church visible and invisible was used to justify a situation that the New Testament does not justify. In Scripture the heavenly church, the body of Christ, is not a church *other than* the visible, rather spiritual reality is expressed in the visible, the members of which are 'saints', 'in Christ Jesus', and possessed of a 'citizenship in heaven'. To the church as visible belong the same nature, the same glory and the same privileges as the heavenly. The fact that this may not be true of some who are found in churches, far from permitting a lowered definition of 'church', only indicates that there are men 'in the church but not of it' (*1 John* 2:19). They have 'crept in unawares'. Thomas Boston was right to question the dichotomy between invisible and visible. 'Christ hath not two churches – one visible and another invisible – but one Church, which is in one aspect visible and in another aspect invisible.'[17] More recently John Murray has forcefully written on the same point: 'It has been customary to define the church, viewed from its visible aspect, in terms merely of profession, and thus to allow for the discrepancy between the church ideally considered and the church realistically considered. This allows for a definition that is embracive enough to include those who are not really members of Christ's body. This, I submit, is an error.'[18] He goes on to give scriptural evidence.

But not only did the seventeenth-century Scots defend the national church idea, they went further. Whatever the defects they recognized in the church as visible, they held that its national unity was essential if the oneness of Christ's kingdom was to be seen. It seems anomalous that they should have combined a low view of church membership with such a high doctrine of visible unity. To them it seemed self-evident that, as Christ has only one church, there has to be a unity in government if that oneness is to be preserved. 'Is Christ divided?' asked Rutherford, quoting Paul. 'There is but one Christ; yea, the Head and the body make but one Christ, so that you cannot divide the body without dividing Christ.'[19] The only alternative they could see to a church that was one in her organization was schism and disunity. Thus James Durham could write:

> It is impossible for those that maintain that principle of the unity of the Catholic visible Church to own a divided way of administering government or other ordinances, but it will infer either that one party hath no interest in the

Church, or that one Church may be many, and so that
the unity thereof in its visible state is to no purpose. This
we take for granted.[20]

What Durham took for granted – that unity depends on
subordination – became the fixed view in Scottish history.
Within a nation there can only be *one church* and thus when a
division occurs the immediate issue becomes the question,
which party in the division continues the true church? Thus
in their Declaration of 1695, the Reformed Presbyterians of
the United Societies rejected what they regarded as the
compromised settlement of the Church of Scotland and called
themselves 'the true Presbyterian church of Christ in
Scotland'.[21] In the Secession of 1733 it was insisted by the
leaders that in reality it was no secession at all: rather they were
the faithful representatives of the one church. In the words of
Ebenezer Erskine,

> We have made a Secession from the judicatories of the
> Established Church; yet we never made a secession from
> the visible Church of Christ in Scotland – by no manner
> of means.[22]

James Walker was correctly representing the Secessionists'
viewpoint when he wrote:

> It was not a separation from the Church of Scotland, that
> ideal Church of 1638, which had so great a hold of all
> good Presbyterians; it was a mere secession from the
> present occupants, as it were, of this divine temple.[23]

The influence of similar thinking was to be found in the
Separatists of the northern Highlands in the early nineteenth
century. These Christians left the parish churches to hold their
own services yet they meant to remain 'within the Church'
and to prove it they would attend communions and take their
children to the regular ministers for baptism.[24]

The church theology of the seventeenth-century men was seen again in the separation of ministers and people from the Church of Scotland at the Disruption of 1843. According to the founders of the Free Church of Scotland they were not a new denomination at all. Their language was: 'We separate as *Members of the Church of Scotland*, from that Church as *now* established by law, because it has ceased to be what it formerly was understood to be.'[25] The official organ of the Free Church of 1843 believed in 'the very great importance of the Free Church adopting no course which might even seem to invalidate her character and claim to be regarded still and always as Scotland's rightful, true, and National Church . . . Scarcely anything could be more pernicious to the position, duties and prospects of the Free Church, than for her to allow herself to acquire the aspect and character of a mere sect.'[26]

The Free Church minority, which refused to join the United Free Church in 1900, repeated the same argument. The minority professed that they rested not on 'the possession of funds or stone or lime', but on the continued testimony of the Church of 1843, which was 'not a new church, but the Church of Scotland, only free'.[27]

WHY THE ARGUMENT FAILED:
1. UPHOLDING THE WRONG PRIORITY

The idea of preserving Christian unity by means of recognizing only one church failed because it elevated the form of church government as a truth of primary importance. Presbyterians of the seventeenth century rightly saw Christian unity as fundamental to Christianity but they erred in thinking that this unity could only be secured by means of one single ecclesiastical structure. In the words of George Whytock, one of their later spokesmen: 'The elders of a particular congregation are to consider themselves subordinate to those of the neighbouring congregations, and these again to a larger body . . . This is not the subordination of one church to another, it is the subordination of a part to the whole.'[28]

In principle, the goal of this view of government is international. In Gillespie's words: 'The line of ecclesiastical subordination is longer and further stretched than the line of civil subordination; for a national synod must be subordinate and subject to an universal synod.'[29] This conviction lay behind the Scots desire to include the Church of England in their plans for reformation in the 1640s.

So definitely was this view of unity believed by a number of the Scots at the Westminster Assembly that, inevitably, they had to regard all who did not share their understanding of church government as opponents of 'Christian unity'. In order to secure unity, they held, there had to be one form of government embracing all churches.

I am not here concerned to discuss the Presbyterian system as such; my point is rather that unity does not take its starting point at the organizational and institutional level. It must start rather with the gospel and with principles directly related to the gospel. Unity begins with believers being in Christ and being indwelt by the Holy Spirit. From that fact, love, sympathy, helpfulness between Christians will naturally follow, and follow as universally as circumstances and the fallibility of Christians permit. For Christ is not divided, nor are his people. They already belong to the one church, 'You are come to . . . the general assembly and church of the firstborn, which are written in heaven' (*Heb.* 12:23). Christians in different parts of the world *are* united in their Head, even though they never meet on earth. The unity is spiritual. It depends not upon participation in a common, universal form of church government but upon spiritual realities – realities that are strengthened by fellowship with Christ and weakened by grieving the Holy Spirit whose presence is the bond of union.[30]

As already said, this was the emphasis of the Reformers against the externalism of the Roman Catholic Church. At that date Roman Catholic authors responded that all would be confusion and disorder if Christians were not kept under the rule of the church. To which it was replied, as for instance by William Tyndale, that there is rule in the church but it is the rule of Scripture and the existence of 'the law of love' between brethren.[31] This rule was a great reality for those in Christ and it bore the spiritual fruit so largely absent in the pre-Reformation church despite all the supposed unity of government that then existed.

In the century following the Reformation, Presbyterian successors to the Reformers unwittingly inverted the gospel priority when they spoke as though there could be no real Christian unity without uniformity in government.[32] As is well known, the debate on uniformity of government at the Westminster Assembly foundered, not because of disagreement on the gospel or on the duties of Christians to one another, but because not all could see that a tiered system of church courts, the lower subordinate to the higher, was laid down in the New Testament as necessary to unity. John R. de Witt states the position of the minority at the Assembly well when he writes:

> The Independents responded that they did not desire a total separation. They would practise the same worship, have the same office bearers, the same qualifications for church members which 'the Assembly itself holds forth to have been in the Primitive Churches, viz., visible Saints, that being of age do profess faith in Christ, and obedience unto Christ,' and the same censures. They would be accountable to the state, and hold communion with the presbyterian churches by an occasional exchange of preachers and sharing of the sacraments both of baptism and the Lord's Supper. In difficult cases they would advise

with the elders of other churches, and should a miscarriage occur they would account to them. This was, the dissenters argued, quite another thing than total separation and did not deserve to be scored with the odious name of schism . . . A schism consists 'in an open breach of Christian love, and not in every diversity of opinion and practice'.[33]

The mistake of the majority at the Westminster Assembly was the attempt to put all the Christians in the British Isles under one common church government and to count any deviation from that government as schism. The sheer realities of Christian experience were to prove that thinking to be wrong. The church is not primarily an external society. Certainly its members will be found joined, wherever possible, to a local church where gospel truth is preached and practised, but to unchurch any such congregations because of different views on how they should be formally connected with others is to elevate questions of government to the same level as the gospel itself. From the seventeenth century onwards, common Christian experience made it impossible to say that there can be no Christian unity without a formal union of churches. There were simply too many Christians, united in the fundamentals of heart and mind and yet with different views on issues of church order, to implement what is now called organic unity.

This recognition was perhaps slower in coming in Scotland. As already noted, as late as 1847 a Free Church of Scotland writer could speak of 'a mere sect' as being the alternative to 'Scotland's rightful, true, and National Church'. Yet by that date the *Free Church Magazine* was no longer speaking with one voice and a better understanding was beginning to prevail. It came to be recognized that no Protestant and evangelical denomination had any exclusive claim to the word 'Church'.

Thus in a leading article on 'Christian Union' in the *Free Church Magazine* it was said:

> It is in vain for any one Church to say: 'we are blameless;' for we have all sinned and violated Christian love and fellowship; but it is not for any one denomination to take upon itself the office of censor, and assert, that though doubtless guilty in some degree, others are more so . . . we humbly, yet very gratefully, regard the increase of evangelical principles among the various denominations, as rapidly producing the only ground on which a truly Christian union can be realized; for as by the prevalence of evangelical principles, union with God will be realized; so by union with him we shall realize union with each other.[34]

The theologians of the Free Church developed this thinking against the older view. William Cunningham wrote:

> Does the unity ascribed in Scripture to the church imply that there must be entire uniformity in all matters of belief and practice among Christians, or that all societies claiming to be regarded as churches must be included in one external visible communion, and subject to one external visible government? It can be easily proved that there is no warrant in Scripture for alleging that the unity there predicated of the church of Christ necessarily implies this.[35]

Similarly James Bannerman in his two volumes on the doctrine of the Church rejected the idea that being a true church depends upon its form of government and its connection with other churches. Where that idea is adopted, he wrote, there 'begins that error which is developed in the intolerant principles of many in the present day who would unchurch all denominations but their own . . . Admit that the possession of a true faith, and that alone, is of the essence of a Church, – and you assign to the truth the place and importance that rightfully belongs to it. But join to the possession of the true faith the administration of outward ordinances, as necessary to constitute a Christian Church, – and you assign to outward ordinances a rank and value which are not justly theirs, and make them of primary, and not, as they truly are, of secondary importance.[36]

It was just such thinking on the relative importance of different truths which brought John Duncan's wise aphorism, 'I'm first a Christian, next a Catholic, then a Calvinist, fourth a Paedobaptist and fifth a Presbyterian. I cannot reverse this order.'[37]

American Presbyterians had reached the same conclusion. R. L. Dabney wrote trenchantly on the subject in his article, 'What is Christian Union?'

As the invisible church is one and catholic, the visible church will strive towards the same unity. But as the bond of union in the invisible church is a common faith and love, and no outward organism, so the unity of the visible church will evince itself in ties of affection and brotherhood rather than in external conformity.[38]

Similarly, A. A. Hodge argued: 'If God had followed our idea, how simple a thing it would have been to make a united Church descending from Adam and Eve!' Instead, he went on, the external organization of the church

is only accidental and temporary, and subject to change and variation . . . the Christian religion which we receive takes various colours and tones from the nationality, from the tribe, and from the race. Undoubtedly there is such a thing as schism . . . All high-churchism, all claims that our Church is the one Church and only Church, are of the essence of schism; all pride and bigotry are of the essence of schism; all want of universal love, all jealousy, and all attempts to take advantage of others in controversy or in Church extension, are of the essence of schism.[39]

A comment from the *Princeton Theological Review* is also worthy of inclusion. Meade C. Williams writing on 'The Multitude of Denominations' said:

> Unity of spirit can prevail where union of organization is not practical . . . To press the necessity of the visible oneness is the very essence of popery. It involves a conception of ecclesiasticism, and of the externality of the kingdom of God, and of what is meant by oneness in Christ, and of the nature of Church ordinances, and of the nature and validity of ministerial function, which is utterly foreign to that on which Christendom has been built.[40]

WHY THE ARGUMENT FAILED: 2. AN IMPOSSIBLE DEDUCTION

There is a further reason why the belief that Christian unity has to mean only one visible church, formally united in a common government, had to fail. Inevitably it encouraged an exclusiveness which was contrary to the spirit of the gospel. If only *one* church can claim to represent the unity of the body of Christ then those who remain outside her fellowship have to be regarded as in a condition of schism and so public co-operation with them is not to be permitted or encouraged. Before there can be communion between two parties thus divided the side at fault has to acknowledge their error. This is not a theoretical possibility. It was just such thinking among the Secession churches of the eighteenth century which gave rise to the principle, 'no communion without union'.[41]

Even in the nineteenth century this principle was still being upheld. Thomas M'Crie, for example, believed that 'no communion without union' followed axiomatically from the unity of the church. He wrote that to allow 'partial or occasional communion' among Christians who otherwise remain separate 'with their distinct constitutions . . . strikes against the radical principles of the unity of the Church, and confirms schism . . . for where communion is lawful, it will not be easy to vindicate separation from the charge of schism.'[42] In other words, if occasional communion is permissible between two denominations, then there ought to be a complete union.

M'Crie, along with earlier authors, thus claimed a scriptural justification for exclusiveness. The painful consequences of this view have been apparent in Scottish history. They appear, for instance, in the rift between the Secession churches and George Whitefield on his visit to Scotland in 1742. The Seceders from the Church of Scotland wanted Whitefield to preach only among their churches on the grounds that to preach in the Church of Scotland would be to condone the injustice they had suffered from the General Assembly of that Church.[43] In their eyes the Secession church was the true church and therefore Whitefield could not be allowed to be in communion both with themselves and with evangelicals who remained in the Church of Scotland.

This same thinking prevented the Seceders recognizing the great blessing given to congregations of the Church of Scotland in the revival of 1742. There are more recent examples of the same kind of attitude and instead of simply condemning it we need to understand how it arises. Wrong principle leads to such practice.

The principle which would restrict fellowship on the grounds of churchmanship has to be wrong for it is alien to the essential instincts of the Christian life and nullifies the duties so well expressed in the Westminster Confession's words on 'the Communion of Saints':

All saints that are united to Jesus Christ their head by his Spirit, and by faith, have fellowship with him in his graces, sufferings, death, resurrection, and glory. And being united to one another in love, they have communion in each other's gifts and graces; and are obliged to the performance of such duties, public and private, as do conduce to the mutual good, both in the inward and outward man (XXVI:I).

One of the finest statements against exclusiveness will be found in the published letter of R. M. M'Cheyne on 'Communion with Brethren of Other Denominations', in which he says:

Where any minister of any denomination holds the Head, is sound in doctrine and blameless in life, preaches Christ and him crucified as the only way of pardon, and the only source of holiness, especially if he has been owned of God in the conversion of souls and the up-building of saints, we are bound to hold ministerial communion with him, whenever Providence opens the way. What are we that we should shut our pulpits against such a man? True, he may hold that prelacy is the scriptural form of church government . . . True, he may have inconsistencies of mind which we cannot account for – he may have prejudices of sect and education which destroy much of our comfort in meeting him (and can we plead exemption from these?) – he may sometimes have spoken rashly and uncharitably (I also have done the same): still, I cannot but own him as a servant of Christ. If the Master owns him in his work, shall the sinful fellow servant disown him?[44]

SOME LESSONS

1. Scottish church history would have been very different if there had not been added to the two biblical usages of the

word *ecclesia* stated in the Confession of 1560 the idea of a national church. Connected with that addition, as we have seen, came the conclusion that separation from the one church had to be schism. Yet while hindsight makes it easy to be critical, the reasons which led the Scottish Reformers to that position have to be appreciated. The only position they had ever known was one in which civil and church communities were identical, and they found justification for this in the theocracy of the Old Testament. Further, they did not believe that Scripture permits civil government to be neutral towards God, with no moral duties.[45] They were also patriots as well as Christians and the issues they faced – the civil and the Christian – were not easily separated. Experience had shown them how Roman Catholicism is a threat to civil liberty as well as to the souls of men.

Thus when the Scottish Parliament (for mixed motives) sided with the Reformation, and was willing to recognize a Reformed national church in place of the church which it dispossessed, the continuance of the former church-state unity appeared very desirable. But the arrangement condoned a national com-prehensiveness with respect to church membership which could not be other than inconsistent with the purity of the church. What John Owen wrote of developments in the fourth century has a real parallel in post-Reformation Scotland:

It came to pass that in the accession of the nations in general unto the profession of the gospel, church-order was suited and framed unto their secular state . . . Herein, I say, did the guides of the church certainly miss their rule and depart from it, in the days of Constantine the emperor, and afterward under other Christian emperors, when whole towns, cities, yea, nations, offered at once to join themselves unto it. Evident it is that they were not wrought hereunto by the same power, nor induced unto it on the same motives, or led by the same means, with those who formerly under persecution were converted unto the faith of our Lord Jesus Christ. And this quickly manifested itself in the lives and conversations of many, yea, of the most of them. Hence those which were wise quickly understood that what the church had got in multitude and number it had lost in the beauty and glory of its holy profession. Chrysostom in particular complains of it frequently, and in many places cries out, 'What have I to do with this multitude? A few serious believers are more worth than them all.'[46]

The church's independence in Scotland was compromised when the civil powers made it national. Even in Andrew Melville's protest to King James VI at Falkland in 1596 the compromise is evident. As proof of Presbyterian defiance of state control, Melville's words to the king, 'There are two kings and two kingdoms in Scotland', are often quoted. In the first of those kingdoms, James was told, 'he is not a king, nor a lord, nor a head, but a member'. Yet in the last word, 'a member', lay a main part of the problem. The King, the magistrates, and civil rulers were all *members* of the same church and history was to show that many of them had no business to be there. An acceptance and reliance upon civil aid, supposedly co-operating in the Presbyterian cause, was to be disastrous in seventeenth-century Scotland. Listen to Rutherford recognizing what had happened when it was too late. Near the end of his life, and reviewing the position up to 1649, he wrote:

When our land and church were thus contending for that begun reformation, these in authority did still oppose the work; and there were not wanting men from among ourselves, men of prelatical spirits, who, with some other time-serving courtiers, did not a little undermine the building; and we doating too much upon sound parliaments, and lawful general assemblies, fell from our first-love . . . Our work in public was too much in sequestration of estates, fining and imprisoning, more than in a compassionate mournfulness of spirit towards those whom we saw to oppose the work. In our assemblies we were . . . more upon form, citations, leading of witnesses, suspension from benefices, than spiritually to persuade and work upon the conscience by the meekness and gentleness of Christ . . . What way the army, and the sword, and the countenance of the nobles seemed to sway, that way the censures were carried . . . We are not for an army of saints, and free of all mixture of ill affected men: but it seems an high prevarication for churchmen to counsel and teach, that the weight and trust of Christ and his kingdom should be laid upon the whole party of such as have been his enemies to our cause.[47]

Rutherford is referring to the period when taking the Solemn League and Covenant (the document framed largely by the Scottish church for the further reformation of Britain) was enforced upon all over the age of eighteen. There is good reason, then, why even the most Presbyterian of later historians should admit that events were marred by 'the mixture of things sacred and civil in the same bond, and the enjoining of it under civil penalties'.[48] Various explanations are given why this ever happened but the conclusion can hardly be avoided that it was bound up with laxity on church membership, and that this had inevitable consequences on the decision-making of the church. On this subject there is significant comment from the nineteenth-century Scottish Reformed Presbyterian leader, William Henry Goold. In writing of the abiding significance of John Owen, Goold was clearly in sympathy with Owen's insistence on 'godliness and spirituality as requisite to membership in the Church . . . It was his belief and hope that not in a vast system, the result of parliamentary enactment, but in separate communities of the faithful, piety, deep and true, might grow and prosper.' On the subject of church membership, Goold believed, 'Owen stands honourably distinguished in Christian authorship.'[49]

2. It is arguable that the low view of church membership that was permitted in the Scottish church led to an undue prominence for ministers and elders as if they alone could be expected to edify others. The emphasis thus came to be on the church as an institution where people were to attend and listen rather than on a fellowship. Knox's weekly meeting where a number might speak early passed out of use as though it could be assumed that gifts for edification belonged only to office bearers, especially ministers. What a recent writer says of Gillespie would be equally true of most of his seventeenth-century colleagues: 'We miss in Gillespie the New Testament description of a giving of gifts by the Holy Spirit to every member of the Body for mutual edification.'[50]

One result of this was that the Christian instinct for fellowship often came to be supplied in Scotland by meetings other than those of the church, although participants were all church members. When this 'irregularity' was opposed as disorderly by some in the seventeenth century, Rutherford defended it on the grounds that 'the Word's working and the Spirit's working are not always confined to the hour of the sand-glass [in church], neither is the Spirit tied to a pulpit, and a gown, and a minister's tongue . . . Private Christians will rub one another's memory and their cold hearts; and often what ministers cannot do in public, God's Spirit with private helps will do at home.'[51]

By the eighteenth century 'fellowship meetings' were a regular part of Christian life in Scotland. We find the need for them urged by such a definite Presbyterian as Archibald Hall (1736–78) who gives eighteen pages to the subject in his *Gospel*

Worship. 'Fellowship-societies,' he writes, are to be held in order that Christians 'may *communicate their gifts and graces* to each other's edification. Hence is that command of the apostle, 1 Peter 4:10: "As every man hath received a gift, even so minister the same one to another, as good stewards of the manifold grace of God." All *talents for public office* are the gifts of an exalted Saviour . . . but there is no evidence that the apostle only, or even principally, intended *such talents* in that passage.'[52] Such meetings were clearly designed to provide what was insufficiently present in the churches.

3. No system of church government can claim to be perfectly scriptural, and each may be said to have its own weakness. The weakness of Presbyterianism (and not only Presbyterianism) is its tendency to the centralization of power. To counter that propensity it was Hugh Martin, a Presbyterian, who argued that it is presbyteries, not General Assemblies, which are the radical courts of the church:

> A Presbytery is more fully equipped with all the functions of a church than the General Assembly is. A Presbytery is, within its bounds, the Church within these bounds. The Assembly is in no sense the Church.[53]

Whatever may be argued from the counsel at Jerusalem in Acts 15, it surely cannot be that all decisions belong to annual national assemblies. In defence of General Assemblies it is always said that they have no authority other than to implement the clear directives of Scripture. The fact, as any honest historian must admit, is that Assemblies have too often acted without scriptural authority.[54] Of course, there is no guarantee that presbyteries will not do the same, but human nature being what it is, a General Assembly gives greater scope for the exercise of pride and ambition. Permanent rule by General Assemblies, and Commissions of Assembly, has encouraged a centralization which is too liable to be misused. There is weight in the argument of Dr Ian Henderson that the call for greater 'unity' has been too often a quest for power.[55]

In the vast quantity of seventeenth-century literature that deals with the subject of the church there are no warnings more permanently important than Rutherford's when he says, '*Why should we strive? For we be Brethren,* the sons of one father, the born citizens of one mother Jerusalem . . . We strive as we are carnal, we dispute as we are men, we war from our lusts, we dispute from diversity of star-light and day-light.'[56]

4. I have spent time on the question of a national church because I believe that in Scotland it has skewed subsequent Presbyterian discussion on the question of denominations. The opinion has lingered down through the centuries that somehow Christian unity means being connected in one single church government. It is not an accident that almost every branch of the Presbyterian communion in Scotland has employed the word 'Church' in the singular in her formal title. Not to do that, it seemed to be assumed, would be to fall short of true unity.[57] And once the word 'church' was equated with denomination it was an easy step to thinking that to the denomination belongs everything said of the New Testament church. Thus to leave a denomination could well be treated as schism.[58]

The effort to bring all the Christians of a nation under one common church government not only failed; it was bound to fail. It could only have succeeded by the use of a compulsion and coercion which is fundamentally alien to the gospel. Its great mistake was to suppose that all right-minded believers must come to the same conclusion, not only on the gospel but also on details of church order. Concerning that mistake R. L. Dabney has written:

Men, being fallible, always have differed, and always will honestly differ in details. How vain is it to expect anything else, when we look soberly over the past history of opinion; when we remember that the different races are reared in different climes, languages, political institutions, and social usages, all of which have an unavoidable effect upon their habitudes of thought; when we consider the limitations and weakness of man's understanding; and, above all, when we bear in mind that he is still at best a sinner, imperfectly sanctified, with passions and prejudices still subsisting. Men cannot be made to think exactly alike, if they think honestly, and this simply because they are men.[59]

Denominations have arisen in Protestantism largely because Christians have differed in their understanding of biblical issues which, although not fundamental to salvation, have been regarded by their founders as involving faithfulness to Christ and his Word. As a Free Church writer noted in 1845, 'Almost every party now existing in Scotland arose out of some peculiar contest, in which some important truth was bitterly assailed, and had to be strenuously defended.' It was far better for Scotland that denominations should be formed, on the basis of conscientiously-held convictions, rather than that freedom to interpret Scripture should be suppressed in the supposed interest of unity.

The justification for a new denomination is the commitment of several congregations to stand together to uphold a truth, or to carry out biblical duties, in a manner which they cannot do as effectively as individual churches or from within another denomination. A denomination is only sectarian when it expects to be regarded as a unique representative of the church universal, and where it shows no regard for maintaining unity of spirit among all who belong to Christ. Cooperation in such inter-denominational activity as requires no suppression of truth, and no condoning of serious error, is surely obligatory for all denominations. The danger of denominations is that with the passage of time commitment to the cause for which it was formed passes out of sight, or no longer ceases to be an issue, and attachment to the denomination becomes an end in itself. When a denomination loses the biblical justification for its existence, as has often happened in history, it forfeits any true claim to the loyalty of its members.[60]

5. The current ecumenical emphasis on the organic union of denominations in order to achieve 'Christian unity' is fundamentally misconceived. Oneness in organization is unnecessary to unity. 'Interdenominational unity in the faith', wrote Principal Donald Maclean, 'is the only unity the New Testament teaches Christians to aspire to.'[61] What are essential are gospel truth and the graces of the Holy Spirit, and the men who are doing most for unity are those who are giving themselves to these great priorities. Whitefield was not ignoring church unity but doing the most to promote it when he emphasized our supreme need of the Holy Spirit:

> Were we but animated, led and influenced by this Spirit, what a blessed union would there be among all the churches of Jesus Christ! It is a want of more of this, that now at present disunites us. I despair therefore of a greater union, till a greater measure of the Spirit be poured from on high. Hence, therefore, I am resolved simply to preach the gospel of Christ, and leave others to quarrel by and with themselves. Love, forbearance, long-suffering, and frequent prayer to your dear Lord Jesus is the best way.[62]

Two centuries after Whitefield's death, Meade Williams argued for the same conclusion:

That Christendom is to be embodied in one great external organism (assuming the Protestant conception of religious truth to endure) is an idle dream. More practical, and far more important, is the cultivation of spiritual unity, and the realization more and more that in the bonds of Jesus Christ all who love Him are already one. It is the remark of an old English Puritan that 'variety of opinions and the unity of those who hold them may stand together'. If the union of Church organizations is not always practicable, spiritual unity is. For spiritual unity, for a fellowship in the Spirit, for fraternity and confidence and good-will and cooperation in testimony and service, we should be ready to go to great lengths.[63]

---

[1] John Macleod, *Scottish Theology* (repr. Edinburgh: Banner of Truth, 1974), p. 31.

[2] Quoted by James Kirk in his chapter on 'The "Privy Kirks"', *Patterns of Reform* (T. & T. Clark: Edinburgh, 1989), p. 12.

[3] See David Calderwood, *The History of the Reformation in Scotland*, vol. 2, ed. T. Thomson (Edinburgh: Wodrow Soc., 1843), pp. 27–9.

[4] John Macpherson, *The Doctrine of the Church in Scottish Theology* (Edinburgh: MacNiven &Wallace, 1903), p. 59, where he discusses the Reformed rejection of Bellarmine's teaching.

[5] Quoted in Johnston, *Treasury of the Scottish Covenant* (Edinburgh: Elliot, 1887) p. 33.

[6] Kirk, *Patterns of Reform*, p. 130.

[7] Hugh Miller, *Scenes and Legends of the North of Scotland* (repr. Edinburgh: B & W, 1999), p. 104. He notes a similar turn-round in 1660 when five-sixths of the Presbyterian Synod of Ross became Episcopalian curates and intolerant of all who failed to conform (p. 106).

[8] Dr Hutton of Paisley, quoted in Johnston, *Treasury of the Scottish Covenant*, p. 198.

[9] *Memoirs of Thomas Boston* (repr. Edinburgh: Banner of Truth, 1988), p. 172. Later in life he wrote: 'I apprehend the malady will be incurable, till the present constitution be violently thrown down' (Ibid., p. 338). See also, pp. 487–8.

[10] J. A. Haldane, *A View of the Social Worship and Ordinances Observed by the First Christians* (Edinburgh: Ritchie, 1805), p. 422.

[11] Calderwood, *History*, vol. 2, p. 27. While the Scots Reformers were concerned to 'damn the error of the Anabaptists' (p. 35), the grounds on

which the administration of baptism to children proceeded were far too broad: 'The father, or in his absence, the god-father, shall rehearse the articles of his faith' (p. 103). The General Assembly of 1597 noted 'the abuse of readers baptizing children gottin in adultery and fornication, before satisfaction made by the offenders' (Ibid., vol. 5, pp. 646–7). There was probably a growing concern among ministers over indiscriminate infant baptism, for when the General Assembly came under the control of the bishops and the King's commissioners in 1616 it ordered that 'every minister shall minister the sacrament of baptism whensoever it shall be required, under the pain of deposition'; and further, that there be punishment for those who do not present a child for communion at the age of fourteen (Ibid., vol. 7, pp. 228–30). These decisions, Calderwood noted, were 'against Protestants and sincere professors'.

[12] Even as near to Edinburgh as Dunbar, English Puritans visiting Scotland in 1568 had been shocked to find that on Good Friday 'they saw certain persons go bare-footed and bare-legged to the church, to creep to the cross'. Reported by Edmund Grindal, *Remains of Edmund Grindal* (Cambridge: Parker Soc., 1843), p. 295.

[13] S. Rutherford, *A Peaceable and Temperate Plea for Paul's Presbyterie in Scotland* (London: Bartlet, 1642), pp. 105–7.

[14] John Brown of Wamphray, 'who it may be was our greatest divine between Rutherford and Halyburton' (Macleod, *Scottish Theology*, p. 148).

[15] Macpherson, *Church in Scottish Theology*, p. 66.

[16] D. Calderwood, *The Altar of Damascus: or, The Pattern of the English Hierarchie, and Church Policie Obtruded upon the Church of Scotland* (1621), pp. 82–3. The variation in the spelling of 'Countie' and 'countrie' is in the original. The difficulties in which this book was produced is reflected in the absence of any place of publication on the title page.

[17] Quoted in James Walker, *The Theology and Theologians of Scotland* (Edinburgh: T. & T. Clark, 1872) p. 121.

[18] 'Nature and Unity of the Church', *Collected Writings of John Murray*, (Edinburgh: Banner of Truth, 1977), vol. 2, pp. 326–7. What Murray calls 'an all-important distinction' is 'that between what a situation may existentially be by reason of the sin, hypocrisy, and infirmity of men, on the one hand, and the terms in which the church is to be defined, on the other' (p. 327). See also, *Collected Writings*, vol. 1, pp. 231–6.

[19] Walker, *Theology of Scotland*, p. 102, quoting from the conclusion of Rutherford on *Liberty of Conscience*.

[20] Ibid., p. 99.

[21] 'The Declaration of a Poor, wasted, misrepresented Remnant . . . ' in *Testimony-bearing Exemplified: A Collection* (Paisley: Neilson, 1791), p. 287.

[22] A. R. MacEwen, *The Erskines* (Edinburgh: Oliphant, 1900), p. 129.

[23] Walker, *Theology of Scotland*, p. 114.

[24] See John Macleod, *The North Country Separatists* (Inverness: Northern Counties Newspaper, 1930), p. 15.

[25] 'Why Separate?' in *The Free Churchman*, 15 Sept. 1843 (Calcutta: Rushton), p. 11.

[26] *Free Church Magazine*, vol. 3 (Edinburgh: Johnstone, 1846), p. 147.

[27] 'The Free Church', *Monthly Record of the Free Church of Scotland*, Dec. 1900, p. 1. Meanwhile the Free Presbyterian Church (a secession of 1893) was making the same claim.

[28] George Whytock, *A Short Vindication of Presbyterial Church Government* (Edinburgh: 1799).

[29] George Gillespie, 'One Hundred and Eleven Propositions', in *The Presbyterian's Armoury: Works of George Gillespie* (Edinburgh: Ogle and Oliver, 1846), , vol. 1, p. 20. R. L. Dabney believed that similar thinking was behind the theories prompting a Pan-Presbyterian Alliance in the nineteenth century and wrote: '*They involve one of the essential elements of popery*. The cardinal doctrine of the Reformers concerning the church was, that only the spiritual and invisible church could be catholic and ecumenical.' *Discussions: Evangelical and Theological* (repr. London: Banner of Truth, 1967), vol. 2, p. 537.

[30] In his exposition of Hebrews 12:22–24, John Owen argues that it is because men do not understand the meaning of this heavenly church, to which all Christians belong, that they fall into confusion and contentions over its earthly expression: 'If this only true notion of the catholic church were received, as it ought to be, it would cast contempt on all those contests about the church, or churches, which at this day so perplex the world.' *Exposition of Hebrews*, vol. 7, p. 352.

[31] Tyndale, *Exposition and Notes* (Cambridge: Parker Soc., 1849), p. 251.

[32] Their mistake appears to have arisen, in part, out of deference to such Church Fathers as Cyprian and Augustine who held that only one single, visible communion is the true catholic church, identified by historical succession from the apostles. Thus in the judgment of these Fathers, 'The Donatists are neither the Church nor even a church.' S. L. Greenslade, *Schism in the Early Church* (London: SCM, 1964), p. 174. As Greenslade points out, there is an untenability in Augustine's position; his criticism of 'churchness' was in conflict with his understanding of grace – a fact illustrated by his words, 'Many who seem to be without are within, and many who seem to be within are without' (*De Bapt.* V, 38). 'The Reformation,' wrote Warfield, 'inwardly considered, was just the triumph of Augustine's doctrine of grace over Augustine's doctrine of the Church.' *Studies in Tertullian and Augustine* (New York: OUP, 1930), p. 130. But even a century after the Reformation this was not clear to all. 'Today,' Greenslade observed, 'with our longer experience of a divided Christianity, most of us find it impossible to deny that the Holy Spirit has been working in communions outside the Church as it is defined by Cyprian' (*Schism*, pp. 181–2). Far greater clarity was brought to the seventeenth-century debate on this point among the Puritans by John Owen's work, *Of Schism: The True Nature of It Discovered and Considered*, 1657 (*Works*, Goold ed., vol. 13).

[33] John Richard de Witt, *Jus Divinum: The Westminster Assembly and the Divine Right of Church Government* (Kampen: Kok, 1969), pp. 162–3. The quotations are from *The Papers and Answers of the Dissenting Brethren and the Committee of the Assembly of Divines . . . for Accommodation, 1645*

(London, 1648). A writer in the *Free Church Magazine* (vol. 4, p. 311) repeats the traditional Presbyterian criticism that at Westminster the Independents sacrificed 'the vast advantages of a common association'; as the above quotation makes clear, their objection was not to association.

[34] *Free Church Magazine, January to December, 1845*, vol. 2, p. 321.

[35] W. Cunningham, *Historical Theology* (repr. London: Banner of Truth, 1960), vol. 1, p. 24.

[36] J. Bannerman, *The Church of Christ* (repr. London: Banner of Truth, 1960), vol. 1, pp. 60–1. His reference to intolerance has to do with Anglo-Catholicism and Roman Catholicism.

[37] William Knight, *Colloquia Peripatetica: Conversations with John Duncan* (Edinburgh: Oliphant, 1907), p. 8.

[38] Dabney, *Discussions,* vol. 2, p. 434. He correctly anticipated the ecumenical movement: 'The Protestant world will soon be educated to set inordinate store by that of which God makes least account – formal union; *at the expense* of what he regards as supreme value – doctrinal fidelity.' (Ibid., p. 538).

[39] A. A. Hodge, *Evangelical Theology* (1890; repr. Edinburgh: Banner of Truth, 1976), pp. 182–3.

[40] *Princeton Theological Review*, vol. 3, 1905, p. 30.

[41] George Patterson, *Memoir of the Rev. James MacGregor* (Edinburgh: Oliphant, 1859), p. 31.

[42] Thomas M'Crie, *Discourses on the Unity of the Church* (Edinburgh: Blackwood, 1821), pp. 94–5. Also in *Works of Thomas M'Crie* (Edinburgh: Blackwood, 1857), vol. 4, p. 177.

[43] As one of their own number wrote on the leaders of the Secession Church: 'Their conduct, in refusing to hold Christian or ministerial communion with Mr Whitefield, on the grounds of diversity of opinion about church government, was quite consistent with their avowed principles.' John M'Kerrow, *History of the Secession Church* (Edinburgh: Fullarton, 1848), p. 159.

[44] Andrew Bonar, ed., *Memoir and Remains of R. M. M'Cheyne* (repr. London: Banner of Truth, 1966), pp. 608–9.

[45] Complications came because the moral obligation of the state was identified with the state's responsibility to support one church and even to coerce people into its membership. Rutherford wrote: 'Now seeing time, favour of men, prosperity accompanying the Gospel, bring men into the Church, so the magistrate may compel men to adjoin themselves to the true Church (*Peaceable Plea*, p. 111). But the obligation of the state to God is that which belongs to all men in their relationship to God as creatures (*Rom.* 2:15; 13:1–3 etc), whereas recognition of Christ's church requires knowledge of Christ as the Redeemer and that means the possession of divine grace (*1 Cor.* 12:1). The older Presbyterians argued that the civil ruler exercises authority on behalf of Christ and that to deny his duty to the church is to condone moral indifference. For an alternative Presbyterian understanding see, *Writings of Thomas E. Peck* (repr. Edinburgh: Banner of Truth, 1999), vol. 2, pp. 275–89.

[46] *Works of John Owen* , vol. 15 (repr. London: Banner of Truth, 1966), p. 199.

[47] 'Mr Rutherford's Testimony to the Covenanted Work of Reformation (from 1638 to 1649) in Britain and Ireland,' a postscript in *Rutherford's Letters* (Glasgow: William Bell, 1796), pp. 525–6. Why this was not included in later editions of Rutherford's letters does not seem to have been recorded. The Scots Westminster divine, Robert Baillie, wrote in 1648: 'I am more and more in the mind, that it were for the good of the world, that churchmen did meddle with ecclesiastical affairs only.' *Letters and Journals of Robert Baillie*, vol. 3 (Edinburgh, Ogle, 1842), p. 38.

[48] Thomas M'Crie, Jr., *Sketches of Scottish Church History* (Edinburgh: Johnstone, 1846), vol. 1, p. 282.

[49] W. H. Goold, 'John Owen on Toleration and Church Government' in *The Evangelical Succession* (Edinburgh, 1883; repr. in *Banner of Truth* magazine, no. 44 (1966), p. 16. To Goold (1815–97) we owe the definitive edition of Owen's *Works*.

[50] W. D. J. McKay, *An Ecclesiastical Republic: Church Government in the Writings of George Gillespie* (Edinburgh: Rutherford House, 1997), p. 279.

[51] *Quaint Sermons of Samuel Rutherford* (London: Hodder and Stoughton, 1885), p. 125. He adds, 'This doctrine should be rightly understood, for it warrants not the conventicles and unwarrantable meetings of Separatists and Brownists.'

[52] Archibald Hall, *Gospel Worship* (Edinburgh: 1770), vol. 2, pp. 225–6.

[53] Speech in the Union Debate, General Assembly of the Free Church of Scotland, 26–27 May 1870. Even Rutherford writes: 'We may grant our General Assembly not to be properly called a National Church, but by a figure, for the believers of the nation are properly the National Church, I mean a mystical believing Church.' *Peaceable Plea*, p. 107.

[54] Alexander F. Mitchell, quotes the words of Rutherford on only Christ ruling in the church, 'and all others that bear office therein ought not to usurp dominion therein, nor be called lords, but only ministers, disciples, and servants', and says that if the full meaning of this had been recognized, 'I cannot but think that the bitter divisions among Scottish Presbyterians would have been fewer, and that there would have been far less occasion for the reproach often cast on them, that new presbyter is but old priest writ large . . . We come short of what we ought to be as men and as Christians, and that would suffice to mar any form of government that could be devised by the wit of men.' *The Scottish Reformation* (Edinburgh: Blackwood, 1900), pp. 220, 238. 'There have been many instances', said William Cunningham, 'in which individuals possessed of authority or influence in the Church, have . . . practised odious and offensive tyranny.' Quoted by J. M. Porteous, *The Government of the Kingdom of Christ* (Edinburgh: Johnstone, 1873), pp. 583–4.

[55] Ian Henderson, *Power Without Glory: A Study in Ecumenical Politics* (London: Hutchinson, 1967). 'Churches [i.e. denominations] are power structures, the relations between churches are power relations, apostolic succession is a power *mythos* . . . Ecumenical inter-Church conversations never mention that the considerations of power ever sullied an ecclesiastic's mind' (p. 182).

[56] Quoted from *Divine Right of Presbyteries* by Macpherson, *Church in Scottish Theology*, p. 67.

[57] We know of no other way to explain how good men could give little attention to the fact that Scripture speaks of the seven *churches* of Asia, the *churches* of Galatia, the *churches* of Macedonia, the *churches* of Judea, but, as Dabney notes, 'says nothing of any visible national church'.

[58] We cannot here enter into the question how far the Scots Reformers were attracted by the apparent expediency of a national church. The advantages for the gospel for a church established by law have often subsequently been argued, but whether these advantages are as great as has been supposed may well be questioned, as Ian Henderson has done: 'Sweden, where there is virtually only one church, has an extraordinarily low record of church attendance, whereas in the United States, where there is an amazing variety of churches, there is an equally high record of church attendance.' *Power Without Glory*, p. 31.

[59] Dabney, *Discussions*, vol. 2, p. 438.

[60] I am arguing that denominations are legitimate where they associate the like-minded for the fulfilment of scriptural purposes. They are a lesser evil than a position of uniformity where such liberty is denied. But they have no *strictly* scriptural status and no particular congregation is to be seen as a true church merely because it belongs to a particular denomination. In his defence of inter-denominational agencies, Jerry White argues that denominations are also parachurch structures, a conclusion with which D. B. Knox, late Principal of Moore College, Sydney, agrees. White, *The Church and the Parachurch: An Uneasy Marriage* (Portland, Oregon: Multnomah Press, 1983), p. 64. D. Broughton Knox, *Selected Works* (Sydney: Matthias Media, 2003), , vol. 2, p. 95.

[61] D. Maclean, *Aspects of Scottish Church History* (Edinburgh: T. & T. Clark, 1927), p. 175.

[62] Whitefield, *Works*, vol. 1 (London: Dilly, 1771), p. 376. For a striking example of the effect on unity of the Spirit outpoured, see the record of the ministry of Daniel Baker, a Presbyterian, preaching in Episcopal and Baptist churches in Beaufort, South Carolina. W. M. Baker, *Making Many Glad: The Life and Labours of Daniel Baker* (repr. Edinburgh: Banner of Truth, 2000), pp. 153–6.

[63] *Princeton Theological Review*, vol. 3, p. 31.

9

Scottish Preaching

Thomas Chalmers Preaching

'It is a striking thing that the whole Church likes those who preach experientially to the life of men, apart from the *details* of their doctrine, and who lay more stress upon their *Christology* than upon anything else. Yes! The Church's heart beats towards its Lord.'

JOHN DUNCAN

'I know my Lord is no niggard: He can, and it becometh Him well to give more than my narrow soul can receive. If there were ten thousand, thousand millions of worlds, and as many heavens full of men and angels, Christ would not be pinched to supply all our wants, and to fill us all.'

'Christ is a well of life, but who knoweth how deep it is to the bottom?'

SAMUEL RUTHERFORD

I t was not, of course, a preacher but a poet who wrote:

> O wad some Pow'r the giftie gie us
> To see oursels as others see us!

While the wish has to be unfulfilled, there are always those outside our circle who may tell us something we do not see. Criticism of Scottish preaching from beyond Scotland is not hard to find. With such criticism as comes from a dislike of the orthodoxy once common north of the Border I am not here concerned. But an observation made by a friend of the gospel, and repeated by more than one, is worth hearing.

It has been asserted, for instance, that Scottish preaching is wearisome. The English evangelical, Richard Cecil, who could say, 'Rutherford's *Letters* is one of my classics', expressed a different opinion of Scottish preaching when he wrote in the late eighteenth century: 'I should not recommend a young minister to pay much deference to the *Scotch divines*. The Erskines, who were the best of them, are dry, and laboured, and wearisome. He may find incomparable matter in them, but he should beware of forming his taste and manner after their model.'[1]

Now reading sermons and *hearing* them preached are two different things and Cecil did not hear the men he strictures, nonetheless his reservations are not without some substance. The American preacher J. W. Alexander, a true friend of the Scottish churches, also thought that the preaching could be on the heavy side, and he pinpointed 'the fondness for scholastic method and minute subdivision, derived from the dialectical turn of the people, and the familiarity of the preachers with the severe manuals of Calvinistic theology'.[2]

William Jay of Bath was one of the most effective English preachers of the nineteenth century and his comment after visiting Scotland was of similar nature to Alexander's. He thought that 'many northern divines' were doctrinally strong but weak in 'the affections and feelings': 'Their sermons have had theology enough in them, and were well methodised [i.e. structured]: but there was little in them to rend or to melt. How much of "The Scottish Preacher" (not the last) might be read through without the troublesomeness of a single emotion?'[3]

In preaching, as in other areas of life, it is common for a weakness to lie close to a strength. The strength of much Scottish preaching was its strictly scriptural character and content. Thus it used to be said of John Brown of Haddington that 'he preached the Bible as though he had read no other book'. But sometimes it was forgotten that teaching truth, as Christ's own example shows, benefits from illustration – illustration from nature or from history. A sermon without illustrations is like a house without windows. William Jay says he was advised by a friend before he went to Scotland, 'that while in the north I must be very careful and guarded, and forbear *freedom*, and especially anecdotes, which would not be relished or endured there'. In the end he found this limitation too hard to bear, as he explains:

> Towards the conclusion of my mission, I was preaching on the Isle of Bute; and near the end of the sermon I mentioned the *caveat* I had received before I left England, adding, that I felt a strong temptation to break through it. I paused, and then said, – 'Well, whatever be the consequence, I will introduce the following anecdote.' I saw that it told; and the ministers coming after into the session-house or vestry, said, 'You have laboured under a great mistake, we are not averse to anecdotes, but to *some*

kinds of them, and to the *manner* of relating and applying them. When they are well chosen, and properly introduced, they are peculiarly acceptable, as they are more unusual with us, and we want excitement more than information.'[4]

The reference to 'excitement more than information' was an admission that instruction was more common than the stimulus which preaching ought to impart. Under God, preaching should subdue and transform the whole man; it ought to strike the heart, move the emotions and affect the will. To inform the mind is not enough.

A century before Jay's visit to Scotland, John Wesley, while in the north, made a similar observation:

> I spoke as closely as I could, both morning and evening, and made a pointed application to the hearts of all that were present. I am convinced that is the only way whereby we can do any good in Scotland. This very day I heard many excellent truths delivered in the kirk, but as there was no application, it was likely to do as much good as the singing of a lark. I wonder the present ministers of Scotland are not sensible of this. They cannot but see that no sinners are convinced of sin, none converted to God by this way of preaching. How strange then, that neither reason nor experience teaches to take a better way.[5]

While these criticisms may indicate recurring tendencies in the Scottish pulpit, the truth is that it is impossible to classify Scottish preaching under any one type. The differences, both in style and content are far too large to admit of such generalization. The various periods of history saw marked changes and, not infrequently, contradictions side by side at the same time. In the Restoration period of the seventeenth century, Bishop Burnet contrasted Presbyterian and Episcopal preaching,[6] and a hundred years later a similarly wide difference existed between the preaching of evangelicals and that of the Moderates whose sermons, Thomas Chalmers once said, were like a winter's day – short, clear and cold. The mid-eighteenth century Church of Scotland evangelical, John Witherspoon, was less polite when he described his Moderate contemporaries as 'poor, flippant, ignorant, worldly men'.[7] In his day, he said, the common ministerial model, was 'a man of most sprightly and lively fancy, of an inexhaustible fund of wit and humour,' free of any kind of gravity, and in the pulpit 'a most genteel and elegant preacher'.[8]

No great weight, then, is to be given to criticisms of Scottish preaching without consideration of the time and men to which they refer. The same J. W. Alexander whose critical comment was given above, could summarize the Scottish pulpit as he knew it in the 1850s as 'at once expository, doctrinal, methodical, and impassioned'.[9]

THE FORM OF THE SERMON

By 'form' I mean not the content but the manner in which the sermon is arranged and structured. In the high-noon of the Reformation, with all the excitement of a rediscovered Bible, and the eagerness of many to hear it explained, no great time or attention was given by preachers to form. Without clear 'heads' and divisions, Calvin spoke freely from a passage, and the one extended sermon by Knox that has survived suggests that he did the same. But it was soon remembered that the mind retains a message better if it is presented in a logical order, with the progression of thought indicated by the statement of distinct and separate points. By the mid-seventeenth century, the pattern indicated in the advice of the Westminster divines 'Of the Preaching of the Word' in *The Directory for the Public Worship of God* (1645) was generally followed in Scotland. A sermon, the divines said, should begin with a text of Scripture, an introduction 'brief and perspicuous', then the text should be analysed into separate points ('doctrines'), and in this care be taken not 'to burden the memory of the hearers in the beginning with too many members of divisions'. All was to be followed by 'application' made to the hearers 'with loving affection'.

A Scot, defending the Puritan view of preaching at Yale in 1876, wrote:

> Men may make themselves merry, indeed, over the long sermons of our Puritan forefathers, with their ninthlies of the thirteenth head, but we should not forget that those who relished the discourses of Howe, and Owen, and Baxter, were the strong heroes who won the liberties of England, and the near kinsmen of the noble pilgrims who laid the foundation of this republic. Depend upon it, if ever the pulpit shall cease to be a vehicle of instruction, and sink into a place for the public reading of little essays, or the utterance of fifteen minutes of rose-water sentimentalism, our people will dwindle into spiritual dwarfs, and the manhood will disappear from their piety.[10]

Despite this rebuttal, it has to be admitted that in Scotland, as elsewhere, the plan of the sermon sometimes became too formal and mechanical. Although they were criticized for it, some seventeenth-century preachers, such as Andrew Gray and Robert Leighton, noted and acted on the additional words by the authors 'Of the Preaching of the Word' which said, 'This method is not prescribed as necessary for every man, or upon every occasion.'

The need was for a medium between a multiplication of divisions and a loose form of speaking in which there is no order and no distinct points. Finding this balance became a perennial issue, and nineteenth-century Scots preachers generally succeeded better than those of the eighteenth. Robert M'Cheyne, noted how, in the zeal of youth, he failed to recognize the need for careful divisions in a sermon: 'I used to despise Dr Welsh's rules at the time I heard them; but now I feel I *must* use them, for nothing is more needful in making a sermon memorable and impressive than a logical arrangement.'[11] On M'Cheyne's practice in this regard, a friend observed:

> The heads of his sermons were not the milestones that tell you how near you are to your journey's end, but they were nails that fixed and fastened all he said, Divisions are often dry; but not so *his* divisions — they were so textual and so feeling, and they brought out the spirit of a passage so surprisingly.[12]

When the son of John MacDonald of Ferintosh was about to be set apart for the Christian ministry, the question of sermon structure was a subject for correspondence between them. MacDonald, Jr., had sent his father an outline of a sermon he had prepared, with the request for advice. The text was 2 Timothy 3:7: 'Ever learning, and never able to come to the knowledge of the truth.' MacDonald commended the 'skeleton' as 'a natural enough plan and arrangement of subject,' but suggested improvements to the first two heads, the first being on 'the knowledge of the truth':

> 1. Its nature and import. 2. Its divine authority. 3. Its excellence. 4. Its purifying or practical influence. The points here are in substance the same as yours; but this seems to correspond more with the language of the text. The words of the enunciation should be attended to. The second head might be worded in greater conformity to the text – reasons why men, notwithstanding efforts made, fall short of this important attainment – efforts made – they are 'ever learning' – and nevertheless fall short. Reasons, 1. That they approach truth with a heart attached

to sin and worldly gratifications. 2. With a legal (self-righteous) spirit – the Jews. 3. With self-confidence as to their own intellectual powers as competent, etc. 4. Early prejudices and preconceived opinions. They bring truth to these, and not these to truth. 5. Not submitting to divine tuition. But perhaps you had better follow your own plan.[13]

Later in the nineteenth century, perhaps in reaction to sermons too formal and predictable in their arrangement, the disuse of clear 'heads' became more popular. W. G. Blaikie handles the subject wisely in his book, *For the Work of the Ministry*. Pointing to the manner in which Christ taught without formal divisions, he asserted it would be foolish 'to represent heads as essential to a good sermon, or to condemn a preacher for not using them, provided he could more effectively draw his remarks, each out of its predecessor, like the folds of a telescope, and in this way he could keep up the attention of his audience'. The preacher, he believed, who used a conversational manner and spoke '*to* the people – right home to the actual feelings of their hearts', has less need of formal divisions. 'It is the heaviest style of preaching that needs most to be broken up into heads . . . Yet in discourses which have the instruction of the audience as one of their leading objects, divisions of some sort are very desirable, both as guiding posts to the preacher and stepping-stones to the audience. Only it must be seen to that instead of signals for inattention they really tend to increase the interest of the audience in the subject.'[14]

While there is no one correct form for the sermon, Scottish preaching calls attention to it, and form is more closely connected with effective preaching than is commonly supposed. 'Find a good plan, and let the plan be your own,' is necessary advice. Whether a sermon sticks in the memory of those who hear it is related to the manner it is constructed, as well as how it is preached. John Moffat tells how, with difficulty, he managed to get into the crowded St John's church, Edinburgh, in the 1850s, to stand in an aisle and hear Thomas Guthrie:

> Services in those days were services. An hour and a half was about the minimum. Five years later I was discussing preachers with a fellow-student, and I mentioned having heard Guthrie, and the particular text from which he preached: 'Not for thy righteousness, nor for the uprightness of thine heart' (Deut. 9:15). 'Why!' said he, 'I was there, and I heard him take that text.' We set to work, and from our combined recollections we reconstructed the sermon from beginning to end. Some preaching is effectual enough to leave life-long impressions.[15]

Guthrie clearly met William Jay's criterion for a good sermon. 'It should', he said, 'both strike and stick.'

EXPOSITORY AND/OR TEXTUAL

The sub-head needs clarification. All true preaching is 'expository' in the sense that it opens and explains Scripture, but in more recent times 'expository preaching' has come more exclusively to mean preaching that proceeds, consecutively and systematically, through a book or large passage of Scripture, over a period of time. In the second half of the twentieth century there was a revival of this type of preaching in Scotland, led by William Still, minister of Gilcomston South Church of Scotland in Aberdeen from 1945 to 1997. His friend James Philip was an eminent example of the same school in Edinburgh. Due to this, and not least to the influence of Martyn Lloyd-Jones elsewhere, 'expository preaching' was adopted in many places around the English-speaking world and often with the excitement as of a new discovery. In fact, the practice was not new at all; for centuries it had been commonplace in Scotland. In one service on the Lord's Day – usually the first – the preacher would sustain a connected series of addresses on a given book or passage of the Bible. Taking the place of a sermon, this address was known as the 'lecture', and not a small number of the best-known works in Scottish Christian literature had their origin in this way, from Leighton on First Peter to Robert Candlish on Genesis.

For the other service on the Lord's Day, the sermon was textual in the sense that it was based on an individual verse, or at most, if the meaning required it, on a few verses, and not necessarily as part of an ongoing series.[16] The purpose of the 'lecture' or 'expository preaching', on the other hand, was to impart a broader grasp of Scripture than is possible in occasional, individual sermons. William M. Taylor explained what he saw as the advantages of this method under the following headings:

> First, *it brings both preacher and hearers into direct and immediate contact with the mind of the Spirit;* second, *it secures variety in the ministrations of the preacher;* third, in following it out *the preacher will be compelled to treat many subjects from which otherwise he might have shrunk;* fourth, *it will promote biblical intelligence among our people;* finally, *in the process of preparing his expository discourses, the preacher will acquire a greater store of materials which he can use for other purposes.*[17]

For a good example of what its author calls an 'expository lecture' we give the following from W. G. Blaikie's advice to his students at New College, Edinburgh:

> Suppose the subject for the lecture is 2 Corinthians 5:1-8, where the apostle contrasts the earthly house of the tabernacle with the house not made with hands. It is plain that, following the order of the passage, we should have

to repeat the same topics: *e.g.,* 'we groan'; v. 4, 'we groan being burdened'; v. 2, 'we earnestly desire to be clothed upon'; v. 4, 'we would not be unclothed, but clothed upon'. We must therefore endeavour to find a single but comprehensive order of topics; laying hold, first, of the leading truth, and grouping the subordinate truths under it. The leading truth is, that in its future state the soul of the believer will be lodged in *a better dwelling* than here. In illustration of this four positions are laid down: I. the present dwelling is imperfect, the soul groans and is burdened in it, but still it desires a dwelling of some kind. II. The future dwelling has many advantages – (1) it is a house not made with hands; (2) a building of God; (3) in the heavens; (4) eternal; (5) in it mortality is swallowed up of life. III. Our fellowship with the Lord is different in the two buildings – in the one we are absent, in the other present with the Lord. IV. We are confidently assured that when one is removed the other will come, for – (1) God has given us the earnest of the Spirit; (2) we walk by faith and not by sight; hence the joyful state of mind even of the suffering Christian, and the earnest desire with which he looks forward to the change when the body is dissolved by death.[18]

Now the question arises, why, if 'expository preaching' has all these benefits, did the practice virtually die out before its revival in the 1950s? The answer might be that as faith in the full inspiration of Scripture decayed in Scotland so did the desire for an exact and full knowledge of its content. But the fact is that even by the 1870s – that is, before unbelief took any general hold in pulpits or churches – we are told that the lecture 'has fallen somewhat into reproach and desuetude [disuse] . . . Expository preaching is not popular. The people do not like it and will not stand it.'[19]

In contrast, textual preaching (we use the phrase for want of a better) at this same date *was* popular, and it is observable that the most popular preacher in Scotland never used the 'expository' method. That preacher was C. H. Spurgeon who, though not living in Scotland, was read there every Thursday as the latest issue of the *Metropolitan Tabernacle Pulpit* was published. The Scots woman who told her husband as he set off for town, 'Dinna forget Spurgeon', was representative of a multitude north of the Border.[20] It was a Scotsman, William Robertson Nicoll, who said: 'The evangelical preacher who has never studied Mr Spurgeon deserves to be placed in the same category with the portrait painter to whom Sir Joshua Reynolds is a stranger.'[21] Spurgeon also supplies evidence that if a sermon is to be directly and pointedly evangelistic, the purpose is better served by individual, well-chosen texts.

It is my opinion that the main reason the 'expository' sermon series fell into disuse was that congregations did not find it as helpful as sermons from individual texts. While it is debatable how far the opinion of the pew should control the pulpit, in the end it is Christian hearers who are the judges of the preaching that edifies them most. After all, as Matthew Henry used to say, 'A good sermon is a sermon that does good.'

This is not to deny that much help was received from the 'lecture'. J. W. Alexander goes so far as to say that in Scotland it was the expository lecture, 'maintained for three hundred years', that had 'done much to mould the religious temper of the nation'.[22] But the value of this form of preaching needs the qualification added by Blaikie. It will only be truly valuable 'when it is really thorough and satisfying'. A qualification likewise appears in the same writer's conclusion: 'Where there is a profound sense of the authority of Scripture, a deep desire to be under its guidance, an earnest desire to know and follow all that the Lord has spoken, *good* expository preaching cannot fail to be highly valued.'

The problem is that time has shown that '*good* expository preaching' (the italics are mine) is by no means common, and in too many instances the deficiencies can outweigh the benefits. There would appear to be a number of reasons why this happens. It may be because a preacher's motives in adopting the method are faulty. Some seem to think that it is the only 'orthodox' way to preach, regardless of the assessment of those who listen. Other preachers argue that it makes life easier because the material for weeks ahead can be known and to hand; no time need be lost in searching for texts. Then, again, the preacher may find 'exposition' more intellectually satisfying; he may enjoy telling his people why he takes a particular view over against this or that commentator whom he has read on the passage. Some even believe this is an easier way to preach, although they may not go as far as the preacher who said, 'I like to take a whole chapter for a text, because when I am persecuted in one verse, I can flee to another.'

In the mid-nineteenth century Charles J. Brown believed that the 'lecture' was in decline because it was being used more as the occasion for a running commentary, or as 'two or three little sermons, on a simply longer text'.[23]

There are several difficulties in the way of good expository preaching; I shall confine myself to one. Effective preaching needs to be compelling – the communication of a message that grips the hearer and sticks in his memory. But such will not be the impression on the hearer unless the text has first taken hold of the preacher himself. This was Spurgeon's chief reason for not preaching through books of Scripture. To preach well he wanted a text that seized him with a degree of compulsion; in his case, he believed, he could not work progressively through a passage, week by week, without losing something vital. It may be objected that this is an altogether too subjective view of how sermons are to be prepared, and that the 'expositor' may handle his material with as much life and fire as the man who stays with single texts. That is undoubtedly true in some instances, but experience would appear to indicate that this method, in the hands of many, is more likely to lead to weariness on the part of hearers.[24]

Far from being an easier way to prepare sermons, exposition in a consecutive series is the more demanding, if it is to hold interest and build congregations. It is imperative that a preacher knows himself, assesses his own abilities, and bears in mind the testimony of Spurgeon:

> I am conscious of not possessing those peculiar gifts which are necessary to interest an assembly in any one subject or set of subjects for any length of time. Brethren of extraordinary research and profound learning may do it, and brethren with none of these, and no common sense, may pretend to do it, but I cannot. I am obliged to owe a great deal of my strength to variety rather than profundity.[25]

On the other side of this question, it is possible to demonstrate the deficiencies of always taking only separate texts, with no continuity, Sunday by Sunday. The tendency of such preaching is to leave hearers knowing only isolated sentences, and without an understanding of Scripture in its several parts. 'We can conceive', writes one Scottish critic of such sermons, 'of a hearer listening during a course of years to every verse in the Bible thus treated, without obtaining thereby any insight into the scope of the sacred writers in the passages from which the texts are selected.'[26] Further, the textual preacher can be tempted, instead of taking the truth that belongs to his text, to use the text merely as a starting point for an address on a general topic.

Scottish preaching thus illustrates that decision on the matter of sermons is not as straightforward as might be thought. Ideally preaching should not be confined either to the expository or the textual method, but make use of both, and both long existed side by side in Scotland.

PASTORAL

Preaching involves more than the opening of Scripture. To be effective it has to be opened in a way relevant to the circumstances of the people. If simply understanding the Bible in its original context was all that is needed in churches, then a supply of good books and commentaries could meet the need. But something more is needed, and hence the work of preaching: divine revelation has to be brought into direct and appropriate contact with the particular lives of the individuals who are gathered to hear it. 'Many otherwise good sermons', one writer rightly observes, 'make no contact because they are to the wrong people at the wrong time.'[27]

This being true, it follows as a general rule that the most effective preachers are men who are devoted pastors, men who know their people and preach accordingly. It is not preachers who have given themselves only to study whose words make the deepest impression, but rather men who are often found among their people and listening to them. Those who make up a congregation that meets on Sundays, come from all manner of circumstances – from the joyful to the sorrowful, the successful to the disappointed, the overworked to the unemployed. The hopes of youth, the cares of parents, and the burdens of the elderly are all likely to be there. In many lives there are decisions to be taken, problems to be resolved, illness, and perhaps bereavement, soon to be faced. It would be a near miracle for a preacher to have no knowledge of these needs and yet address his people regularly with true sympathy. 'Every pulpit needs to be vitalised by close contact with living people', is an indisputable statement. [28]

Scottish church history certainly bears this out. Burnet, critic though he was of seventeenth-century Presbyterian preachers, speaks of their closeness to their people: 'They used to visit their parishes much . . . they lived in great familiarity with their people, and used to pray and talk oft with them in private, so it can hardly be imagined to what degree they were loved and reverenced by them.'[29]

For a seventeenth-century example of the closeness of pastors and people *Samuel Rutherford's Letters* are unforgettable. Separated from his parish in days of persecution, he was forced to resort to letters, and the personal issues about which he writes show how his pastoral work was conducted. The spiritually cold, the sorrowing, the individual struggling with temptations, the believer lacking assurance, and many more, all have his attention and sympathetic interest. To an old man about whom he had some doubt he can write:

> My soul longeth exceedingly to hear how matters go betwixt you and Christ; and whether or not there be any work of Christ in that parish that will bide the trial of fire and water. Let me be weighed of the Lord in a just balance, if your souls lie not weighty upon me. Ye go to bed and rise with me: thoughts of your soul, my dearest in our Lord, depart not from me in my sleep. You have a great part of my tears, sighs, supplications and prayers. Oh, if I could buy your soul's salvation with any suffering whatsoever, and that ye and I might meet with joy up in the rainbow, when we shall stand before our Judge![30]

One illustration of the way such preachers thought about their people is indicated by a phrase that has now passed entirely out of use. They referred to them as their 'books'. By which they meant that, next to the Bible, their flock were what they had to 'read' week by week.[31] Far from diminishing preparation for the pulpit they saw this as a vital part of it. An abundance of biographies show this to have been the continuing practice of the evangelical Scottish ministry. In

Glasgow, Thomas Chalmers practised his axiom, 'A house-going minister makes a church-going people.' Facing a parish of 11 to 12,000 people, he determined within a year or two to be in every home. To accomplish this he dispensed with clerical tradition: his visits were necessarily short but people, often for the first time in their lives, could talk with a gospel minister face to face.[32] Before Chalmers' day the tradition for a minister's visit, if he visited at all, was for him to conduct a formal mini-service in the home.

Chalmers' students and successors followed his example. Charles J. Brown, a leading preacher in Edinburgh in the 1840s, was in the habit of visiting twelve families a week. The purpose was an opportunity for free conversation with his people, 'and, as far as possible, make their familiar acquaintance'.[33] One of M'Cheyne's hearers, over forty years after his death in 1843, remembered how the last time they had met in the street his minister had said to him, 'Jimmy, I hope that all is well with your soul. How is your sick sister? I am coming to see her again shortly.' M'Cheyne's devotion to his people continued to his last hours when, although delirious, he would pray, 'This parish, Lord, this people, this whole place!' Again, one of the ablest preachers in the Scottish Highlands in more modern times, Kenneth MacRae of Stornoway, normally gave three hours to visiting every day, five days a week.[34]

The relevance of such practice to preaching is obvious. Good preaching, it may be said, is not so much preaching *to*, far less *at*, people, but speaking *with* them, and putting such questions to them as they might themselves ask. The Bible has to be brought into the present, and preaching which fails to do this, Blaikie well argues,

> is little better than a piece of dry antiquarianism. The real object is to illuminate the present by the lights of the past . . . It depends much on sympathy, – one of the chiefest

of a true preacher's qualities. By means of sympathy he will read his Bible with and for his people, and see as he reads, what meets their wants. His people will never be far from his mind, and by his sympathy he will know their feelings almost as if they were his own . . . We own to a suspicion of the preachers who are always urging on their people the duty of regularity [in attendance] . . . the question comes up, If their people found God's Word brought to bear on their actual wants, their sorrows, their bitterness of soul, their weariness, their unsatisfied hearts, would they not be more attracted, and not need to be scolded into regularity?[35]

SERMON CONTENT

If preaching is truly a delivery of the Word of God, then the first business of the preacher is to be sure that he has that Word, and that what he speaks is the truth of the text he has announced: 'If anyone speaks, he should do it as one speaking the very words of God' (*1 Pet.* 4:11). Authority and conviction in preaching does not come from the preacher. On the contrary, the more powerful the preaching the more the man himself recedes from view, which is presumably what Chrysostom meant when he said that in sermons, 'God ought to speak much, and man little.' Dr Kidd of Aberdeen had something similar in mind when he interrupted a student for the ministry whom he had taken with him on prison visitation. The need, Kidd had previously explained, was to let men hear Scripture itself but, instead of this, the young trainee launched into inappropriate exposition. When his mentor could bear it no longer he exclaimed, 'Young man, will you hold your peace and let the Holy Ghost speak!'

A preacher in our day is making the same point when he says that his continual advice for men beginning to preach is,

'Quote the text! Quote the text! Say the actual words of the text again and again. Show the people where your ideas are coming from.'[36]

Behind such thinking lies a fundamental principle. The first business of preaching is to engage men's minds with the truth about God and about themselves. Knowledge and teaching ('doctrine') are therefore of pre-eminent importance. Certainly, preaching fails if it does not touch the emotions, but preaching that consists in moving the emotions alone is a disaster, for it is a result that will not last. It is reported of an eloquent preacher, who had failed to grasp this, that he once confessed: 'There must be something wrong with my preaching. I can paint the sufferings of Christ on a Sunday, so that my whole congregation shall weep, and on Monday morning I hear them swear to my face.'

The existence of real Christianity requires a stronger basis than feeling. The nature of that basis is clear in Paul's injunctions to Timothy and Titus: it is 'sound doctrine', 'sound words', 'the word' (*1 Tim.*1:10; *2 Tim.* 1:13; 4:2–3; *Titus* 1:9; 2:1).

The reason for this apostolic priority is twofold: first, as already said, it is the mind of man that has first to be engaged and convicted; second, it is the Word of God that the Spirit of truth honours and nothing will convince without his witness. These convictions were the starting point for the evangelical preachers of Scotland. They did not see themselves as in charge of the situation. They were only the spokesmen for God and real preaching must have with it something more vital than their speaking. It must be 'in demonstration of the Spirit and of power: that your faith should not stand in the wisdom of men, but in the power of God' (*1 Cor.* 2:4-5). Andrew Bonar understood this when he noted in his diary, 'It is one thing to bring truth from the Bible, and another thing to bring it from God himself through the Bible.'

If the content of preaching is biblical, it follows that it will be 'theological', that is to say, it will concern the knowledge of God. 'Brethren,' Spurgeon could tell his students, 'if you are not theologians, you are in your pastorates just nothing at all. We shall never have great preachers until we have great divines.' Closeness to Scripture and love for sound doctrine belong together.

History has proved that when the influence of true preaching is at its greatest, commitment to sound doctrine will ever be present. Thus the Puritan period produced men such as Robert Douglas, a commissioner to the Westminster Assembly, who was reputed to have committed the whole Bible to memory. The same was said of some of the Secession preachers. George Lawson of Selkirk, for instance, 'had nearly the whole of God's Word on his mind,' and he would quote 'from any part of the sacred volume with perfect accuracy.'[37] Of Chalmers it was said that the Bible seemed to be transfused into the man. While even an approximation to such attainments is no necessary characteristic in evangelical preachers, all ought to share in the ambition to have 'a large and ever increasing portion of the Scriptures *gotten by heart*'.[38] And it was this mastery of Scripture that promoted clear, doctrinal preaching. It began with God, and the glory of his character, man's broken relationship with God, entailing his judgment upon man as a sinner, and leading to the divine provision of a Mediator – a Second Adam who would restore all, and more, that the first Adam lost. For the experience of that restoration the gospel is to be preached and, while transcending thought, its component parts could be stated as Ruin, Redemption and Regeneration.

It was the distinct way these truths were spelt out, and their mutual relationships made clear, both by preaching and by the Shorter Catechism, that produced a theologically minded population in many parts of Scotland. What J. W. Alexander said of the Presbyterian tradition in general was eminently true in Scotland: 'The day was when churches were much more concerned than we, about the truths conveyed, and much less about the garb of the truths. Doctrine, rather than speaking, was what drew the audience.'[39]

Yet when all this is said about the content of preaching, the main thing remains. Doctrinal preaching, as such, does not necessarily make it evangelical and a warning against being 'too orthodox to be evangelical' is still needed. Truth is only saving and sanctifying when seen and believed in relation to Jesus Christ. 'Sound words' are no end in themselves. Without Christ, living and present, words become just another system of thought. The great business of preaching is to present Christ, to announce who he is and what he has done for the sinful and the lost; thus Luke could sum up apostolic preaching in the words, 'they ceased not to teach and preach Jesus Christ' (*Acts* 5:42). How else is Paul's 'determination not to know any thing among you, save Jesus Christ and him crucified' to be explained? (*1 Cor.* 2:2).

Even this is not all. True preaching, according to the New Testament, does not mean simply hearing about Christ, it is hearing Christ *himself*: it is Christ speaking, Christ inviting, Christ calling to repentance. The preacher is present only as a messenger; Christ is present to be believed, to be obeyed and to be worshipped. Where preaching does not lead to that, and only begins and ends with the sermon, it has failed.

It is here that the greatest demand is made upon the preacher. Without real communion with Christ, 'preaching Christ' will just become another subject, delivered without faith in his actual presence. The message may be orthodox but it will be without joy or freshness. Preaching will lose its happiness and be only a duty. The best of Scottish preaching has ever come from men who believed, with John Flavel, that 'The excellency of a sermon lies in the plainest discoveries and liveliest applications of Jesus Christ'. And they knew that for such preaching their first need was for more personal enjoyment of Christ, and more likeness to him. A hearer once said of Rutherford, 'He showed me the loveliness of Christ.' It would not have been possible without a life of private devotion, and the old saying has to be true, 'A minister's life is the life of his ministry.' In his private notes on 'Personal Reformation', Robert M'Cheyne wrote: 'I am persuaded I shall do most for God's glory and the good of man . . . by being filled with the Holy Spirit at all times, and by attaining the most entire likeness to Christ in mind, will, and heart, that is possible for a redeemed sinner to attain to in this world.'[40] On this vital point W. G. Blaikie draws the conclusion:

> Ought not preachers themselves to live on the great fundamental truths of the gospel? Ought not our souls to be continually fed from them, and our hearts continually thrilling with them? Ought not a fresh glow to come over our hearts every day as we think of Him who loved us, and washed us from sin in His blood, and made us kings and priests unto God and to the Father? Give us the plainest preacher that ever was; let him preach nothing that a whole congregation do not know; but let him preach with a thrilling heart; let him preach like one amazed at the glory of the message; let him preach in the tone of wonder and gratitude in which it becomes sinners to realise the great work of redemption, – not only will the congregation listen with interest: they will listen with profound impression . . . We greatly need preachers for the people. A preacher to the people needs to be very clear in his views, homely in his style, full of illustration, direct and courageous in his application, rich in brotherly sympathy, and very warm and vigorous in delivery. Alas! they are not common. I believe that if only every tenth student that passes through our hands were a man of this

stamp, we should soon see a change on the face of society.[41]

Eras in Scotland have been ushered in by preaching, preaching that has affected whole communities and even the national character. At such points in history the preaching was *new*, new to an unbelieving age in its message, and new in its freshness and attractive power. We can only doubt the future if we fail to believe it was Chirst who made these preachers what they were. The aged John Brown of Haddington said, 'Were it not for a God in my nature, I would reckon the present case of the Church very hopeless; but in view of Christ, I am persuaded that she will yet remarkably revive on earth.'[42] The basis of that hope remains today. Jesus, seeing the multitudes, was 'moved with compassion', and said to the disciples, 'The harvest truly is plenteous, but the labourers are few; pray ye therefore the Lord of the harvest, that he will send forth labourers into his harvest' (*Matt.* 9:36–38). 'How much more shall your heavenly Father give the Holy Spirit to them that ask him?' (*Luke* 11:13).

---

[1] *Remains of Richard Cecil*, ed. Josiah Pratt (London: Knight, n. d.), pp. 99–100. Admitting that their sermons were 'wild and unpruned', W. G. Blaikie, nevertheless said: 'Seldom has gospel truth been preached with the fullness of view, the rich flavour, the fervour and earnestness of Ralph and Ebenezer Erskine.' *For the Work of the Ministry: A Manual of Homiletical and Pastoral Theology* (London: Nisbet, 1885), p. 42.

[2] J. W. Alexander, *Thoughts on Preaching* (repr. Edinburgh: Banner of Truth, 1975), p. 263.

[3] *Autobiography of William Jay*, eds. G. Redford and J. A. James (repr. Edinburgh: Banner of Truth, 1974), p. 145.

[4] Ibid., pp. 139–40.

[5] Quoted by C. H. Spurgeon in *The Sword and the Trowel* (London: Passmore & Alabaster, 1877), p. 562. To which Spurgeon added the words, 'Scotland would not now deserve such a record, but there are many places in these islands of which it is sadly true.'

[6] See Bishop Burnet, *History of His Own Time: From the Restoration of Charles II to the Peace at Utrecht* (London: Evans, 1809), vol. 1, pp. 217–221. [7] Ibid., vol. 1 (Glasgow: Ogle, 1857), p. 12.

[8] John Witherspoon, *Ecclesiastical Characteristics,* in his *Works,* vol. 6 (Edinburgh: 1805), p. 212. He is describing, of course, the so-called 'Moderates', of whom he said, 'I never knew a moderate man in my life, that did not love and honour a heretic, or that had not an implacable hatred at the persons and characters of heresy-hunters' (p. 156). Notwithstanding this, Witherspoon says, it was claimed for a Moderate (as it would be for similar teachers in later generations) that he was 'a man of a good heart'.

[9] *Thoughts on Preaching,* p. 263.

[10] William M. Taylor, *The Ministry of the Word* (London: Nelson, 1876), p. 128.

[11] Andrew Bonar, *Memoir and Remains of Robert Murray M'Cheyne* (repr. London: Banner of Truth, 1966), p. 31.

[12] Ibid., p. 64.

[13] John Kennedy, *'The Apostle of the North',* p. 239.

[14] W. G. Blaikie, *For the Work of the Ministry,* pp. 119–20. There has been no unanimity on whether a sermon's divisions should be announced in advance. At all costs, tediousness is to be guarded against, and effort made to avoid sermons becoming predictable. As Blaikie says, 'Young preachers can have but a faint notion of the amount of inattention that prevails in an ordinary congregation.'

[15] Robert U. Moffat, *John Smith Moffat,* pp. 39–40.

[16] Sometimes, as in the case of Jonathan Edwards' sermons, the same text might be taken for more than one Sunday.

[17] Taylor, *The Ministry of the Word,* Lecture VII.

[18] *For the Work of the Ministry,* p. 132.

[19] Ibid., pp. 157, 176,

[20] R. L. Stevenson speaks of how, when his father was engaged with workmen in a building project on a remote part of the Scottish coastline, it was a Spurgeon sermon that would be read on the Lord's Day.

[21] 'The Yale Lectures on Preaching', *British and Foreign Evangelical Review,* vol. 27 (London: Nisbet, 1878), p. 528.

[22] *Thoughts on Preaching,* p. 264.

[23] Charles J. Brown, *The Ministry: Being Addresses to Students of Divinity* (Edinburgh: Maclaren, 1872), p. 44. More recently, Martyn Lloyd-Jones gave the same warning.

[24] It is no help in this regard when the preacher, instead of an introduction fresh to his hearers, begins with a summary of the previous week's sermon.

[25] 'On the Choice of a Text', *Lectures to My Students,* First Series (London: Passmore and Alabaster, 1875), p. 99. Referring to expositions of Hebrews that he once heard he adds: 'I wished frequently that the Hebrews had kept the epistle to themselves, for it sadly bored one poor Gentile lad. By the time the seventh or eight discourse had been delivered, only the very good people could stand it.'

[26] The words occur in a review (possibly by the editor, William Cunningham) of the *Autobiography of William Jay, British and Foreign Evangelical Review,* vol. 3 (Edinburgh: Johnstone and Hunter, 1854), p. 875. J. W. Alexander is critical of William Jay for the same reason (*Thoughts*

on Preaching, p.239), and quotes the strong words of the Scot, John Mason, who, on retiring from his church, charged them concerning a successor, 'Do not choose a man who always preaches upon insulated texts . . . You have been accustomed to hear the word preached to you in its connection. Never permit that practice to drop. Foreign churches call it lecturing; and when done with discretion, I can assure you that, while it is of all exercises the most difficult for the preacher, it is in the same proportion, the most profitable for you (Ibid., p. 252).

[27] Fred. B. Craddock, *Preaching* (Nashville: Abingdon Press, 1985), p. 92.

[28] Theodore L. Cuyler, *How to Be a Pastor* (London: Nisbet, 1891), p. 12.

[29] Burnet, *History of His Own Time*, vol. 1, pp. 217–8.

[30] *Letters of Rutherford*, p. 344. Rutherford's language is, of course, dated but the spiritual lesson is abiding. In Calvin's words, 'No man shall ever be meet to be a teacher, unless he has put on a fatherly affection.'

[31] The terminology dates at least from the seventeenth century. We read that when David Dickson became a professor of divinity his preaching 'fell off in sweetness and force; no wonder, he said, for I have lost my books; he missed pastoral intercourse with his people, the knowledge which he thus acquired of their wants, and the encouragement to further preaching from learning how they had been helped before.' W. G. Blaikie, *The Preachers of Scotland* (repr. Edinburgh: Banner of Truth, 2001), pp.105–6. When there was a rumour circulating among the Christians in the Highlands of Scotland in 1864 that their much loved preacher, John Kennedy of Dingwall, might be going to London, one correspondent wrote of it to a friend: 'The poor North of Scotland has need of him; and were he to go elsewhere he would find that he had left much of his "library" in Scotland and would miss them. Alas! Minister's libraries are very thin compared to what they were in his younger days.' Alexander Auld, *Ministers and Men in the Far North* (Inverness: Free Presbyterian Church, 1956), p. 298.

[32] Hanna, *Chalmers*, vol. 2, p. 110. One observer wrote: 'Till Dr Chalmers came to Glasgow, parochial Christian influence was a mere name . . . The people were let alone' (p. 121).

[33] Charles J. Brown, *The Ministry*, p. 67. Responsible for a large congregation in Edinburgh, Brown initially took seven years to visit every member but with the change, spending 'not more than twenty minutes' in a home he reduced the time to nine months, visiting twelve families a week 'with almost undeviating regularity'.

[34] See *Diary of Kenneth MacRae*, ed. Iain H. Murray (Edinburgh: Banner of Truth, 1980).

[35] *The Preachers of Scotland*, p. 341.

[36] John Piper, *The Supremacy of God in Preaching* (Grand Rapids: Baker, 2004), p. 88. 'One of the biggest problems I have with young preachers whom I am called on to critique is to get them to quote the parts of the text that support the points they are making' (p. 44).

[37] John MacFarlane, *Life and Times of George Lawson* (Edinburgh: Oliphant, 1862), pp. 234–6. This knowledge certainly included a considerable part of the Hebrew and the Greek text. When Lawson lectured to

students he would often quote chapter and verse without repeating the words. 'I do not quote them,' he would say, 'trusting that you remember them' (p. 301).

[38] C. J. Brown, *The Ministry*, p. 59. Those with this aspiration were far from satisfied with their attainment. Horatius Bonar wrote: 'We have given a greater prominence to man's writings, man's opinions, man's systems in our studies than to the Word. We have drunk more of human systems than divine. We have held more communion with man than with God.' *Words to Winners of Souls* (repr. Phillipsburg, NJ: 1995), pp. 43–4. J. W. Alexander makes the same point forcefully in a sermon on 'Distrust of the Word': 'If ever Christianity is destined to revive in this age, it will not be until we give new attention to the Scriptures of truth.' *The Living Pulpit, Eighteen Sermons by Eminent Living Divines,* ed. E. Wilson (Philadelphia: Sherman, 1859), p. 126.

[39] *Thoughts on Preaching,* p. 32.

[40] *Memoir and Remains,* p. 150. I have sought to address elsewhere 'The Holy Spirit and Preaching' (*Pentecost Today? The Biblical Understanding of Revival,* Edinburgh: Banner of Truth, 1998). Writing on 'Power in the Pulpit', Henry Fish asked: 'Is there a man living that would not name, as the *first* requisite to increased pulpit efficiency, "a new baptism of the Holy Ghost"? How many men, now weak and common-place ministers, would become mighty in word and doctrine, if only "filled with the Holy Ghost"!' *British and Foreign Evangelical Review,* vol. 11 (1862), p. 582.

[41] *The Preachers of Scotland,* pp. 305, 320.

[42] *The Life of John Brown, with Select Writings,* ed. W. Brown (Edinburgh: Banner of Truth, 2004), p. 136. The same preacher said: 'Were God to present me with the dukedom of Argyle on the one hand, and the being a minister of the gospel, with the stipend which I have had, on the other, so pleasant has the ministry been to me, notwithstanding all my weakness and fears of little success, I would instantly prefer the latter' (p. 133).

Edinburgh from the Pentland Hills

The Problem of the 'Elders'

Ordination of Elders, by Robert Lorimer

'When I first entered the ministry among you, I had very inadequate views of the duty of ruling well the house of God. I thought that my great and almost only work was to pray and preach . . . I now feel very deeply persuaded that two keys are committed us by Christ; the one the key of doctrine, by means of which we unlock the treasures of the Bible; the other the key of discipline, by which we open or shut the way to the sealing ordinances of the faith. Both are Christ's gift, and neither are to be resigned without sin. And I am deeply persuaded that that church will flourish best, that is ruled best.'

ROBERT MURRAY M'CHEYNE

For many the 'elders' were never a theological problem. Elders were to be found in all the Presbyterian churches of Scotland in the centuries following the Reformation. They numbered about twenty thousand by the 1870s. Through the generations these men quietly carried out their accustomed duties: commonly, they were at the church door on Sundays; served with the minister on the session (where all new communicants were first examined); exercised spiritual care and discipline; and were the regular visitors to the homes in the congregation allocated to them. From the sixteenth century onwards their work was set out in books and sermons. According to John Knox's *Book of Common Order*, 'The elders must be men of good life and godly conversation, without blame and all suspicion, careful for the flock, wise, and above all things fearing God.' 'Men of best knowledge of God's word and cleanest life', said the First Book of Discipline (1562). Attention centred on the work involved rather than on the office itself.

'The duties of a ruling elder', William Guthrie told his people at Fenwick, Ayrshire, 'be of two sorts, some that are personal, and relate to his conversation as a Christian, others that are official and relate to his ruling as an office-bearer in the house of God.'[1] There were instances, without doubt, when the 'personal' qualification was neglected; the elder failed to be a 'blameless' Christian, and the name became an empty title. In many other cases, however, the elder contributed no small strength and comfort to both ministers and people. Dr Archibald Charteris wrote of what three faithful elders meant to him in his early ministry as 'wise counsellors of a young minister in every difficulty.' And he concluded, 'It is not possible to over-estimate the effect of this constant upholding by the elders.'[2] Thomas Boston, and so many others, would have endorsed that judgment.

To the extent that problems existed over the eldership, they were personal and practical rather than theological. The office as such was taken for granted, and for some time that was my own attitude. I regarded the eldership as a mainstay in the Presbyterian form of church government, and thought of congregations that lacked elders as biblically deficient. Certainly I had, while reading, come across indications that the matter was not entirely straightforward, and I knew something of the controversy between John Whitgift and the Elizabethan Puritans. But I remained unimpressed by any doubts until my thinking received a sudden and severe jolt.

The occasion was a visit to St Andrews on a summer's day in the 1970s. Calling at a second-hand bookshop, a slim title among a number of old books caught my eye, and I purchased *The Theory of Ruling Eldership* by Peter Colin Campbell. The author was Principal of the University of Aberdeen at the time of its publication in 1866.[3] I had only to turn one page to find this author calling my understanding of the eldership 'a specious theory'. The challenge was enough to require further reading and, by the time I had finished, I knew I had a problem. There is truth in the saying, 'The wider the reading, the greater will be the modesty.'

THE PROBLEM DEBATED

We turn to the problem with which Principal Campbell hit me so unexpectedly, but first a personal word. It is the propensity of youth, and one not without merit, to take for guidance the opinion of leaders of spiritual stature. For me, and not least on questions of church government, the Puritans were standard bearers, and it was my belief that at least the majority of their number took the same position on the eldership as their Scottish brethren advanced at the meetings of the Westminster

Assembly. On the basis of that assumption, I also supposed that the understanding reached and set out by the Assembly reflected the Scots' (and my own) position! For clarity I shall call this the 'presbyter/elder theory'. According to this understanding, the office of the New Testament *presbyteros* has two parts to it: all presbyters are to oversee (rule) the church but, in addition, some have the added calling of being preachers of the Word. The proof text advanced was 1 Timothy 5:17, 'Let the elders that rule well be counted worthy of double honour, especially they who labour in the word and doctrine.' This text, it was claimed, distinguishes two classes of presbyters, and to indicate the difference between them the Scottish tradition gave the title 'elder' to those who 'rule', while 'minister' designated those who preached as well as ruled.

I found Campbell challenging this understanding on two grounds, the first *scriptural*. He argued that while many texts in the New Testament refer to the work of *presbyteroi*, in no instance, apart from the alleged reference in 1 Timothy 5:17, is there any indication of there being two sorts of presbyters – one restricted to 'ruling' and the other with the additional calling to preach. On the contrary, *all* the other Pauline references to the work of elders *join* teaching with ruling. Aptness to teach is a qualification for the office (*1 Tim.* 3:2). The elders at Ephesus are to counter the threat of 'grievous wolves' by feeding the church of God with the truth (*Acts* 20:28). Elders in Crete are to 'hold fast the faithful word' and 'be able by sound doctrine both to exhort and to convince the gainsayers' (*Titus* 1:9). If the words of 1 Timothy 5:17 distinguish two groups of presbyters, then it is the *only* text to do so; and, this being so, it follows that the meaning attributed to it by the presbyter/elder theory needs re-examination. Campbell, along with most modern exegetes, believed that the words could well bear a sense other than the one that stipulates two classes of men and work. They pointed out that 1 Timothy

5:17 says nothing about any presbyter being *restricted* to ruling; only that those who 'labour in the word and doctrine' (giving their very best to it) are worthy of 'double honour'.

The NIV translation of 1 Timothy 5:17 reads: 'The elders who direct the affairs of the church well are worthy of double honour, especially those whose work is preaching and teaching.' On this reading the meaning is plain. All elders 'direct the affairs of the church', or rule, but there are some 'whose work is preaching'. But the original is by no means so clear, and the NIV translators are doing here what they seem to do too often, namely, interpret rather than translate. The words 'whose work' does not accord with the original. The KJV's 'especially they who labour in the word and doctrine' stays closer to the original, and can well be understood as saying, 'All elders who do well as leaders are worthy of double honour, especially those who are *painstaking* in preaching – who "toil" *(kopiao)*, unweariedly, "in the word and in teaching".' On this understanding, the difference is not between elders who only rule and others who preach, it simply gives special commendation to those who are outstanding in their efforts in the preacher's calling. The text gives no leave to some elders not to preach at all. They are not relieved of the duty.[4]

Campbell's second ground for rejecting the theory I had accepted was *historical*. I first gave attention to his passing remark that the theory was 'deliberately repudiated' at the Westminster Assembly. It did not take long to establish that, broadly speaking, his statement was correct. In November and December 1643 the divines gave prolonged attention to the subject. The case that 1 Timothy 5:17 distinguished 'preaching elders' from 'ruling elders' was thoroughly argued by the Scots commissioners, although Samuel Rutherford 'admitted that there were over a dozen possible interpretations' of that verse.[5] After one of the debates, another Scot, Robert Baillie, commented: 'I profess my marvelling at the great learning, quickness, and eloquence, together with the great courtesy and discretion in speaking, of these men.'[6] Yet despite every effort by the Scots, along with the Independents and others, the Assembly remained unconvinced of the case they presented. A carefully worded finding on the issue, while not explicitly repudiating the theory, was clearly intended to give it no support. In 'The Form of Church Government' which they published there is a section entitled 'Pastors' but none with the title 'Elders', and the section entitled 'Other Church Governors' tells us the reason why:

> As there were in the Jewish church elders of the people joined with the priests and Levites in the government of the church; so Christ, who hath instituted government, and governors ecclesiastical in the church, hath furnished some in his church, beside the ministers of the word, with gifts for government, and with commission to execute the same when called thereunto, who are to join with the minister in the government of the church. Which officers reformed churches commonly call Elders.[7]

For proof texts for this statement, the Westminster divines did not cite the instances of presbyters (elders) in Acts, 1 Timothy, or Titus. They restricted proof-texts to the references to gifts of ruling and government (*Rom.* 12:7–8 and *1 Cor.* 12:28). Commenting on this decision (which came in November 1644), John Lightfoot, one of the members, noted:

> There fell a debate about naming Church governors, whether to call them 'Ruling Elders' or no, which held a very sad and long discussion; at last it was determined by vote thus, – 'such as, in the Reformed Churches, are commonly called elders'. Then Mr Gillespie moved that they should be called 'Ruling Elders', but this prevailed not.

In other words, the Westminster divines – or at least the majority[8] – would not identify those 'commonly' called 'elders' with the New Testament name. Only in accommodation to a common usage in Scotland and elsewhere would they refer to these persons as 'elders'. Instead of endorsing the theory that the office of presbyters ought to exist in two forms, they wished it to be understood that all presbyters are set apart as servants or 'ministers' of the Word.

To assess how a common identification of 'elder' with 'presbyter' arose, there is need to go further back than Westminster. Long before the Assembly met, opponents of the Puritans attributed the 'ruling elder' idea to Calvin and Geneva. There were enough men at Westminster versed in history to show the charge was wrong and Campbell's book details some of the evidence. Early in church history there were, alongside presbyters and deacons, 'seniors' (*seniores*) in the churches of North Africa. A document of AD 313–5 refers to *presbyteri, diaconi et seniores* – 'presbyters, deacons, and seniors'. Presbyters were sometimes also called 'clergy', but neither name was given to the 'seniors'. Thus letters were addressed *clero et senioribus*, 'to the clergy and seniors'; and Augustine (AD 395) could speak of 'Peregrinus, the presbyter, and the seniors of the Mustican district.' These seniors were 'trustworthy' men who shared in the discipline of the churches. Hilary affirmed, 'The Church had seniors, without whose counsel nothing was done in the Church.'[9]

Calvin was well aware of this evidence and saw in it the fulfilment of the gift of government:

> The governors I understand to have been *seniors selected from the people,* to unite with bishops [=presbyters] in the censure of manners and the exercise of discipline. For this is the only meaning that can be given to the passage, 'He that ruleth with diligence'. From the beginning, therefore,

each Church had its senate council, or consistory, composed of pious, grave, and venerable men, invested with that power of correcting faults.[10]

The idea of rulers in the churches, other than preachers, was thus not original to Calvin, and, of course, it had a parallel in the Old Testament. Before the Reformation it had also been known in the Waldensian and Bohemian churches. Yet the critics who blamed Calvin for 'ruling elders' were not entirely wrong, for in addition to instancing gifts of government to justify the office, he also appealed to 1 Timothy 5:17. The theory that there are two classes of presbyters/elders thus came to have the weight of his reputation behind it in Reformed churches, and the usage became so common that the Westminster divines had to make allusion to it, while wishing to put the term 'church governors' in the place of 'elders'.

CHURCH GOVERNMENT AND THE RULE OF SCRIPTURE

At first sight, all I have discussed above may seem a mere dispute about words. Does it matter, after all, whether 'seniors' and 'church governors' are given the same name as presbyters/ elders? At the Westminster Assembly it certainly mattered and for a good reason. At the Reformation it was a leading principle for the recovery of the church that nothing should be imposed in her government and worship that lacked express biblical authority. Calvin's counsel to pastors was widely regarded, 'Be particularly careful not to attempt anything which His Word does not permit.' As we have noted, this was Knox's emphasis, and many Puritans suffered in England and Scotland for acting on it.

Among the members and Scots commissioners at the Westminster Assembly there was no disagreement over the need for men, in addition to those in the regular ministry, to serve in the care of the people. The importance of their office was not in doubt, the point of contention was over where the scriptural authorization for the office was to be found. All agreed that Scripture, not tradition, must rule. Precedents from the early centuries were no safe guide. But while a majority thought that 'gifts of government', coupled with the fact that the Old Testament church had representatives of the people (elders), was enough justification, others were alarmed that, if 1 Timothy 5:17 was rejected as a proof text equating these persons with presbyters, there was no express biblical institution for their office. In the view of the minority, the affirmation of 'church governors' in such general terms as the majority proposed amounted to allowing prudence and expediency to rule instead of express Scripture. There was plain New Testament warrant for the institution of presbyters and deacons, but if 'church governors' could not be identified with presbyters, where was there any New Testament institution of their office? If there was none, they believed a serious departure from the biblical pattern was being tolerated.

This difference over the precise nature of biblical authority explains the length of time the Assembly gave to the eldership question. The Scots and others were far from satisfied that an office of 'church governor' could be established in England, where it did not exist, or maintained in Scotland, chiefly on the grounds of prudence and expediency. Robert Baillie's private comment in a letter written in the midst of the eldership debate in November 1643 is significant:

> All of them were ever willing to admit Elders in a prudential way; but this to us [i.e., the Scots commissioners] seemed a most dangerous and unhappie way, and therefore was peremptorilie rejected. We trust to carry at last, with the contentment of sundrie once opposite, and silence of all, their divine and scriptural institution. This is a point of high consequence.[11]

But the hope of Baillie and the other Scots commissioners was not fulfilled. Later he had to add to the same letter: 'We have been in a pitifull labyrinth these twelve days, about Ruleing Elders.' When he wrote again, in December 1643, the position had not changed: 'How many and learned debates we had on these things, in twelve or thirteen sessions from nine to half two, it were long to relate.'[12] The sticking point was the attempt to establish ruling elders by 'divine right' (*jus divinum*). When it was taken up at committee level the problem was the same. Dr Stanton reported, 'It was not the mind of the committee to stamp *Jus divinum* upon the ruling presbiter.' In the outcome, a year later, as we have seen above, the Assembly's 'Form of Church Government' gave no ground to those who wanted to assert divine institution from 1 Timothy 5:17.

In the Westminster Assembly's 'Form of Church Government' the point which the Scots commissioners had regarded as of 'great consequence' was 'quietly buried'. The Scots had to return north satisfied that at least the office of those the 'reformed churches commonly call elders' was endorsed. For the time being the debate was over and 'elders', not 'church governors', continued to be the accepted term in Scotland. The common assumption was that where the word 'elder' occurred in the English New Testament, it designated the same men as they knew by that name. Such passages as 1 Timothy chapter 3, and Titus chapter 1, with their references to the calling of elders, were thus considered correct for reading at the appointment of ruling elders, and most would have been very surprised had they been told that the Westminster documents authorized no such understanding.

THE ISSUE SURFACES AGAIN

Only in the 1840s did the controversy at the Westminster Assembly over elders break out again on a large scale, this time among the descendants of the Puritans and Presbyterians on the other side of the Atlantic.

The renewed debate appears to have been prompted by a new work on the eldership by Samuel Miller, Professor of Ecclesiastical History and Church Government at Princeton Theological Seminary, published in 1821, and then in an enlarged edition in 1831, with the title, *The Warrant, Nature and Duties of the Office of the Ruling Elder*. British editions followed in 1835 and 1842. Contrary to the judgment of the Westminster Assembly (which he did not mention), Miller gave as proof texts for the office the *same* texts as were universally accepted as the basis for the ministerial office, including 1 Timothy 5:17. The consequence of this claim was not missed. If pastors and elders were one and the same in office, with different functions, then there ought to be parity between them that did not exist. Elders were not ordained by the laying on of hands; did not preside at the Lord's Table; participate in the ordination of ministers; or chair ('moderate') meetings of session. An awakening to this recognition set in motion an agitation within the Presbyterian Church in the United States to redress what now appeared to be an 'unscriptural' inequality. Instead of accepting elders and ministers as two separate offices, able leaders such as R. J. Breckinridge and J. H. Thornwell pleaded for a recognition of *one* office. This revived the long-forgotten controversy and the Editor of Thornwell's *Collected Writings* says that, in the early 1840s, 'The whole Presbyterian Church in this country was agitated upon the question.'[13]

On many occasions Thornwell gave eloquent calls for a change. In particular he wanted ruling elders to be ordained in the same way as ministers, and he also argued for the equal participation of elders in the ordination of ministers. Ordination, he urged, was an act of presbytery and ruling elders are presbyters as truly as those men who preach.[14]

A full response to Thornwell was not immediately forthcoming, though the direction it would take was clearly indicated in an article by Charles Hodge, 'The Rights of Ruling Elders', published in 1843.[15] Hodge followed the Westminster divines in denying that ruling elders and ministers held the same office, with diversity only in their duties. That same year Hodge made the friendship of the Free Church of Scotland leader and theologian, William Cunningham, when the latter visited the United States. When Hodge's eldership article was published in a separate form he sent a copy to Cunningham, who replied in a letter of July 1844:

> I received the pamphlet on the Eldership, and am much obliged to you for it. I have never been able to make up my mind fully as to the precise grounds on which the office and functions of the ruling elder ought to be maintained and defended. For some time before I went to America I had come to lean pretty strongly to the view that all ecclesiastical office-bearers were presbyters, and that there were sufficiently clear indications in Scripture that there were two distinct classes of those presbyters, *viz.* ministers and ruling elders; though not insensible to the difficulty attaching to this theory from the consideration that it fairly implies that wherever presbyters or bishops are spoken of in Scripture ruling elders are included. I have been a good deal shaken in my attachment to this theory by the views I have heard from you, but I have not yet been able to abandon it entirely.[16]

Whether Cunningham was ever able to come to a decision is not on record. The truth is he was greatly occupied with other matters. Meanwhile the controversy went on in America. In 1860 there came a full and formidable reply to Thornwell's call for ruling elders to be regarded as New Testament presbyters from Thomas Smyth, a Presbyterian minister of

Scots-Irish descent in Charleston, South Carolina. The best-known Presbyterian journal in the land, *The Biblical Repertory and Princeton Review*, edited by Charles Hodge, published Smyth's first article on 'Theories of the Eldership', fifty-one pages in length, in the April issue of 1860. The next month at the General Assembly of the Presbyterian Church, Thornwell and Hodge collided in a monumental debate on this and kindred themes belonging to the definition of Presbyterianism. In July 1860 *The Biblical Repertory* continued Smyth's material on the eldership and Hodge also sought to answer Thornwell in print with an article on 'Presbyterianism'.[17]

R. L. Dabney now joined the debate, taking the same side as Thornwell, with a long article, 'Theories of the Eldership' published in the *North Carolina Presbyterian*, September 1860.[18] Perhaps Dabney would have been wiser to wait, for Smyth was not yet finished. The *Biblical Repertory and Princeton Review* of the following month brought his third and concluding article, making 130 pages in all from his pen. In an editorial note on the work of the Charleston preacher, Hodge said: 'Smyth's purpose was to oppose the new doctrine, that ministers and ruling elders are one in office. In this opposition we cordially agree with him.' Charles Hodge's own final thoughts on 'Warrant and Theory of Ruling Eldership' appeared in 1867.[19]

This point in time brings us back to Scotland and the book with which this chapter started. Principal Campbell had been following the debate in the United States and his own book came out in 1866. He quotes with approval Smyth's words, 'The whole burden of proof rests on those who generalise the term presbyter so as to include "ruling elders".'[20] Campbell was not the only Scot to call attention to the position that had been determined at Westminster two hundred years earlier. A few others had done so, and the Scottish Congregationalists had already given up the position on elders that had been adopted by their predecessors in the 1640s. Ralph Wardlaw, in his book *Congregational Independency in Contradistinction to Episcopacy and Presbyterianism* (1847), had a forty-five page chapter on 'No Evidence for Ruling Elders'.

Little else seems to have appeared after Campbell, with the exception of a lengthy article by the Scots-Irish Presbyterian, Thomas Witherow. Witherow had abandoned the argument that 1 Timothy 5:17 authorized a class of elders not authorized to preach, but claimed that, for practical reasons, while all might take the pulpit, only some ought to do so. When the First General Presbyterian Council met in Edinburgh in 1877 it gave a long afternoon session on 5 July to 'The Eldership: Its Theory and Practice'. Able addresses were given by men from both sides of the Atlantic, followed by contributions from the floor. Professor Simpson, an Edinburgh Free Church elder, believed that 'it was one of the grand advantages of the Presbyterian system that it had a capacity for laying hold of the living power of all its membership to join together to do the work of their common Saviour and Lord'. 'An elder', he went on, 'should be first and foremost a man of God', but this did not mean he should be 'capable of taking the minister's place in the pulpit'. A Pastor Dusek from Bohemia spoke of the value of the elders in his country since 1456. In days of persecution, he told the Assembly, 'the elders were the chief helpers in the work of the Lord. The ministers were easily put aside, but in their stead there stepped forward instantly the elders, showing the people how, if necessary, they ought also to die for the sake of the gospel.' It was his conviction that as long as the Reformed churches 'continue to have elders who would do their duty for Christ, the Churches will stand; but if the elders become corrupted the Church is then rotten and dead!'

It was impossible that one afternoon could settle differences discussed and unresolved over weeks at Westminster and 'the

Rev. Mr Sprott, North Berwick', referring to the differences, moved that the Council appoint a committee to look at the elders' office prior to the next Assembly. But the Assembly's published reported tersely noted, 'After a short discussion Mr Sprott withdrew his motion as to the appointment of a Committee.' Perhaps the men were just tired of committees, but the truth is that issues of church government no longer had the attention of nineteenth-century Scotland. As we shall see in the next chapter, a much more serious controversy was already ignited in Edinburgh and one which would relegate questions about proof-texts on church government to the past.

SOME OBSERVATIONS

1. The debate over eldership is one that cannot be settled by the etymology of words, and by supposing a word always has a fixed meaning. It might be thought that the meaning of the Hebrew word for 'elder', translated into the Greek New Testament as *presbyteros,* must determine how the latter word is to be understood, and that its primary meaning has reference (as the Old Testament word does) to age. But that is an assumption that cannot be established. Words can change in meaning. It may be that the first elders in the Jerusalem church (*Acts* 11:30) represented a continuation of the elder of the Jewish synagogues, but the eldership at the time of the Pastoral Epistles was by no means a mere continuation. The youthfulness of Timothy as an 'elder' is proof enough of that fact. As T. M. Lindsay has written, 'It must always be remembered that Christian 'elders' had functions entirely different from the Jewish . . . nothing but the name was borrowed.'[21] The primary sense of *presbyteros* is not about age; it is about overseeing or ruling.

This ruling, it is no less clear, is connected with teaching. As William Tyndale says in a marginal note on Titus, chapter one, presbyters (which he translates as 'elders' or 'overseers') are 'chosen to govern the congregation in doctrine and living'. Implicit in this is an important check on abuse of office in the church. Whereas rule in the affairs of the world is exercised by persons solely in terms of the authority of their office, rule in the church is to be by the teaching of Scripture. In Protestant churches obedience is not required on the authority of the church or of any of her office-bearers: 'God alone is lord of the conscience.' Thus the warning to Christ's first disciples, 'Ye know that the princes of the Gentiles exercise dominion over them, and they that are great exercise authority upon them. But it shall not be so among you' (*Matt.* 20:25–26). Servants of Christ are not 'lords over God's heritage' (*1 Pet.* 5:3).

As Scripture is the authoritative instrument of government, the teachers of the churches have a primary responsibility in ruling, yet it does not follow that there is no need for 'church governors' as well as 'presbyters'. The support of others, as in the Presbyterian and other systems of government, has long been found beneficial.

2. This debate is misunderstood if it is thought to be a question of 'clergy' versus 'laity'. Those who opposed the presbyter/elder theory were not men jealous for the rights of the full-time officers of the church. The lesson of the domination of the clergy suffered under Roman Catholicism was not forgotten. The proof of that is the fact stated by Charles Hodge, that Presbyterian government gives more voting power to the men called elders than it does to ministers:

> In our system the people have not only the right to elect their own Church officers, but they have controlling influence in the government of the Church; exercising that influence through the elders, who are their representatives . . . In the primary Church court, the session, they are

always the majority, and in all other courts they are, as a general rule, as numerous as the ministers. Nothing can be done without their concurrence. They may admit and exclude from the Church, in opposition to the ministers; they may even secure the admission or deposition of ministers, in opposition to the pastors. For if in any presbytery, the elders, being more numerous than the clergy, should vote for the ordination of a man, and all the ministers against it, he must be ordained.[22]

The opposition to treating elders as presbyters was not due to a concern to support the 'vested interests' of ministers, although it cannot be denied that such a spirit can arise in times of declension. The concern was rather that the preaching office, which receives the highest priority in the New Testament, should not be weakened. The view that treated all elders as presbyters left no room for the distinct calling and appointment of preachers. If all the references to presbyters in the Pastoral Epistles are to a shared office, embracing non-preaching elders *and* preachers, where else is anything to be found on the calling of those who are distinctly to be ministers of the Word?

The preacher must be first in leadership, even though he cannot act in independence of the people. Where non-preaching 'elders' are given equality in office with preachers, the New Testament priority is affected.

3. It may be objected that if 1 Timothy 5:17 speaks only of presbyters who are ministers of the Word, how is a plurality of such men in every congregation, found in the New Testament, to be explained? Does a congregation need a team of preachers? Is the plurality not more easily explained if the elders are understood to include non-preaching presbyters?

It is true that we have no record of a church in the New Testament possessing only one presbyter. Nor do those who say the New Testament elder is a preacher have any objection, in principle, to more than one preacher. Calvin attributed to the 'ignorant' and the 'godless', a remark that three preachers were enough for Geneva.[23] Two preachers in a congregation were to be found in a number of cities in Puritan times, and William Guthrie believed that it was simply 'want of maintainance' that prevented that practice from being more common.[24]

Whether two preachers can be taken as the equivalent of the plurality to be found in New Testament churches may be uncertain, yet it has also to be borne in mind that 'the church' in towns did not necessarily consist of only *one* congregation, any more than the congregation at St. Peter's, Geneva, comprised the whole church in that city. The limitation in our information is not enough to prove that there should be a multiplicity of preachers in every congregation.

There is also a good biblical reason to show why, in practical terms, a whole team of preachers in one congregation is not feasible. Preaching is so important that some need to give their whole time to it, and for that reason Scripture enjoins their support in temporal things. That is the clear biblical duty of a congregation wherever possible: 'The Lord ordained that they which preach the gospel should live of the gospel' (*1 Cor.* 9:14; see also *Gal.* 6:6). Now, if an average congregation were to treat equally a whole team of preachers, how could they possibly fulfil this obligation? Is it better to have a whole group of preachers, none of whom is full-time, or to have one or two preachers who can give themselves wholly to the work of the gospel because their temporal needs are provided for?[25]

It can also be said that where the experiment has been tried of having many preachers of equal authority in one congregation the system has not lasted long. It has not been appreciated by the people themselves, and has too often led to discord, if not disaster. Theoretically a group of Christian preachers should be able to settle among themselves who preaches, and how often, but this discounts the place which Scripture and nature gives to the leadership of individuals. Commenting on the reference to 'bishops and deacons' in Philippians 1:1, Calvin wrote:

> I acknowledge, indeed, that, as the minds and manners of men are, there cannot be order maintained among ministers of the word, without one presiding over others. I speak of particular bodies [i.e., congregations], not of whole provinces, much less of the whole world.[26]

Similarly John Owen writes of the New Testament situation:

> It is evident that in all their assemblies they had one who did preside in the manner before described; which seems, among the apostles, to have been the prerogative of Peter . . . it is certain that the order very early observed in the church was one pastor.[27]

Owen did not regard the 'one pastor' as necessarily un-scriptural.[28] He conceded that 'in each particular church there may be many pastors with an equality of power, if the edification of the church do require it,' but added the significant caution, 'The absolute equality of many pastors in one and the same church is liable unto many inconveniences if not diligently watched against.'[29] He believed in 'the necessity of precedence for the observation of order'.[30]

Where Christianity exists in a healthy state, it is certain there will be many ministries and gifts being exercised throughout a congregation; and all the speaking will not be left to one man. But, too often, the modern outcry against 'the one-man ministry' lies in a failure to recognize the supreme importance of the preacher's office and the need for leadership. Spurgeon wrote, 'Ministers do not claim to be a class of sacred beings, like the Brahmins of India,' yet he was not being inconsistent when he also said, 'The outcry against the "the one-man ministry" cometh not of God, but of proud self-conceit, of men who are not content to learn, although they have no power to teach.'[31]

4. We have noted that the crux of the debate over the office of the 'elder' was the question of scriptural authority. This was the issue both at Westminster and again when the controversy revived in the United States in the 1840s. Thornwell argued that if 1 Timothy 5:17 does not give us the institution of ruling elders, then the office has no definite biblical authority, and therefore no 'divine right' (*Jus divinum*), and, for him, the implications were enormous: 'To say that a Ruling Elder [in Presbyterian churches] is not entitled to the appellation of Presbyter . . . is just to say that the fundamental principle of our polity is a human institution . . . Presbyterianism stands or falls with the distinction between Ruling and Teaching Elders.'[32]

This argument proceeds on the same basis as the one adopted by the Scots at the Westminster Assembly: church government must be determined wholly by Scripture, otherwise it has no claim to divine authority. So, Thornwell and others later argued, the biblical claims for Presbyterianism must fail if an office so central to its organization lacks express sanction. Similarly Witherow asserted, 'The introduction into the church constitution of an official who can plead no warrant for his office from the Scripture, opens a wide door for the creation of other offices, as expediency may suggest or human wisdom determine.'[33]

The reply of Charles Hodge to this was basically the same as the reply made at Westminster. He believed that gifts of governing (*Rom.* 12:8, *1 Cor.* 12:28) were sufficient warrant for men to share in the ruling of the churches. The fact that there was no express institution of their office would invalidate Presbyterianism only if it claimed divine right for all its parts and details. In Hodge's opinion – and he was equally a Presbyterian with Thornwell – no such claim should be made. 'The reasoning of our brethren', he wrote, 'seems to be founded on the high, *jus divinum*, principle, that there is a definite and complete form of government, laid down in the word of God, from which the Church has no right to deviate; either by introducing new officers, or judicatories, or by modifying the duties of those therein mentioned.' He saw this as a real mistake:

> Christ has not made his grace to depend on external organization; nor has he bound his church to any one exact model of ecclesiastical discipline. If in the early church it was expedient and easy to have several presbyters in the same church, all clothed with the same office; and if we find it better, in our circumstances, to have one minister, assisted by a bench of elders, we have a divine right so to order it.[34]

Hodge, of course, is here using 'divine right' in a broader sense than Thornwell would allow, but it seems to us that Thornwell is also not without difficulty in claiming divine right, in the strict meaning of that term, for every part of his position. For if the presbyters of 1 Timothy 5:17 constitute one office, where is there to be found any *distinct* authority for ministers of the Word? There are no texts other than those referring to the appointment of *all* elders, be they ruling or preaching, according to his understanding. Yet when Thornwell and Dabney are not dealing with the eldership problem, but writing on the call to the ministry of the Word, they both make it plain that they regard this as something quite different from the call to the eldership. Where are the Scriptures to support that opinion to be found, given their interpretation that the office is common to all elders? They have to be inconsistent to give to the preaching office the weight that the New Testament gives to it.[35]

To return to the autobiographical for the moment, this is why Peter Campbell's little book on *The Theory of Eldership* was so important to me. It set me, reluctantly, on a course which led to my believing that Hodge was closer to the truth than Thornwell. I believe that the Presbyterian system, in its general principles, can appeal to Scripture, and is a wise form of church government, but it is not to be denied that some of its features rest on experience and prudence rather than on proof-texts.

5. It is worthy of note that a reason why 'elders' have endured in Presbyterian churches, while they early failed in those of the Independent or Congregational order, was in part, at least, because of the safeguards that experience and expediency had built into Presbyterian organization. If, as in Independency, the preacher shares the same office with a number of elders of equal authority, his preaching may be directed, and even his removal decided, by these fellow officers. In Presbyterian government, the checks and balances are such that a minister cannot be removed by his local session. Where there have been no such safeguards, elders have too often contributed to problems, and this seems to have led to their demise in Independent churches, as in New England where the office had virtually died out by the time Cotton Mather published his *Magnalia Christi Americana* in 1702. 'The inconveniencies into which many churches have been plunged by elders', Mather wrote, 'have much increased a prejudice against the office itself.'[36]

A notable example of such 'inconveniencies' occurred under the ministry of James and Robert Haldane who attempted to restore 'apostolic eldership' in the Independent congregations they gathered in Scotland at the beginning of the nineteenth century. James Haldane, pastor of the Edinburgh Tabernacle, argued in 1805 that 'the elders are all equal in office, but an equality of gifts among them is not to be expected. Where the elders and the church are of a proper temper, there will be no disputing on this head.' Yet disputes there evidently were. It was not necessary, James Haldane believed, that several elders 'should, in *their turn*, conduct the public service'. Where that system had been allowed to operate there had been 'great injury to the power of religion, even in the members of the church'.[37] He was speaking from unhappy experience and observation.[38] The attempt to secure a plurality of elders at Haldane's Tabernacle did not succeed, and Robert Haldane was to say in 1821 that 'the system did not work'.[39]

6. That discussion over eldership became a 'labyrinth', both at Westminster and at other times, has to teach us that we all understand less about the government of the apostolic churches than has often been admitted. Our knowledge is too imperfect to justify the dogmatism that has too often led to prolonged controversy. The Presbyterian T. M. Lindsay, in his book *The Church and the Ministry in the Early Centuries*, has written, 'The organization of the Primitive Christian Church . . . has no resemblance to any modern ecclesiastical organization, and yet contains within it the roots of all, whether congregational, presbyterian (conciliar) or episcopal.'[40] This may be an over-statement but there is important truth in it. Calvin, preaching on the eldership, could say: 'There is yet a great distance between us, and the order that was practised in the apostles' time.'[41]

A measure of uncertainty is good for us if it leads us to moderate controversy about lesser things. Names and titles are of less importance than the right use of the gifts which Christ gives to his church. Historic Methodism with its class leaders and local preachers differed considerably from the Presbyterian system, yet spiritual gifts were often present in a notable degree. It was not without reason that, when eldership was discussed at the First General Presbyterian Council in Edinburgh, it was noted that, in England and America, Methodism had led to 'the infusion of a lay element into their councils and boards'. Likewise the gifts which Presbyterianism finds in 'elders' have been found no less in the many churches which call those who exercise the same gifts 'deacons'. One candid Presbyterian writer, Dr Thomson of Coldstream, comparing Scottish and English churches, points this out: 'Two sorts of officers are recognized by both: – and what are deacons in the one are just elders in the other. Names are nothing.'[42]

All this does not mean that all Christians should not desire to be as close as possible to Scripture, but it ought to be a check on the dogmatism and 'ultraism' that has too often prolonged controversy and diverted the churches from their main duty, which is to see men united to the church which is 'the heavenly Jerusalem'. Without that, as Owen says, 'All contests about church-order . . . are vain, empty, fruitless.'[43] In different words, James Haldane was to profess similar sentiments in his last illness:

It was his conviction that the Spirit was given as the Lord saw good to all Churches – that it was the preaching of sound doctrine which the Lord blessed, and not particular systems of church-government. 'Great good', he said, 'was done by itinerating, but we were permitted for a time to attach too much importance to some things connected with Church order; and whether it was that we were not worthy, or whatever was the cause, our efforts to restore apostolic Churches and primitive Christianity were unsuccessful.'[44]

This was a salutary warning from a faithful man, and to it may be added the words of Richard Baxter: 'While we wrangle here in the dark,' he wrote, 'we are dying and passing to the world that will decide all our controversies; and the safest passage thither is *by peaceable holiness.*'[45]

[1] 'A Treatise of Ruling Elders and Deacons', *Works of William Guthrie* (Glasgow: Hunter, 1771), p. 321. This appears to have been the first edition of the works of Guthrie (1620–65).

[2] Quoted by G. D. Henderson, *The Scottish Ruling Elder* (London: James Clarke, 1935), p. 232.

[3] *The Theory of Ruling Eldership, or The Position of the Lay Ruler in the Reformed Churches* (Edinburgh and London: W. Blackwood, 1866).

[4] This understanding of 1 Timothy 5:17 has gained wide acceptance. In a book he wrote in 1856, *The Apostolic Church, Which Is It?*, Thomas Witherow claimed: 'Any unprejudiced person may see from 1 Timothy 5:17, that the office of the eldership divided itself into two great departments of duty in primitive times, even as at the present.' But in 1873 on the same text he said this of the 'distinction between two classes of elder': 'To us it seems clear that the whole theory rests on a misconception of the force of the passage, 1 Timothy 5:17, and therefore cannot be any real justification for the difference that actually exists between the ruling elder and the minister.' He now believed the text made no exception whatever: 'Every elder must be able to rule, and also fit to teach.' 'The New Testament Elder,' *British and Foreign Evangelical Review* (London: Nisbet, 1873), p. 204.

[5] For discussion of the debate see Henderson, *Scottish Ruling Elder;* John R. de Witt, *Jus Divinum: The Westminster Assembly and the Divine Right of Church Government* (Kampen: Kok, 1969); and Robert S. Paul, *The Assembly of the Lord: Politics and Religion in the Westminster Assembly and the 'Grand Debate'* (Edinburgh: T. & T. Clark, 1985).

[6] Robert Baillie, *Letters and Journals*, ed. David Laing, vol. 2 (Edinburgh: Ogle, 1841), p. 110.

[7] 'The Form of Presbyterial Church-Government . . . Agreed . . . at Westminster', 1645, usually bound up with the Westminster Confession of Faith.

[8] Whether there was a majority, or whether a majority gave way to a minority view for the sake of unity, has been questioned, i.e. J. R. de Witt, *Jus Divinum*, p. 85. Richard Baxter, on the other hand, wrote, 'As far as I can understand, the greater part, if not three for one of the English ministers' opposed the minority view of the Scots and the Independents, *Five Disputations of Church Government and Worship* (London, 1659), Preface, p. 4.

[9] Campbell, *Theory of Ruling Eldership*, pp. 6–12. See also, T. F. Torrance, *The Eldership in the Reformed Church* (Edinburgh: Handsel Press, 1984).

[10] I am here giving Campbell's translation of the 1543 edition of the *Institutes* (Book IV, iii. 8). Calvin's final words on the passage will be found in the Battles translation of the *Institutes* (Philadelphia: Westminster Press, 1960), vol. 2, p. 1061.

[11] Baillie, *Letters and Journals*, vol. 2, p. 111.

[12] Ibid., pp. 115–7.

[13] *The Collected Writings of J. H. Thornwell* (1875, repr. Edinburgh: Banner of Truth, 1974), vol. 4, p. 14. All Thornwell's writing on the eldership will be found in this volume. See also B. M. Palmer's *The Life and Letters of J. H. Thornwell* (repr. Edinburgh: Banner of Truth, 1974).

[14] *Collected Writings*, vol. 4, p. 119.

[15] *The Biblical Repertory and Princeton Review*, pp. 313–32. Reprinted in Charles Hodge, *The Church and Its Polity* (London: Nelson, 1879).

[16] A. A. Hodge, *The Life of Charles Hodge* (London: Nelson, 1881), p. 425.

[17] Hodge, *Church and Its Polity*, pp. 118–33; also in Thornwell, *Collected Writings*, vol. 4.

[18] *Discussions of R. L. Dabney* (London: Banner of Truth, 1967), vol. 2, pp. 119–57.

[19] Reprinted in *The Church and Its Polity*, pp. 262–71.

[20] *Theory of Ruling Eldership*, p. 54.

[21] T. M. Lindsay, *The Church and the Ministry in the Early Centuries* (London: Hodder and Stoughton, 1903), p. 153.

[22] *Church and Its Polity*, pp. 262, 264.

[23] *Sermons of Calvin on the Epistle to Timothy and Titus* (London, 1579; repr. Edinburgh: Banner of Truth, 1983), p. 512.

[24] *Works of Guthrie*, p. 329.

[25] It is not required of the pastor, says Owen, 'only that he preach now and then at his leisure, but that he lay aside all other employments, though lawful, all other duties in the church, as unto such a constant attention on them as would divert him from this work, that he give himself unto it, – that he be in these things labouring to the utmost of his ability.' How can such an ideal be fulfilled other than by the tradition which has been most common in the Protestant churches?

[26] *Commentaries on Philippians, Colossians and Thessalonians* (Edinburgh: Calvin Trans. Soc., 1851), p. 23.

[27] Owen's *Works*, vol. 16, p. 46.

[28] Ibid., p. 141, 'There may be, and oftentimes is, but one teaching elder, pastor, or teacher in a church.'

[29] Ibid., p. 105.   [30] Ibid., p. 105.

[31] Spurgeon, *The Metropolitan Tabernacle Pulpit*, vol. 36 (London: Passmore and Alabaster, 1890), p. 255, and vol. 8 (1863), p. 195.

[32] *Collected Writings of J. H. Thornwell*, vol. 4, pp. 115, 125.

[33] *British and Foreign Evangelical Review*, 1873, p. 219.

[34] Hodge, *Church Polity*, pp. 275, 284.

[35] See 'The Call to the Ministry' in Thornwell, *Collected Writings*, vol. 4; 'What Is a Call to the Ministry?' and 'The Standard of Ordination', in Dabney, *Discussions*, vols. 2 and 3.

[36] Mather, *The Great Works of Christ in America* (Edinburgh: Banner of Truth, 1979), vol. 2, p. 239.

[37] J. A. Haldane , *A View of Social Worship and Ordinances Observed by the First Christians, Drawn from the Sacred Scriptures Alone* (Edinburgh, 1805), pp. 254–8.

[38] On this subject see Alexander Haldane, *The Lives of Robert and James Haldane* (1852; repr. Edinburgh: Banner of Truth, 1990), pp. 356–61. Some of the congregations allowed any man to speak in public worship, 'a system', writes J. Haldane, 'which appears to me destructive of the pastoral office and of all order in the house of God'.

[39] Ibid., p. 379.

[40] *Church and Ministry in the Early Centuries*, p. 155.

[41] *Sermons on Timothy and Titus,* pp. 508–9.

[42] Quoted by Ralph Wardlaw, *Congregational Independency in Contradistinction to Episcopacy and Presbyterianism: the Church Polity of the New Testament* (Maclehose, 1864), p. 185. Wardlaw points out, with justification, that the work of the diaconate has been poorly regarded in many Presbyterian churches. T. F. Torrance takes the matter further when he writes, 'It would seem to be the case that our elders now fulfil a ministry which in the New Testament itself is ascribed to deacons . . . Consider, for example, the Epistle to the Philippians 1:1, in which St Paul mentions only "bishops and deacons". Are we to include "elders" here under "bishops" or under "deacons"? That is the issue, and when faced with it, Reformed commentators have regularly included them under "deacons". It might be said, then, that what we call "elders" are really "elder-deacons".' *The Eldership in the Reformed Church*, p. 10.

[43] *Works,* vol. 24 *(Exposition of Hebrews,* vol. 7), p. 342.

[44] *Robert and James Haldane*, p. 583.

[45] Richard Baxter, *The Cure of Church Divisions* (London, 1670), p. 256.

The Tragedy of the Free Church of Scotland

Free Church College Library, Edinburgh

The age's progress fears no God,
No righteous law, no Judge's throne;
Man bounds along his new-found road,
And calls this universe his own.

Old misbelief becomes earth's creed;
The falsehood lives, the truth has died;
Man leans upon a broken reed,
And falls in helplessness of pride.

He spurns the hand that would have led,
The lips that would have spoken love;
The Book that would his soul have fed,
And taught the wisdom from above.

Eternal Light, hide not Thy face;
Eternal Truth, direct our way;
Eternal Love, shine forth in grace,
Reveal our darkness and *Thy* day!

HORATIUS BONAR

In the last quarter of the nineteenth century a change of belief over the Bible took place in the Free Church of Scotland, with more far-reaching consequences than anything that had happened since the Reformation. In the public arena the change may be said to have begun in 1870, when the General Assembly appointed a new professor to the vacant professorship of Hebrew at the denomination's college in Aberdeen. While such an occasion did not normally attract much attention, this appointment had all the features of the unusual. At the age of twenty-three, the foremost candidate, William Robertson Smith, who had just finished his training as a student in theology, was being spoken of as a 'phenomenon'. Certainly, assessments of his ability represented him as out of the ordinary. Moving his appointment to the professorship, Dr James Walker of Carnwath, himself no lightweight theologian, declared, 'I doubt if such testimonials have ever been presented to us.' While Robertson Smith's abilities were remarkable, Walker believed there was also 'a guarantee of the highest and surest kind for his orthodoxy'.[1]

AN ENCYCLOPAEDIA EXPLODES IN THE CHURCH

Robertson Smith was appointed, and such were his gifts that only five years later he was asked to contribute the biblical articles for the ninth edition of the *Encyclopaedia Britannica*. When these began to appear, the reliability of the 'guarantee' of which Dr Walker was persuaded became an issue that plunged the Free Church into controversy. First, an article on 'Angels' seemed to suggest that the author might not believe in their personal existence, and it was noted that he had nothing to say on fallen angels. But it was his entry on 'Bible' that raised what was to be the main issue in the years ahead. It proposed an understanding of the construction of the Old Testament with which 'the Church was entirely unacquainted'.[2] Robertson Smith taught that the Book of Deuteronomy was 'put in the mouth of Moses' by unknown authors many centuries after the period to which it was supposed to belong, and that it contained much of which Moses could have known nothing. Further, the writer seemed to question the importance of the predictive elements in the Old Testament prophets; he wished prophets to be understood as preachers to their own times. Nor was it only the Old Testament that had to be freshly understood: the four Gospels, Smith believed, were not written by the authors after whom they are named; rather they were 'non-apostolic digests of spoken and written apostolic tradition'.

Smith's statements were referred to the College Committee of the Free Church and, while this body vacillated, other publications and reprints deepened the controversy. Dr Marcus Dods, minister of Renfield Free Church, Glasgow, entered the field in support of Robertson Smith. In a sermon entitled, 'Revelation and Inspiration', he argued that the element of 'inspiration' in Scripture was limited to matters of salvation.[3] Dr Hugh Martin replied with two publications demonstrating that, according to the Confession of Faith, it was not part but the whole of Holy Scripture that it 'pleased the Lord' to commit 'wholly unto writing'.[4] In the words of the Larger Catechism, 'The holy scriptures of the Old and New Testament are the word of God.' 'There are those in Scotland', Martin wrote, 'who would die of sorrow if they could no longer believe this, and who will die with gladness for the truth of it.'

The issue was quickly taken up in Presbyterian churches beyond Scotland. Dr Robert Watts, of the General Assembly's Theological College in Belfast, put his finger on the question that was to come to the fore more largely at a later date: if only part of Scripture is trustworthy, 'Is it not manifest that the minds of men must suffer great distraction in the reading of the Scriptures? The question will not be the simple one, "What does this Scripture say?", but the soul-disturbing one, "Is this truly and properly a part of Scripture?"' The new school in the Free Church, Watts believed, had 'framed a theory of inspiration in palpable contradiction to the Confession of Faith, and yet claim for themselves liberty to teach it to a rising generation of Scotland's ministry'.[5]

The extent to which the doubt over Scripture had already taken hold in the Free Church was soon to be apparent. Senior ministers, such as Dr Moody-Stuart,[6] and the Bonar brothers, calmly sought to refute the new views, while younger men were noticeably uncertain. In 1879 Horatius Bonar wrote two articles in the *Christian Treasury* in defence of the Pentateuch. 'I feel', he said, 'a vastly greater certainty, as the years roll on, with regard to the Divine authority and verbal inspiration of the Word of God.' But Bonar's words no longer carried the weight they had once done, and the same was true of other authors.[7] One contemporary tells us, 'The young bloods of the Scottish pulpit in quest of popularity found neither material nor method in the preaching of Dr Bonar.'[8]

At the General Assembly of 1880, by a majority of only nine, it was determined not to proceed with any charge of heresy against Robertson Smith. By this time feelings ran high and when the result of that vote was announced, 'For a time the conduct of the business was absolutely arrested, and nothing was heard but cheers, accompanied by the waving of hats and handkerchiefs.'[9] Smith was only to be admonished for 'the unguarded and incomplete statements of his articles'. So little did this mean to the Professor of Hebrew that a further article from him which soon appeared contained opinions no less inflammatory. The Assembly of the following year, wearied with the effect of the dispute upon the Church, decided that it was not expedient to retain him in his professorship at Aberdeen.

The chair of Hebrew was declared vacant and Smith continued on full salary. Before long he was to leave Scotland for Cambridge.

As far as dealing with the real issue was concerned, the removal of Robertson Smith in 1881 was futile. It had involved no determination of truth or error in his teaching. Further, other Free Church professors, or lecturers, with views akin to Robertson Smith's were already in position, including Alexander Balmain Bruce and Henry Drummond. Their numbers were soon to be increased. Among the most notable were Marcus Dods, who succeeded George Smeaton at New College, Edinburgh, in 1889, and George Adam Smith who went to the Glasgow College in 1892.[10] Their appointment to train men for the ministry was a sure indication of how both mood and opinion were changing in the denomination. Dods was appointed despite his already known views on Scripture. Dr Robert Rainy, Principal of New College, favoured his appointment, although privately conceding there was some 'risk' and saying that Dods had 'uttered many things that are disturbing'.[11] The risk was real enough. In his inaugural lecture as professor in New College, Dods described the doctrine of verbal inspiration as 'a theory of inspiration which made the Bible an offence to many honest men, which is dishonouring to God, and which has turned inquirers into sceptics by the thousand, – a theory which should be branded as heretical in every Christian Church.'[12] Only one year after his appointment Dods, together with A. B. Bruce, was examined before the General Assembly on grounds of heresy in 1890. Both were cleared.

Similarly, in 1897, James Denney was elected Professor of Systematic Theology in the Glasgow College, despite the fact that his view of Scripture was largely in sympathy with the one so recently introduced. He had told the General Assembly that 'for verbal inerrancy he cared not one straw'.[13]

Various attempts continued to be made by a dwindling older generation to arrest this tide, but without success. By the 1890s all the leaders of the Disruption era had passed away. The last major trial before the General Assembly (of what was now the United Free Church)[14] came in 1902, when a judgment against the teaching of Professor George Adam Smith was rejected by a vote of 534 to 263. The conservative minority, although still considerable, would never muster that number again. It seemed that G. A. Smith had been proved right in the assertion he had made when lecturing at Yale in 1899, 'We may say that Modern Criticism has won its war against the Traditional Theories.'[15] The eight lectures he delivered on that occasion became the book that formed the basis of the charge from which he was cleared in 1902. The controversy of the preceding thirty years was virtually over.

In recent times there have been suggestions that belief in the verbal inspiration of Scripture only *became* common among evangelicals in the late nineteenth and early twentieth centuries.[16] But in Scotland, as elsewhere, that suggestion is untrue. Carnegie Simpson, no friend of inerrancy, writing in his massive *Life of Principal Rainy*, on the belief concerning Scripture now introduced into the Free Church, said: 'It was absolutely new. Traditional views as to the history, the authorship and even the verbal inerrancy of the Bible had remained unchallenged in the Scottish Church since the Reformation.'[17]

THE SPEED OF CHANGE

From what we have considered the question arises, How could such a change be accepted in such a comparatively short time? Two answers present themselves:

First, the time frame in which the change occurred was not quite as short as public events would suggest. The new teaching did not originate with Robertson Smith in the 1870s. It had

been going on quietly under the teaching of A. B. Davidson at
New College, Edinburgh, since the 1850s.[18] Those who had
sat as students under Davidson were not surprised at the
more public presentation of what they had already heard in
seminal form. But while Davidson was only a single individual,
there was in Germany a galaxy of professors, of brilliant
erudition, thought to be leading the world in Old Testament
studies. In Scotland the real drift of their work was not
immediately apparent.[19] Thus, when Dr Walker commended
Robertson Smith for the Aberdeen professorship in 1870, one
of the points he made was that the candidate 'has a thorough
acquaintance with and mastery of the critical works of
Germany', and that Professor Ritschl had praised his 'extraordinary versatility of mind'. However, Smith's 'versatility' did
not go as far as subjecting his German mentors to criticism. It
was not without reason that Julius Wellhausen, one of the most
eminent of his teachers, liked to speak of him as 'a British pupil
of mine'.[20]

The novelty of Robertson Smith's opinions, his youthfulness,
backed by the prestige of German scholarship, affected a whole
rising generation of students. As one of them wrote, 'The Free
Church was certainly the most scholarly Church in Scotland',[21]
and, for it to remain so, it was thought Smith was the man to
follow. 'They were proud of his gift,' wrote another
contemporary.[22] Smith had spent two summer semesters in
Germany in the 1860s, and in the next decade a stream of the
Church's ablest students followed. The vogue for German
thought seemed to be irresistible, and this despite the fact that
the state of the churches in Germany was poorer than in
Scotland.[23]

A second reason why the change in the Free Church
occurred as it did was the repeated claim that, in all that
was most fundamental, there was really no change at all. If the
Free Church stood for scholarship, no less did she stand for

evangelical Christianity. Her whole existence, as we have seen in earlier pages, was related to that fact. The strength of Free Church support for Moody in 1873–4 seemed to reflect the way in which evangelism was still regarded as a high priority. From Robertson Smith to Henry Drummond, A. B. Bruce, Marcus Dods, and G. A. Smith, all the best-known advocates of the new teaching represented themselves as strong evangelicals. If they used any term for their position it was 'The New Apologetic', and the name, 'Higher Criticism', as a term describing destructive belief, only gradually came into use by those of the other side.

The united claim of these men was that they were giving new and pre-eminent attention to Christ. 'In this country at the present day nearly every leader in Old Testament criticism – and remember that some are as advanced as any on the Continent – ', G. A. Smith asserted, 'is a believer in evangelical Christianity.'[24] The promise was of a 'better' understanding of the Bible – one that would not only uphold evangelical belief but would greatly promote it in the years ahead. The outcome, Smith assured men, would be a basis for 'faith more stable than ever the older was ever imagined to be – richer mines of Christian experience and truth, better vantage grounds for preaching the Gospel of Christ'.[25] Marcus Dods, in answering the heresy charge that he faced in 1890, struck the same note: 'I have an evangelistic function which I cannot decline to discharge.'[26] In the words of the admirer who quoted that statement, 'His aim was high and worthy, to restore to men faith and joy in the truths of the Divine Word.'

Henry Drummond, especially, was held up as an example of how one could hold the new views and still be an evangelical. People were reminded of how prominent Drummond had been as a helper among young people at the time of Moody's mission in the 1870s. How far his beliefs changed after that date was played down by his admirers. Yet the evidence was clear enough by the time one of those admirers, G. A. Smith, wrote Drummond's biography in 1899. Speaking of the 1870s, Smith observed, 'The Evangelical movement had many defects, which in his younger days Henry had shared, and which we shall see him unlearning'[27] What that 'unlearning' involved is to be seen in the same biography as well as in other sources. It was not only 'a narrow mechanistic view' of the Bible that had to go; there was much else. Professor Robert Watts of Belfast wrote that Drummond and his school had 'no adequate recognition of the innate depravity of man in his natural condition, or of the agency of the Holy Spirit in Regeneration.'[28] C. H. Spurgeon commended a reviewer for 'laying bare the device of deleting the atonement of Christ with the idea of promoting the imitation of Jesus'.[29] 'It is apparent', G. A. Smith could conclude in 1899, 'how far Drummond had travelled from the positions of the older orthodoxy.'[30] The 'evangel' was still professed but it was not that of historic Christianity. As Drummond himself wrote: 'We have a Gospel in the new Evangelism for which for a hundred years the world has been waiting.'[31]

Yet for all this, Drummond, Bruce, and all their associates, continued to claim that the Bible was 'a divine book', and that they only aimed to deepen faith in its message. The inspiration and authority of the *message* (as distinct from the *Book*), was not in question, or so they claimed. G. A. Smith could say at his trial in 1902, 'From the bottom of my heart I believe in the Bible as the revelation of God to sinful men.' Yet Smith taught that Moses had nothing to do with the composition of the Pentateuch, nor David with the Psalms; that the historicity of Abraham was very unlikely and his story must be regarded as romance. Instead of the Bible beginning with the revelation of the living God, the Hebrew people were first polytheists, worshipping a tribal god. It was so obvious, he believed, that the Old Testament contained 'errors and immoralities', as

Marcus Dods had said years before, that there was no longer any need to say it.

But what of the claim that Higher Criticism gave true prominence to Christ? 'I have been looking at the Church in the dazzling light of the King and the Kingdom,' A. B. Bruce affirmed at his trial before the Assembly in 1890.[32] Ten years earlier it had been pointed out by Moody Stuart that, as Christ had explicitly spoken of Moses *writing* the precepts in Deuteronomy (*Mark* 10:5), this 'ought to have been revered as a Divine arrest on the new theory'. How could the authority of Christ be upheld if Moses never wrote what he attributed to him? By the time the question came more fully into the open, those who thus claimed to be exalting Christ had either to confess his fallibility, or question the authenticity of statements attributed to Jesus by the Gospel writers.

The real issue was now clear: it was not the Bible that the new teachers praised, but only *parts* of the Bible, and it lay in the hands of other 'scholars' to determine which parts these were to be. No statement of Scripture, as such, could be taken as trustworthy; all had to go into the critics' sieve. What would endure after that sieving no one could be sure. A 'trustworthy' Bible, as reconstructed by the latest opinion, was not in sight, either in Germany or in Scotland. As a reviewer of G. A. Smith wrote: 'The "revelation" in which Prof. Smith believes is one that sits enshrined in the cloudland of conjecture.'[33] Another reviewer of Smith and his associates put it still more plainly:

> The Bible which Christ taught and on which He fed and sustained His religious life is not their Bible. They have cut it into fragments and discredited its history, and reconstructed it on a different basis and on new lines, till no one would recognise it as Christ's Bible. There can be no doubt how their analysis and reconstruction of the Bible would have been regarded by Him who in all His

teaching and example assumed its truth and trust-worthiness.[34]

A LANDSLIDE AT HAND

In this situation, two reactions were possible. The first was that represented by C. H. Spurgeon who had often visited Scotland and been a long-time admirer of many of her preachers and authors. He wrote in 1889:

> The Free Church of Scotland must, unhappily, be for the moment regarded as rushing to the front with its new theology, which is no theology, but an opposition to the Word of the Lord. That Church in which we all gloried, as sound in the faith, and full of the martyrs' spirit, has entrusted the training of its future ministers to two professors who hold other doctrines than those of its Confession. This is the most suicidal act a Church could commit . . . Unless the whole church shall awake to its duty, the Evangelicals in the Free Church are doomed to see another reign of Moderatism.[35]

Others in the Free Church, less certain than Spurgeon, were nevertheless also apprehensive over what might happen if people in the pew came to believe what was being taught in the Colleges. Robertson Nicoll, the Free Church minister who became the first editor of the *British Weekly*, was one of those troubled, even although he largely shared the new view of Scripture and counted a number of its advocates as his friends. In a letter to a friend in 1908 he spoke of his concern that Professor James Denney declined to affirm that Jesus is God, and went on: 'There is a singular vein of scepticism in him, for all his apparent orthodoxy. For instance, he does not believe in the existence of the devil and of evil spirits. Nor does he believe in the Second Advent.'[36]

Even Dr Rainy, who played a large part in the toleration of error and was Principal of New College before Dods, seems to have had short-lived concerns. In the words of his biographer: 'Dr Rainy said that undoubtedly the effect of removing the old basis would produce a species of "land-slide" in many minds regarding characteristic evangelical doctrines, but he believed they would re-emerge.'[37]

A second reaction was quite different. Supposing the text of the whole Bible is too questionable to make it a basis for fixed beliefs, does that really matter? Are beliefs, after all, so important? Is it not enough for individuals to 'experience' the living presence of Christ, and to know God, without dogmatism over belief? Some of the leaders of the higher criticism clearly thought that these were the right questions, and they seem to have reached their own conclusions. Sometimes they spoke of the historicity of the life of Christ as though it were of no great importance. So A. B. Bruce could say:

If any one finds it impossible to believe in the resurrection of Christ, but easy to believe in His present life and power, it would only be mischievous to require of him a faith he cannot give in addition to a faith which brings him into real fellowship with Christ.[38]

B. B. Warfield, reviewing Marcus Dods, asked, 'What Christ we are to believe in', if we only have a fallible Bible?[39] If the import of the question disturbed the Higher Critics they seldom revealed it. Professor James Candlish, of the Glasgow Free Church College, believed that while a 'love of goodness' cannot exist where there is 'moral and spiritual death', it can be found where there is no *Christian belief* at all. Thus he affirmed:

Examples may be found in Buddha, and in some of the modern and atheistic philosophers, who have a high sense

and regard for moral excellence, to show that ignorance
and denial of God does not necessarily imply the absence
of the highest life of the soul . . . We are not, therefore,
entitled to deny that there may be real spiritual life outside
the pale of those who have received the revelation of God's
grace, and in men who know not the living God.[40]

Henry Drummond took the same line. 'Christ allows us to
be indefinite about our beliefs,' he asserted.[41] Even if the
upshot of this should be that the ministry of the Church itself
is no longer necessary, that thought did not dismay A. B. Bruce
overmuch. Bruce wrote, 'I am even disposed to think that a
great and steadily increasing portion of the moral worth of
society lies outside the Church . . . Many, in fact, have left the
Church in order to be Christians.'[42] In 1907 Denney wrote to
Nicoll of those who wanted to get 'a religion free from
historical certainty'. He instanced the teaching of Schmiedel
who had written, 'The inmost religious good that I possess
would not be injured at all if I had to admit the conviction
today that Jesus never lived.' He went on: 'The number of
people that are on the slope that ends here, and who suppose
that they are Christians while it is all the same to them if Jesus
never lived, is appalling.'[43]

THE MOTIVES OF THE HIGHER CRITICS

How is the intention of these teachers to change the belief of
the Church to be interpreted?

It is not necessary to impute any deliberate intention to turn
men away from truth and faith. The sincere motive of many
who supported the new thought was a concern to reduce the
'essentials' that Christianity needed to defend in an age when,
they feared, scientific and philosophic thought was making faith
in the Bible impossible. Even in Scotland, G. A. Smith believed
that by 1884 traditional Christian belief no longer claimed the
commitment of the educated. Given the strength of opposition

to Scripture, the best defence was thought to be a supernatural message, not a supernatural Book. In the words of Warfield, Dods belonged to a school of men who 'have sought to ease the situation by casting away what they have deemed the husk in the hope of saving what appeared to them the kernel. They have commended to us, therefore, a new and reduced Christianity, documented in a new and reduced body of Scriptures.'[44] The thinking was: 'We cannot hold the Bible in the face of modern assault. Let us hold to a shadowy Bible within the Bible, which is removed beyond the reach of scientific tests.'[45]

When Warfield wrote the words just quoted in 1894, some saw the issues more clearly but their numbers were in decline. The damage was done; too late did others come to see that an acceptance of the German criticism could not be held along with a continued belief in the authority of Scripture. The popular illusion was that an acceptance of the new views need not interfere with the maintenance of the Bible's authority. In 1881, for instance, after Robertson Nicoll had talked with Wellhausen in Germany, the Scot reported in a letter: 'We spoke of Robertson Smith. I said that Smith held the Bible to be inspired and historically accurate, along with Wellhausen's views, and that he also held to the truth of miracles. W. shook his head.'[46]

As late as 1895 there were many in the Free Church who still failed to see why the German professor shook his head. Thus, in that year, the Free Church minister and historian, Norman L. Walker, thought he was writing truthfully when he affirmed, 'By none of our critics has the supernatural authorship of the Bible been for a moment called in question.'[47] By 1902 Walker knew he had been wrong. At that date, after the acquittal of George Adam Smith in the General Assembly on charges arising out of his Yale lectures, *Modern Criticism and the Preaching of the Old Testament,* Walker wrote:

The critics have not said their last word, and the last concession has not been made to them. We are on an inclined plane and in the end little may remain of the Book [i.e. the Bible] . . . Written apparently for the purpose of relieving the perplexities of such preachers as have been disturbed by the higher critics, [Smith's book] has unquestionably failed in that aim. Many preachers will continue to have as many difficulties as before. Prof. Smith fails to meet the situation. He has done worse than that. He has awakened doubts where none had previously existed and seriously hindered the evangelistic work of the Church.[48]

Yet if the higher critics are not indiscriminately to be charged with insincerity, there is more that needs to be said. It cannot be doubted that some employed a measure of deliberate concealment, and equivocation, as they waited until times were more propitious. Beliefs destructive to faith in the Bible were aired among students long before they became more public. Dr A. B. Davidson, for instance, was the mentor of most of the men who became prominent in the later controversies. G. A. Smith spoke of him as the Church's 'greatest teacher – one man against an ancient and honoured system'.[49] But it was Davidson's policy to say almost nothing questionable outside the walls of his class at New College, and when Marcus Dods spoke of 'errors and immoralities' in the Old Testament, he was not pleased, as he let it be known in private.[50] Davidson's policy is well stated by another of his pupils. Robertson Nicoll wrote:

Dr A. B. Davidson, the recognised master of Old Testament learning in this country, a man who joins to his knowledge, imagination, subtlety, fervour, and a rare power of style, had been quietly teaching the best men among the students that the old views of revelation would have to be seriously altered. He did not do this so much directly as indirectly, and I think there was a period when any Free Church minister who asserted the existence of errors in the Bible would have been summarily deposed. The abler students had been taking sessions in Germany, and had thus escaped from the narrowness of the provincial coterie.[51]

How Nicoll could avoid commenting on the morality of this procedure I cannot understand. Another of Davidson's students tells us that even when higher criticism became a matter of trial in the General Assembly his lips remained 'so firmly sealed'.[52] And Davidson was by no means alone in this policy of caution. When the sermon of Marcus Dods on *Revelation and Inspiration* in 1877 challenged the full authority of Scripture, he 'agreed to suppress it in deference to the advice of his brethren'.[53] By the time Dods went to New College in 1889 he judged that such caution could be thrown aside. I find it impossible not to believe that the higher critics were conscious that teaching they introduced was incompatible with the commitment they had made to the Westminster Confession at the time of their ordination. The convoluted language in which some of them expressed their views, and their habit, at times, of quoting the destructive views of others, without saying explicitly that *they* agreed with them, also suggests they were aware of the anomaly of holding an office entered by a commitment to ordination vows. It is no wonder they pressed for the passing of a Declaratory Act in 1892 which loosened commitment to the Confession.

The essence of rationalism is its concern to explain everything without reference to the supernatural. It has to be said that some of the Scottish higher critics of the Free Church reflected deference to such thinking. Warfield had cause to speak of Marcus Dods' 'chariness with regard to the super-natural', and, speaking of Dods's view of the Bible, he went on, 'He wishes apparently as little supernatural a book as he can, as a Christian man, manage to get along with. The writers of Scripture, it is undeniable, held the diametrically opposite view. There was no antecedent opposition to the supernatural in their minds.'[54] In other words, there was a spirit evident that cannot be harmonized with the spirit of a child of God as given in Scripture. Norman Walker, in 1902, was touching on the same subject when he commented on Professor G. A. Smith's 'readiness to give up everything to the critic without a struggle, without apparently even a pang . . . We were not prepared for the spectacle here presented to us – that of an orthodox teacher going over to the higher critics without a blow.'[55]

CONSEQUENCES

The school of men who undid the commitment of the Free Church to the Bible did not stem the attack of naturalistic thinking on Christianity. Instead they accelerated it, and introduced the unbelief of the world into the Church. They did so, as we have seen, while ever promising the opposite result. Yet this very assurance was being given when the results of higher criticism upon the German churches were already known and visible. Horatius Bonar had drawn attention to the fact when he was Moderator of the Free Church in 1883. In speaking of the fruit in Europe, he instanced the life of one of the most influential of the German higher critics, Ferdinand Christian Baur (1792–1860):

> In youth he was full of evangelical zeal. He came in contact with Strauss, and gradually the spiritual life went from him. Unbelief took the place of faith. He found he could not even pray; and when his wife was dying he had to send for an earnest pastor in the neighbourhood to pray with her, and supply his lack of service. He found

himself dumb in the presence of his dying wife. Unbelief could do nothing for him. It had closed his lips; and it had hidden the face of God.[56]

This reading of history was by no means confined to those who shared Bonar's convictions on Scripture. Carnegie Simpson, a sympathizer with the change of thought in the Free Church, wrote: 'In other countries where the higher criticism has asserted itself – in Germany under Wellhausen and others, or in Holland under Kuenen – the Churches were permeated by what is vaguely called rationalism.'[57]

Still more significant is the testimony of Marcus Dods himself. He became Principal of New College, Edinburgh, in 1907 (two years before his death), and closed that academic year with an address on 'The Work of the Ministry'. Speaking of the age of transition in which they lived, he quoted the 'statement recently made on a German platform that faith in God is fast disappearing'. The ministry that his students were to enter upon, he told them, faced 'a revolution from which Christendom will emerge either old, worn-out, and shattered, with hopes blasted and faith dead, or with the glory of a new dawn upon its face, remade, renewed in youth, immovable in a re-found faith'. By faith in God he hoped it would be the latter, although an 'extraordinary theological movement has by no means spent itself', and 'problems of the most momentous kind still await solution'. Then, with an illustration he summarized the change that he believed his generation had succeeded in making:

> In America a house is sometimes shifted bodily to a new site. That is always a precarious operation. But still more fraught with risk and consequence is the shifting of theology from the basis of a Book to that of a Person . . . You begin where we left off . . . And to you is this great grace given, to help with quiet, cautious steadiness in the task of leading

the people of Scotland into a surer standing in Christ Jesus, a standing which will bear the test of the fiercest light that beats upon it. It is a hard and precarious task.[58]

But just how 'precarious' the future would be without a reliable Bible, Dods did not admit. It is only in a private letter that he is on record as saying: 'The churches won't know themselves fifty years hence. It is to be hoped some little rag of faith may be left when all's done.'[59] The same year as his address to the students, he wrote to another correspondent: 'It's a strange, unintelligible world, and the one fixed point on which hope can rest is that God is Father of all. If it is not so, then the solid foundation truly is rottenness.'[60] As a recent writer concludes concerning Dods, 'His *Later Letters* seem to reveal a man who had lost his way.'[61]

Who can say how many others were led into the same doubt? Dods' 'rag of faith' admission had been foreseen more than twenty years earlier, when Moody Stuart had warned in words he did not live to see fulfilled:

When the historical truth [of Deuteronomy] is once abandoned, there is no ground left on which to defend the Divine authority; and however individual men, retaining their loyalty to their Lord, may hold fast the truth after they have undermined its foundation, it is to be feared that the greater number will follow out consistently the path on which they have been persuaded to enter, will go on to reject the historical and prophetical truth first of the Old Testament and then of the New, and will either roam in a dreary path that has no solid ground beneath it, or fall into the dark abyss of hopeless unbelief.

The Word of the Lord is pure, and out of this trial it will come forth in all its brightness as silver out of the furnace. But, meanwhile, an unutterable calamity may overtake us, for our children may lose the one treasure we were bound to bequeath; and for long years they may wander 'through dry places seeking rest, and finding none', before they recover their hold of the Word of Life.[62]

CONCLUSIONS

1. The thinking of the theological professors of the Free Church became dominated by the wrong concerns. Instead of their priorities being determined by the spiritual needs of the people whom their students were to serve, their preoccupation was too largely with the intellectual climate of the times, and how the faith was to be accommodated to that climate. In 1908 James Denney believed that Unitarianism already had 'all the science and all the philosophy of the universities on its side', and he saw the best hope in the kind of conciliatory policy followed by his colleague in Glasgow, G. A. Smith.[63] If my case in this chapter is true, that policy did not contain unbelief. Instead it gave it a reputation in the theological colleges.[64] This led to 'teaching for doctrines the commandments of men' (*Matt.* 15:9), a consequent loss of authority in the pulpit, and spiritual famine across the nation.

2. In all controversies, leading biblical duties are likely to become obscured and this surely happened at this period. The plain New Testament duty of contending for the faith and refuting error was put aside. Instead, hesitancy on matters of belief came to be regarded as more Christian than 'dogmatism'. What was attributed to A. B. Bruce as a virtue was shared by a number of his associates: 'Bruce had learned to have the greatest possible respect for honest intellectual difficulty.'[65] But this 'respect' had the effect of cancelling the affirmation made by every Free Church minister before his ordination. To each the question was put, 'Do you sincerely own and believe the whole doctrine of the Confession of Faith . . . and will you

firmly and constantly adhere thereto, and to the utmost of your power assert, maintain and defend the same?'

The Bible calls, not for discussion and conciliation with error, but opposition. In the words of Horatius Bonar: 'Fellowship between faith and unbelief must, sooner or later, be fatal to the former . . . We may tamper with doubt, we may trifle with certainty, and we may succumb to public opinion; but what will the end be? . . . We are apt to forget that error is sin; that truth does not reverse itself; that inspiration and non-inspiration are two opposite poles, admitting no medium; that infidelity ought not to cloak itself under the name of candid inquiry; and that candid inquiry should beware of being landed in unbelief.'[66]

2. Warnings given to the church by Christ were not regarded: 'Beware of men'; 'Call no man Master'; 'By their fruits you will know them'; and other such injunctions received minimal regard. The attention was elsewhere as men with out-standing natural gifts were treated with near-reverence. Previously the Free Church had always emphasized scholarship; though it was not learning, as such, that had been praised. But now, what was said on the acquittal of George Adam Smith and his book in 1902, was the pattern: 'The Assembly's action virtually resolved itself into unbounded adulation of *the man*, instead of a quiet, judicial sifting of the statements and tendencies of *the book*.' The same writer, a Scottish presbyter, summarized the mood of the Assembly in these words: 'Let us remember how "popular and impressive" the author is; let us think what a cataclysm there would be in our Church if we were to presume to admonish him; "let us give God glory for the man."'[67] What Bonar had foreseen coming in 1868 had reached its harvest: 'The Church's danger has ever been to substitute a ministry of the intellect for a ministry of the Spirit; to confide in the human instead of the superhuman.'[68]

It was pride in man that so dazzled the Church that they could not see what was before their eyes. Therein lies the secret cause of all apostasy. To idolize 'scholarship', professors, preachers, or the Church herself, is to depart from God. The terrible decline of the Free Church ought to be no mystery. 'Because of unbelief they were broken off', Paul wrote of the Jews, and for every Christian Church he added the warning, 'You stand by faith. Be not high-minded, but fear. For if God spared not the natural branches, take heed lest he also spare not you' (*Rom.* 11:20–21). Looking back on the history of the Free Church, Horatius Bonar wrote: 'It would have been better for us had we, as a Church, forborne some of our subsequent boasts, and allowed our doings and success to speak for themselves.'[69] And when the decline was already advanced, Andrew Bonar was surely interpreting events rightly when he observed: 'I sometimes think that the Lord has let this state of things come to pass in order to complete our weaning from all earthly things, from *church* as well as *self*. My soul longs for the Church of the first-born.'[70]

3. We have noted above that Robertson Smith had nothing to say on fallen angels, and that even James Denney did not believe in the existence of the Devil or of evil spirits. Yet, if the Bible is true, the ultimate influences behind error and unbelief are superhuman. It was the serpent who 'deceived Eve by his cunning' and, far from teaching that such a possibility was no longer to be feared, Christ and the apostles spoke of the work of the 'evil one' as ever present (*Luke* 22:31; *2 Cor.* 11:3; *1 Pet.* 5:8). Even disciples may speak in Satan's interest without knowing it (*Matt.* 16:23). In his Yale lectures, G. A. Smith asserted that a 'war' had been waged to secure the change in belief of which he approved, but it was not war of the kind he supposed. 'The Spirit expressly says that in later times some will depart from the faith by devoting themselves to deceitful

spirits and teachings of demons' (*1 Tim.* 4:1). 'Beloved, let us not believe every spirit, but test the spirits to see whether they are from God, for many false prophets have gone out into the world' (*1 John* 4:1). Can it be without significance that the very weapon that higher critics believed could be laid aside was the one used by Jesus and the apostles to resist Satan? 'It is written' was Christ's threefold answer to the demonic (Luke 4:4, 8, 10). Men who thought it no longer necessary to 'take the sword of the Spirit, which is the word of God' (*Eph.* 6:17) were being led by another spirit. The pride which leads anyone to put his reason above Scripture has its origin in the sin that began with the question, 'Has God said?' (*Gen.* 3:1).

4. In this book I hope I have shown something of the strength and influence of Scottish character. But the lesson of this chapter is that natural gifts alone are of no account in the kingdom of God. It is not in terms of nationality that the degree to which Scots men and women brought blessing to the world is to be explained. In the mid-nineteenth century, and later, the Scot had a reputation for a national character second to none. He was serious and upright, dependable and honest in labour; in the words of one observer in the 1850s, 'destined by nature to religious depth of thought'; this trait was said to be as permanent 'as the rocks of his native land'.[71] It was not true.

What was most admired in Scottish character had been built through generations of Bible reading and Bible believing. Even Robert Burns, after describing how the Scottish peasantry of Ayrshire would read the Bible in family worship, wrote

> From scenes like these, old Scotia's grandeur springs,
> That makes her lov'd at home, rever'd abroad.[72]

The testimony of an Anglican visitor to Scotland in the 1860s had many confirmations. The Rev. William Haslam wrote:

I may say that, coming from the South, I was surprised to find so much Bible-knowledge, especially among the working classes. Their intelligent acquaintance with Christian doctrine also surprised me, though not so much when I saw in the little shop windows the children's lesson book, with the 'A,B,C' on one page, and a short Catechism on the opposite page. I believe that this early planting or teaching of God's truth, coupled with the daily reading of the Bible, is the secret of Scottish stability and influence. Even in secular matters, it helps to form that steadfast and indomitable character which distinguishes this people from the English the world over, and still more from the Irish.[73]

It is the light of revelation that lifts a people heavenwards. God and his Word elevated this little land and gave it the position it came to occupy in the world. Let grace be taken away and the Scottish character degenerates into what it was when 'each one of them [was] hangman to other'. Robert Moffat understood this when, speaking of the heathen he came to help, he wrote: 'Degraded as they are, they merit not the epithets which have been heaped upon them, by those who are unmindful that *their* position only, has prevented them from becoming Hottentots and Bushmen themselves.'[74]

Scripture holds up Israel as an example to all nations. Her greatness was not of herself. She was taught to say, 'A Syrian ready to perish was my father' (*Deut.* 26:5). It was her highest privilege to receive the Word of God and when that was disbelieved she forgot that 'There is none righteous, no not one.' Grace does not belong to nature. National character is not permanent. Scotland was a witness to what the Bible can do, and she has since shown how, without that light, a people once godly, serious and upright, can become as earth-bound and frivolous as any other nation. Thus numbers of one-time

Edinburgh church buildings are today restaurants, theatres and health clubs.

But 'the end is not yet'. Today also, while the books of higher critics lie unwanted, the writings and biographies of many of the men who were faithful to Scripture are republished and read across the earth. So it is that the promise made to the man whose 'delight is in the law of the LORD' is being fulfilled: 'His leaf shall not wither; and whatsoever he doeth shall prosper' (*Psa.* 1:3). With that same Word, God will send men for his churches till the end of time.

> A glory gilds the sacred page,
> Majestic, like the sun:
> It gives a light to every age;
> It gives, but borrows none.

> The hand that gave it still supplies
> The gracious light and heat;
> His truths upon the nations rise,
> They rise, but never set.

[1] 'Speech on Mr Robertson Smith's Appointment', James Walker, *Essays, Papers, Sermons* (Edinburgh: T. & T. Clark, 1898), pp. 257, 263.

[2] Norman L. Walker, *Chapters From the History of the Free Church of Scotland* (Edinburgh: Oliphant, Anderson, Ferrier, 1895), p. 273.

[3] Marcus Dods, *Revelation and Inspiration: The Historical Books of Scripture* (Glasgow: L. MacKinlay, 1877). This was in a third printing by June 1877.

[4] Hugh Martin, *The Westminster Doctrine of the Inspiration of Scripture* and *Letters to Marcus Dods* (both books, London: Nisbet, 1877).

[5] R. Watts, *The New Apologetic and Its Claims to Confessional Authority* (Edinburgh: Maclaren, 1879), pp. 31, 34.

[6] *Our Old Gospel: Moses on the Plains of Moab* (Edinburgh: Maclaren, 1880).

[7] In an obvious attempt to influence opinion, Thomas Chalmers *On the Inspiration of the Old and New Testaments* was reprinted in 1879 (Edinburgh: Elliot), with a Preface by George Smeaton.

[8] *Memories of Horatius Bonar*, p. 123. Robert Haldane, *The Books of the Old and New Testaments Proved to be Canonical and their Verbal Inspiration Maintained*, came out in a seventh edition ((Edinburgh: Maclaren, 1877).

[9] Walker, *Chapters from the History*, p. 284.

[10] Further on G. A. Smith see, I. D. Campbell, *Fixing the Indemnity: The Life and Work of Sir George Adam Smith* (Milton Keynes, 2004).

[11] Patrick Carnegie Simpson, *Life of Principal Rainy* (London: Hodder and Stoughton, 1909), vol. 2, pp. 109–10. It is regrettable that this work, favourable to the change of belief in the Free Church, has no counterpart from the other side.

[12] Quoted in Henry F. Henderson, *The Religious Controversies of Scotland* (Edinburgh: T. & T. Clark, 1905), p. 238.

[13] Simpson, *Rainy*, vol. 2, p. 115.

[14] In 1900 the Free Church (excepting 25 mainly Highland ministers) joined with the United Presbyterian Church to form the United Free Church.

[15] G. A. Smith, *Modern Criticism and the Preaching of the Old Testament* (London: Hodder and Stoughton, 1901), p. 72. How Smith applied the theory of evolution to Old Testament theology can be seen in his words: 'His Spirit sympathises with His children's rude and painful struggles after light; with their discontent with the earlier achievements of religion, and with their revolts against ancient dogmas. Moreover, it rewards the rebel by the gift of new aspects of truth, and by guidance to firmer and more original faith in God' (p. 296).

[16] This seems to be the opinion of D. W. Bebbington, *Evangelicalism in Modern Britain* (London: Unwin Hyman, 1989), pp. 189–90. It is extraordinary that this author should say: 'The resistance to the higher criticism was not grounded in a doctrine of inerrancy because, at least among the educated, inerrancy held no more attractions than the conclusions of the higher critics' (p. 190).   [17] Simpson, *Rainy*, vol. 2, p. 311.

[18] Initially a lecturer, and assistant to John Duncan, Davidson was appointed Professor of Hebrew in 1863.

[19] This needs to be borne in mind. Speaking of Alexander Whyte's support of Robertson Smith in the 1870s, G. F. Barbour noted: 'The fact that Robertson Smith was not at this time interested in the restatement of dogma but only in the reinterpretation of the Bible, meant that the new outlook on Scripture had time to prepare the way for the reconstruction of belief. It also enabled men like Whyte to take their stand unhesitatingly at his side.' In other words, they did not anticipate the doctrinal change that would inevitably follow. G. F. Barbour, *Life of Alexander Whyte* (Hodder and Stoughton, 1923), p. 205.

[20] Simpson, *Rainy*, vol. 1, p. 354.

[21] *Rainy*, vol. 1, p. 307.

[22] Walker, *Chapters from Free Church*, p. 277.

[23] See, for instance, *Krummacher; An Autobiography*, trans. M. G. Easton (Edinburgh: Clark, 1871): 'I fear there is darkness here in the future of the Church . . . The mass of the candidates here before their second examination are not believers . . . Art thou not constrained to regard Scotland as the bright point of light in the dark church-picture of the present? It is truly more blessed than we are' (pp. 278, 290). I have written more on the effect of German theological influence in *Evangelicalism Divided: A Record of Crucial Change in the Years 1950 to 2000* (Edinburgh: Banner of Truth, 2000).

[24] *The Preaching of the Old Testament to the Age* (London: Hodder and Stoughton 1893), p. 33. If German critics were rationalists, he argued, it was not due to their studies but to some other cause. He also offered comfort in the assurance that 'great parts of the Old Testament remain unquestioned by criticism. Unquestioned? I should rather say, fortified, explored, and made habitable by modern man' (p. 37).

[25] G. A. Smith, *The Life of Henry Drummond* (London: Hodder and Stoughton, 1899), pp. 241–2.

[26] Quoted in Henderson, *Religious Controversies of Scotland*, p. 245.

[27] Smith, *Drummond*, p. 39. One of the things he had to 'unlearn' was the value of Bonar's *God's Way of Peace* (p. 27). There was severe criticism for the representation of Christian in Bunyan's *Pilgrim's Progress*: 'Christ's conception of Christianity was heavens removed from that of a man setting out from the City of Destruction to save his soul.' Quoted by Murdo Macaskill, *The New Theology in the Free Church* (Edinburgh: Hunter, 1892), p. 13.

[28] *Presbyterian and Reformed Review* (Philadelphia), January 1892, p. 167.

[29] *The Sword and the Trowel*, 1891 (London: Passmore and Alabaster), p. 340.

[30] Smith, *Drummond*, p. 243.

[31] Henry Drummond, *The New Evangelism and Other Papers* (London: Hodder and Stoughton, 1899), p. 41.

[32] Henderson, *Religious Controversies*, p. 267.

[33] *Presbyterian and Reformed Review*, Oct 1904, p. 604.

[34] Ibid., Jan.1902, p. 139.

[35] Spurgeon, *The Sword and the Trowel*, 1889 (London: Passmore and Alabaster), p. 634. The two professors to whom he referred were A. B. Bruce and Marcus Dods. For further comment on Bruce, see p. 660 of the same volume; and on G. A. Smith, p. 291: 'Mr Adam Smith has, in somewhat veiled language, taken away from Holy Scripture the inspiration which is the ground of our faith.' Spurgeon was, at this time, engaged in a parallel conflict in England; see my *Forgotten Spurgeon* (2nd. ed., Edinburgh: Banner of Truth, 1973).

[36] T. H. Darlow, *William Robertson Nicoll, Life and Letters* (London: Hodder and Stoughton, 1925), p. 364. For the statements that gave rise to Nicoll's concern, see *Letters of Principal James Denney to W. Robertson Nicoll 1893–1917* (London: Hodder and Stoughton, n. d.), p. 102. Denney's position is problematical. While he remained gospel-orientated, his reluctance to ground doctrinal belief on the authority of Scripture alone seriously weakened his teaching. See the survey of Denney's writings by C. Wistar Hodge, 'Dr Denney and the Doctrine of the Atonement', *Princeton Theological Review*, Oct. 1918, pp. 623–41. There are insights into Denney in A. P. F. Sell, *Defending and Declaring the Faith: Some Scottish Examples* (Exeter: Paternoster, 1987).

[37] Simpson, *Rainy*, vol. 2, p. 116.

[38] Henderson, *Religious Controversies*, pp. 234–5.

[39] B. B. Warfield, *Critical Reviews* (New York: OUP, 1932), p. 125.

[40] J. Candlish, *The Work of the Holy Spirit*, pp. 82–3, quoted by Macaskill, *The New Theology*, p. 10.

[41] Smith, *Drummond*, p. 491. But on the same page Drummond qualified his statement. Belief in evolution, he said, Christ himself taught as a certainty: 'He has asserted his purpose to carry on the evolution of the world . . . The man who joins the Christian Life finds security and something which, as a Law of the World, will evolve the animal into the perfect man.' In writing elsewhere on 'The Problem of Foreign Missions', he said: 'The advantage of speaking of "the Christian evolution of the world," instead of , or, at least, as a change from, "the evangelization of the world" will appear as we go on.' *New Evangelism*, p. 123.

[42] Bruce, *The Kingdom of God*, p. 141. Quoted by Henderson, *Religious Controversies*, p. 261.

[43] *Letters of Denney*, pp. 99–100. In contrast with most of his professorial colleagues, Denney is said to have appreciated Spurgeon.

[44] Warfield, *Critical Reviews*, p. 119.

[45] *Presbyterian and Reformed Review*. Oct 1894, p. 651.

[46] Darlow, *Nicoll, Life and Letters*, p. 41.

[47] N. L. Walker, *Free Church of Scotland*, p. 297.

[48] *Presbyterian and Reformed Review*, October 1902, p. 596.

[49] Quoted by Campbell, *Fixing the Indemnity*, p. 28. After his ordination Davidson had entered the work of College teaching without ever being called to a congregation – a mistake that has sadly been often repeated in the appointment of men to train preachers and pastors.

[50] W. Robertson Nicoll, *Princes of the Church*, London, 1921, p. 239.

[51] In Henry Drummond, *The Ideal Life and Other Unpublished Addresses* (London: Hodder and Stoughton, 1897), pp. 7-8.

[52] Simpson, *Rainy*, vol. 1, p. 355.

[53] Henderson, *Religious Controversies*, p. 238.

[54] *Critical Reviews*, p. 124.

[55] *Presbyterian and Reformed Review*, Oct. 1902, p. 589.

[56] Bonar, *Our Ministry*, pp. 56–7.

[57] Simpson, *Rainy*, vol. 1, p. 307.

[58] Marcus Dods, *Christ and Man: Sermons* (London: Hodder and Stoughton, 1909), pp. 268–70.

[59] *Later Letters of Marcus Dods* (London: Hodder and Stoughton, 1911), p. 67. The contrast between this and Dods' public statements about the future throws some doubt on the words of Robertson Nicoll: 'Dr Dods told you frankly all that was in his mind. He was not keeping back any secret unbelief. He was grandly and frankly and constantly truthful.' *Princes of the Church*, p. 239.

[60] *Later Letters*, p. 256.

[61] *Marcus Dods*, in *Dictionary of Scottish Church History & Theology*.

[62] Moody Stuart, *Our Old Bible*, pp. 70–1.

[63] *Letters of Denney*, p. 116. These letters show Denney's closeness to Smith, who had characteristics, such as kindness, that he greatly appreciated.

[64] Alexander Auld, biographer of Kennedy, records that when he was a theological student, a Christian well-wisher in the North wrote to warn him of 'the great pot' out of which the sons of the prophets get their food, for there is 'death in it', which could only be cured by casting meal into it

(*2 Kings* 4:40-1): 'The pot is the college; the death in it is learning without grace, and the meal is the good food ground on Calvary between the millstones of law and justice, which can be gotten only by the hand of faith.' *Ministers and Men in the Far North* (repr. Inverness: Free Presbyterian Publications, 1956), p. 125.

[65] Henderson, *Religious Controversies*, p. 251.
[66] Bonar, *Our Ministry*, pp. 97–8.
[67] *Presbyterian and Reformed Review*, Oct. 1904, pp. 597–8.
[68] *Life of Milne*, p. 102.
[69] Ibid., p. 86.
[70] *Diary and Letters*, p. 286.
[71] Krummacher, *Autobiography*, p. 290.
[72] *The Cottar's Saturday Night*, xix.
[73] W. Haslam, *'Yet Not I'* (London: Marshall and Scott, n.d.), p. 124.
[74] Moffat, *Missionary Labours and Scenes*, pp. 282–3.

ADDITIONAL NOTE

For further comment on the theme of this chapter, see R. L. Dabney, 'Refutation of Prof. W. Robertson Smith', and, 'The influence of the German University System on Theological Literature', in *Discussions: Evangelical and Theological*, vol. 1 (repr. London: Banner of Truth, 1967), pp. 399–465.

Index of Persons & Authors

Some Scottish Christian Classics
Published by the Banner of Truth Trust